Theorizing Adaptation

Theorizing Adaptation

KAMILLA ELLIOTT

OXFORD
UNIVERSITY PRESS

OXFORD
UNIVERSITY PRESS

Oxford University Press is a department of the University of Oxford. It furthers
the University's objective of excellence in research, scholarship, and education
by publishing worldwide. Oxford is a registered trade mark of Oxford University
Press in the UK and certain other countries.

Published in the United States of America by Oxford University Press
198 Madison Avenue, New York, NY 10016, United States of America.

Library of Congress Cataloging-in-Publication Data
Names: Elliott, Kamilla, 1957– author.
Title: Theorizing adaptation / Kamilla Elliott.
Description: New York : Oxford University Press, 2020. |
Includes bibliographical references and index.
Identifiers: LCCN 2019049084 (print) | LCCN 2019049085 (ebook) |
ISBN 9780197511176 (hardback) | ISBN 9780197511183 (paperback) |
ISBN 9780197511206 (epub) | ISBN 9780197511213 (On-line)
Subjects: LCSH: Literature—Adaptations—History and criticism. |
Film adaptations—History and criticism.
Classification: LCC PN171.A33 E44 2020 (print) |
LCC PN171.A33 (ebook) | DDC 808—dc23
LC record available at https://lccn.loc.gov/2019049084
LC ebook record available at https://lccn.loc.gov/2019049085

1 3 5 7 9 8 6 4 2

Paperback printed by Marquis, Canada
Hardback printed by Bridgeport National Bindery, Inc., United States of America

To the loves of my life,
Lucas Elliott Denman and Christina Janette Pedder

Contents

Contents

Acknowledgments

In many ways, this entire book is an acknowledgment of my indebtedness to other adaptation scholars: without their work, this metacritical history, metatheoretical theory, and rhetorical study of theorizing adaptation could not exist. My study adapts their work and will be itself adapted in future scholarship.

I am particularly indebted to scholars who have worked to establish adaptation studies as a field, many of whom have been mentors and editors establishing me as an adaptation scholar. Despite failing health, George Bluestone read my PhD thesis, offering invaluable advice and supporting my scholarship even when it disagreed with his own. Joss Marsh was superbly supportive of my early career and an inspirational co-author. Robert Stam's formidable scholarship and editorial encouragement of my fledgling scholarship offered a heartening boost at a difficult time in my career. Neil Sinyard, whose focus on adaptation as a mode of criticism greatly influenced my scholarship, maintains kind and regular contact. Although I did not meet Dudley Andrew until 2010, his essay, "Adaptation," is one to which I have repeatedly returned, finding new insights with each revisitation. Linda Hutcheon's dazzling display of insightful and wide-ranging scholarship in *A Theory of Adaptation* is an accomplishment to which this book can only aspire.

I am especially grateful to Deborah Cartmell and Imelda Whelehan for founding the Association of Adaptation Studies and the Oxford journal *Adaptation*, providing a field home to which I regularly return and in which I can meet with and read the work of other adaptation scholars, and for offering my work a home in their edited collections and journal. The Literature/Film Association and the *Literature/Film Quarterly*, founded by James M. Welsh and Tom Erskine, now under the leadership of David T. Johnson and Elsie Walker, and the Linnaeus University Centre for Intermedial and Multimodal Studies, led by Lars Elleström, have been other homes to which I return regularly and gratefully.

I am indebted to other scholars, including Marie-Laure Ryan, John Glavin, Pascal Nicklas, Oliver Lindner, Jørgen Bruhn, Anne Gjelsvik, Eirik Frisvold

Hanssen, Ariane Hudelet, Shannon Wells-Lassagne, Julie Grossman, Barton Palmer, Thomas Leitch, Dennis Cutchins, Katja Krebs, Eckart Voigts, Ljubica Matek, Željko Uvanović, Ann Lewis, and Silke Arnold-de Simine, for including my work in edited collections and, in many instances, for encouraging me to write it in the first place. Countless other adaptation scholars have informed my scholarship with theirs and called mine to account, encouraging me to keep going in a field that has been far more difficult than any other in which I have worked. Explaining why is the subject of this book.

No one has inspired, challenged, and encouraged my work more than Thomas Leitch. As a press reviewer of this manuscript, Tom's incisive, rigorous, constructive criticism has greatly strengthened it. Tom is also largely responsible for my finishing what I came to refer to as "the never-ending book," which I wanted to abandon many times. I was worried that this manuscript might not find a publisher, since it challenges the humanities mainstream and takes many leaps and risks. I am extremely grateful to my other press reviewer (unnamed) and to Norm Hirschy of Oxford University Press for taking a gamble and agreeing to publish it.

My home institution, the University of Lancaster, has been supportive of my scholarship in many ways, fostering a culture that encourages independence and diversity of thought and offering regular sabbatical leave to its employees. This book also owes a debt to my students at Lancaster. It cites scholarship by former PhD candidates, now Dr. Dawn Stobbart and Dr. Annie Nissen, and by former MA student, now Dr. Marcus Nicholls. It is a joy to see the directions in which these and other emerging scholars are taking adaptation studies. I am also grateful to my former PhD student, now Dr. Abigail Oyston, for help in proofreading the bibliography, to OUP's meticulous copy editor, Debbie Ruel, and to James Deboo for expert assistance with the proofs and index. Without their support, this might indeed have been the never-ending book.

Introduction

The Problem of Theorizing Adaptation

According to the Modern Language Association's *International Bibliography*, humanities[1] adaptation studies has expanded exponentially since 1990. Of the 25,241 hits produced for "adaptation" as a subject term, 13,903 were published since 1990 and 11,145 since 2000.[2] Adaptation studies is on the move.[3] In 2008, two new adaptation journals published their first issues: the Oxford University Press journal *Adaptation: The Journal of Literature on Screen* and the Intellect *Journal of Adaptation in Film & Performance*. In 2015 saw the launch of the *Palgrave Studies in Adaptation and Visual Culture* book series, edited by Julie Grossman and R. Barton Palmer, and of Bloomsbury's *Adaptation Histories* series, which joined its *Screen Adaptation* series (established in 2009), both edited by Deborah Cartmell.

And yet the following passages attest to a persistent and pervasive opinion that humanities adaptation studies is unscholarly, uninformed, and unconvincing—simultaneously dogmatic and uncertain, narrow and fragmented, obsessive and unfocused, undeveloped and superannuated.

> Personal preferences, snap judgments, isolated instances, and random impressions . . . characterize most of the writing in the field. (Asheim 1951, 289)
>
> The mysterious alchemy which transforms works of fiction into cinematic form is still being widely practiced without, perhaps, being sufficiently understood. (Bluestone 1957, 215)
>
> The overwhelming bulk of what has been written about the relationship of film and literature is open to serious question. (Giannetti 1975, 89)
>
> [O]ne is tempted to call for a moratorium on adaptation studies. (Orr 1984, 72)
>
> [W]hat has always troubled us about adaptations . . . and . . . theoretical talk about them [are] . . . blatant omissions, ludicrous revisions, absurd miscarriages. (Boyum 1985, 22)

Theorizing Adaptation. Kamilla Elliott, Oxford University Press (2020). © Oxford University Press.
DOI: 10.1093/oso/9780197511176.001.0001

In view of the nearly sixty years of writing about the adaptation of novels into film ... it is depressing to find at what a limited, tentative stage the discourse has remained. (McFarlane 1996, 1)

The critical literature on adaptations . . . has not, even now, reached a happy compromise. (Whelehan 1999, 4)

[T]he very subject of adaptation has constituted one of the most jejeune areas of scholarly writing about the cinema. (Naremore 2000b, 1)

Why has this topic, obviously central to humanities-based film education, prompted so little distinguished work? (Ray 2000, 38)

Despite the theoretical sophistication of recent literary critical discourse, adaptation studies have remained stubbornly rooted in often unexamined values and practices. (Bortolotti and Hutcheon 2007, 443)

[A]daptation theory has progressed very little since the 1950s. (Albrecht-Crane and Cutchins 2010, 11)

Adaptation studies, rather like Don Quixote, continue[s] to fight the day before yesterday's battles. (MacCabe 2011, 7)

Spurned by the progressive wings of . . . host disciplines, adaptation studies turned in on itself, becoming in the process increasingly intellectually parochial, methodologically hidebound, and institutionally risible. (Murray 2012a, 2)

This book proposes to challenge . . . negative inclinations . . . within the field of adaptation studies . . . by offering a new theoretical orientation, a new framework. (Hodgkins 2013, 8)

[M]ost of the problems that were raised in adaptation studies in the 1990s (if not before) still await a solution today. (Cattrysse 2014, 14)

[Adaptation is] too literary, too filmic, lacking rigor, too elitist, too preoccupied with debased forms of culture, too left-wing and postmodern, not adept enough at close reading, too theoretical, too naive. In short it contains multitudes of sins. (Whelehan, qtd. in Cartmell, Strong, and Whelehan 2018, 267)[4]

Most critics have placed the blame squarely upon adaptation scholars for engaging the "wrong" theories and for lagging behind the theoretical times. In 1998, Lloyd Michaels critiqued James Griffith's *Adaptations as Imitations* for its "unmistakable air of datedness" and Brian McFarlane's *Novel to Film* for its "out-of-fashion structuralist methodology" (429). In 2000, Robert B. Ray assessed that the field of literature-and-film (then the main focus of adaptation studies) was floundering and marginalized by both literary studies and film studies because it lacked "a presiding poetics" (44) and because its scholars had failed to turn with the theoretical turn in the humanities.[5] While no humanities discipline has entirely ceded to the claims of the theoretical turn, adaptation studies at the turn of the twenty-first century was seen to be especially behindhand: Thomas Leitch assessed that the "founding fallacy of adaptation studies" at that time was the belief that "[t]here is such a thing as contemporary adaptation theory" (2003a, 149).

Both before and since 2003, contemporary theories have been engaged widely and extensively in adaptation studies, including dialogics (Stam 2000; Bruhn 2013), intertextuality (Leitch 2003a; Aragay 2005b; Sanders 2006), hypertextuality (Park-Finch 2012), trans/intermediality (Voigts-Virchow 2009; Elleström 2013; Schober 2013; Fortier 2016; Cochrane 2018; Cutchins 2018), postmodernism (Hutcheon 2006; Slethaug 2014), poststructuralism (Donaldson-McHugh and Moore 2006; Hurst 2008; Vartan 2014; Geal 2019), postmodern cultural studies (Cartmell, Whelehan, et al. 1996–2010), gender theory (Cartmell et al. 1998; Ferris and Young 2010; Primorac 2012; Cobb 2015; Lofgren 2016), queer theory (Hankin 2009; Agane 2015; Coatman 2018; Demory 2018; 2020), postcolonialism (Gibson 2004; Wells 2009; Jeffers 2011; Ponzanesi 2014; Setiawan 2017), ethnicity theories (Wells 2009; Newstok and Thompson 2010; Pittman 2011), reception theories and fan studies (Hutcheon 2006; Lee 2016; Meikle 2017; Pope 2019), industry and economic theories (Higson 2006; Murray 2008 and 2012a; Ponzanesi 2014; Kennedy-Karpat and Sandberg 2017), avant-garde theory (Verrone 2011), meme theory (Hutcheon and Bortolotti 2007; Gratch 2017), affect theory (Hodgkins 2013), identity and performance theory (Krebs 2018), polysystems theory (Cattrysse 2014), Deleuzian theory (Fortier 1996; Hodgkins 2013), translation and cross-cultural theory (Chan 2012; Della Coletta 2012; Raw 2012; 2013; 2017; Krebs 2012; 2013; Lee, Tan, and Stephens 2017), new media theories (Parody 2011; O'Flynn 2012; Gratch 2017; Newell 2017; Meikle 2019a; Schäfke and Fehle 2019), mediaturgy (Collard 2014), theories of perception (Nicklas and Baumbach 2018), biopolitics (Nicklas 2015), embodiment theory interacting with media technologies (Ruud 2018; Richard 2018), the posthuman adaptations of artificial intelligence systems (Voigts 2019), and connections between film adaptation and adaptations of migrancy and climate change through a rhetoric of recycling (Meikle 2019b). The last two citations (Voigts 2019 and Meikle 2019b) were papers presented at the annual Association of Adaptation Studies conference in Brno, Czech Republic in September 2019, at which other papers treated other cutting-edge theories, including digimodernism and metamodernism. These theories, papers, and publications are illustrative rather than exhaustive.

Even as many new theories have proliferated in twenty-first-century adaptation studies, the discourse of theoretical failure and lack has continued and expanded. In their introduction to the first issue of the Oxford journal *Adaptation* in 2008, editors Deborah Cartmell, Timothy Corrigan, and Imelda Whelehan increased Ray's two reasons why adaptation studies remains academically marginalized to ten. Although they faulted wider academic and cultural factors as well, they too blamed adaptation scholars for engaging the wrong theories (1-2). In 2010, Brett Westbrook perceived that a "lack of theory about adaptation studies" stands "in direct contrast to the rise of theory in and of itself" in the humanities (25). In 2012, Rainer Emig critiqued adaptation studies for not engaging sufficiently with the theories of the theoretical turn. In 2011, Fredric Jameson discussed "Adaptation as a Philosophical Problem"; in 2014, Margot Blankier complained of "the limits of existing adaptation theory" (108). In 2017, Brian Boyd identified fidelity criticism as the "perennial problem" of adaptation studies (587), while Mary H. Snyder designated it the chief obstacle to uniting adaptation theory with adaptation practice (2017).

For all the protests against adaptation studies' marginalization by single humanities disciplines (for example, Naremore 2000b, 15; Corrigan 2017, 30), it is troubling that the most strident field critiques have come from *within* adaptation studies. I know of no other field whose scholars are so pervasively dismissive and denigrating of fellow scholars. In 2008, Simone Murray assessed that "worryingly, adaptation studies is currently experiencing a welter of criticism not only from outside its own ranks but also from within" (4), but here and in *The Adaptation Industry* (2012a), she joined the internal criticism, as her epigraph to this introduction attests. I must also include my own essays, "Theorizing Adaptations/Adapting Theories" (2013) and "Adaptation Theory and Adaptation Scholarship" (2017), in this critique.

What is particularly troubling is that the theoretical critique of adaptation studies and scholars extends to *adaptation itself*. I am not the first scholar to raise this concern. In 2006, building on seminal essay collections edited by Deborah Cartmell, Imelda Whelehan, Ian Q. Hunter and Heidi Kaye (Cartmell et al. 1996-2001), Linda Hutcheon addressed "the constant critical denigration of the general phenomenon of adaptation—in all its various media incarnations" (xi), puzzling why "disparaging opinions on adaptation as a secondary mode . . . persist," since "all the various manifestations of 'theory' over the last decades should logically have changed this negative view of adaptation" (xiii).

My research finds that adaptation has been condemned by theories of all kinds, including new ones, and by diametrically opposed as well as compatible theories. Adaptation has been castigated both for failing Romantic originality and poststructuralist deconstructions of originals and copies; it has been excoriated both for violating aesthetic purity and medium specificity theory and for supporting those principles by postmodern and radical theorists; it has been decreed a semiotic impossibility under formalism, structuralism, and poststructuralism alike; it has been charged with political incorrectness by both conservative and radical scholars; it has been accused of philosophical untruth by both modernist and postmodern theorists. In the disciplinary wars, film adaptations of literature have been condemned both as bad literature and bad film. I know of no other field whose subject matter—quite apart from its scholarship—has been so lambasted for theoretical nonconformity of all kinds.

In any other domain of intellectual enquiry, such dynamics would have been contested, if not condemned. For example, had all theories of women, including all feminist theories, been as critical of and hostile towards women *themselves* for violating theoretical precepts as they have been of adaptation, someone somewhere would have posited the failure of theorization to account for women. Yet there has been little discussion regarding the failure of humanities theorization *generally* to account for adaptation—not just particular theories with which we do not agree. Instead, the blame has been cast on adaptation scholars, adaptation studies, and adaptation itself.

While I too have critiqued adaptation scholarship, including my own (2017), I have become increasingly convinced that the problem of theorizing adaptation derives primarily from *a dysfunctional relationship between theorization and adaptation in the humanities.* This dysfunctional adaptation scholarship more problematic than scholarship in other fields and renders it impossible to find the "right" theories. That the sciences and social sciences have no equivalent discourse of adaptation as a theoretical problem supports this argument, as does the fact that internationally renowned theorists such as Vachel Lindsay, Béla Balázs, François Truffaut, Seymour Chatman, and Dudley Andrew in the twentieth century and Robert Stam, Linda Hutcheon, Fredric Jameson, and Mieke Bal in the twenty-first have struggled to theorize adaptation as satisfactorily as they have theorized other fields.

This study focuses less on adaptation's secondariness to other media forms and more on its secondariness to *theorization*, critiquing the largely undeconstructed, hierarchical relationship between theorization and adaptation in the humanities that persists even in the wake of the theoretical turn. Because the *content* of much recent humanities theorization has been ideologically, politically, and culturally revolutionary and deconstructive, it has obscured the ongoing, top-down, hierarchical philosophical, cultural, and institutional relationship of theorization to what it theorizes. This hierarchy persists even in piecemeal, pluralistic, skeptical, indeterminate theorization.

The persistence of the hierarchy is also evident in that, while adaptation has been so unilaterally lambasted for theoretical failure, almost no one has pondered the possibility that humanities theorization may have failed adaptation. Rather than blaming adaptation scholars for using the "wrong" theories and exhorting them to use the "right" theories, this study examines how and why humanities theories and theorization have been wrong for adaptation. A dysfunctional relationship between theorization and adaptation in the humanities has meant that no matter what new theories are brought to bear on adaptation, or what old theories are discarded, the problems remain. Adaptation studies has floundered not because scholars have failed to use the correct theories, I argue, but because *the practices and processes of adaptation are at odds with those of mainstream humanities theorization.*

I develop the argument in two parts: Part I, "Theorizing Adaptation," offers a metacritical history of theorizing adaptation, tracing the changing theoretical fortunes of adaptation from the sixteenth century to the present. It finds that humanities adaptation, theoretically valued in earlier centuries, began to be cast as a bad theoretical object in the late eighteenth century. In contrast to biology, which moved away from theories of divinely created, hierarchized, separate species to embrace theories of adaptation, the humanities went in the opposite direction: after centuries of celebrating aesthetic adaptation as a primary means of artistic and cultural progress, humanities theorists pitted pseudo-scientific theories of the arts as separate species and pseudo-religious theories of original creation against adaptation. In the twentieth century, modernism atomized adaptation into allusions, structuralist semiotics declared it to be a theoretical impossibility, and formalist theories declared it to be bad art. In the late twentieth century, adaptation served as a weapon in disciplinary, cultural, and theoretical wars. While its recent growth in academia owes a great deal to the rise of new media, franchise entertainment, and globalization, it is also the product of radical political theories, postmodern pluralism, and intertextual and intermedial theories. Yet in spite of its rise, adaptation studies remains marginalized by and dispersed across disciplines and their theories, a diaspora pursued intermittently and variably across media, national, geographical, and historical borders. By comparison to other fields, including interdisciplines such as cultural, intertextual, and intermedial studies, adaptation lacks a field of its own and a body of shared, accumulated knowledge upon to build, although this is beginning to change. In the twenty-first century, as adaptation studies has oscillated between theoretical nostalgia and theoretical progress and between theoretical pluralism and theoretical abandonment, the discourse of adaptation as a theoretical problem persists, as this introduction attests.

Rejecting the usual conclusions to histories of theorization in the humanities, in which the author adjudicates among theories and selects one to rule them all or declares theorization to be progressing well, my history points to a need to *retheorize and refigure what theorization is and does in the humanities*, which is the focus of Part II, "Adapting Theorization." My history of theorizing adaptation makes clear that, when theorization values adaptation, it does so only when adaptation conforms to its tenets, disciplining and punishing it when it does not.

The dysfunctional relationship between theorization and adaptation, however, is not solely the product of humanities theorization's especially hierarchical stance towards what it theorizes. Theorization and adaptation, my research finds, are rival, overlapping, mutually resistant, cultural processes each vying to subject the other to their operations. I demonstrate this relationship by subjecting adaptation to the three stages of theorization (definition, taxonomization, and theoretical principles), demonstrating how and why adaptation has refused to conform to them and calling for a process in which we define, taxonomize, and theorize adaptation adaptively, as adaptation, according to adaptation's principles, going further to ask whether these processes might, in turn, adapt theories of what theorization is and does in adaptation studies and in the humanities more generally. Adaptation studies, I argue, needs not new theories but a new *relationship* between theorization and adaptation.

"Refiguring Adaptation" turns from the larger arcs of metacritical history and metatheoretical theory to the minutiae of rhetoric, examining how parts of speech have situated adaptation and theorization in relation to each other and pondering how rhetoric might rework that relationship. Figurative rhetoric, I argue, holds especial potential for refiguring their relationship.

Already central to humanities theorization and theories of adaptation, fig-uration, an ancient process on a par with those of theorization and adap-tation, not only offers ways to refigure their relationship but also to redress specific theoretical problems in adaptation studies. Indeed, the two parts of this book, "Theorizing Adaptation" and "Adapting Theorization," construct a figure when conjoined: an antimetabole. Antimetabole is a figure that allows for opposition and mutuality to co-exist; its mirrored horizontal relations dismantle hierarchies and preclude revolution through a process of inversion and exchange, in which each inhabits the other mutually and reciprocally. In the final analysis, this book turns out to be as much about adapting theoriza-tion as it is about theorizing adaptation.

A Note on Methodology

In 2000, Ray credited adaptation studies' lack of a "presiding poetics" in part to "the endless series of twenty-page articles" that has characterized adap-tation scholarship (44). Even monographs tend to unfold as chapter-length case studies of particular adaptations, following a theoretical introduction. Assessing that "individual readings . . . rarely offer . . . generalizable insights into theoretical issues" (2006, xiii), Linda Hutcheon broke ranks in *A Theory of Adaptation*, using micro-case studies to illustrate a variety of theories across a range of media forms. In spite of Hutcheon's influence and impact on the field, chapter-length case studies of single adaptations continue as the main format for adaptation publications.

I discuss some reasons for this later in this book. The point to stress here, by way of introduction, is that just as every field benefits from a variety of theo-ries, epistemologies, and subject matter, so too every field benefits from a va-riety of viewing distances. Adaptation studies needs more macroscopic and more microscopic studies because methodological diversity is as essential to academic freedom as cultural, historical, ideological, and social diversity. While many larger theoretical narratives have been didactically totalitarian in their claims to university, it is *methodologically* totalitarian to allow only local studies to theorize a field. Moreover, just as there are both local and global tyrants, so too some case studies have been as just as theoretically dog-matic, autocratic, and absolutist as large-scale studies. The size and scale of a study does not determine its truth value. Larger views need not be universal or totalizing: they can simply be larger views, every bit as historically and culturally contingent and situated as local case studies. My history of theorizing adaptation does not lay claim to totality or to absolute truth: rather, it is a selective, metacritical history offering particular perspectives on particular questions. Similarly, my metatheoretical discussion does not seek to establish which theoretical tenets are true: rather, it works to explicate and redress the dysfunctional relationship between theorization and adaptation in the humanities.

A variety of viewing distances is all the more important (and difficult) in a field such as adaptation studies, which inhabits and crosses many fields, and is, in the process, situated both as a sub-field of other fields and as a larger field encompassing these fields. Both angles of view are required to study adaptation. Macroscopic views reveal transhistorical, transdisciplinary, and transtheoretical dynamics that do not manifest in localized case studies, while microscopic studies can erase or refocus differences and oppositions that case studies may maximize. For example, in *Rethinking the Novel/Film Debate* (Elliott 2003a), tracing a longer history of interart relations from eighteenth-century debates over poetry and painting through nineteenth- and twentieth-century debates over prose fiction and illustration and twentieth-century debates over words in film clarified a paradox of twentieth- and twenty-first-century novel/film studies that theorizes novels and films as both sister arts *and* separate species, while microscopic studies of pictorial initials break down oppositions between words and images maintained at the level of whole words and complete pictures. My research questions in this book are similarly illuminated by adopting larger and closer views.

I am keenly aware that any larger view cannot be comprehensive: it must omit materials and neglect nuances and details. Conversely, any closer view must lose the bigger picture. Yet case studies are equally selective and incomplete—no case study has ever addressed every aspect of even one aspect of a single adaptation. That we do not critique case studies for their incompleteness is testimony to our methodological prejudices and blind spots, which are the products of the aesthetic formalist, (post)structuralist, and postmodern cultural theories that champion case studies as the best—even the only—way to promote their tenets.

But my main reason for not following the case study format is that I do not want to replicate the hierarchical relationship that case studies maintain between theorization and adaptation: one in which theorization decrees, while case studies support, illustrate, and defer to it, and in which theorization is "discovered" to be always already lurking in what it theorizes. To challenge the hierarchy of theorization over adaptation, theories *are*, for the most part, the case studies in this book. Rather than focusing on how aesthetic works have adapted other aesthetic works or have been adapted to new cultural, historical, and media contexts, this study forges case studies of how adaptation and theorization in the humanities have sought to adapt each other.

PART I
THEORIZING ADAPTATION

1

Histories of Theorizing Adaptation

David N. Rodowick has written: "Every historical moment of theoretical awakening is . . . to some degree metacritical or metatheoretical" (2014, xv). A study of theorizing adaptation that unfolds solely within the domain of theory is partial, in both senses of that word. History offers a perspective on theorization that theorization, often ahistorical in its claims to universality or working within closed systems, lacks, indicating how deeply enmeshed purportedly transcendent and timeless theories have been in particular historical contexts and the social, cultural, economic, and political agendas that theories have served. As history subjects the universal claims of theories to the scrutiny of the temporal and local, concomitantly, a diachronic history provides longer purviews beyond the immediate and local, which have so often been the focus of adaptation studies under the various formalist and cultural studies theories that have dominated the field. A diachronic, metacritical history of theorizing adaptation is also illuminating because it is not limited to a particular point in time but examines theoretical questions and issues across different theories over time.

A history of theorizing adaptation is essential to identifying and redressing the one-way, hierarchical discourse of "theorizing adaptation." Historicization presents a third term to mediate between adaptation and theorization: indeed, tensions between historicization and theorization in the humanities resemble and inform tensions between theorization and adaptation. Like theorization and adaptation, theory and history have sought to "-ize" each other—that is, to subdue and reduce each other to their own principles and processes. Theories have been historicized as the discursive products of historical forces, with no intrinsic truth value; conversely, history has been theorized as the product of theoretical paradigms. Theory has challenged history's claims to objectivity, impartiality, and factuality; history has challenged theory's claims to totality and universality. Theory has questioned historical narratives of evolution and progress; history has subjected theory's atemporal narratives to the scrutiny of chronology.[1]

Theorizing Adaptation. Kamilla Elliott, Oxford University Press (2020). © Oxford University Press.
DOI: 10.1093/oso/9780197511176.001.0001

While history and theory may police each other with equal rigor in many humanities fields, they have not done so in adaptation studies. Adaptation studies has been dominated by ahistorical, even anti-historical, theories such as aesthetic formalism, Romantic originality, New Criticism, narratology, auteur theory, and postmodern cultural theory. Although postmodern theory stresses historical situatedness and is keenly concerned with historical contexts, it is skeptical of historical chronologies, challenging their claims to cause and effect, factuality, and progress. And yet it is not enough to understand historical situatedness in a particular moment: we are also transhistorically situated, as theoretical forebears inform and inflect present theories, meaning that histories of theorizing adaptation offer essential insights into theorizing adaptation today. For example, a longer chronological history of theorizing adaptation challenges the narratives of theoretical progress that characterize histories of theorization in the humanities generally and in adaptation studies specifically. Histories of theorization tend to adopt the progressivist view that newer theories have corrected the errors and omissions of older ones. Far from challenging postmodern theories of history as a process of recycling, pastiche, and palimpsest, my chronological history of theorizing adaptation supports them. However, it goes beyond supporting postmodern tenets to challenge narratives of theoretical progress with narratives of theoretical *adaptation* that themselves engaged in processes of repetition with variation. Just as Richard Hurd acknowledged in 1757 that his theoretical principles were taken from a prior century—"In delivering this rule I will not dissemble that I myself am copying, or rather stealing from a great critic" (57)—so too my history finds theorists repeating, appropriating, and *adapting* prior theories. A history of theorizing adaptation reveals recessive theoretical "genes" resurfacing in new historical, political, cultural, and academic contexts, repeating and varying in them to ensure their survival. As so many critics have noted, albeit in other diction, postmodernism is modernism adapted and neo-narratology is classical narratology adapted, both of them to the cultural and philosophical revolutions of the late twentieth century. Adaptation studies is even more characterized by these tendencies than other fields, as theories resolutely discarded by the theoretical mainstream and other disciplines have shown remarkable persistence in academic, industry, artist, consumer, pedagogical, and political discourses of adaptation and as twenty-first-century adaptation studies continues to oscillate between theoretical progressivism and theoretical nostalgia (see

Chapters 3 and 4). It therefore turns out that a history of theorizing adaptation is *already* a history of adapting theorization.

Researching this history has further clarified why histories of theorizing adaptation are underdeveloped. Adaptation has tended to be studied within single disciplines or between two disciplines. It became a broader interdisciplinary field in a post-historical age, when chronological, empirical historicism was under attack by New Historicism and ahistorical postmodernism and, prior to that, it was studied under formal theories that marginalized, footnoted, or denigrated historical study. Deeply researched chronological histories of adaptation such as H. Philip Bolton's *Dickens Dramatized* (1987) and Martin Meisel's *Realizations: Narrative, Pictorial, and Theatrical Arts in Nineteenth-Century England* (1983) have therefore been rare and remained childless when academia became preoccupied with the theoretical turn. In other fields, traditional histories exist to be challenged and rewritten; the belated arrival of adaptation studies into academia, especially adaptation studies beyond literature and film, has meant that we lack longer, wider histories, as most field histories only start with the birth of film.

When in 2006 Linda Hutcheon expanded adaptation studies beyond literature, film, theater, and television to all manner of media (graphic novels, theme park rides, historical enactments, virtual reality, art installations, videogames, and all manner of new and digital media) and pursued pluralistic theorization in *A Theory of Adaptation*, she did not accompany her disciplinary and theoretical expansion with a historical expansion. Although she acknowledged that adaptation pre-existed the birth of film, she did so in a single paragraph (2006, 20).[2] As Glenn Jellenik has observed, adaptation scholars "suggest rather than explore the roots of adaptation," with single-sentence gestures to an unspecified, "long" history or "a history as old as narration," an "expanded scope" that he considers "renders theorizing adaptation almost impossible" (2017a, 36).

There are practical as well as theoretical reasons why historical adaptation studies are scant. While all histories are time-consuming to research, histories of adaptation theorization are particularly so. Adaptation has no home discipline, but is scattered across many. A disciplinary bastard, it has been called by many different names across many nations and centuries, making it a challenging subject to locate, let alone historicize. Additionally, adaptation's conscription in disciplinary wars has often distorted and obscured its history, as well as theirs (Elliott 2003a, Chapters 2–4). More pertinent to the research questions of this book, it has also been used as a weapon in theoretical wars at the expense of being itself theorized. For all the calls to free literary film adaptation from literature and study it as film in its own right, adaptation has rarely been studied as a subject in *its* own right. Instead, we have developed ahistorical mythologies of adaptation theorization that serve theory against the evidence of history.

Mythologies versus Histories

In lieu of a theoretical history tracing what scholars have actually written about adaptation, many adaptation critics[3] have substituted a myth that adaptation studies has until now, at the time that they are writing, been wrongly and culpably preoccupied with "the ideal of a single, definitive, faithful adaptation" (Stam 2005, 15) and that this theoretically culpable preoccupation is the chief reason that adaptation theorization is lacking. As Kara McKechnie puts it, fidelity is the "F-word" of adaptation studies (2009, 193).

A history of theorizing adaptation makes clear that, while some adaptation scholars have certainly championed this notion of fidelity—for example, James M. Welsh challenged: "Can there—or should there—be any more central issue in the field of adaptation studies [than fidelity]? Even for nonbelievers and infidels?" (2006, 1)—and while many have engaged in comparative criticism to assess degrees of fidelity between adapted and adapting works, the vast majority of adaptation scholars have opposed strict fidelity to source texts and championed *infidelity*, as the following passages illustrate.

> There are many and varied motives behind adaptation and few involve faithfulness. (Hutcheon 2006, xiii)
> Most striking in reading back over 50 years of academic criticism about adaptation is not the dead hand of fidelity criticism, but—quite the opposite—how few academic critics make any claim for fidelity criticism at all. (S. Murray 2008, 5)

Some go farther to expose propagating the fidelity myth as a false claim to originality, endlessly repeated:

> Practically every recent book on adaptation pretends it has revolutionized adaptation studies by deconstructing fidelity and the supremacy of the original. (Van Parys 2007, n.p.)

Endless attacks on fidelity [are] common to almost all the new literature on the subject. (MacCabe 2011, 7)

[Adaptation critics] all seem to have one fundamental starting point, namely the denunciation of the notion of fidelity to the original text. (Jameson 2011, 216)[4]

Today, adaptation scholars continue to propound the myth of fidelity criticism against the evidence of history. For Brian McFarlane the survival of the fidelity myth points to a lack of actual historical research: "The authors of such works have not adequately surveyed the critical field of recent decades" (2007, 15). Greg Jenkins, whose historical survey of literary film adaptation theory is the most thorough I have read for the period that it addresses, confirms that "most critics . . . are rather open-minded with respect to the fealty of adaptations. While they expect to notice some affinity between novel and film, the level of fidelity is rarely thrust to the forefront of a critique" (1997, 7). Even in the years 1909–1977, when one would expect to find ample evidence of the fidelity criticism excoriated by the myth, a simple count of entries treating adaptation in Jeffrey Egan Welch's annotated bibliography of literature and film studies in that period (1981) makes clear that publications advocating fidelity and opposing infidelity constitute a *minority* of adaptation scholarship, that many more promote infidelity than fidelity, and that quite a few studies are unconcerned with either. Continuing to rebut the fidelity myth eight years on, what Simone Murray finds

most striking in reading back over 50 years of academic criticism about adaptation is not the dead hand of fidelity criticism, but—quite the opposite— how few academic critics make any claim for fidelity criticism at all . . . the ritual slaying of fidelity criticism at the outset of a work has ossified into a habitual gesture, devoid of any real intellectual challenge. . . . It appears more likely that the standardized routing of fidelity criticism has come to function as a smokescreen, lending the guise of methodological and theoretical innovation to studies that routinely reproduce one set model of comparative textual analysis. (2008, 6)

Joining Colin MacCabe's critique in *True to the Spirit: Film Adaptation and the Question of Fidelity* on "the endless attacks on fidelity, common to almost all the new literature on the subject" (2011, 7), Fredric Jameson's reference to "the scarecrow of fidelity" attests further to its mythical status (2011, 215).

The fidelity myth has done extensive damage to adaptation studies, presenting our field and our scholarship as myopic, pedantic, outmoded, uncreative, and puerile, right up to the present time. In 2019, I reviewed several works submitted to presses or journals claiming that fidelity is *still* the chief or even sole preoccupation of adaptation scholarship today. An actual history of theorizing adaptation reveals otherwise. Historicizing recent in/fidelity debates, David T. Johnson has shown not only how prominent valorizing *infidelity* has been but also how complex and nuanced interplays between fidelity and infidelity are in adaptation (2017). A longer history of theorizing adaptation reveals that fidelity was not only excoriated on theoretical grounds but that it was also judged to be illegal.

Jellenik locates the historical origin of adaptation studies in a review of a novel adapted to a play in 1796, on the basis that the review is the first publication to use "adaptation" as a noun to describe a whole aesthetic work. Immediately, that rationale constrains adaptation to aesthetic products, away from a much older discourse of its processes in verbs of adapting, and to formalist theoretical preoccupations with whole works. The incipient focus on adaptation as a product rather than a process coincided with the rise of industrialism, capitalism, and commodification in the late eighteenth century, and was by no means the beginning of adaptation theories, practices, or discourses.

Jellenik locates the birth of fidelity criticism of the sort critiqued by Stam (2017, 47) and many others in this review, arguing that the reviewer was concerned solely with backward fidelity to the novel. However, his official argument is at odds with his own perceptive analysis of the review, which equally discusses the play's failure in forward fidelity to the conventions of the stage. As biblical translators had done in the seventeenth century, adaptation critics of the eighteenth century stressed the importance of an adaptation's fidelity to new aesthetic and cultural contexts more forcefully than backward fidelity to sources, going farther to use fidelity to new *contexts* as justification for infidelity to source *texts*. The chief criterion of theoretical value at that time, and for centuries after, was *aesthetics*, not fidelity of translation. Adapters valued source texts only insofar as they provided aesthetic value for the adapting work. The leading argument and opening line of the review is that "the adapter knows not how to select with taste and arrange with judgment," not that he has been unfaithful to the novel (Litchfield 1796, 20). Indeed, the chief task of the adapter is to know what to select *and what to discard* from a source text, which requires not only aesthetic taste and judgment but also infidelity to the source. An adapter must know when to be unfaithful to a source in order to make an aesthetically good adaptation. Further evidencing this, when John Litchfield reprinted his review to confute the playwright's published rebuttal of it, the lengthy introduction and summary of the review prefacing it *do not mention fidelity to the novel at all*: rather, they locate "the cause of [the playwright's] failure" in the play's lack of "dramatic application and effect" (iii–iv), its "radically dull and defective" unfolding on the stage, which was the fault of the writing rather than the acting (it was too badly written to be well acted) (13), its piecemeal composition (opposed to tasteful, judicious selection) (17), bolstering its failure to adapt both from and to with evidence that the audience hated the play (11–12). Robert B. Ray's survey of Welch's bibliographies affirms that the primary criterion of value in adaptation in the twentieth century continued to be *aesthetics*, not fidelity in translation (2000, 44).

While Jellenik locates fidelity in history, other scholars have pitted history against fidelity. The title, blurb, and introduction to Anne-Marie Scholz's *From Fidelity to History: Film Adaptations as Cultural Events in the Twentieth Century* (2009) claim to be moving adaptation studies away from textual fidelity studies to history and contextual studies. However, hers is not a diachronic history, but an application of historically based Marxist theories to selected 1950s adaptations and of feminist theories to selected 1990s adaptations. There are no case studies of adaptations made between the 1950s and 1990s, nor does the book offer a history of prior scholarship that has similarly applied Marxist and feminist theories to adaptation.

Other scholars, who have brought real theoretical innovation to adaptation studies, nevertheless undermine their scholarship with the fidelity myth. For example, John Hodgkins invaluably introduced affect theory to adaptation studies in 2013, while Samantha Pearce and Alexis Weedon offered new insights into fan adaptation studies in 2017. Yet by invoking the fidelity myth instead of setting these new theories in dialogue with *actual* prior theories, they weakened their own theoretical interventions. Similarly, even as Brian Boyd built fruitfully on prior discourses setting humanities and scientific adaptation theories in dialogue, advancing his contributions as solving "adaptation studies' perennial problem of 'fidelity discourse' " (2017, 587) left them unanchored to actual adaptation theorization. It may be that Boyd was referring to *debates* over fidelity, which are certainly adaptation studies' perennial problem, but the more accurate wording would be "the perennial problem of 'infidelity discourse.' "

The fidelity myth is adaptation studies' fake news: to use the *Oxford English Dictionary*'s Word of the Year for 2016, it is "post-truth" and post-historical history. The myth continues to be retweeted, without evidence, often in 140 characters or fewer, as in Yvonne Griggs's *Bloomsbury Introduction to Adaptation Studies: Adapting the Canon in Film, TV, Novels, and Popular Culture*: "Prior to the 1957 publication of George Bluestone's highly influential text, *Novels into Film*, discussion of adaptations to screen in particular, revolved around issues of fidelity" (2016, 2). That this account is inducting new scholars into adaptation studies promises to keep perpetuating the fidelity myth in lieu of actual field history.

My history of theorizing adaptation does more than (yet again) refute the fidelity myth: it explicates its persistence in histories of field theorization, arguing that the myth of fidelity criticism is the product of humanities theorization's centuries-long preference for difference and abiding hostility to similarity. It was infidelity that differentiated adaptation from forgery and plagiarism in law and from (mechanical) reproduction in culture. More central to the focus of this study, difference supports a host of theoretical values from Romantic originality to political nonconformity and from aesthetic formalist medium specificity theory to postmodern diversity; sameness attaches to a panoply of theoretical taboos: aesthetic derivation, political conformity, false philosophy, cultural homogenization, soulless mass production, and more. Because theories in the humanities, however else they may differ, have by and large championed infidelity (difference) over fidelity (sameness), making fidelity the history, theory, hallmark, and totality of adaptation studies has fed a transtheoretical, antagonistic relationship between adaptation studies and theorization—one perpetuated masochistically by adaptation scholars ourselves. Equally detrimental to adaptation studies, it neglects adaptation's similarities while fetishizing its differences, distorting study of adaptation as a process combining repetition with variation (Hutcheon 2006, 4). When adaptation is defined as repetition with variation, a transtheoretical insistence on difference and opposition to sameness in adaptation represents not only a demand that adaptation should conform to theorization, as all subject matter must, but also a demand that it repress or denigrate half of its very identity. In the final analysis, the fidelity myth supports theorization's occlusion, abuse, and oppression of adaptation and masks the demand that adaptation and adaptation studies *be faithful to theories.*

Prior Histories of Theorizing Adaptation

Julie Sanders has written: "The effort to write a history of adaptation necessarily transmutes at various points into a history of critical theory" (2006,
18). Although the fidelity myth often substitutes for an actual history of our
field, there have been prior histories of theorizing adaptation that do much
more. Even so, most historicize the field as theoretically lacking and call for
theoretical progress. George Bluestone (1957), Brian McFarlane (1996),
Guerric DeBona (2010), Simone Murray (2012a), and John Hodgkins (2013)
all present prior adaptation theorization as something to be challenged,
overthrown, or ameliorated by the theories that they propose. Their accounts
of prior theorization are scant, invoked chiefly to reject them, while they ex-
pansively illustrate and support the theories that they champion in case study
chapters that bulk out their books.

Histories of theorizing adaptation have been reduced in other ways: most
prioritize recent theorization. Some begin with the first academic monograph on literary film adaptation, George Bluestone's *Novels into Film* (1957)
(Leitch 2007, 1;[5] S. Murray 2008, 4; Slethaug 2014, 1; Griggs 2016, 2); one
commences in the late 1990s, implying that adaptation theory before that
time does not warrant comment (Saint Jacques 2011b).[6] Here, theoretical
progressivism does away with theoretical history.

By contrast, field overviews in edited collections, handbooks, companions,
and student readers (e.g., Beja 1979; McDougal 1985; Giddings, Selby, and
Wensley 1990; Stam 2005; Aragay 2005b; Corrigan 2007; 2011; Cartmell
2012c; Leitch 2017b) and monographs treating the adaptations of a particular genre, author, filmmaker, period, or nation (e.g., G. Jenkins 1997;
Niemeyer 2003; Donaldson-Evans 2009; Archer and Weisl-Shaw 2012) have
provided more capacious, less dismissive histories of theorization. The most
comprehensive field history of literary film adaptation that I have read is
Greg Jenkins's introduction to his 1997 book on Stanley Kubrick and adaptation. It includes radical adaptation scholars of the 1970s and 1980s omitted
by theorists claiming to be pioneering these theories in the 1990s, 2000s,
and 2010s. However, since few would think of turning to a book on Kubrick
adaptations for their introduction to adaptation theory, scholars have missed
out on the best field overview available in 1997—and for years after that. Yet
Jenkins's history is partial in another way, addressing only the history of theorizing literary film adaptation. Additionally, this excellent history is now
more than twenty years old.

The title of Bert Cardullo's collection of reprinted essays, *Stage and Screen: Adaptation Theory from 1916–2000* (2011) is misleading: only two of its essays treat adaptation at all; the rest are general comparative studies of theater and film, while many seminal essays treating adaptation theory in this period do not appear in the volume, probably because of copyright issues. Timothy Corrigan's student readers on *Film and Literature* (1999; 2011) offer a fuller range of historical essays on literary film adaptation. Bloomsbury Press's series The History of World Literatures on Film, edited by Bob Hasenfratz and Greg Colón Semenza, offers longer histories of national literatures adapted to film. Two have been published (Semenza and Hasenfratz 2015; Leitch 2019), with more to follow,[7] invaluably expanding historical literary film adaptation studies.

However, we need histories that go back farther than the birth of film and that treat adaptation in other media. While historical studies of theorizing adaptation prior to the birth of film and in other media abound, they reside within single disciplines and are seldom included in histories of adaptation studies more generally. We need to set histories of theorizing adaptation across media in dialogue. Reaching farther back to ponder older interart discourses of poetry, painting, theater, and illustrated fiction in *Rethinking the Novel/Film Debate*, Elliott (2003a) clarified theoretical problems in novel-and-film studies that I could not understand in their twentieth- and twenty-first-century contexts. It was not until I discovered that George Bluestone had carried Gotthold Ephraim Lessing's eighteenth-century categorical distinctions between poetry and painting wholesale into literature-and-film studies, without adapting them to their new media contexts, that I understood why worded films had been dubbed "visual" and illustrated fiction "verbal" (Elliott 2003a, 11–16).

Table 1.1 indicates the results yielded by a subject term search of the *Modern Language Association International Bibliography* (henceforth *MLA International Bibliography*) for "adaptation" and historical periods.

The earliest publication on this list dates only as far back as 1892. Adaptation theorization, of course, precedes that date by many centuries, and the table includes 61 entries discussing adaptation prior to 0 CE. The Romans adapted Greek poetry, theater, and visual art and theorized their adaptations (Cooke 1775, 135; Grube 1965, 151ff.). For Kara Reilly, "even the ancient Greek playwrights can be seen as adapters. Audiences knew the myths already and went to the theatre to see how the stories were told" (2017, xxi). The Greeks too theorized their adaptations.

Table 1.1 *MLA International Bibliography* adaptation studies by period

Period	No. of Publications	Earliest Publication
2000–2099	1,106	1999
1900–1999	13,488	1923
1800–1899	5,204	1910
1700–1799	977	1903
1600–1699	1,009	1897
1500–1599	3,611	1892
1400–1499	786	1896
1300–1399	876	1896
1200–1299	858	1896
1100–1199	843	1896
1000–1099	762	1896
900–999	762	1896
800–899	762	1896
700–799	729	1896
600–699	726	1896
500–599	724	1896
400–499	722	1896
300–699	55	1955
200–299	91	1947
100–199	67	1947
0–99 AD	66	1947
BCE	78	1947

Note: Search date December 23, 2019. All searches exclude dissertations. Some entries span more than one century and therefore appear under more than one date range.

My history of theorizing adaptation, even after years of research, cannot reach back to the classics: it is limited by my academic expertise, the brevity of my academic career, begun in mid-life, the constraints of publication, the research questions of this study, and its tripartite structure. My national, historical, and disciplinary expertise lies in British literature of the long nineteenth century in relation to other arts and media. Yet even within these constraints, I can glimpse discourses of classical adaptation in nineteenth-century Britain:

Whether Homer stole the best things in the *Iliad* and *Odyssey* from the temple of Vulcan, in Memphis; whether Virgil dipped into Nicander's lucky-bag for the gems of his *Georgics*, and derived his pathos from Apollonius; whether Horace foraged amongst the minor Greek poets,— these and many similar questions have been discussed hotly enough by critics. (Russell 1869, 44)[8]

My history of theorizing adaptation, like prior histories, is limited. It stretches back only to the sixteenth century, beginning in earnest in the late seventeenth century, continuing to the twenty-first. While it does include some non-Anglophone theorists and goes beyond adaptations of literature, it focuses primarily on my areas of expertise. I hope that others, expert in other fields, periods, and nations, will historicize adaptation theorization further.

Even within these parameters, there remains much that I have not read, and I cannot discuss everything that I have read. In *Elegy for Theory*, which investigates the status of film theory following David Bordwell and Noël Carroll's *Post-Theory* (1996), David N. Rodowick turned to history, tracing theory's genealogy back to the eighteenth century in an effort to understand its operations in the twenty-first century. He too made selections:

> My attempts to understand the conceptual vicissitudes of theory have veered wildly in perspective, sometimes plunging into one or two texts in florid detail . . . then retreating to the horizon to frame the most panoramic view possible. (2014, 201)

My history's long temporal reach and particular questions means that it omits works that other scholars may consider essential and condense theories to which others have devoted tomes and lifetimes.

My history, being metacritical, is further limited by what has taken center stage in adaptation studies. A metacritical history must prioritize dominant discourses, although mine also recovers forgotten and dissenting voices and works to connect discourses of adaptation across media and disciplines. Adaptation studies has been dominated by twentieth-century Anglophone literature and film, as Tables 1.2 through 1.4 attest. The reasons for this are manifold and include the global dominance of the English language, British literature, and American film. Table 1.2, created from subject search terms indicated in the left column, reveals the dominance of film and novel adaptation, while also documenting that adaptation scholarship has a substantial presence in other media.

Table 1.2 *MLA International Bibliography* adaptation studies by media format

Subject Search Terms	No. of Publications
Film adaptation	15,320
Novel adaptation	10,777
Theatrical adaptation OR dramatic adaptation	4,048
Television adaptation	2,163
Short story adaptation	1,404
Poetry adaptation	1,272
Music adaptation OR musical adaptation	1,319
Operatic adaptation	916
Comics adaptation OR graphic novel adaptation	762
Radio adaptation	265
Dance adaptation OR ballet adaptation	254
Ballet adaptation	116
Video game adaptation	162
Illustration adaptation	99
Painting adaptation	44
Photography adaptation	20
Visual arts adaptation	16

Table 1.3, created from subject search terms for "adaptation" and various nationalities, attests to the dominance of English adaptation studies, markedly higher than American adaptation studies, with France a distant runner-up. Between them, English and American adaptation studies publications outnumber those of all other nations combined. Although European nations occupy seven of the top eight spots, the next five are non-European, and the table confirms that adaptation studies are nationally diverse.

The national diversity of Table 1.3 diminishes significantly in Table 1.4, which affirms the dominance of canonical British authors in adaptation studies, while showing the prominence of canonical authors hailing from Europe, above that of US authors. A subject search for "adaptation" paired with Indian, African, and Arabic authors located the following: Rabindranath Tagore (18); Salman Rushdie (14); Wole Soyinka (14); Chinua Achebe (7).

Shakespeare publications are in the thousands rather than the hundreds, outnumbering all other authors combined, explaining why Shakespeare adaptation scholarship is often the richest and deepest, developed as it has been over centuries. Even so, scholars such as Jennifer Clement are beginning to

Table 1.3 *MLA International Bibliography* adaptation studies by nation

Nation	No. of Publications
England	8,837
USA	6,059
France	3,087
Germany	2,221
Spain	1,122
Italy	921
Russia	850
Canada	449
Japan	462
China	379
Africa*	328
India	276
Argentina	217
Australia	208
Brazil	198
Sweden	140
Mexico	126
Denmark	121
Turkey	103
Norway	107
Portugal	113

Note: Subject search terms were "adaptation" plus, for example, "English," "Brazilian," etc. With above 30 and below 100 citations are Cuba (77), Czech Republic (77), Korea (72), New Zealand (67), Chile (64), the Netherlands (62), Hungary (58), Austria (47), Finland (46), Croatia (51), Israel (32), and Slovenia (32). While a search by Arabic nations yields few results, a subject search for the subject terms "adaptation" and "Arabic" yields 94 publications.

* I am aware that Africa is a continent rather than a nation; however, studies of African adaptation often do not specify a particular nation (e.g., Dovey 2009), and a search by individual nations produces the following: South Africa (94), Nigeria (55), Egypt (45), Algeria (17), Morocco (7), Tanzania (4), Ghana (4), Kenya (3), Tunisia (3), Ethiopia (2); other African nations have one or no publications.

challenge Shakespeare's primacy within Early Modern adaptation studies, citing databases such as Early English Books Online to demonstrate that adaptation was central to early modern culture more generally (Clement 2015). Although women appear far less frequently than men in the table, Jane Austen occupies the second spot. Similarly, although popular authors do feature, the majority of adaptation studies cluster around canonical authors.

Table 1.4 *MLA International Bibliography* adaptation studies by literary author

Author	No. of Publications*
William Shakespeare	3,288
Jane Austen	406
J. R. R. Tolkien	291
Charles Dickens	235
Arthur Conan Doyle	225
Miguel de Cervantes	172
Joseph Conrad	158
Mary Shelley	155
Bertolt Brecht	146
Stephen King	139
Bram Stoker	130
Virginia Woolf	126
Samuel Beckett	123
Thomas Mann	121
Franz Kafka	118
Anton Chekov	112
Edgar Allen Poe	105
Émile Zola	100
Harold Pinter	99
Lewis Carroll	95
Herman Melville	95
Victor Hugo	94
Leo Tolstoy	94
Vladimir Nabokov	92
Fyodor Dostoyevsky	91
J. K. Rowling	90
Oscar Wilde	89
Charlotte Brontë	82
Geoffrey Chaucer	79
Dante Alighieri	75
Marcel Proust	73
F. Scott Fitzgerald	71
Henrik Ibsen	71
H. G. Wells	70
William Faulkner	69
John Steinbeck	69

Continued

Table 1.4 *Continued*

Author	No. of Publications*
Annie Proulx	67
Honoré de Balzac	63
Harriet Beecher Stowe	57
Emily Brontë	57
Gustave Flaubert	56
Lope de Vega	55
Edith Wharton	53
Graham Greene	52

Note: The following authors have generated between 30 and 50 publications: Alexandre Dumas (49), John Milton (48), Federico García Lorca (46), Gabriel García Márquez (46), Molière (46), Margaret Mitchell (43), George Bernard Shaw (41), Guy de Maupassant (40), Friedrich Schiller (40), George Eliot (38), D. H. Lawrence (37), Eugene O'Neill (35), Nathaniel Hawthorne (33), C. S. Lewis (35), Mark Twain (35), Daphne du Maurier (31), Alberto Moravia (31), Alice Walker (31), Günter Grass (28), Giovanni Boccaccio (27), Jules Verne (26), August Strindberg (25), Roald Dahl (24), and Henry Fielding (21).

* There are more entries for *Frankenstein* (159) than for Shelley.

Agreed canons provide a focal point for scholarly discourse and debate, whether they are the canons developed by high-art humanist theories or the newer canons generated by feminist, postcolonial, and other radical theories. Even scholars who oppose the high-art humanist canon understand its centrality to establishing and connecting adaptation studies. Deborah Cartmell and Imelda Whelehan, who have campaigned from 1996 to expand adaptation studies beyond canonical literature and film to popular and trash fiction, film, television, and novelization, devote a substantial proportion of their many publications to adaptations of canonical works, as do other adaptation scholars who are keen to move the field beyond canonical literature (Aragay 2005b; R. Carroll 2009; Albrecht-Crane and Cutchins 2010a; Frus and Williams 2010). Scholars treating adaptation in other media (opera, ballet, art, radio, and television) also tend to foreground canonical works; newer arrivals to adaptation studies such as comics and videogames are also developing canons as a shared ground for their emerging fields (L. Burke 2015; Papazian and Sommers 2013; Flanagan 2017; Stobbart 2018). Studies of literary film adaptation in other nations also tend to limit their studies to canonical literature and film (Rentschler [1986] 2015; Umrani 2012; Faulkner 2004; Deppman 2010; Archer and Weisl-Shaw 2012).

In such a widely dispersed field as adaptation studies, with such a long history spanning so many media, we tend to borrow our canons from other disciplines; we do not yet have an *adaptation* canon of our own: we tend to discuss the adaptation of works canonized in single disciplines rather than ponder what a canonical, exemplary, or paradigmatic *adaptation* might look like. Developing an adaptation canon across media, nations, and periods would indubitably build adaptation studies as a field—all the more so if this canon were contested and debated.

Returning to adaptation studies past and present, comparing Table 1.4 to Table 1.5 underscores prior adaptation studies' far greater interest in literary authors than in film directors, and supports claims that literary film adaptation scholars have prioritized literature over film. Directors who adapt Shakespeare feature prominently, while a search for celebrated theater directors who are not also playwrights yields scant results.

In contrast to the previous table, here US directors dominate, with twice as many appearances as British directors, in second place, with New Zealand director Peter Jackson in the top spot and Australian director Baz Luhrmann in fourteenth place. Western Europeans make far fewer appearances in the directors' table than in the authors' table. Taiwanese director Ang Lee tops the list of Asian directors with 142 citations; however, his work outside of Asia and English language adaptations go a long way to establishing that count. Japanese director Akira Kursawa comes next at (104), followed by Indian director Vishal Bhardwaj (34): both are renowned for their adaptations of Shakespeare. Indeed, the prevalence of Shakespeare adaptation studies generally influences the directors' table, with several known solely for their Shakespeare adaptations. Zhang Yimou tops Chinese mainland adaptation studies by director: his subjects are Chinese rather than Western (16). Other searches for Asian, African, and Middle Eastern directors yielded fewer than 10 hits.[9]

These tables represent twentieth- and twenty-first adaptation studies, and a handful of studies from the 1890s. A longer history of theorizing adaptation reveals continuities with and variations of these trends. While literary film adaptation dominates twentieth-century adaptation studies, adaptations of prose fiction to theater dominate discourses written in the nineteenth century, which are important precursors vitally informing discourses of literary film adaptation. In the late seventeenth and eighteenth centuries, the most frequently discussed adaptation practices were intramedial ones: poetry to poetry-and theater-to-theater adaptations.

Table 1.5 *MLA International Bibliography* adaptation studies by film director

Film Director	No. of Publications
Peter Jackson	253
Stanley Kubrick	234
Kenneth Branagh	187
Orson Welles	180
Ang Lee	142
Alfred Hitchcock	139
John Huston	127
Victor Fleming	125
Francis Ford Coppola	123
Steven Spielberg	121
Laurence Olivier	112
Luchino Visconti	111
Akira Kurosawa	104
Baz Luhrmann	91
Roman Polanski	87
Franco Zeffirelli	87
Rainer Werner Fassbinder	85
Peter Greenaway	77
David Cronenberg	75
David Lean	74
Martin Scorsese	73
Luis Buñuel	70
James Ivory	68
Julie Taymor	67
Peter Brook	62
John Ford	61
William Wyler	53
Jean Renoir	52

Note: "Adaptation" and director name were both entered as subject search terms. With between 20 and 50 citations are Joel and Ethan Coen (49), Jane Campion (48), François Truffaut (46), Howard Hawks (43), Michael Winterbottom (43), Robert Bresson (42), D. W. Griffith (39), Derek Jarman (39), Spike Jonze (39), Michael Almereyda (38), Steven Soderbergh (33), Jean-Luc Godard (37), F. W. Murnau (34), Max Ophüls (35), Alain Resnais (35), Vishal Bhardwaj (34), Bernardo Bertolucci (33), Mira Nair (32), Michael Haneke (30), Joseph L. Mankiewicz (30), Billy Wilder (30), Michelangelo Antonioni (29), Terence Davies (24). Fritz Lang (24), Vittorio de Sica (23), Satyajit Ray (23), and Sergei Eisenstein (21).

A Historical Turn in Adaptation Studies?

For Semenza and Hasenfratz, "the scholarly fantasy of arriving at a grand theory or methodology tends to trump real, sustained attention to the stubborn realities of historical specificity" (2015, 7). In spite of claims that adaptation studies is theoretically lacking, theory has outweighed history in adaptation studies. Pedagogical publications are more likely to be organized by theoretical than historical categories: by formal and narrative theories focused on literary and film genres (Desmond and Hawkes 2006, reprinted 2015), by different theoretical approaches (K. Brown 2009), by aesthetic theories celebrating canonical novels and/or films or by cultural theories celebrating popular ones (Cutchins, Raw, and Welsh 2010b), by a combination of theories (Cutchins, Raw, and Welsh 2010a), or by blending theoretical paradigms with pragmatic pedagogical advice (Cartmell and Whelehan 2014). Given the charges outlined in the introduction that adaptation studies is atheoretical, theoretically lacking, or theoretically superannuated, the fact that scholars have prioritized theory over history presents our field as even more historically than theoretically lacking.

In 2015, Semenza and Hasenfratz called for "a historical turn in adaptation studies" that moves beyond the formal, ahistorical readings of texts promoted by aesthetic formalism and New Criticism and beyond postmodern restrictions to adaptations in particular, localized cultural contexts to engage diachronic histories of adaptation (6, 9), a call that is being realized in the Bloomsbury series they co-edit, *The History of World Literatures on Film*. In 2017, Peter Lev observed: "There are hundreds of books and thousands of articles about film adaptations of novels and plays, but only a tiny percentage consider adaptation from a historical perspective" (661). For Lev, "historical" does not mean historically located case studies: these are legion. Nor does it mean historical surveys of adaptations of individual authors or filmmakers: these too proliferate (Bolton 1987; Marsden 1995; Jenkins 1997; Parrill 2002; Rothwell 2004; Kidnie 2009; Osteen 2014). Nor does it mean surveys of adaptations within a particular historical period: these too are well established (Giddings et al. 1990; Del Villano 2012; Bolton 2000; Simonova 2015; Cartmell 2015). For Lev, "historical" means corpus studies based in archival research that ask and answer historical questions: for example, whether there was a shift in adapting plays to adapting novels in the 1930s. Scholars have been answering calls for adaptation studies to take a historical turn individually (Tutan 2017; Leitch 2018) and collectively, as the

Adaptation special issue edited by Jeremy Strong, "Adaptation and History" (2019), attests.

In 2018, Semenza again called for "a greater balance between theory and history—as well as a more historically informed . . . practice of theory" and for "much larger [histories] that would take into account changing conceptions of adaptation" (62, 64). My history of theorizing adaptation, partial as it is, undertakes this challenge. More than anything, however, my history seeks to redress the one-sided, top-down discourse of "theorizing adaptation" with an inversely reciprocal discourse of "adapting theorization," telling a story of how theorization has adapted over time and across history.

2

Theorizing Adaptation in the Sixteenth to Nineteenth Centuries

Traditionally, theorization proceeds in three stages: definition, taxonomization, and the development of theoretical principles. Even post-structuralist theorist Paul de Man, who opposed fixed meaning, conceded that theorization must begin by defining the subject matter to be theorized (1986, 5). In practice, however, theorization rarely follows this sequence: a priori theoretical principles often determine definitions and taxonomies. Even so, these stages help to structure a discussion of how adaptation was theorized in the sixteenth to nineteenth centuries.

Historical Definitions: Hierarchies, Processes, and Products

A history of defining adaptation also initiates the explication of why adaptation has been so difficult to theorize in the humanities. While theory seeks to identify and fix subject matter for theorization, history makes clear that definitions are not stable or fixed, but change over time and are contested within historical periods.

The *Oxford English Dictionary* locates the first use of the noun "adaptation" in 1597. Then, as now, adaptation was not confined to any one discipline or discourse, but was invoked in many, from alchemy to theology, from philosophy to physiology. Although its earliest definition, "the action of applying one thing to another or bringing two things together so as to effect a change in the nature of the objects" (*Oxford English Dictionary* (hereafter *OED*), 2nd. ed., s.v. "adaptation," definition 1, accessed June 5, 2017, http://www-oed-com/view/Entry/2115) was considered obsolete by the *Oxford English Dictionary*'s second edition (1989), it was prominent historically and is, perhaps, the most resonant one for this study, which seeks to bring theorization and adaptation together in order to effect a mutual, reciprocal change in

Theorizing Adaptation. Kamilla Elliott, Oxford University Press (2020). © Oxford University Press.
DOI: 10.1093/oso/9780197511176.001.0001

each. Indeed, that this definition is now deemed obsolete only reinforces the need for such a definition today. By 1654, the term "reciprocal adaptation" was in use (*OED*, "adaptation," definition 2.a) and my history confirms that relations between adaptation and theorization were more reciprocal then than they were in the twentieth and twenty-first centuries.

Adaptation's most prominent definition today was established in 1610, two centuries before Charles Darwin (1809–1882) was born: "The action or process of adapting one thing to fit with another, or suit specified conditions, esp. a new or changed environment, etc.; (also) an instance of this" (*OED*, "adaptation," definition 2.a). This definition helpfully differentiates adaptation from other kinds of intertextuality and intermediality: while intertextuality and intermediality treat textual and media relations of all kinds, adaptation focuses more specifically on changes made to suit new environments. Adaptation's environments include not only historical and cultural contexts but also textual and media ones. More pertinent to this project, adaptation's environments also include theoretical environments.

The *Oxford English Dictionary*'s earliest documented usage of the noun "adaptation" to refer to literary works is 1799 (*OED*, "adaptation," definition 4); however, Glenn Jellenik has located a theater review that used it in this sense in 1796 (see Chapter 1). Adaptation in the humanities extends beyond literature in performance: John Aikin nominated poetry adapted to musical settings "adaptation" in 1774 (14–16), while an unnamed author used it to address religious music adapted to bawdy songs in 1765 (Percy 2.119–20). These may not be the earliest uses of the noun "adaptation" to describe whole aesthetic works.

Even if they are, restricting adaptation to its application to whole aesthetic works delimits a history of theorizing adaptation. Much earlier and more prevalently than the noun, the verb "adapt" was engaged to describe changes to aesthetic works to suit new environments. The *Oxford English Dictionary*'s earliest recorded usage of the verb in 1531 refers to music (*OED*, 2nd rev. ed., s.v. "adapt" 1, accessed November 19, 2017, http://www-oed-com/view/Entry/2110). That the verb predates the noun by more than sixty years indicates the priority of the *process* of adaption over adaptation as a *product* in the sixteenth century, an emphasis that influenced how adaptation was theorized.

Although Figure 2.1's Ngram is not limited to humanities adaptation discourses, it demonstrates the rise of the noun to overtake the verb between 1775 and 1825 more generally, a period marked by the rise of industrialism

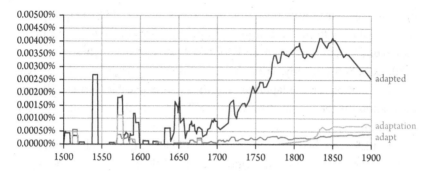

Figure 2.1 Google Books Ngram of adapt, adapted, adaptation, 1500–1900, generated December 8, 2018.

and Romanticism in Europe. What is striking, however, is how prevalent the verb "adapted" was in these centuries compared to other forms of the word. This may be because the past tense of "adapted" fuses the process and product of adaptation by rendering both complete.

However, 1531 does not mark the origin of adapting aesthetic works to new environments: practices and discourses of adaptation are much older than the words "adapt" and "adaptation" and there is a much longer history of theorizing adaptation under other names. Along with the verb "adapt," Early Modern, Restoration, and eighteenth-century artists and scholars picked up and continued ancient classical practices and discourses of adaptation titled and discussed under other names, including "translation," "imitation," "metaphrase," and "paraphrase" in literature, while developing new terminologies for dramatic adaptation such as "alteration." That twentieth- and twenty-first-century critics studying these historical discourses and practices, otherwise named in their day, now nominate them adaptations supports this argument (e.g., Kelly 1978; Marsden 1995; Roglieri 2001; Del Villano 2012; Kousser 2015; Simonova 2015).

Twentieth-century critics were not, however, the first to render other historical terminologies interchangeable with adaptation. The *Routledge Encyclopedia of Translation Studies* attests that many translation historians locate the initial terminological divide between adaptation and translation in debates between Cicero and Horace in the first century BCE, where adaptation describes freer translations in opposition to more literal ones (1998, 3). In Samuel Johnson's "Life of Alexander Pope" ([1781] 1830), the verb "adapt" defines Pope's "mode of imitation, in which the ancients are familiarized, by *adapting* their sentiments to modern topics" ([1781] 1830, xxi, emphasis added). Johnson located the origin of Pope's practice "in the reign of Charles the Second by [John] Oldham and [John Wilmot, Earl of] Rochester" ([1781] 1830, xxii). Subsequently, Britain's International Copyright Act of 1852 rendered imitation and adaptation *legally* interchangeable terms ("Recent Legislation on the Law of Contracts" 1875, 441), both distinguished from adaptation.

Yet a history of theorizing adaptation would lose a great deal by conflating all terms or substituting "adaptation" for all of them, since terminological variations invaluably illuminate how adaptation was being *theorized*. While the twentieth-century theoretical mainstream prioritized formal adaptation studies, earlier centuries used different terminologies to distinguish formal from cultural adaptation. "Imitate" articulated the relationship of adapted to adapting form, while "adapt" expressed the relation of both adapted and adapting works to a new cultural context. In titles such as Edward Burnaby Greene's *The Satires of Juvenal: Paraphrastically Imitated, and Adapted to the Times* (1763), "imitated" describes the work's relationship to its source text, while "adapted" describes its relationship to its new reception context, and "paraphrastically" indicates the type of adaptation practice engaged.

Similarly, while recent critics have pursued continuities between adaptation and translation fruitfully (O'Thomas 2010; Raw, 2012; Krebs 2012; 2013; Minier 2013), earlier scholars differentiated them in ways that are equally fruitful for theorization. As T. R. Steiner has written: "The evidence weighs very strongly that translation and imitation were different and were generally so recognized by seventeenth- and eighteenth-century theorists (1975, 175). According to Steiner, "translation implied use only of the modern language in its modern idiom . . . whereas imitation meant radical modernizing, of customs, places, allusions, etc." (148).

Distinctions were also useful for marketing adaptations. An early nineteenth-century Pickering & Chatto catalogue indicates that publishers made similar distinctions between translation and adaptation: for example, an advertisement for *The Distressed Family* indicates that it was "*translated* from the French" in 1787 and that "Mrs. Inchbald in 1791 *adapted* this translation for the English Stage," adding: "she distinctly improved the piece" (Pickering & Chatto [1800?] n.d.,[1] 481, emphasis added). "Adapted" was also used to describe relations between works written in the same medium, nation, and language but different historical periods, as in the advertisement for *Double Falshood* [*sic*] (1728), "Written originally by W. Shakespeare, and now revised and *adapted* to the Stage by Mr. Theobald, the Author of Shakespeare Restor'd" (Pickering & Chatto [1825] 1903, 292, emphasis added). "Revised" indicates what was done to the text, while "adapted" points to the new cultural environment.

The word "adapted" was not limited to literary works dramatized for the stage: in 1825, *Illustrations of Shakespeare* offered 230 vignette engravings "adapted to all editions" (Pickering & Chatto [1825] 1903, 293). A 1789 advertisement discussed the adaptation of lyrics to music, claiming that the volume of songs *The Jolly Companion; or a Cure for Care* was "calculated to Please Every Body, and Offend No Body, adapted to well known [*sic*] and approved Tunes" (Pickering & Chatto [1789] 1896, 178). Even in such discussions of form, "adaptation" is keenly attuned to consumer reception, tastes, and values ("well known" and "approved"). Commenting on the 1691 opera *King Arthur* (written by John Dryden, music by Henry Purcell, choreography by John Priest), a critic assessed that "The play was adapted to the times by the omission of politics" (Pickering & Chatto [1825] 1903, 101). An advertisement for a book of sermons by Thomas Wilson, Bishop of Sodor and Man (1663–1775) remarks: "His style and language is [*sic*] adapted to the understanding and capacity of all orders and degrees of men" (Pickering & Chatto [1825] 1903, 379). These glimpses make clear that adaptation was richly and diversely understood as a complex nexus of formal and cultural interchanges, even by publishers.

In the nineteenth century, differentiating terminologies became a matter of law. The International Copyright Act of 1852 aligned imitation and adaptation and contrasted both to translation. In 1870, a judge ruled that this Act "clearly distinguishes between a translation and an adaptation. . . . A translation means a delivery from one language into another, having regard to the difference of idioms," while an adaptation accommodates a work to "the tastes and feelings of an English audience . . . according to English notions. . . . That is the broad distinction between the two." Translation makes the work formally intelligible to an English audience; adaptation makes it culturally acceptable to them. In this case, the judge ruled that the translator had gone beyond translation to "an imitation and adaptation to the English stage" (James 1870, 648):

> That is, you transfer the scene to England, you make the characters English, you introduce English manners when our manners differ from French manners, and you leave out things which you say would not be suitable for

representation on the English Stage. . . . [T]his is not a translation. . . . [A]
translation must be sufficiently literal to enable an Englishman to see from
it the character of the original work. (James 1870, 643; 641)

Thus, even when both translation and adaptation occur in same medium
and technology (the case concerns two published theatrical texts), translation emphasizes formal, semantic, and linguistic changes, while adaptation foregrounds social, cultural, and ideological ones. Attempting to sever
formal from cultural adaptation studies in 2006, Linda Cahir made a similar
distinction, rejecting the term "adaptation" in favor of "translation" in order
to focus on media rather than cultural changes (14). While it is impossible
to separate the two definitively, since formal and aesthetic theories are invariably intertwined with historical, cultural, and political ideologies, and
cultural ideologies themselves have formal and structural properties, the law
did distinguish them. Separating formal and cultural aspects into separate
spheres and theorizing them as separate species in the twentieth and twenty-
first centuries delimited the study of adaptation, which cannot be understood without considering both *in relationship to each other*. However, other
taxonomies were proposed to theorize adaptation prior to that.

Historical Taxonomies and Fidelity in Adaptation

Definition is followed by the second stage of theorization, taxonomization.
Taxonomies build on, nuance, and complicate baseline definitions prior
to the development of theoretical principles. Like definitions, taxonomies
often derive from, rather than precede, the formation of theoretical principles. Taxonomies of literary translation, imitation, and adaptation in the
seventeenth century had their roots in medieval theologies of biblical translation, themselves inflected by classical theories of literary translation and
imitation (Hopkins 2000). As Ruth Morse has noted, "By a process of adaptation, Christian writers legitimated the use of classical patterns" (1991,
135). Samuel Johnson's dictionary (1755) shows the centrality of theology
to adaptation's aesthetic definitions and taxonomies, engaging Richard
Hooker's taxonomy of biblical translation ([1636] 1821) to explicate it.[2]
Quite strikingly for proponents of the fidelity myth in adaptation studies (see
Chapter 1), Hooker argued that true fidelity is *incompatible with* literal translation of a source text:

Now the principal thing required in a witness is fidelity.... Touching translation of Holy Scripture ... the judgment of the church ... hath been ever,
That the fittest for public audience are such, as following a middle course
between the rigor of literal translators and the liberty of paraphrasts, do
with greatest shortness and plainness deliver the meaning of the Holy
Ghost. (Hooker [1636] 1821, 2.47)

Hooker's taxonomy reveals that the faithful, literal translation that so many
late twentieth- and twenty-first-century "histories" of the field have claimed
constitutes the majority of all adaptation scholarship, right into the 2010s,
was *not even favored clerics policing the translation of the Bible in the 1630s, or
at any prior point in the history of the Christian church* ("the judgment of the
church hath ever been").

Yet Hooker did not dismiss fidelity as a concept: rather, he valued it and
redefined it, arguing that fidelity *requires* a departure from the literal in order
to convey a text's meaning and to ensure its favorable reception in new cultural and historical contexts. In later centuries, "the meaning of the Holy
Ghost" would become a discourse of fidelity to the spirit of a literary text,
theorized variably as author intent, tone, thought, personality, and style; textual meaning, including psychological subtexts; reader response; the spirit
of an age or its cultural ideologies; postmodern indeterminacy; and deconstructive aporia (Elliott 2003a, 136–43).

Douglas Kelly attests that the "[r]einterpretation of earlier material was
traditional in medieval adaptation" and that adaptation was often "justified as an improvement on the original version," with "effective adaptation"
sometimes amounting to "correction" of sources (1978, 107; 157; 83). It is not
within the scope of this history to reach back into the Middle Ages; its discussion of taxonomies begins with John Dryden (1631–1700), poet laureate,
playwright, literary adapter, and celebrated Augustan critic, whose highly influential taxonomy of literary translation ([1680] 1795) shaped many subsequent taxonomies of adaptation right into the twenty-first century. Like
Hooker's, his taxonomy spans degrees of resemblance between adapting and
adapted texts from the literal to the free, with metaphrase being the most literal, imitation the least, and paraphrase forging a middle way between them.[3]
Dryden favored the middle way, condemning strict fidelity to source texts
as the worst of the three because it fails to *adapt to* new cultural contexts.[4]
For Dryden, to imitate is "not to translate his words, or to be confined to his
sense, but only to set him as a pattern"; the imitator "assumes the liberty not

only to vary from the words and sense, but [also] to forsake them both as he sees occasion; and, taking only some general hints from the original, to run division on the ground-work, as he pleases" ([1680] 1795, 348). While Dryden admired some imitations, he favored paraphrase because it valorizes adapting *from* and adapting *to* equally. In so doing, it values adapting and adapted works equally. Literal translation (metaphrase) disproportionately favors the source text; free adaptation (imitation) disproportionately favors the adapted text. Dryden's middle way is valuable for contemporary adaptation studies in offering a discourse that esteems adapted and adapting works equally and values equally adaptation as a process of adapting *from* and a process of adapting *to*.

Johnson subscribed to Dryden's view when he praised Pope for pursuing a "middle composition, between translation and original design, which pleases when the thoughts are unexpectedly applicable, and the parallels lucky" ([1781] 1830, xxii). Dryden's taxonomy of translation can be set in dialogue with Geoffrey Wagner's taxonomy of literary film adaptation published nearly three hundred years later. Wagner too produced a tripartite taxonomy tracing relative degrees of closeness to sources and was as influential in establishing adaptation taxonomies in his day as Dryden in his.[5] Even when subsequent theorists changed the names (Klein and Parker 1981; Desmond and Hawkes 2006), they followed his and Dryden's tripartite structure of close, less close, least close.

However, while Wagner agreed with Dryden in pronouncing the most literal mode (transposition) the worst, he differed from him in valuing the freest adaptation (analogy) the most highly. Wagner's analogy resembles Dryden's imitation: it too "represent[s] a fairly considerable departure for the sake of making another work of art. . . . [It] cannot be indicted as a violation of a literary original since the director has not attempted (or has only minimally attempted) to reproduce the original." As with Augustan imitation, analogy must be "worthy of the original" and at least take "hints from [its] sources" (1975, 223).

Wagner's valuation of the least faithful category of adaptation over the middle way attests to a theoretical sea change that began in the second half of the eighteenth century and continues to the present. Twentieth-century revivals of medium specificity theory and Romantic originality pioneered in the second half of the eighteenth century allied to value *most* those adaptations that resembled their sources the *least*. By contrast, even as Dryden allowed that the least faithful mode of adaptation, "imitation," may produce a work "perhaps more excellent than the first design" and that "[i]mitation of an author is the most advantageous way for a translator to shew [sic] himself," he expressed concern that imitation may be "the greatest wrong which can be done to the memory and reputation of the dead" ([1680] 1795, 349). For Dryden, the middle way of "paraphrase" establishes a genealogy between adapted and adapting authors and works, carrying forward what is valuable in the adapted work while adding new value to it. Paraphrase functions similarly to theories of biological adaptation developed two centuries later, in which adaptation carries forward valuable inherited traits while adding variations that contribute to survival in new and changing environments.

Five years on from Wagner, film scholar Dudley Andrew, finding the extremes of "fidelity and transformation . . . tiresome" (1980, 12), like Dryden, favored the middle way in his tripartite adaptation taxonomy (borrowing, intersecting, transforming) because it values adapting and adapted works equitably (10–13).[6] While other adaptation scholars have worried that adaptation theory may *invariably* favor adapted (source) work over adapting work (to name only a few: Whelehan 1999, 3; Ray 2001, 126; Cardwell 2002, 64; Stam 2005, 131–45; Hutcheon 2006, 7; Leitch 2007, 4; Cartmell and Whelehan 2010, 49; Snyder 2017, 208), Andrew's intersecting promotes a middle way that values both equally. Although he does not mention Dryden, his discussion of "borrowing" resonates with Dryden's comments on the cultural prestige of adaptation: "the adaptation hopes to win an audience by the prestige of its borrowed title or subject. But at the same time, it seeks to gain a certain respectability, if not aesthetic value, as a dividend in the transaction" (1980, 10). Throughout the history of theorizing adaptation, aesthetics have been far more important than fidelity to source texts in assessing the value of an adaptation. In seventeenth-century France, scholar, poet, and man of letters Gilles Ménage (1613–1692) celebrated "*les belles infidèles*"—translations that are beautifully unfaithful to their sources (Lhermitte 2004, par. 8).

Andrew's essay also revives the Augustan focus on cultural adaptation lost following the formalist turn in twentieth-century humanities theorization when it calls adaptation studies to "take a sociological turn" (10). More recently, while the title of Lawrence Venuti's article, "Adaptation, Translation, Critique" (2007), recalls Wagner's taxonomy (analogy, transposition, critique), it integrates the cultural and social conditions of the materials as well with the interpretive, hermeneutic agency of the adapter/translator.

Early nineteenth-century taxonomies of adaptation continued to denigrate textual fidelity and elevate contextual fidelity. In 1801, an anonymous critic of Scottish poet, publisher, and playwright Allan Ramsay (1656–1758) intriguingly denigrated *exact translation* while praising *exact adaptation*:

> This composition, which, from its fidelity to the thought, and happy imitation of the style of the original, might almost fall under the description of a translation, is distinguished from that species of writing, solely, by this peculiarity, in which lies *the chief merit of the copyist, an exact adaptation* of the different characters in the original to modern times and to the manners of his own country. ("Remarks on the Genius and Writings of Allan Ramsay" 1800], xcvi, emphasis added)

Valorized fidelity is limited to a secularized version of Hooker's fidelity to "the meaning of the Holy Ghost": "fidelity to the thought" of the author and "happy imitation" of "the style of the original." By contrast, *exact fidelity* in adapting the source text *to* a new historical and cultural context is highly commended.

Historical Theoretical Principles

Following taxonomization, the third and final stage of theorization is the development of theoretical principles. As we will see, adaptation experienced variable fortunes under changing—adapting—humanities theories from the sixteenth to the nineteenth century. The *Routledge Encyclopedia of Translation Studies* locates "the golden age of adaptation" in the seventeenth and eighteenth centuries (1998, 3). It was also a golden age of adaptation theorization, for better and for worse.

Theorizing Adaptation as a Good Theoretical Object: The Augustan Age and Its Legacy

My introduction to this book attests that adaptation has been excoriated as a bad theoretical object in the humanities, in and of itself, quite apart from its scholarship. A longer history of theorizing adaptation, however, reveals that this has not always been the case. Prior to the mid-eighteenth century, adaptation was a good theoretical object, a valued aesthetic and cultural practice. The Romans adapted Greek poetry, theater, art, sculpture, and architecture (Kousser 2015); the Anglo-Saxons adapted classical legends (O'Connor 2014, 3); Medieval and Renaissance Europe abounded in celebrated adaptations of the Judeo-Christian Bible in art (Jeffrey 2017) and of Greek and Latin authors in literature (Grafton, Most, and Settis 2010; J. Clark, Coulson, and McKinley 2011; Rhodes 2013), while many other adapted forms received high theoretical and critical praise (L. Campbell 2017). Of course, that adaptation as a practice was valued aesthetically, politically, and culturally did not mean that all adaptations were valued any more than any form of art has ever been unilaterally praised. John Dryden valued adaptation (imitation) as a *general* practice even as he denounced *particular* adapters of the Roman poet Horace (65 BCE to 8 BCE) in the preface to his play, *All for Love*, itself an adaptation, "written in Imitation of Shakespear's Stile" [*sic*]" (1678, vii).[7] Dryden was an adapter as well as a critic of adaptation, modernizing Chaucer's poems in 1700 and adapting Shakespeare's *The Tempest* with William D'Avenant in the 1660s and Sophocles's *Oedipus* with Nathaniel Lee in 1678.

Critics viewed adaptation as fostering an innovative, progressive, national, aesthetic culture. Literary adaptations of the period focused largely on Greek, Roman, and older English "classics," upon which adapters sought to progress toward aesthetic perfection, infusing works already imbued with the wisdom and skill of aesthetic forebears with the progressive knowledge of later cultures (Del Villano 2012, 177). Against later notions of adaptation as secondary in every derogatory sense of that word—historically behind-hand, culpably nostalgic, inferior in status, aesthetically derivative and unoriginal, intellectually and ideologically conformist—adaptation was viewed as progressive, modernizing, and aesthetically and morally improving not only of prior works but also of art generally. In 1874, John Diekmann retroactively credited Dryden with giving "elegance and harmony to English poetry," praising him for establishing a "new versification," after which "English poetry had no tendency to relapse to its former savageness" of "forced thoughts and rugged met[er]" (1874, 9). Diekmann heroized Dryden via late nineteenth-century, bourgeois theories of masculinity, independence, and justice: "though his predecessors did much, they left much to do. . . . It was reserved to Dryden manfully to claim and to vindicate the freedom of a just translation." Praising Dryden's adaptations, Diekmann also invoked adapting the spirit over the letter of a text: "Not to copy servilely the very words, but to transfuse the spirit of the author" (10).

Similar discourses unfolded treating other art forms. Sigismund Thalberg, Vice-President of the Austrian Imperial Conservatory for Music and Drama and music juror at the Great Exhibition of 1851, assessed that "the adaptation for the pianoforte of all the best orchestral compositions" had contributed to "the advance of the art, and the improvement of the piano . . . until it is now beyond all question the first of musical instruments, both to the profession and to the cultivated classes of society" (1852, 326).

Adaptation was not only theorized as a means of improving particular aesthetic works and whole aesthetic genres and forms but also as formative of those who produced them, offering a way for fledgling poets, dramatists, artists, sculptors, and musicians to learn their art and for mature ones to demonstrate their superiority to the predecessors whose works they adapted (Bassnett 2013, 4). Like Dryden, many theorists and critics were also practitioners of adaptation, reflecting on their own adaptations in prefaces and notes and reviewing and theorizing adaptations by others. Drama critic James Robinson Planché (1796–1880) was the prolific author of 176 plays, libretti, and theatrical entertainments; he also pioneered new adaptation forms, including adapting well-known paintings to theatrical scenes (tableaux vivants) and contemporary novels to critically acclaimed operas. He saw himself as working in a long lineage of distinguished adapters: "no one can deny that it has been the practice of the greatest dramatists in every age and every country to found their plays upon the popular tales of their own or of former times" (1872, 47).[8]

Planché was not the first to make this point: William Shakespeare, John Milton, and Alexander Pope were widely celebrated *as adapters* rather than as original artists, even after the rise of Romantic theories of originality. Discussing Shakespeare's *The Merchant of Venice* in 1857, Richard Grant White remarked that

> the story of this comedy, even to its episodic part and its minutest incidents, had been told again and again long before Shakespeare was born. . . . What then remains to Shakespeare? and what is there to show that he is not a plagiarist? Every thing [sic] that makes *The Merchant of Venice* what it is. The people are puppets, and the incidents are all in these old stories . . . [but his characters], and the poetry which is their atmosphere . . . are Shakespeare's only. (139–40)

For White, it was adaptation that allowed Shakespeare to show forth his genius by comparison to the authors of his sources and thereby to forge aesthetic progress. Similarly, David Masson assessed that "Milton's imitation of Theocritus [in *Lycidas*] . . . excels Virgil's" (1874, 3.448), while in 1729, Henry St. John, first Viscount Bolingbroke, claimed that Pope was "above all writers I know, living or dead" (Warton [1782] 2004, 117), including Horace and Homer, whose *Iliad* Pope had adapted to English heroic couplets (1715–1720). Far from diminishing Pope's reputation, adaptation established it.

The contribution of adaptation to the reputations of celebrated authors and artists continued when their selection *for* adaptation by later artists was credited with carrying them into posterity, not only by recent critics such as Jean Marsden (1995) and Michael Dobson (1992) but also by eighteenth-century critics. In 1769, an unnamed critic claimed that David Garrick's adaptations of Shakespeare's plays (which were extensive rewritings, not simply performances or editions of Shakespeare's writings) "gave a new existence to several inestimable works, which had otherwise remained perhaps in everlasting obscurity" ("The British Theatre" 1769, 407).

Critics from Ben Jonson (1623) to Harold Bloom (1998) have argued that Shakespeare's longevity and popularity with adapters is due to the fact that his writing is universal; however, much of the credit for his global reach and historical longevity must go to adaptation—both his adaptations of prior works and others' adaptations of his. While Jonson hailed Shakespeare as "not of an age, but for all time!" in his preface to the first folio of Shakespeare's plays (1623), White adapted that eulogy to foreground adaptation: "Jonson said . . . that Shakespeare was not a man of his age, but that what he wrote was for, *adapted to*, all time" (1865, 1.cxcv, emphasis added). Earlier theorists figured literary immortality not as a divine, metaphysical process but as a genetic, genealogical afterlife akin to biological adaptation, based in earthly, mutating, human endeavors.

Shoring up the theory that it is adaptation that ensures the survival of works into future generations rather than universality or aesthetic merit, even bad adaptations were credited with preserving the works they adapted. In 1764, as attitudes to adapters were changing for the worse, poet and historian Walter Harte (1709–1774) assessed that author Gervase Markham (1568–1637) "appears to be the first English writer who deserves to be called a hackney-writer. All subjects seem to have been alike easy to him. Yet, as his thefts were innumerable, he has now and then stolen some very good things, and in great measure preserved their memory from perishing" (1764, 32).

Theorizing Adaptation as a Good Theoretical Object: Apotheosizing Adaptation in the Early Eighteenth Century

The eighteenth century witnessed a shift in theorization that, at one end of the century and spectrum, valued adaptations more highly than their sources to a theoretical climate that, at the other end, celebrated original works and denigrated adaptations. In the first half of the eighteenth century, the Augustan theoretical balance valuing adapted and adapting works (almost) equally began to tilt so far in favor of adaptations over their sources that it paved the way for a virulent reaction elevating sources immeasurably over their adaptations in the second half.

As we have seen, Restoration and early eighteenth-century critics considered the best adaptations to be superior to what they adapted: adaptations were theorized as harbingers of cultural, moral, and intellectual progress and formal, aesthetic, and stylistic advancement. Increasingly, comments promoting adaptation as a mode of advancement from venerated sources ceded to those theorizing adaptation as a censorious correction of sources. In a series of essays published in *The Spectator* (1711–12), Joseph Addison roundly critiques Milton's diction, along with Aristotle's:

> A second fault in [Milton's] language, is that he often effects a kind of jingle in his language ... some of the greatest ancients have been guilty of it ... [including] Aristotle himself. ... But ... it is, I think, at present universally exploded by all the masters of polite writing. ("Defects" 1712, 48)

For Addison, the "polite" progress of adaptation had universally (and violently) "exploded" prior writing styles.

The progressivist discourse of adaptation's superiority to what it adapts is reflected in adaptation's changing terminologies. By the mid-eighteenth-century, "alteration" was displacing "imitation" as adaptation's companion term in theatrical discourses and titles such as Edward Salmon's *The Historical Tragedy of Macbeth (Written Originally by Shakespear [sic]), Adapted to the Stage, with Alterations* (1753) and John Dalton's *Comus: A Masque (now Adapted to the Stage): As Alter'd from Milton's Masque at Ludlow Castle* (1750). Although "altered from" articulates the relation of adaptation to its source text and "adapted to the stage" focuses on adaptation's reception context, it is impossible to separate alteration from adaptation definitively, since alteration describes what was done to the text in order to adapt it to modern audiences and stage conventions (actresses, elaborate scenery and costumes, sentimental melodrama, a preference for action over speeches, music, seating, licensing, and new forms of censorship).

"Alteration" expresses a more critical attitude to its sources than "imitation," which connotes respect for them. Imitation is optional; alteration is necessary; imitation aspires; alteration corrects, like a tailor altering clothing for a new or changing body. These adaptions were not simply performances: they were rewritings. Marsden attests that, from 1660–1777, "playwrights augmented, substantially cut, or completely rewrote" Shakespeare's plays, including the introduction of "new characters, new scenes, new endings, and . . . new words" (1995, 1).[9] Nahum Tate's dedication to his *The History of King Lear*, which displaced Shakespeare's play on the British stage from 1681 to 1838, nominates the adaptation a "revival . . . with alterations" to Shakespeare's diction (described as "a heap of jewels, unstrung and unpolished") as well as to the play's plot and genre. Of his decision to give Shakespeare's tragedy a happy ending, he defends "so bold a change" on the grounds that it was "well received by my audience," while Dryden, the most prominent critic of the day, credited him with "art and judgment" for it (Tate [1681] 1761, n.p.).

These alterations and critiques were not simply concessions to contemporary language and tastes but also conformations to prevailing *theories* of adaptation. In *Alterations and Adaptations of Shakespeare* (1906), American scholar Frederick Wilkinson Kilbourne explains: "It was the universal opinion that, owing to his having lived in a barbarous age—that is, from the eighteenth-century point of view—and his own lack of education, Shakespeare was ignorant of the 'rules of art'" (10). Therefore, adaptations of his "plays began to conform more or less strictly to certain so-called rules of art based on Aristotle and others of the ancients and modified by French ideas and usages . . . to which the playwrights of the time endeavored to make Shakespeare's plays conform by means of alteration" (6–7). Eighty-five years on, in *The Re-Imagined Text: Shakespeare, Adaptation, and Eighteenth-Century Literary Theory* (1995), Marsden delineates how seventeenth- and eighteenth-century critics used Shakespeare adaptations as exemplars of their *theories*, so that "the criticism of Shakespeare written during the Restoration and eighteenth century arises out of the same literary consciousness as the adaptations" (7). Here, adaptation theory and practice were tightly intertwined.

Aesthetic value in this period was by no means a purely aesthetic, formal affair: aesthetic values were inseparable from moral, national, and class values—didactically so. Literary adapters laid claim to moral and cultural as well as stylistic civilization of their celebrated sources. In 1699, Colley Cibber adapted Shakespeare to the moral conventions of his day, which could not tolerate Shakespeare's moral ambiguity, rendering King Richard a simplistic, unequivocal villain in his adaptation of *Richard III* (Kilbourne 1906, 107–112). Garrick, who played Richard III in Cibber's adaptation 213 times from 1741–1776, also saw the task of adaptation as one of correcting both Shakespeare's aesthetic and moral failings. The advertisement to his Shakespeare adaptation, *Romeo and Juliet by Shakespear [sic]: With Alterations, and an Additional Scene*, declares that Garrick has made both formal and moral improvements to his source: "to clear the original as much as possible, from the jingle and quibble which were always thought a great objection to performing it" and to remove "a blemish in [Romeo's] character" (1750, 3).

The narrative of moral and aesthetic progress via adaptation so confidently championed by Restoration and early eighteenth-century critics was itself subjected to critical revisionism by later theorists. Hailed by leading critics in 1691, in 1838, the final year in which Tate's adaptation of *Romeo and Juliet* was performed, condemnation of it was so established that it appeared in that year's *Cabinet Cyclopaedia*: "this author, utterly destitute of imagination and taste, a mere plodder and mechanic in literature, had the courage, not only to make extensive alterations in the Lear of Shakespeare, but to justify them boldly in print" (Lardner 1838, 195). Encompassing the preface that theorized his changes, this critique dismisses Tate's theoretical principles along with his adaptation practices.

Even when critics claimed to be overthrowing aesthetic theories in favor of "nature" in the late eighteenth century, they did so in the service of new theories. In 1765, an anonymous theater critic rejoiced that,

> though a number of profound scholars declared that it was shameful to laugh or to cry where the unities were sacrificed . . . the feelings of the heart triumphed over the laws of the stagyrite, and the simple dictates of nature bid defiance to the unbending severity of criticism. ("The British Theatre" 1769, 407)

In spite of the overt message that academic, neoclassical theories had ceded to "the feelings of the heart" and "the simple dictates of nature," these were proto-Romantic theoretical principles. The new theories were more than a pitting of affect against decorum and nature against culture: they served the material, economic, and political interests of the rising middle classes. The superiority of the ruling classes was demarcated by land ownership; new theories of nature allowed everyone to "own" land through a psychological identification with nature, mediated by art and the imagination. In *The Elements of Dramatic Criticism*, Will Cooke asserts: "application to the study of nature alone . . . is the only infallible guide to theatrical success" (1775, 138). While earlier adapters had represented themselves as craftsmen resetting the "unstrung jewels" of Shakespeare's language with polish and sophistication or as aesthetic medics "reviving" his works, now they positioned themselves as authoritative correctives to Shakespeare's *theoretical* errors, outlined in a rhetoric of unworthiness, weak concessions to public taste, and disconnections between his writing and his "true" self. Critiquing Shakespeare, Cooke declared that "a play is an imitation of nature, and since no man, without premeditation, speaks in rhyme, neither ought he to do it on the stage." He further faulted Shakespeare's signature word play: "a play of words is unworthy of that composition which pretends to any degree of elevation; yet Shakespeare has made this sacrifice to the age he lived in, in many instances" (1775, 76). Cooke insists that Shakespeare wanted to write as Cooke's theory prescribes, but that he was forced to adapt his will and better judgment to his cultural context. Here, cultural adaptation is far more powerful than formal expression: even Shakespeare is seen to be delimited by it and must await general cultural and theoretical progress before his authorial intentions can be realized.

In contrast to the retroactive return to nature, critics continued to theorize adaptation as a progressive and improving process, aligning it to how the middle classes conceptualized their adaptation to new economic, political, and social spheres: they were improved by and sought to improve these environments. More aggressively, they engaged adaptation both offensively and defensively to dominate other classes and: to bring down, aspire to, and possess the representational elitism of the landed aristocracy (Elliott 2012b, 161–63), to raise up and to keep down the lower orders (Elliott 2012b, 285–87), and to defend the nation from foreign influences.

Theorizing Adaptation as a Bad Theoretical
Object: Romantic Originality

Theories of adaptation as a return to nature were accompanied by theories of adaptation as a return to origins. In 1765, an unnamed critic claimed that Garrick had not only improved Shakespeare's "original," but that he had further "restore[d] Shakespeare to himself" ("Review of David Erskine Baker," 214–16). Here, Garrick's adaptation is figured as truer to Shakespeare's self than Shakespeare's own writing. Elsewhere, Garrick boasted of correcting Shakespeare *as an adapter*, justifying his alterations to *Romeo and Juliet* by claiming that he had restored the play to one of Shakespeare's sources (1750, 3). These and other proto-Romantic theories of adaptation as a return to natural, true origins supported middle-class rejections of Augustan aesthetic lineages, which were tied to social and political prerogatives based in family lineage. In their place, theorists championed both newly created, self-made individuals and original aesthetic works. In 1791–2, Thomas Paine claimed equal rights for all men, arguing that their origins in nature overrides any lineal identity: "all men are born equal and with equal natural right, in the same manner as if posterity had been continued by creation instead of generation" (29). Romantic concepts of great art as the individual expression of original genius located in the imagination rather than in aesthetic traditions manifest the values of the rising middle classes, appealing to their assertive, ambitious individualism (Crocco 2014, 99). Acts of aesthetic self-making are aligned with economic self-making; successful authors and artists do both, amassing fortunes and establishing celebrity status apart from family lineage.

Mid-century, proto-Romantic theories of originality emerging in works such as Edward Young's *Conjectures on Original Composition* (1759), William Duff's *An Essay on Original Genius* (1767), and Alexander Gerard's *Essay on Genius* (1776) mounted a reactionary attack upon adaptation as a vehicle of historical progress. Romantic theories located aesthetic value in nature and the imagination, figuring the best art as the original, spontaneous, inspired product of natural genius, generated by the imagination rather than by prior works. Romantic "theories of literary creation . . . assumed an analogy, if not an equality, with divine creation, whereby the literary work is created from beyond the material or phenomenal context" (MacFarlane 2007, 1). By contrast, "Literary resemblance [was] held to be suggestive of unoriginality, and unoriginality reveals in the writer both an intellectual servility and an imaginative infertility" (MacFarlane 2007, 3). Good art, real art, true art had to be an entirely new creation generated by imagination of what has not yet been rather than from memory of what has—a solipsistic original without source or origin. Like the aspirational middle classes, good art was based in aspiration and possibility rather than tradition and inheritance.

The history of art, with its aesthetic genealogies and canons, collaborative creations, and intertextual engagements, was nothing; whether adaptations were literal or free made no difference; they were alike rejected as derivative, inorganic, servile, and uninspired. The Augustan balance of power between adapted and adapting works gave way to a binary opposition between originals and copies that devalued all adaptations—not just unaesthetic or culturally obtuse ones. Tate was condemned not solely for being a bad adapter but also for not being an original author: "Of all the plays he produced not one was original. They were all either compilations from other sources, or old plays remodeled" (Lardner 1838, 195).

Romantic theories of originality extended beyond literature to other media. Luigi Antonio Lanzi's *History of Painting in Upper and Lower Italy* is infused with Romantic theories of originality, lamenting that, in the late sixteenth century, "imitation was . . . the sole means of attaining to distinction. Every school was the slave of its founder" (1831, 2.236). Elsewhere, a music critic assessed: "an imitation . . . wants the majestic simplicity of the original. . . . [T]he style is common place and unworthy [of] the sublimity of the subject" ("Reviews of New Music" 1826, 421). An opera reviewer opined: "Literary men of talent will not descend to the drudgery of cobbling up these adapted pieces; which, accordingly—with an exception or two—are full of ignorance, awkwardness, and bad taste" ("Fashion in Music" 1833, 272). A review of Henry Austin's *Thoughts on the Abuses of the Present System of Competition in Architecture* sets adaptation against imitation: even the best imitations "want truth and life—that fine adaptation of material and form to particular circumstances . . . can only can be found when the Art is creative where invention is not trammelled by rules devised for entirely different ends" ("Review of Henry Austin" 1841, 787). The anonymous critic of this review went further to condemn the Augustan theory of adaptation as a gradual progress toward perfection ("the gradual progress of imitation is the relinquishment of all attempt at invention or combination") and to deny imitation the status of art ("We mistake imitation for Art") (787).

Even judges weighed in on the debate. Adjudicating a copyright case, Walter Copinger (1847–1910) ruled that "the original [musical] air requires the aid of genius for its construction, but a mere mechanic in music can make the adaptation or accompaniment" (Copinger 1870, 108). Financial settlements were made (or not made) on the basis of these theories. These and other discussions make clear that it was not infidelity to sources that led to condemnations of adaptation, but fidelity to sources that precluded adaptation from theoretical value, and that aesthetics remained the main criterion of value in adaptation theory, even as aesthetic theories—ideas of what made good art and bad art—altered markedly in changing cultural, economic, and political environments.

Romanticism's binary of originals and copies wiped out Dryden's triadic taxonomy and mediating middle way. Where Ben Jonson's translation of Horace had served as Dryden's eschewed category of metaphrase in 1680 (a "servile, literal translation" 6.349), for Henry Home, Lord Kames in 1762, Jonson was "a servile *Imitator*, little better than a painful Translator" (2.115, emphasis added). No longer did imitation mean a free, creative, independent type of adaptation, as Dryden had defined it; it became barely distinguishable from literal translation: both alike became bad theoretical objects. By 1790, Immanuel Kant claimed universality for theories of original creation in totalitarian rhetoric: "*Everyone* agrees that genius is *entirely* opposed to the spirit of imitation" (187, emphasis added).

Critiques of individual adaptations became platforms for denigrating adaptation along binary lines of originals and copies, not infidelity and fidelity. A review of Peregrine Post's *A Four Days Tour through Part of the Land of Dumplings*, for example, reads:

> This is a whimsical composition and intended as another imitation of Mr. Sterne's peculiar mode of writing; *like all imitations*, it only serves to set off the excellence of the *original* from which it *copies*, at the evident expense of its own immediate author. (1769, 324–5, emphasis added)

This figures *all* adaptations inferior to *all* originals. Adaptation had become an essentially and intrinsically bad theoretical object.

By 1835, the assumption that adapters were inferior to original creators was not restricted to academic discourse: it was pronounced "usual" by the adapter-defendant in the case of *D'Almaine v. Boosey*, which contested violation of a musical copyright. Boosey conceded:

> It is in the usual course of trade to call such compositions by the name of arrangements or adaptations; and that the persons who make or compose

them, possess an inferior degree of talent to the original composer of the opera, who, from his superior talent, would not occupy his time or attention upon such a subject. (Younge and Collyer 1836, 292)

The assumption here is that any talented artist in any medium would never stoop to adapt and that, concomitantly, all those who do lack talent.

Adaptation became not only a hallmark of inferior talent but also an aesthetic "sin":

[L]ike their fathers before them,—ay, from Shakespeare to Sheridan,— they have sought for their plots on the foreign stage, or in the popular novel. . . . [I]t is not the style of execution, but the act itself which is so un- sparingly reprobated. . . . [W]hy, we will ask, have the few writers of original comedies . . . gradually fallen into the same sinful ways of translation and adaption? ("Drama: Drury Lane" 1829, 847)

Whether adapting works from past history, foreign cultures, or other media—whether resonantly composed and powerfully produced, adaptation was figured as a fall, not from fidelity to sources, but from original creation.

Leading twenty-first adaptation scholars have rightly faulted Romantic theories of originality for adaptation's falling theoretical fortunes. In 2005, Robert Stam argued that "the subaltern status of adaptation" is due in part to "a priori valorization of historical anteriority and seniority" (4), which values source texts over their adaptations purely by virtue of having come first. In 2006, Linda Hutcheon too lamented that adaptation's secondary tem- poral position caused it to be viewed as inferior, belated, and derivative (xv). Recent Romantic theorists have affirmed that artistic originality "continues as one of the most important shibboleths of our culture" (McGann 1983, 91). Robert MacFarlane has written:

This conceit of making *ex nihilo* has remained a compelling literary cre- ation myth, proving highly resistant to attempts to discredit or obliterate it. . . . [It] continues to prosper in the literary-cultural consciousness. If an- ything, indeed, it is more unshiftably ensconced there than 200 years ago. (2007, 3)

However, it was not Romanticism alone that scuttled the theoretical fortunes of adaptation. Adaptation was under attack in other ways, as eighteenth-century aesthetic theorists aspired simultaneously to theologies of original creation and to the precision of biological species classification, working to recategorize the arts, hitherto theorized as sisters, as separate species.

Theorizing Adaptation as a Bad Theoretical Object: Neoclassical Medium Specificity

In *Laocoön: An Essay upon the Limits of Painting and Poetry* ([1766] 1962[10]), German philosopher, dramatist, and art critic Gotthold Ephraim Lessing (1729–1781) applied Linnaean biological taxonomies to poetry and painting, rejecting the sister arts theories that had encouraged their mutual emulation and interchange of sources, principles, subject matter, and techniques, re-taxonomizing them not as siblings but as separate species that could not and should not mate or mix. He justified this taxonomical revolution by pressing the higher priority of resemblances between form and content within each art form over formal resemblances between the arts. Each art, he argued, must highlight its difference from other arts by foregrounding its own unique formal properties through a corresponding choice of subject matter and eschew imitating or adapting other arts and their subject matter. Each art should remain in its own sphere, doing what it does best, and not seek to emulate other arts. For Lessing and many others, medium specificity was the basis of aesthetic worth. Politically, it was a conservative move that did not encourage class mobility or mixing.

A few years prior, Scottish philosopher and judge Henry Home, Lord Kames (1696–1782) had also prioritized form-content relations over interart affinities: "Words being intimately connected with the ideas they represent, the greatest harmony is required between them" ([1762] 1785, 496). Allying Romantic originality to neoclassical medium specificity theory, he categorized and hierarchized the arts according to their degree of originality (2.489).[11] A hierarchy predicated on originality rather than inherited aesthetic traditions valorized the self-making classes above all others, including the aristocracy: his own title was not inherited but was conferred on him for his work as a judge. A hierarchy based in originality meant that adaptation did not even feature in it: literature adapting other literature was downgraded as unoriginal; adaptation between the arts was theorized as monstrous, unaesthetic miscegenation.

It was this powerful *alliance* between pseudo-religious Romantic theories of original creation and pseudo-scientific theories of medium specificity, not Romantic originality alone, that scuttled the fortunes of adaptation, rendering adaptation a doubly bad theoretical object by the end of the eighteenth century. Romantic originality eviscerated adaptations within the same medium; medium specificity theory denounced adaptations between media. Even though neoclassical categoricity is philosophically at odds with Romantic organicism, it colluded with Romantic originality against adaptation, just as scientific theories of separate species would collude with theologies of divine, original creation against biological adaptation two centuries later. Neoclassical theories tightened the bond between form and content within each art against theories of sibling resemblances between the arts, infusing their separations with the essentialism of Romantic theories of organic unity to oppose interart adaptation. Romantic theories of art spiritualized the union.

Theoretical Defenses of Adaptation: Sister Arts Theory and Adaptive Originality

There were, however, dissenting voices. In 1827, architect and author of architectural works Christopher Davy (1803–1849) protested: "Why should the sister arts be separated, when they are so generally acknowledged to share each other's beauties and when the perfections of one are comparatively cold and insignificant without the embellishment of the other?" (147). In the nineteenth century, Augustan continuities between the theory and practice of adaptation were eroding. Nineteenth-century culture was an environment in which adaptation practices flourished, so that even when adaptation was excoriated in theory, as it often was, it thrived in practice. More than this, as adaptation practice defied medium specificity theory, theorists arose to champion its theoretical violations. By mid-century, "The relationship between the sister-arts, particularly between the visual arts and literature, was never more incestuous, or more accepted, than in the mid-Victorian period," as "popular tradition . . . directly challenged Lessing's proscription of the sister-arts analogy" in paintings from novels and illustrated fiction (Curtis 1995, 225). Nowhere were sister-arts relations more celebrated than in drama. Superseding even the integration of illustrations and prose, critics identified drama as both epitome and zenith of sister arts theory. H., author of "The Drama: Historically Considered in Reference to Its Moral and Intellectual Influence on Society," decreed that

> the sister arts are generally so harmoniously blended in these representations, that we have in them at one grasp the very essence of the arts. Music, adapted to, or assisting poetry of the highest order, spreads its glowing and soul-subduing influence over our best feelings and affections, while painting illustrates and realizes the vivid conceptions which her magic sisters have created. (H. 1836, 10–11)

Romantic theories of organic unity opposed Lessing's theory that the essence of each art can only be seen separately. Far from confusing the essence of the arts, drama was credited with distilling and accentuating their individual essences *by combining them*.

Poet Thomas Campbell's (1777–1844) valedictory stanzas for actor John Philip Kemble (1757–1823) on his retirement from the stage similarly hail drama as "the youngest of the Sister Arts, / Where all their beauty blends," arguing that each art compensates for the representational lack of the others:

> For ill can Poetry express,
> Full many tone of thought sublime,
> And Painting, mute and motionless,
> Steals but a glance of time.
> But, by the mighty actor brought,
> Illusion's perfect triumphs come,—
> Verse ceases to be airy thought,
> And Sculpture to be dumb. (Campbell [1817] 1851, 138)

Yet even though sister arts theory and medium specificity theory are categorically and taxonomically opposed (in the first, the arts are close relations; in the second they are separate species), proponents of each alike canvassed the impossibility of adaptation: if separate species cannot mate, neither can those of the same gender.

Medium specificity theorists argued, then and subsequently, that intermedial adaptation always and inevitably produces bad art. The familiar twentieth-century maxim that you can't make a good film from a good book (discussed in Elliott 2003a, 12) had precursors in discussions of novel-to-stage adaptation. In 1825, pondering "the peculiar difficulties of the dramatic art, and . . . impediments which lie peculiarly in the way of the novelist who aspires to extend his sway over the stage," Scottish poet, novelist, playwright, historian, and critic Walter Scott (1771–1832) argued:

> Though a good acting play may be made by selecting a plot and characters from a novel . . . we know not any effort of genius, which could successfully insert into a good play, those accessories of description and delineation, which are necessary to dilate it into a readable novel. ([1825] 1852, 21)

His argument is based in medium specificity theory:

> Description and narration, which form the essence of the novel, must be very sparingly introduced into a dramatic composition, and scarce ever have a good effect upon the stage. The drama speaks to the eye and ear; and when it ceases to address these bodily organs, and would exact from a theatrical audience that exercise of the imagination which is necessary to follow forth and embody circumstances neither spoken nor exhibited, there is an immediate failure, though it may be the failure of a man of genius. (21)

Thirty-nine years later, the English poet, novelist, playwright, adapter, critic, and politician Edward Bulwer-Lytton (1803–73) forged a prototype for the subsequent twentieth-century maxim that good films can only be made from bad novels:

> Any story can be told, but comparatively very few stories can be dramatized; and hence some of the best novels in the world can not [sic] be put upon the stage, while some, that have very little merit as novels, have furnished subject-matter for the greatest plays in the modern world. ([1863] 1864, 325)

Even as attacks on intermedial adaptation increased under medium specificity, defenses of intramedial adaptation were mounted against Romantic theories of originality. In some discourses, adaptation *to* cultural contexts mitigated theoretical opprobrium for adapting *from* prior works. An article on British architecture distinguishes derivative imitation of past works from creative adaptation of them, which was seen to give them new life: "We mistake imitation for Art"; even the best imitations "want truth and life—that fine adaptation of material and form *to particular circumstances*, which only can be found when the Art is creative, where invention is not trammeled by rules" ("Review of Henry Austin" 1841, 787, emphasis added).

Prior to Romanticism, adaptation had been widely credited with originality. For example, poet, dramatist, and Oxford Professor of Poetry Joseph Trapp (1679–1747) had claimed that poetry "by lively Copies produces new Originals" (1742, 9). Protesting against wholesale reverence for originality and scorn for adaptation, Scottish classical scholar William Laudér (c. 1680–1771) argued:

> Scarce an eminent writer can be instanced who has not been indebted to the labors of former authors; but how absurd would it be to urge this as an argument that there is no merit in their productions? For as one may be what is called an original writer, and yet have no pretensions to genius, so another may make use of the labors of others in such a manner as to satisfy the world of his own abilities. (1750, 7–8)[12]

An anonymous critic writing at the turn of the nineteenth century drew ingeniously on Romantic theories to argue that adaptations made by original geniuses must resemble their makers and must, therefore, be original: "The genius of Ramsay was original; and the powers of his untutored mind were the gift of nature" ("Remarks on the Genius and Writings of Allan Ramsay" 1800, lx):

> The adaptation, by the Scottish poet, to the scenery and manners of his own country . . . displays a singular felicity of genius. Of this most beautiful composition I have no scruple to affirm, what I believe will be assented to by all, who are competent to judge of poetry alike in either language, that it surpasses the merit of the original. ("Remarks on Allan Ramsay" 1800, xcviii–xcix)

In this account, the adaptation exceeds its source, not via Augustan theories of incremental progress but via Romantic theories of original creation in which adapted works were made in the image of their original spirit of their maker.

In 1819, another anonymous periodical writer claimed similarly that high Renaissance painter and architect Raphael (Raffaello Sanzio da Urbino, 1483–1520), "in his wise adaptation, as well as in his genius, surpassed all other painters since the revival of the arts" because he had conformed to

Romantic theories of genius and nature and adapted his work to the spirit of his historical context: he "rendered whatever he derived from the Ancients subservient to nature, and the spirit of the age in which he lived." "Wise adaptation" joins natural genius to elevate Raphael above prior artists. Even more controversially in terms of the Romantic apotheosis of originality, the article asserts: wherever "imitation is not gracefully adapted to the spirit of modern times, art must fail in originality" (W. C. 1819, 51). Here, Romantically valorized originality *depends* upon adaptation to historical and cultural contexts.

The president of the Boston Music Academy 1840, Samuel Atkins Eliot (1798–1862), similarly rendered adaptation the epitome of high art in music: "Adaptation is the merit and the end and aim of music, and whenever the composition or the performance fails to adapt itself . . . it fails to produce the highest effects of art" (Eliot 1840, 338). Here, adaptation becomes a cardinal aesthetic principle: it is the primary value and goal of music, both in its textual production (composition) and contextual reception (performance); without it, he argues, there is no high art.

Discussing dramatic adaptation mid-century, White returned to the theological roots of Romantic theory to refigure adaptation as original creation. Just as God did not create humans out of nothing, he argued, neither did Shakespeare. His sources were "heaps of dry bones" that he "clothe[d] with human flesh and breathe[d] into them the breath of life" (1857, 140). More than a century later, Harold Bloom (1998) likewise credited Shakespeare with the "invention of the human"; unlike White, he did not credit this invention to Shakespeare's facility with adaptation.

In 1864, Bulwer-Lytton went further than White, arguing not only that adaptation is creative but also that originality is a fiction:

New combinations are, to all plain intents and purposes, creations. It is not in the power of man to create something out of nothing. . . . It is, then, not in the invention of a story, nor in the creation of imaginary characters, that a dramatist proves his originality as an artist, but in the adaptation of a story found elsewhere to a dramatic purpose. (307; 323)

In 1869, an anonymous theater critic concurred:

If originality is to signify absolute initiation of what is essentially new . . . there would seem to be a tolerably strong case against believing such a thing to be, or ever to have been since the first germs of human thought began to move in distant prehistoric ages. ("Originality" 1869, 364)

While postmodern and poststructuralist intertextual theorists too claim that no aesthetic production can be original (Hutcheon 2006, 21), this critic went further to define adaptation *as* originality: "Originality is . . . not an isolated act of bare initiation, but an act or process of adaptation or moulding so perfect as to resemble a new creation, and *in fact to be one*" ("Originality" 1869, 365, emphasis added). Adaptation practitioners too laid claim to originality: for example, American playwright Augustin Daly (1838–1899) subtitled his adaptation of a French play "an original adaptation in four acts" (1868, title page).

Even so, critics of the day cautioned against using exceptional adapters to valorize all adaptations. Edward R. Russell remarked: "It is not of much use to point to Shakespeare's borrowings and Molière's thefts as an excuse for writers who cannot plead even by the most distant analogy Shakespeare's and Molière's merit" (1869, 44). Russell prefigured Wagner (1975) in valuing adaptations according to their degree of originality and differentiation from their sources: "There are adaptations which are nearly original, and there are others which are the merest translations" (1869, 44). Both Russell in 1869 and Wagner in 1975 valued most those adaptations that were most original and least derivative of their sources.

Further prefiguring later theories, Russell turned to reception to define and assess adaptation, arguing that originality is a phenomenological effect in the eye and ear of the beholder, rather than an ontological essence. Taking a longer historical view, he observed that perceptions of originality change over time: "The world is always content, at any rate after a century or two, that an author should have borrowed if he has in borrowing created a genuinely independent book. Nowadays, nearly all adaptations are taken to be mere copies" (44–45). Yet in future epochs, he assessed that these too may be deemed original and "genuinely independent" (45). Writing in the same year, the anonymous author of "Originality" disagreed that time must pass before an adaptation can be deemed original: "It is clear that adapted plays may individually show originality now as truly (though no doubt in a different manner and degree) as the similar process showed it in Shakespeare's time" (1869, 365). These discourses were theoretically radical—and yet, published in periodicals, they were widely read.

Theories of originality in adaptation carried from critical discourses into court cases fought over copyright. In the case of *Wood v. Boosey*, determining whether a published pianoforte score by Franz Bressler violated the copyright of an opera by Otto Nicolai, the judge determined that "the real question . . . is whether the opera and the adaptation are one and the same work" (Maskelyne 1868, 87)—whether the piano score "is a mere mechanical adaptation of the original composition" or "a new and substantive work, and just as much entitled to the benefit of copyright . . . as the original opera" (86–87). Deciding that "the opera was Nicolai's and the arrangement was Bressler's," the judge ruled that "the defendant was entitled to succeed, as the pianoforte arrangement was a production requiring independent knowledge and skill on the part of the composer" (85). Arguing that "he cannot be both pirate and composer," the verdict ruled that "there is an authorship in Bressler" (85; 88). Theories of adaptation, then, had economic consequences.

Theoretical Defenses of Adaptation: Realization and Intermedial Adaptation

Late eighteenth-century medium specificity theory was much more contested than it would be in the twentieth century: not only was intermedial adaptation rampant in the period, unparalleled until the digital age in the late twentieth century, but critical discourses also supported the sister arts. In 1824, illustrator Richard Plowman positioned neoclassical medium specificity theory as a brief aberration when he argued that

> the Art of Painting has in all ages been employed, more or less, in explaining and enforcing the imagination of the poet, and . . . the poet has, in his turn, found resource in the designs and conceptions of the painter. Assuming this position to be established, the usefulness of bringing the sister arts into union with each other, by what is generally termed Illustration, seems evident at first sight. (5)

Martin Meisel's *Realizations: Narrative, Pictorial, and Theatrical Arts in Nineteenth-Century England* (1983) documents how leading Victorian painters and poets blithely violated Lessing's taxonomization of them as separate species, disproving theories that violating medium specificity produces bad art. Celebrated artists including Arthur Hughes, William Holman Hunt, John William Waterhouse, and Sidney Harold Meteyard flocked to paint Alfred, Lord Tennyson's poems, while Dante Gabriel Rossetti produced poems and paintings treating the same subjects. Mid-century, distinguished painters not only painted from poems but also designed illustrations for prose fiction: for example, John Everett Millais, Frederick Leighton, and Hubert Herkomer illustrated novels by Anthony Trollope, George Eliot, and Thomas Hardy, respectively.[13] As adaptations of adaptations (engravings of paintings of fiction), illustrations extended and intensified the focus on the ways in which the arts represented *each other*, diminishing priority on their representation of the world or ideas. As new print technologies allowed engravings and prose to be bound, sold, and consumed together, eventually on the same page, illustrated works became hybrid intermedial forms that adapted themselves internally (Elliott 2003a, Chapter 2; 2016). Engraved adaptations of paintings furthermore produced an economic downward mobility for adaptation, as many who could not afford to purchase or view paintings in galleries could consume mass-produced art in illustrated books and periodical literature (Elliott 2016, 539–40). Here and elsewhere, intermedial adaptation became increasingly varied and complex.

Even so, adapters and critics wishing to valorize intermedial adaptation could not ignore medium specificity theory. Instead, they challenged pseudo-scientific theories of the arts as separate species with pseudo-religious theories of incarnation, expressed in a rhetoric of realization. Meisel defined realization as

> both literal re-creation and translation into a more real, that is more vivid, visual, physically present medium. To move from mind's eye to body's eye was realization, and to add a third dimension to two was realization, as when words became picture, or when picture became dramatic tableau. (1983, 30)

Meisel did not invent the word but gleaned it from a periodical article published in 1866,[14] in which an anonymous critic noted "the desire for realization, which, at the present day, either from a wish for novelty, or from a tendency to idealized materialism, is grown almost a passion with our young artists and poets" ("The Drama and the Stage" 1866, 26). In 1844, an anonymous reviewer had argued: "The great end of all literature has been to idealize the actual. The new and higher literature must aim at the realization of the ideal" ("Mrs. Butler's Poems" 1844, 512).

Adaptation as realization is far from naïve realism: it highlights the artifactuality of forms by focusing on aesthetic forms representing other aesthetic forms rather than nature or reality. Coupling pseudo-religious incarnational theories with Victorian realism, realization brings the abstract into the material, working concomitantly to idealize materialism. In "idealized materialism," the value of an adaptation lies not in its identity as a medium-specific or even hybrid form, but in its capacity to hybridize the abstract and the perceptual, the ideal and the material, without dissolving either, making the ideal seem real without losing its ideality and the abstract material without losing its imaginative and illusory dimensions. Realization does not make real or descend from the ideal to the real; rather, it makes the ideal *appear* to be real.

Although Meisel's study focuses on written, visual, and dramatic art, theories of realization extended to other media in this period. As later practitioners and critics would argue with regard to Shakespeare and film, British actor and dramatist Morris Barnett (1800–1856) claimed that, "had the operatic stage existed in his time, Shakespeare would have adapted some of his more fantastic subjects entirely for musical representation" (1850, 39). Barnett considered that characters such as "the delicate sprite Ariel" were more realistically conveyed by music than by theater's "visible and corporeal form," concluding that "the representation of the drama in an operatic form" is therefore "a more perfect realization" of the ideal than "a represented play" (39). By contrast, the "visible and corporeal" monster Caliban is "a wonderful realization, in look, gesture, and bearing" (42). Realization, then, was not always a one-way process from more abstract to more phenomenologically palpable representational forms, as in Meisel's account: it could refer to adaptation from a less abstract art to a more abstract one that produced a greater illusion of realizing the spirit world.

At the other end of the phenomenological spectrum, adaptation extended to commodities, becoming tangibly and commercially possessable. While the Arts and Crafts movement adapted contemporary, classical, and medieval works to household objects (Sommer and Rago 1995), the less wealthy consumed mass-produced tie-in merchandise spawned by popular literature. In 1891, the Anglo-Irish author, critic, painter, and sculptor Percy Fitzgerald (1834–1925) recalled tie-in merchandise sold in conjunction with Charles Dickens's *The Pickwick Papers* in the 1830s:

Pickwick chintzes figured in linen-drapers' windows, and Weller corduroys in breeches-makers' advertisements; Boz cabs might be seen rattling through the streets. . . . There were to be seen "Pickwick canes," "Pickwick gaiters," [and] "Pickwick Hats." (1891, 25)

There were even forms of adaptation akin to what we call cosplaying today, as " 'Pickwick clubs' [sprang up] all over the kingdom" (Fitzgerald 1891, 25).

As realization aspired to incarnate Romantic genius, prove its reality, and realize material profits, it was a perfect theory of adaptation for an age of invention, industrialism, and commodification. A poem published in *Punch* indicates that contemporary critics were well aware of these connections:

A realistic age! It acts;
Nor taste to approve importunes;
The painters realize their facts
The managers their fortunes. ("Theatrical Reflections" 1864, 187)

Here and elsewhere, theatrical realization came in for a great deal of aesthetic criticism—nowhere more so than in realizations of Shakespeare's plays. Although this was adaptation within the same medium (theater to theater), the aesthetic principles of realization still prevailed. In 1840, playwright and drama critic Frederick G. Tomlins (1804–1867) complained:

Modern critics, a class always more celebrated for their logical than their imaginative power, have been for reducing every thing [*sic*] to reality: they triumphantly announce realization to be the end and object of the imitative arts, and more particularly of the drama. (42–43).

Tomlins praised early modern English classical drama for prioritizing the performed word over stage spectacle: "splendid dramatic literature" (1840, 103) expressed by gesture and dialogue" (1840, 7). He was not alone in this opinion, citing critics from Walter Scott to Friedrich Schlegel who agreed with him in his Appendix (150–52).

The critic who defined realization as idealized materialism was even more censorious of it: under its influence, "the poetical, the expanding, the analyzing mode of the poetical drama comes to be treated by fanatical and ignorant realists, as a mass of absurdity" ("The Drama and the Stage" 1866b, 26). For this critic, realization brought about a *loss* of the real:

> Our plays no longer represent human nature, although it is the chief aim of the existing stage to realize actualities. . . . [W]hile there is a loud call for real tables, real chairs, real carpets; clocks that will go; looking-glasses that actually reflect; real silks and satins for the women's dresses; coats made by Poole; and even for real horses and dogs on occasions . . . yet there is no call for real human emotion, nor a true and deep exemplification of human nature. There is an amazing desire in audiences to see the real outside of everything; and the caterers for the public, the managers . . . pander to this demand with even a reckless extravagance. . . . The consequence is that all mental development is abandoned; all the internal conflict of emotion is left undeveloped; and the figures pass before the audience real as to clothes, and real as to speech as far as it goes; but with no more of their inward human nature shown than one could learn in a thronged thoroughfare. ("The Drama and the Stage," 26)

For this critic and many others, "human nature" is defined as interior thought best expressed by verbal soliloquys ("they avoid soliloquys," 26), supplemented by classical theatrical gestures ("none of the old and antique dramatic expression is allowed that would show us their minds, their reasoning, their impulses, and their feelings," 26). In another article published a few months later, the same critic ruminates on theater's double nature, "bounded as it is on the one side by literature and on the other by showmanship." Pitting "poets and scholars" against "posture-makers, mummers, and showman," the essay laments that "the showman's party are in the ascendant" ("The Drama" 1866a, 185).

Today, with the hindsight of history, these critiques seem reactionary, with religious and philosophical roots in logophilia and iconophobia (Mitchell 1986),[15] where what is most sacred and valued is accessible only to verbal language, which pictorial images are seen to profane and devalue. Similar charges have been made by literary film adaptation scholars such as Lellis and Bolton (1981)—charges resonantly critiqued by Stam (2000, 58; 2005).

More pertinent to this book than battles between words and images is the battle waged between adaptation and theorization. Rather than adapt theoretical principles to changing practices of adaptation, for the 1866 critic of realization and many others, a priori theoretical principles should dictate "the nature of art" and practitioners should follow them:

> The nature of art . . . is not a nature we see exemplified in any actual objects; but it is the *ruling principle* which forms a new set of objects, things, and occurrences. . . . [T]he poetical, the expanding, the analyzing mode of the poetical drama comes to be treated by fanatical and ignorant realists, as a mass of absurdity, and burlesque. ("The Drama and the Stage," 26, emphasis added)

Theater generally, and adaptation particularly, are charged with falling from these principles. Rather than seek new theoretical principles to explicate new forms of adaptation, adapters who practice against the "ruling principle" of theorization are "fanatical and ignorant"; their work is condemned as "a mass of absurdity" *because theoretical tenets cannot explain it*. Yet why is it not the theorist who is ignorant, unable to explain realization via his theory? That the practice of adaptation is threatening to humanities theorization is apparent in the charge that it is *burlesquing* theory. Burlesque has long been theorized as a low and derided mode of adaptation; however, it is double-edged, also bringing down and deriding what it burlesques.

As in prior centuries, whenever art defies theoretical principles, theorists deny it the status of art, exiling it from their domain: "It is, in truth, to reduce art to artisanship" ("The Drama and the Stage," 26). Two months later, a sequel to this article denied "the definition of art" to theatrical spectacles, because to do so would be to credit "the property-man, the costumier, and the gas-lighter . . . rather than the intellectual critic" ("Theatric Art" 1866c, 88). Here, we see the cultural and economic basis of opposition to realization: the manual laborers who produce realization in the theater threaten the power of "the intellectual critic" and theorist over drama. Manual laborers are declared incapable of generating theoretical principles: "Undoubtedly, there are rules and principles for producing such effects, but they cannot be included in the fine arts. . . . Mechanism is everywhere; art nowhere" (88). At a time when the urban male working classes were petitioning effectively and threateningly for *political* representation, a franchise that would be granted the following year in the Representation of the People Act of 1867, attempts to exclude them from *aesthetic* representation and domains monopolized by the already enfranchised bourgeoisie intensified. The phobia expressed by this bourgeois critic is palpable: first, fear of manual theatrical laborers' ability to create aesthetic power neither generated by nor under the control of his theoretical words; second, fear of and contempt for the power of mass public taste to shape art and the diminishing power of the bourgeois critic to dictate public taste:

> The stage, our modern stage, is certainly much more indebted to the artisan than to the artist for effects.... Is there any principle of art in them? The predominant power is derived from light and color; and these affect audiences as they might savages or infants. Glare, direct contrasts, color in its simplest expression, the glitter of gems, the shine of metal, the blaze of unmodulated light, are the preponderating qualities. Here is no art for the uneducated eye; which, like that of the unjudging infant, is merely gorged with crude matter.... Such devices lay bare the deplorable vulgarity of the age; which is not confined to the uneducated class, but is, perhaps, most paraded by those calling themselves, *par excellence*, the cultivated. ("Theatric Art" 1866c, 88, emphasis in original)

In a third article published in November, the critic again condemned the taste for realization as "childish and barbarous, being very like that of the savage," and expressed outrage that realization was "outrageously popular" ("The Drama" 1866a, 187) and disgust that such taste encompassed all classes: "The elegant people in the stalls are no whit before the roughest youths in the gallery" ("The Drama" 1866a, 185). I doubt that Virginia Woolf had read this article when, eighty years later, she described early cinema audiences similarly as "the savages of the twentieth century," at "no great distance . . . from those bright-eyed naked men" ([1926] 1966, 268). Rather, the similarities manifest deeply engrained class prejudices, phobias, and rhetoric infusing theories, continuing across media and over time.

What this and other discourses reveal is that theorists fought not only with each other and practitioners over theorizing adaptation but also with the public. As a critique of downward mobility from mind to matter, from divine to human, from analytical to absurd, from ideal to real, from abstract to material, from poetical to literal, and from art to artisanship, the critique of realization was inextricable from critiques of the downward mobility that adaptation in the form of realization brought to the arts, a downward mobility made possible by the social, economic, and cultural upward mobility of the masses. Bourgeois critics especially feared the downward mobility of realization into the lowest and most marginalized classes and its ability to represent their views and desires, just as they feared and resisted extending political representation to them, which would allow their views and desires to be represented in the political sphere (Elliott 2012a, Chapter 3). They therefore tutted over "the realization of the Newgate calendar" in the theaters and opposed theatrical representations of "the deepest atrocities, the most squalid miseries, the most revolting adventures ... [of t]he lives of gamblers, murderers, and gaol-breakers" (Tomlins 1840, 65). This was realization and downward mobility a step too far.

Aesthetic theory in Britain had long excluded the lower classes from its canons of taste. Even as Kames sought "to establish principles that ought to govern the taste of *every* individual" ([1762] 1785, 1.vi, emphasis added), he excluded the working classes, asserting that "those who depend for food on bodily labor, are totally void of taste; of such a taste at least as can be of use in the fine arts." Supporting connections between aesthetic and political representation in the period, he argued further that "many by a corrupted taste are unqualified for voting" (1762. 2.499–500). Kames equally excluded "the opulent, the proud" ([1762] 1785, 2.499–500) from aesthetic taste, implicitly reserving it for the honorific and higher bourgeoisie, like himself. Yet while Kames and his ilk had exerted theoretical sway in the eighteenth century, a century on, bourgeois critics were losing their authority to direct the tastes of even their own class, and the 1866 drama critic was aghast at the "extraordinary rage for realization" among "*genteel people* at a theatre named after Royalty" ("The Drama and the Stage," 26, emphasis added).

As bourgeois intellectuals feared the rise of classes beneath theirs through aesthetic and political representation and losing power over even their own class, they adapted prior theories of adaptation as a culturally improving force to impose them on the lower classes. Adaptation was no longer theorized as the hallmark of the highest transhistorical and transcultural progress but as a concession to downgraded popular tastes and fleeting fashions. As Cooke had condemned Shakespeare for making concessions to his age, critics now condemned their contemporaries for doing likewise. Discussing an English version of Charles-François Tiphaigne de la Roche's (1722–1744) novel *Giphantia*, a reviewer focused not on the adaptation of text to text, but of text to cultural context: "Nothing more remain[s] but to adapt things to the taste and mode of the age" ("Review of *Giphantia*" 1761, 223). A century on, a music and drama critic critiqued popular taste for producing adaptations of adaptations: "Nowadays it isn't enough to translate a piece; it must be done second hand, adapted from an adaptation[:] translate from a translation, or it stands no chance of popularity" (J. V. P. 1860, 373). Numerous twenty-first-century critics have discussed attacks on adaptation for its secondariness (Klein and Parker 1981; Whelehan 1999; Stam 2005, 1–8; Cahir 2006, 13; Hutcheon 2006, xii; Cartmell and Whelehan 2010, 8); in this period, even as second-hand adaptations were devalued and downgraded *theoretically*, they were highly prized *economically*.

Theorizing Adaptation as an Equivocal Theoretical Object: Portable Property, Medium Specificity Theory, and Copyright

Neoclassical medium specificity prohibiting intermedial adaptation in theory paradoxically aided intermedial adaptation in practice, as adaptations of works to other media forms were classified as separate species who could not reproduce or evolve into each other and were therefore were not seen to impinge on copyright, unless they took the same form of printed words or music exactly reproducing the words and notes of a prior printed work. Even here, it depended on the proportion of copied material printed. Copyright did not extend to the spoken word of performances, which meant that dramatic adaptations of fiction were not viewed as violating copyright and, until 1833 in Britain, anyone could speak the words of another's play on stage without breaching copyright as well. Copyright laws therefore allowed adaptation to flourish, making free use of prior aesthetic works without crediting their makers, paying royalties, or sharing profits. Copyright laws as we understand them, requiring formal permission to adapt an aesthetic work to another form or medium, were not passed until 1911 in Britain and 1909 in the United States.

Stam has argued that derogatory rhetoric nominating adaptation a " 'betrayal,' 'deformation,' 'violation,' 'bastardization' " is predicated on charges of infidelity to sources (2005, 3); however, this was not the case in this period, when adaptations were far more often castigated for appropriating sources *too faithfully and literally*, without crediting or remunerating their producers, as protests against copyright law increased. Prior to the second half of the eighteenth century, the most celebrated and discussed adaptations were intramedial ones of classical and historical works in the public domain. We have seen that adapters sought to enter and elevate distinguished aesthetic lineages and to bring about cultural progress in the arts through adaptation.

Subsequently, the ambitious, rising middle classes who sought power apart from lineage used theories of original creation to claim economic and legal ownership of their aesthetic work and campaigned to redefine aesthetic productions as the property and progeny of their makers and render their adaptation by others a criminal act of theft or kidnapping. Author and composer rights could be, and were, sold to publishers, so that court cases were fought chiefly by publishers protecting their economic interests; even so, the rights belonged to their creators to sell.

That adaptation was historically common practice and legally and socially condoned is evident in that, prior to 1710, there was no government copyright legislation[16]: the Statute of [Queen] Anne in Britain passed in that year was the first in the world. The statute protected authors, musical composers, and their publishers from anyone "printing, reprinting, or publishing books, and other writings, without the consent of the authors or proprietors, to their very great detriment, and too often to the ruin of them and their families" (Copinger 1870, 14). It gave ownership to authors for a fixed period of time (fourteen years); a series of amendments to the statute made copyright renewable throughout their lifetimes. George William, Lord Lyttleton (1817–1876) summarized changes in British law from 1710 to 1833:

> The law of copyright was one wholly founded upon statute, dating from the time of Queen Anne. The first Act gave to authors of books and their heirs the sole right of publication for fourteen years, and if the author outlived the expiration of that term the right was extended to another fourteen years. That was the general state of the law up to the present day with two alterations and extensions. By the [Copyright Act of 1814] the period was extended from fourteen to twenty-eight years, and in the event of the author being alive at the expiration of that time the copyright was extended over the remainder of his life. (Hansard 1866, 360)

Democracy, Romanticism, individualism, and capitalism, which fed the growing social and economic power of the middle classes, intensified debates over copyright in the late eighteenth and early nineteenth centuries (Woodmansee 1984). Theories of natural rights entered copyright debates in the case of *Millar v. Taylor* (1769), when Lord Mansfield asserted that it is "*just*, that an Author should reap the pecuniary Profits of his own Ingenuity and Labour" and that "It is *just*, that another should not use his name, without his consent. It is *fit*, that he should judge when to publish, or whether he will ever publish" (*Millar v. Taylor* 1769, 4 Burr. 2399, emphasis in original). In a decision that granted ownership to individual genius and labour, against royal statute and the public, Mansfield affirmed common law copyright against the Statute of Anne, ruling that no works should *ever* enter the public domain. When a subsequent case overruled this decision (*Donaldson v. Becket* 1774), it did so on the basis of opposing publisher monopoly and encouraging free trade; both rulings, therefore, favored bourgeois capitalism.

In the United States, there was minimal copyright law prior to 1790. Here too, its advent was driven by a rising middle class. In 1783, following a petition from authors, Continental Congress announced that "it was persuaded that nothing is more properly a man's own than the fruit of his study, and that the protection and security of literary property would greatly tend to encourage genius and to promote useful discoveries" (Continental Congress 2016 [1914], 24: 326). This law tied Romantic theories of original creation and individual genius to individualistic theories of private property and to a bourgeois work ethic that valued intellectual exertion above manual labor.

American copyright laws protected works within the same medium, but not adaptations between different media. Until the early twentieth century, "copyright, whether one considered it a common law or a purely statutory right, operated to prevent the unauthorized reproduction of a work *in the same medium* in which the protected work was given tangible form" (Deazley 1833, n.p., emphasis added). Lyttleton underscored that although the Dramatic Copyright Act of 1833 "conferred the same privileges upon the authors of plays not printed and published as had previously been conferred upon authors by the [1814 Act]" even as it "applied distinctly to dramatic pieces," it did not apply "to the adaptation of books of fiction, and their alteration into another form" (Hansard 1866, 360).[17]

Indeed, the result of the 1833 Dramatic Copyright Act, which protected plays from being performed and printed by other dramatists, was to *increase* dramatic adaptations of novels, as performing plays written by others was no longer legal: the law stated didactically that "no person may, without the author's written consent, represent the incidents of his published dramatic piece, however indirectly taken, yet no action will lie, at the suit of the author of a novel, against a person who dramatizes it and causes it to be acted on the stage" (Copinger 1870, 160).

Economic damage was nothing; medium specificity was everything, so that when novelist, playwright, essayist, adapter, and frequent copyright litigator Charles Reade (1814–1884) brought a suit that a dramatization of his novel *It Is Never Too Late to Mend* had "injured" the sale of his book, while making profits for the theater, the judge ruled against him (Copinger 1870, 160). Even when theatrical adapters took words verbatim from novels and put them in the mouths of stage actors named after novel characters; even when the plots were identical, this did not violate copyright, because the spoken word and printed word were decreed to be different media forms by medium specificity theory: "The only way in which it appears possible for an author to prevent other persons from reciting or representing as a dramatic performance the whole or any portion of a work of his composition is himself to publish his work in the form of a drama, and thus bring himself within the scope of the dramatic copyright clauses" (Copinger 1870, 163). Thus, in spite of assaults upon it from Romantic organic unity, sister arts theories, and theories of realization, medium specificity theory prevailed in the courts and directed the economics of the adaptation industry.

However, as the case of *Tinsley v. Lacy* (1863) affirms, although "anyone might have told the story or acted the drama" or "read the book aloud" without prosecution (*Tinsley v. Lacy* 1863, 328), if adapters *printed* too many or the most "striking" words of a novel, medium specificity theory was no defense: they had breached the novel's copyright by the act of printing and selling them. In this landmark case, Mary Elizabeth Braddon's publisher, William Tinsley, sued Thomas Hailes Lacy for publishing stage adaptations of her best-selling novels *Lady Audley's Secret* (1862) and *Aurora Floyd* (1863), which were printed and sold to the public. Judge Vice-Chancellor Sir William Page Wood ruled in favor of the plaintiff on the basis that "a very large portion" had been "taken word for word from the novels." Not disputing that the publisher "was entitled to do this for the purpose of a mere acting drama," the judge ruled that "he is not so entitled for the purpose of printing or selling his compilation." The defense had argued that, "From the time of Shakespeare it has been the practice for dramatic authors to borrow their plots from published novels" (*Tinsley v. Lacy*, 328), but the judge found that "the very stage directions in the plays are . . . taken directly from the narrative portions of the novels, so that the supposed distinction between a play and a narrative almost disappears," further remarking that playwright William E. Suter (1811?– 1882) "can scarcely maintain that he, like Shakspeare [*sic*] has clothed the narratives of others in original language of his own, and given 'to airy nothing a local habitation and a name'" (330). He therefore issued a perpetual injunction banning further sales.

In this and similar cases, judges in courts of law made judgments based on aesthetic theories as well as legal precedents. Wood drew on Romantic theories of aesthetic vitalism, organicism, and originality in his ruling:

> An abridgement of a work might be published without infringing the author's copyright . . . in the case of scientific or historical works; but this doctrine was . . . inapplicable to a work of fiction the creation of the author's brain . . . all the vital parts of the novels, the very pith [essence] of the stories, had been appropriated . . . in the identical language in which the original author composed it. (Chambers, Streeten, and Haynes 1863, 536; 538).

He further linked Romantic aesthetic theories to bourgeois theories of labor and property, which medium specificity theory and adaptation threatened: "It is said that this is a play, and not a novel, and therefore the story being repeated *verbatim* out of the novel" does not infringe copyright. However, "this lady, having acquired *by her genius for novel-writing* a copyright in a work of fiction in which there are stirring events described in stirring language, has a right to the property herself for all purposes whatever" (Chambers et al., 538).

Wood likewise dismissed the Robin Hood defense that the defendant "is a public benefactor who lets the public have at a cheap rate what the author sells dear" (Chambers et al., 539), retorting that copyright law was established precisely to *prevent* this. He equally rejected the defense that "he who assists in diffusing an outline of the knowledge which the author gives in full is . . . to be considered as a sort of an assistant to the author" (539), since the adapter claimed authorship of the plays without crediting the novelist. He even advised Braddon how to forefend against dramatic adaptations in the future, suggesting that she "take a pair of scissors and cut out certain scenes and publish a little drama of her own" in order to "come within the protection of the Dramatic Authors' Copyright Act" of 1833 (537).

Other values were engaged to defend works against adaptation. Champions of the 1833 Dramatic Copyright Act prioritized the value of the adapter's hard work over Romantic theories of the spontaneous, effortless creation of natural genius. Prior to the Act, Bulwer-Lytton protested that the dramatic author

> had no power—no interest in the results of his own labour—a labour often more intense and exhausting than the severest mechanical toil. Was this a

just state of things? . . . The commonest invention in a calico—a new pattern in the most trumpery article of dress—a new bit to our bridles—a new wheel to our carriages—might make the fortune of the inventor; but the intellectual invention of the finest drama in the world, might not relieve by a groat the poverty of the inventor. (Hansard 1831, 246–47)

The image of the nation's greatest literary hero "starving in a garret," joined to unfavorable comparisons to copyright law in France and Belgium (Hansard 1831, 247), persuaded nationalist politicians to pass the law.

Even after the law was passed, theoretical debates continued in other court cases over the relative economic value of originals and copies. The case of D'Almaine v. Boosey (1835) was fought over the British copyright of a French opera belonging to the publisher D'Almaine. Boosey had published melodies from the opera adapted to dance music. The defense was predicated on the originality and labor of the dance music: "There is considerable exercise of mind in these adaptations independently of what is derived from the original composition" (Younge and Collyer 1836, 296). The judge rejected these arguments, decreeing:

It must depend on whether the air taken is substantially the same with the original. . . . [T]he mere adaptation of the air, either by changing it to a dance or by transferring it from one instrument to another, does not, even to common apprehensions, alter the original subject. The ear tells you that it is the same. (Hansard 1831, 302)

On the basis of the adaptation's too-great fidelity to the original composition, the judge ruled in favor of the plaintiff. Fidelity in adaptation was not only lambasted on aesthetic grounds by theorists: it was also judged to be *illegal* in courts of law.

Writing in 1860, Reade conjoined three bourgeois value systems to argue that the superior *aesthetic* value of an original work derived from its greater *work ethic* and therefore warranted its higher *economic* value. Asking, "Why give all the proceeds to one collaborateur, the less meritorious of the two in respect both of skill and labour," he conceded:

I grant that a competent adaptation requires labour and skill, and therefore ought to be properly remunerated; but for the same reason the longer labour and higher skill of the inventor ought also to be remunerated. . . . For

invention is the highest and rarest effort of the human mind, and adaptation is neither high nor rare; and as for labour, time is its best standing test
throughout the world: show me the French play I cannot adapt to our stage
in six days, as skilfully as any living Englishman can, and you shall cut my
hand off to make donkey soup; but to invent the same thing would cost me
a hundred days' labour, or more. (1860, 62)

While proclamations of a middle-class work ethic jarred with Romantic
notions of spontaneous genius, both held that original creation is more valuable than adaptation. Aesthetic value thus allied with economic value to devalue adaptation.

However, higher aesthetic value did not always translate to greater economic value: theater manager and actor Charles James Mathews (1803–78)
wrote to the dramatic authors of France: "You must bear in mind that we
have to pay our authors as much, per act, for good adaptations from the
French as for original productions" (Mathews 1852, 31). All the same, belief that adaptation required work, even of a lesser kind, prevented it from
being classified legally as theft. Discussing *Tinsley v. Lacy* and *Toole v. Young*
(1874),[18] Thomas Scrutton wrote: "It is only the presumed intellectual labour
in dramatizations of novels that hinders them from being held infringements
of playright [the legal right in a play] or copyright" (1896, 77).

While the most common synonyms for adaptation in earlier periods had
been translation, imitation, and alteration, a rhetoric of criminality began
to characterize adaptation discourse in the nineteenth century. When stage
adaptations of fiction were made without permission, acknowledgment,
or financial remuneration, albeit legally, prose fiction authors retaliated in
writing, sometimes within the very fiction that was being adapted to the
stage. Charles Dickens's famous diatribe against unauthorized, uncredited
stage adaptations of his novels in *Nicholas Nickleby* concludes:

Show me the difference between such pilfering as this and picking a man's
pocket in the street; unless, indeed, it be that the Legislature has a regard
for pocket handkerchiefs, and leaves men's brains (except when they are
knocked out by violence) to take care of themselves. (1839, 2: 478–79)

Reade, who was involved in numerous copyright suits as both plaintiff
and defendant, published more protests against copyright laws than any
other author, including a book-length treatise, *The Eighth Commandment*

(1860): "Thou shalt not steal."[19] The book nominates adaptation "plagiarism" (page 53, with eleven other instances) and criminalizes it as "theft" (39, with ten other instances), "steal[ing]" (page 18, with thirty-three other instances), "fraud" (page 70, with sixteen other instances), and "swindle" (page 36, with thirty-two other instances, including ten references to "the adaptation swindle").

What was figured as criminal pickpocketing, theft, fraud, and swindling at home was nominated piracy abroad. Following the International Copyright Act of 1852,[20] which extended the license given to adapters at home to those in other nations, Reade protested: "The pirates are now robbing English dramatists and English composers, and calling it 'adaptation'" (1860, 331). A later treatise advocating changes to copyright law proposed that "Adaptation shall be considered piracy and treated in the same manner" (Bowker 1886, 27).

It was not only aggrieved authors who contested the morality and legality of adaptation: Article IV of the United Kingdom's International Copyright Act of 1852 distinguished between "fair imitations or adaptations" and "piratical translations," decreeing that "the question whether a work is an imitation or a piracy shall in all cases be decided by the courts of justice" (Charles James Mathews 1852, front matter, n.p.).

In the case of *Tinsley v. Lacy*, Judge Wood acknowledged and sympathized with the outrage of novelists:

> It has been thought a grievance by many authors that their works, the benefit of which they thought they had secured, might be taken, and the very language might be used (by what is called dramatizing) upon the stage, without any possibility of the authors interfering to prevent that use being made of what in another shape was secured to them as their property.
> (*Tinsley v. Lacy*, 537)

As is so often the case, the law was much slower to change than authorial, public, and even unofficial legal opinion. Although Reade and other authors formed a Copyright Association in 1872, campaigned and published extensively on the subject, and championed bills to amend the law in the 1880s and 1890s, it was not until 1911 that authors were given exclusive rights over adaptations of their work to other media in Britain.

The public joined authors in criminalizing adaptations. In a letter to the *Athenaeum* dated December 17, 1866, S. R. T. Mayer protested:

> Three out of four of the so-called "original" tales in the penny journals are reprints of American novels, slightly . . . altered. . . . The injustice of this contemptible pilfering . . . prevents a fair price for [authors], as it is so very much cheaper to steal . . . old stories than to purchase new ones. (841)

Here, the slight alterations of adaptation legalize theft; like Fagin's boys picking handkerchiefs from middle-class pockets and unpicking the initials for resale, penny journals are condemned for pilfering, unpicking, and re-embroidering middlebrow literature.

Critics went further to cast adaptation in a rhetoric of violent crime. The *Quarterly Review* represented stage adaptations of novels as having "not merely plundered, but maimed, mutilated, [and] mangled romance" ("Review of Scott's *Lives of the Novelists*" 1826, 361). Aesthetic works bore their makers' names, like children, and Reade accused adapters of "robbing me of my child by kidnapping" (1860, 378).

Elsewhere, Augustan theories of adaptation forging an elite, fertile lineage of art and artists were eviscerated in a rhetoric of illegitimacy and miscegenation. Novelist, playwright, drama critic, pedagogue, and academic James Brander Matthews (1852–1929) referred to English adaptations of French plays as "a bastard hybrid . . . we may say of this adapted drama what the Western wit said of the mule, that it has no pride of ancestry, and no hope of posterity" (1894, 54). Drama may be a composite of the sister arts working harmoniously together, but adaptation—especially international adaptation—is here charged with illegitimacy, baseness, and sterility. Since the adaptations Matthews critiques were from drama to drama, the protest was not against adaptation violating the formal borders proscribed by medium specificity theory, but against adaptation violating national, cultural, and class borders.

Theorizing Adaptation as an Equivocal Theoretical Object: Originality, Medium Specificity, Class, and Nation

From the late eighteenth century, adaptation discourses and practices became less concerned with colonizing historical time through contemporary, national, aesthetic progress than with colonizing contemporary spaces, moralizing and civilizing foreign works for domestic consumption and adapting bourgeois works to civilize the lower classes at home. Johnson's dictionary defines "imitation" as "a method of translating looser than paraphrase, in which modern examples and illustrations are used for ancient, or domestick [sic] for foreign" (Johnson 1755). In the question asked by an early nineteenth-century critic as to why original dramatic authors had "gradually fallen into the same sinful ways of translation and adaptation" ("Drama: Drury Lane," 1829, 847), the rhetoric of sin serves not as a metaphor for infidelity to a source text but as a metaphor for violating cultural and aesthetic theories of originality, while translation represents a fall from the separate species advocated by nationalism. As Bianca Del Villano has argued, nationalism in this period was interwoven with "the shift from imitation to originality": "part of a complex ideological pattern in which the British *political*, rather than literary identity was at stake" (2012, 182, emphasis in original).

Class wars within Britain were also waged via a dichotomy of adaptation and originality, in which the bourgeois classes arrogated originality and aesthetic value for themselves and allocated adaptation and low aesthetic value to the lower classes. Tying originality didactically to moral values, they shifted it away from aesthetic and toward the cultural values by which they laid claim to superiority over both higher and lower classes, as in this passage:

> Wherever . . . imitation is not gracefully adapted to the spirit of modern times, art must fail in originality . . . and miss her great end, a power of exercising a *moral* influence over the understanding, through her hold upon the heart. (W. C. 1819, 51, emphasis added)

Medium specificity, then, allied with Romantic originality to theorize adaptation culturally as well as formally. Augustan theories arguing that adaptation brings about a gradually improving lineage of aesthetic works over time, as well as of society, ceded to categorical discourses that tied the separate species of art forms to similar categorical classifications of nations and classes as separate species, as Lord Kames tied his hierarchical classification of the arts (1762) to class hierarchies.[21]

As alliances between Romantic originality and medium specificity became nationalized and classed, they theorized adaptation equivocally and variably as a good or bad endeavor, depending on who was doing the adapting and for whom. There was, therefore, as much discourse about adaptation's global and domestic improving potential as there was about its debasing tendencies, rendering it a thoroughly equivocal theoretical object.[22] When adaptation aimed to moralize scandalous foreign works or elevate the lower orders at home, it was decreed a good theoretical object; when it challenged national with foreign values or the prerogatives of the dominant classes, it was condemned. Theorized variably as civilizer and corruptor, home guard and colonizer, adaptation was both recommended to raise the lower classes and condemned for debasing them; it was simultaneously conscripted to resist foreign invasion and to invade foreign nations.

Franco–English relations were the most commonly canvassed in English adaptation discourse.[23] Publications such as *Sermons, Altered and Adapted to an English Pulpit from French Writers* (Partridge 1805) and *French Cookery, Adapted to English Tastes and English Pockets* (Macdonald 1835) treat ideological, economic, and gustatory adaptations: copyright cases drew on such rhetoric. Adapting foreign plays to the English stage was viewed as a way to demonstrate a superior national identity (Del Villano 2012, 184). In Britain, this superiority was presented as a moral one. In 1870, a case was brought against a theater manager who had purchased exclusive rights to stage an English translation of the French drama *Frou Frou*. Other English dramatists who also wanted to stage the play made the case that, because translator Sutherland Edwards had gone beyond formal, linguistic translation to cultural adaptation, he had voided his exclusive right to the play. However,

> His Honour decided that the defendants have a right to their translation, that . . . [to preserve] all, or nearly all, the allusions and *double entendres* [would] render the work totally unfit to be put before an English family; and [make] the International Copyright Act . . . a dead letter. . . . To declare that Mr. Edwards, who is an excellent French scholar, forfeited the rights thus purchased because he left out the vice of the original, would be about as just as to make a housewife forfeit a fish or a fowl, because she had cleaned, gutted, and prepared it for domestic consumption. ("Literary Intelligence" 1870, 260, emphasis in original)

Far from being devalued for lack of originality or violation of medium specificity, adaptation is heralded as a guardian of English domesticity and an eviscerator of French culture. Astonishingly, the judge determined that to uphold the *legal* distinction between translation and adaptation would be more egregious than to violate the law which he had vowed to uphold; here, he placed national defense above the law, as in times of war. The judge acknowledged that "this may be a great wrong, but we shall consider it a great gain if it excludes—as indeed it will—the great body of the highly spiced modern French literature from English homes and readers" ("Literary Intelligence" 1870, 260). Adaptations, then, could serve as home guards preventing immoral French culture from invading moral English homes.

Adaptation in such instances was a good theoretical object, essential to English nationalism. In his preface to *The Patriot Father, Freely Translated from the German of Augustus von Kotzebue*, Frederic Shoberl (1775–1853)[24] similarly affirmed:

> I am but too sensible of the imperfections of this translation, or rather adaptation—for I have not scrupled to omit, to add, or to alter, wherever the original seemed to be susceptible of improvement, or not congenial to English taste and feelings. (1819, ii–iii)

Shoberl and others deemed textual infidelity a national virtue mandated by fidelity to English cultural contexts, a valorized infidelity that turned unfaithful translators into national heroes.

Theater critic Charles James Mathews was one of many to affirm that such international adaptations required skill:

> Literal, word-for-word translations, are of no use whatever, and have never, nor will they ever, had much success on the English stage. The taste of the two countries is so essentially different, that it requires a very skillful hand to adapt, expand, retrench, and arrange even the most available foreign dramas. (1852, 31)

Translation may make a foreign work intelligible to the English, but only adaptation to English ideologies, conventions, and customs can make it acceptable to the public. As the rhetoric of adaptation and arrangement joined a territorial, militaristic rhetoric of expansion and retrenchment, adaptation took on colonizing properties.

Adaptation practices and discourses were vested in exporting English culture as well as in Anglicizing foreign works for domestic consumption. In the second half of the eighteenth century, the discourse of adaptation engaged an increasingly colonizing rhetoric, carrying adaptation from its role as home guard to one of aggressive, nationalist, aesthetic colonizer. Shakespeare was epitome and zenith of such discourses, as practitioners and critics expanded their preoccupation with civilizing Shakespeare's works for home consumption to celebrating Shakespeare as a both a national and universal poet, "thus supporting a nationalist policy . . . projected on a world scale through colonialism" (Del Villano 2012, 182). Blending nationalist superiority with universal aesthetic theories, adaptation was conscripted in the service of world domination. Shakespeare's popularity among foreign adapters was (and still is[25]) theorized as the logical consequence and proof of the universality of his works, rather than proof of the universality of adaptation or the would-be universality of British colonial endeavors. As a theater critic (cited earlier) claimed that Garrick's adaptation restored Shakespeare to himself in 1764, a century on, critics were claiming that Shakespeare was restoring other nations to their essential, universal selves. Shakespeare's touted universality authorized the British to invade other nations via adaptation precisely because he was theorized to have always-already been there via his universality.

The Victorians readily acknowledged the importance of adaptation to their colonizing literary nationalism. We have seen that Ben Jonson's homage to William Shakespeare, "He was not of an age, but for all time!" (1623), was adapted by Victorian Shakespeare scholar Richard Grant White to read: "What he wrote was for, *adapted to*, all time" (1857, 1.cxcv, emphasis added). White, however, did not view Shakespeare as a global writer but as an intensely national one: "Only his race could have produced him (for a Celtic, a Scandinavian, or even a German Shakespeare is inconceivable)."[26] In a sleight of word, Shakespeare serves as both original and adaptation of the English branch of the "Anglo-Saxon race [which] is distinguished by a sober earnestness and downrightness of character, which manifests itself even in its narrative, dramatic, and poetical literature" (1857, 198). "Sober earnestness and downrightness of character" are specifically Victorian bourgeois values that would not have been defined as quintessentially English in Shakespeare's day.

Robert Shelton Mackenzie claimed similarly of Charles Dickens's writings that "there are no other works, in the language, so well *adapted* for all classes and ages" (1870, 333, emphasis added). Yet even as Mackenzie celebrated Dickens as already adapted to all ages and classes, he protested against adaptations of Dickens by foreigners and for lower-class markets. French adaptations of Dickens reversed the moralizing trajectory of English adaptations of French literature:

Jules Janin—famous critic, then and now! . . . assailed the play, as if Dickens himself had written it, and branded him as an immodest writer! Now, immodesty was the very last offence with which Dickens could honestly be charged, at any time. (Mackenzie 1870, 116)

As English adaptations sanitized French literature, French plays spiced up English fiction. Mackenzie was particularly mortified that French adaptations undermined Dickens as national literary hero and subjected him to the moral castigation of high-minded, bourgeois French critics.

At home, originality and aesthetic hierarchies were likewise classed and moralized. Aesthetic quality, defined in terms of originality, was made the prerogative of the bourgeois classes, most notably by novelist, playwright, adapter, and critic Wilkie Collins (1824–1889). In "Dramatic Grub Street," originality is synonymous with greatness and both are the province of the educated middle classes:

> I read at home *David Copperfield*, *The Newcomes*, *Jane Eyre*, and many more original stories, by many more original authors, that delight me. . . . I go to the theater, and naturally want original stories by original authors . . . [but] I must have the . . . adaptation. . . . [T]he adapted drama, is the sort of entertainment I do *not* want. . . . The fast young farmer has his dramatists, just as he has his novelists in the penny journals. We, on our side, have got our great novelists (whose works the fast young farmer does not read)—why, I ask again, are we not to have our great dramatists as well? (1858a, 266, emphasis in original)

Here, originality is not only the hallmark of aesthetic greatness, it is also the "natural" taste of the bourgeoisie, while adaptation is the domain of low quality, low prices, and the lower classes. While Collins did not deem the dichotomy between originality and adaptation or between classes to be impassable ("Why is my footman not to have the chance of improving his taste, and making it as good as mine?" 1858a, 266), he did theorize improvement as a one-way affair, a progress from adaptation to originality and lower-class to middle-class taste.

Similarly, in a report to the English government, Irish actor and playwright Dion Boucicault (1820–1890) blamed "the decline of the drama, and the decline of the fine arts generally, and literature itself" on the economic rise of the lower classes: at a lower stage of "intellectual development," they had become "greater consumers of thought" and "thinkers [had] condescended to supply the market; so that in that way literature [had] descended, and the theatres

[had] reduced their prices to meet the demand." However, he was patron-
izingly optimistic: "The lower classes cannot rise, but we can stoop . . . and
raise them gradually" (1866, 150). Seventeen years on, in "Concerning the
Unknown Public," literary and cultural critic Thomas Wright[27] assessed that
"the taste of the penny public has been and is being educated. . . . They have
become desirous of having better work and are capable of appreciating it"
(1883, 294).

As adaptations were valued for inculcating bourgeois ideologies in the
lower classes, "original" bourgeois fiction was adapted for lower-class
budgets and tastes, not only in plays based on fiction (Bolton 1987) but also
in chapbooks, penny dreadfuls, shilling shockers (Haywood 2004), and
penny journals, which adapted and abridged fiction for the lower classes. In
the inaugural issue of the *Dublin Penny Journal,* editor Philip Dixon Hardy
announced that

> our *brazen* Journal is adapted to be read by *every body* [sic]. . . . [O]ur Journal
> circulates from house to house of the working class, it will be raising up a
> *new* generation of readers, and be the means of creating a thirst for know-
> ledge where it never existed before. Thus will it be the means of extending
> the blessings of civilization. (Hardy 1832, 3, emphasis in original)

Like Collins, bourgeois critics were more likely to complain of than to celebrate these purportedly civilizing adaptations. Mackenzie complained not
only of French adaptations of Dickens's fiction but also of its adaptations for
the lower classes at home:

> Long before "Nickleby" was completed, some unscrupulous and impudent
> scribbler brought out in penny weekly numbers, a new version of what he
> called " 'The Nickleby Papers, by Poz." They were stupid to a degree, but the
> low price was in their favor, and they had a large sale. . . . Nothing could
> have been more clumsily written, but the book had thousands of readers—
> among the non-respectables in London. (116)

Downwardly mobile adaptation, adapting to lower aesthetic forms, lower
prices, lower tastes, lower classes, and lower age ranges, was roundly
condemned here and elsewhere. Even when that downward mobility
was seen as improving of lower nations and lower classes, there was usually a sense that what had been adapted was diminished by it. Claims of

adaptation's secondariness focused less on the aesthetic and textual than on the economic and cultural contexts to which texts have been adapted—less on the secondariness that arises from violating originality and medium specificity theory than on the secondariness of classes considered to be separate human species.

In 1858, Collins mocked and feared "The Unknown Public" who read penny journals, characterizing them as "a monster audience of at least three millions" incapable of responding to quality literature even when it was serialized for their pockets (Collins 1858b, 121). Especially galling to Collins, penny journals were filled with uncredited adaptations laying claim to originality and therefore "great" art (1858b, 121). Collins attacked mass popular literature doubly by aligning it rhetorically with various scorned and marginalized social groups and charging it with violating medium specificity theory at the level of genre, characterizing it as "a combination of fierce melodrama and meek domestic sentiment; short dialogues and paragraphs on the French pattern, with moral English reflections of the sort that occur on the top lines of children's copy-books" (1858a, 221). This rhetoric degrades adaptations and hybrid literature by associating them with violence ("fierce"), women ("meek domestic sentiment"), foreigners ("French"), and children ("children's copy-books"). Adaptation is not just for lesser nations and the lower classes but also for the lesser gender and lower ages. The reference to "children's copy-books" doubly attacks adaptation as infantile and derivative. But his most devastating double-edged attack was in using adaptation to attack the lower orders and, conversely, the lower orders to attack adaptation, enclosing them in a circle where each devalues the other. Foreign adaptations too were doubly bad: "That our stage should become the receptacle for bad adaptations of immoral French buffoonery, we feel a national degradation" ("To the Reader" 1860, 2). Bad adaptations of morally and intellectually bad French plays allied to produce "national degradation."

Collins blamed lower-class taste both for the prevalence of dramatic adaptations by comparison to original plays and for the invasion of foreign literature that adaptation enabled:

I go to the theatre, and naturally want original stories by original authors. . . . Do I get what I ask for? Yes, if I want to see an old play over again. But, if I want a new play? Why, then I must have the French adaptation. The publisher [of novels] can understand that there are people among his customers who possess cultivated tastes, and can cater for

them accordingly, when they ask for something new. The manager, in the
same case, recognizes no difference between me and my servant. (Collins
1858a, 266)

Adaptation outraged Collins and other members of the bourgeoisie because
it did not recognize class distinctions.

Others charged foreign adaptation with bringing down the aesthetic
standards of English arts and for preventing the development of national
arts: "This rage for adaptation is as great an obstacle to the possession of a
National Opera, as the French vaudeville is an impediment to the regener-
ation of the English Drama" (Telesforo de Truera y Cosío, 1831, 607). Mass
culture and the public shared the blame: once foreign opera became the
fashion,

> the public would no longer rest satisfied with what Bishop, or any other
> English composer could do for them. Since then, the state has been de-
> pendent for its support on *adaptations* of foreign operas. . . . To transfer,
> therefore, the music of one country to the language of the other is to make
> a forced marriage which can never be happy. . . . All this is most injurious to
> the art, as it breaks that union between sense and sound which is essential
> to good vocal music. ("Fashion in Music" 1833, 272, emphasis in original)

Medium specificity here joins national specificity to produce a nationally
separatist theory of adaptation.

The "fashion," however, was by no means fleeting and the lower classes were
blamed for it: "The English Opera still seeks to court half-price visitors by
foreign frivolities" ("The Theatres" 1841, 302). Illustrating the argument, this
critic recounts:

> On Thursday we endured the pain of . . . an English version—we cannot
> call it an adaptation—of a prurient piece of intrigue from the Opera
> Comique. . . . [S]uch things are alike unsuited to English talent and to
> English taste; and to attempt them is only proclaiming the inferiority of our
> artists in a worthless kind of entertainment, in which excellence is scarcely
> to be coveted. ("The Theatres" 302)

The review complains not only of adaptation but also of the *failure* of adaptation: it has failed because it has been too faithful to its foreign source—so

much so that it does not merit the name "adaptation." Insufficiently adapted, it has obscured "English talent" and offended "English taste." But foreign invaders have been enabled by English traitors: it is the bad taste of the lower classes that has allowed the nation to be invaded by foreign powers who have exposed "the inferiority of our artists." The lower classes have colluded with England's historical foreign enemy to undermine English opera, making it less aesthetically competitive on the international stage. Even after conceding English inferiority, this hyper-nationalist critic pronounces the French art "worthless."

In the final analysis, whatever the prevailing aesthetic values, whatever the theories underpinning them, critics sought to monopolize cultural value for their nation, their class, their gender, and their generation. They feared not only the downward mobility of art to classes beneath their own but also that adaptation was carrying their own class beyond their theoretical control. There is evidence that adaptations in penny journals were not read solely by the lower classes. Rebutting Collins's mid-century diatribe against "the unknown public" in 1883, Wright assessed that "those who have reasoned themselves into the belief that the patrons of the penny fiction journals must be a race apart, have failed in their search for such a race," confessing to having read them himself (1883, 288; 285).[28] Perhaps the greatest threat of adaptation was not that it belonged to one side or another in theoretical and cultural wars, but that it occupied both. In Victorian culture, adaptation's greatest threat to formal aesthetic and cultural political divides lay in its insistence on straddling them.

Conclusion

These are only some of many discourses of adaptation in the sixteenth to nineteenth centuries, but they are sufficient to indicate that adaptation theory was diverse, complex, nuanced, contested, and often ingenious. They furthermore attest that adaptations have not always been bad theoretical objects or always theorized as inferior and secondary: indeed, they were often decreed superior to what they adapted, for a variety of reasons. They further make clear that adaptation was seldom theorized as a solely textual, backward-looking affair but was more often theorized as a forward-looking cultural one, and that the fidelity of adaptation to new cultural contexts was prized more highly than the fidelity of adaptation to earlier texts.

Adaptation discourses in this period also demonstrate that theoretical logic and consistency often took second place to political, economic, and cultural values. The doubleness and multiplicity of adaptation enabled it to serve a variety of conflicting agendas and contradictory theories and to have it both ways. Adaptation allowed seventeenth- and eighteenth-century theorists to look both nostalgically back and progressively forward, simultaneously revering and castigating earlier artists for theoretical incorrectness, both emulating and correcting them in the name of aesthetic and cultural progress. Theories of Romantic originality were also doubly engaged to attack and defend adaptation; theories of adaptation as realization were invoked both to shield intermedial adaptation from medium specificity theory and to denigrate adaptation when it became too downwardly mobile for the ruling classes. In the long nineteenth century, theories that adaptation improved society vied with theories that adaptation harmed it; as medium specificity theory spread from aesthetic forms and human phenomenology to biologized, cultural categories of class, nation, race, gender, and age, adaptation became an equivocal theoretical object.

Adaptation's refusal to take sides bridged warring political, religious, and aesthetic theories, as well as enabling it to serve in their wars. Del Villano has shown that Restoration adaptations constructed ideological bridges between warring Cavalier and Puritan values,[29] dissonant classical and Christian ideologies, and Aristotelian poetics and French neoclassical theories (2012, 177). Adaptation also has potential to bridge warring theories and ideologies today.

We can learn from historical adaptation studies to theorize adaptation as a good theoretical object. Augustan theories of adaptation navigated far more equitably between adapted and adapting works and granted more equal attention to adaptation's formal and cultural dynamics than subsequent theories. As the Augustans imitated and adapted their forebears, it would behoove adaptation scholars today to imitate and adapt some of their theories to reconstruct adaptation as a good theoretical object.[30] Indeed, as this history has shown and will continue to show, the history of theorizing adaptation does not unfold as a linear history of progress but rather as a process of adaptation itself, with a remarkable number of recessive theoretical genes resurfacing—sometimes across centuries. The recessive dimensions of theoretical history become even more apparent in the twentieth and twenty-first centuries. Beyond theoretical repetitions, a history of theorizing adaptation reveals constants in *relations* between adaptation and theorization: whatever the theory, whatever the historical period, adaptation rose and fell according to how well it conformed to dominant theories of the day.

This history has shown that the laws governing adaptation lagged behind the theoretical and industry times. Even as bourgeois individualism championed original creation and individual ownership of art, and theories of realization and revivals of sister arts theories declared the interrelatedness of the arts and the naturalness and inevitability of interart adaptation, neoclassical medium specificity theories governed the copyright laws that rendered them economically independent, legalizing what many considered to be criminal acts of adaptation. Intriguingly, just as early twentieth-century copyright law finally rejected medium specificity theory, twentieth-century semioticians and formalists were reviving and adhering to it, as Chapter 3 attests.

3

Theorizing Adaptation in the Twentieth Century

Adaptation and Modernism

Although modernism (not to be confused with modernity, which began with the seventeenth-century shift from feudalism to capitalism in Europe) is defined as a single theoretical and aesthetic movement encompassing many arts and nations, there are many modernisms, modernist theories, and modernist practices.[1] Modernism is most commonly located in the years 1910–1945, with proto-modernism arising in the 1890s and the period after 1930 designated late modernism (Levenson [1999] 2011). However, this dating maps better onto British literature than the literature of other nations, since French poets such as Charles Baudelaire (1821–1867) and American poets such as Walt Whitman (1819–1892) were writing proto-modern literature in the 1850s. Modernism's dates also vary across art forms. Proto-modernism in visual art began with impressionist painting in the 1860s and modernist art continued long after 1945: indeed, art historians largely agree that it culminated in the 1960s with abstract art.[2] Modernism also continued in music and dance well into the 1960s (Albright 2004).

Modernism's end date in each art form is usually determined not by the cessation of modernist art but by the rise of postmodernism in that field. And yet modernist theory and practice did not end with the rise of postmodernism any more than neoclassical theories of medium specificity, Romantic theories of originality, and Victorian high-art humanism disappeared with the rise of modernism. Just as twenty-first-century theorists have argued that Romantic originality holds even more firmly now than it did in its own day (McGann 1983, 91; MacFarlane 2007, 3), so too artists and theorists continue to practice and publish according to modernist principles: "We are still learning how not to be Modernist" (Levenson [1999] 2011, 1). Modernism continues both in its own right and as an aspect of postmodernism: the two are commonly seen as interpenetrating continuously and discontinuously.

Theorizing Adaptation. Kamilla Elliott, Oxford University Press (2020). © Oxford University Press.
DOI: 10.1093/oso/9780197511176.001.0001

Ihab Hassan has written: "The Term postmodernism is . . . Oedipal. . . . [I]t cannot separate itself completely from its parent. It cannot invent for itself a new name. . . . [I]t remains a conflictual 'dialogue' with the older movement [modernism]" (2001, 8).

In adaptation studies, while studies of particular modernist adaptations are legion, few have addressed relations between adaptation and modernist theories. While Martin Halliwell's "Modernism and Adaptation" informatively contrasts the fertile relationships between modernist authors and film to the "love–hate relationship" between Anglo-American modernist fiction and film in literary film adaptation (2007, 90), it applies modernist theories to adaptation as if they were self-evident truths. Similarly, although the *MLA International Bibliography* yields 103 hits from a search for the subject terms "adaptation" and "modernism," a search for the subject term "adaptation" and the primary *theories* engaged by modernists produces few: astonishingly, searches for the subject term "adaptation" combined with "aesthetic formalism," "formalist approach," "New Criticism," or "medium specificity" yield *no hits at all.* Searches for related theoretical terms produce scant results: one hit for "adaptation" and "narratology"; two for "adaptation" and "formalism"; two for "adaptation" and "hermeneutic approach"; two for "adaptation" and "structuralist approach" (none for "structuralism"); and three for "adaptation" and "phenomenology" (on which medium specificity theory is predicated). This stands in striking contrast to Robert B. Ray's assessment in 2000 that a majority of literary film adaptation studies had been conducted according to theoretical principles laid down by aesthetic formalism and New Criticism, a view borne out by Jeffrey Egan Welch's annotated bibliographies of literature and film studies spanning from 1909 to the late 1980s. Similarly, a search pairing the subject terms "adaptation" and "narrative theory" yields only 35 results, in contrast to the legion adaptation studies pursuing narrative theories. These findings suggest that *MLA International Bibliography* contributors and indexers may not recognize older, hegemonic theories *as* theories. By contrast, they are more attuned to identifying the theories of the theoretical turn as theories: "adaptation" and "postmodernism" produces 94 hits; "adaptation" and "feminism" 125; "adaptation" and "queer theory," 71; "adaptation" and "psychoanalytic approach," 70; "adaptation" and "historical approach," 68; "adaptation" and "postcolonial approach," 49. While many variables go into producing subject terms, one conclusion can be drawn: there is a marked lack of theoretical self-reflexivity among aesthetic formalists and New Critics. As this chapter illustrates, they often see their theories and methodologies not as theories but as demonstrating essential and universal truths about art and humanity or self-evident manifestations of good taste and interpretive acumen. A search combining the subject terms "adaptation" and "humanism," a predominant theoretical position in the history of adaptation studies, yields only 15 results. Humanism is not a natural or essentialist state of mind: it is a philosophy, an ideology, a particular world view (T. Davis 2017), as are aesthetic formalism and New Criticism, and my history shows that they are sharply at odds with other theories.

Historical approaches to modernism and adaptation have been more theoretically self-aware. Richard Hand's "Adaptation and Modernism" (2012) treats modernism as a historical movement. Figuring film adaptation as "an obsession" in "the epoch of Modernism" (54), Hand's chapter agrees with Halliwell's that their relationship contains both positive and negative elements: "Adaptation provided a springboard into creativity for a diverse range of artists of the modern period, yielding experiments and explorations that remain exciting and innovative to the present day" (68), while Henry James and Joseph Conrad failed to adapt their writing to film (60). These assessments are arrived at by subjecting adaptation practices to aesthetic humanities theories: my study in this section focuses on how modernist theories affected adaptation discourses and practices more generally.

Just as changing copyright laws were opening discursive and legal spaces to legitimize intermedial adaptations (1909 in the United States and 1911 in Britain), modernist theories drastically diminished the theoretical fortunes of adaptation in ways from which it has still not recovered today. Central to adaptation's declining theoretical fortunes was modernism's rejection of the past and celebration of the new. Modernism's rejection of past styles and aesthetic traditions included the Augustan theories that had celebrated adaptation as a progressive, lineal, incremental means of improving the arts and society over time. Under modernism, aesthetic progress was achieved by radical rupture from and revolution against the past, most famously articulated in Ezra Pound's call to "Make it new!"[3] No longer could adaptation be defended as a *type* of originality: aesthetic works must be radically, wholly, even antagonistically new. Nor did adaptation fare well under modernism's "quest for the pure, self-referential art object" (Berman 1988, 30), for adaptation always and inevitably refers to something other, which it has both incorporated and left behind.

Adaptation, however, survived in modernism under other names. In his introduction to *The Routledge Companion to Adaptation* (2018), Dennis

Cutchins observes that "something like adaptation studies was . . . present at the inception of the modern era in literary scholarship" in "forensic . . . [i]nfluence studies" (1). However, while the chapter rightly figures modernist attention to literary allusions as an "antecedent" of twentieth-century adaptation studies, a longer history of theorizing adaptation positions it as a *shattering* of older adaptation studies and a reconstituting of new ones from their broken pieces. Because the modernist quest for the new was not theorized as springing spontaneously from Romantic genius and imagination but from destroying and revolutionizing what had gone before, modernist modes of adaptation were often shatteringly violent. T. S. Eliot concluded his modernist poem and manifesto *The Waste Land* (1922) with the words, "These fragments I have shored against my ruins" (Eliot [1922] 2010, 83). As modernists shored fragmented allusions to past writers and artists against the ruins of Augustan theories of adaptation, they perpetuated adaptation practices piecemeal, in keeping with modernist fragmentations and reconstructions of other aesthetic traditions. Pericles Lewis has affirmed that "the modernists were highly self-conscious about their relationship to literary tradition," describing *The Waste Land* as an attempt "to make a new poem out of the inherited language of tradition" (2011, 132). In "Tradition and the Individual Talent" (1919), Eliot argued that modernist poetry must cast all earlier poetry in a new light (P. Lewis [2007] 2011, 131). The past was not completely rejected and destroyed: it was adapted. Even as Pound hailed *The Waste Land* as "the justification of the 'movement' of our modern experiment, since 1900" (P. Lewis [2007] 2011, 129), a break with the aesthetic traditions of western culture, it not only adapted those traditions but also their *adaptation* traditions, as well as its official rejection of them, shattering and incorporating them. In the historical and theoretical contexts of modernism, allusions indubitably constitute piecemeal, modernist adaptations that not only apply modernist theories of fragmentation to adaptation practice but also continue—and revolutionize—longstanding traditions of adapting prior aesthetic productions, as well as of adapting adaptation practices to new theories.

Some adaptation theorists exclude allusions from their definition of adaptation (Hutcheon 2006, 9). Yet just as scholars study modernism's fragmentation of past aesthetic traditions, adaptation studies would benefit from investigating modernism's fragmentation of past adaptation practices and discourses. Linda Hutcheon's insistence on defining adaptations at the level of whole works adapted to other whole works is a legacy of modernist theory, particularly New Critical theories of textual organic unity, one that postmodernists, including Hutcheon herself, have challenged elsewhere. Adapters had for centuries cut, pasted, combined, and overwritten prior works; modernist theories continued such practices, atomizing and reconstituting them by "assembling 'fragments' or 'broken images' from the past into a sort of mosaic" (P. Lewis [2007] 2011, 136). Even if we concede Hutcheon's definition of adaptation as a "creative and an interpretive," "acknowledged," "extended intertextual engagement" with "a recognizable other work or works" (2006, 8), James Joyce's *Ulysses* (1922), which adapts Homer's *Odyssey*, meets her criteria. A history and theory of modernist adaptation, set in dialogue with older practices of adaptation, awaits fuller formulation not only in literary studies but also in other disciplines. Marcus Nichols has written a brilliant PhD thesis theorizing decadent practices of fragmentation, mosaic, and collage as modes of adaptation that determined "which parts of the adapted forms endure, survive" (2018, 282). His study finds decadent adaptation to be "excessive yet particulate" (291). For Nichols, decadent adaptation encodes both decay and artifice in its processes, as heavily encrusted, ornamented surfaces overlay entropic texts that thereby become increasingly susceptible to further fragmentation and decay (297). Thus, it is not only modernism that undertook adaptation as a process of fragmentation: decadent theory and practice did likewise.

If we are to pursue a longer, wider theoretical history of adaptation, definitions of adaptation need to expand. A lack of engagement with modernist reworkings of adaptation theory and practice undoubtedly contributed to adaptation's declining theoretical fortunes in the twentieth century, although scholars in the twenty-first have begun to redress this neglect (joining Halliwell, Hand, and Nichols is Nissen 2018). Yet scholarly neglect of modernist adaptation is not the only problem that adaptation studies faced: modernist theories actively assaulted both adaptation and the theories that had valorized adaptation in the past.

Adaptation, the Formalist Turn, and Medium Specificity Theory

The formalist turn in the humanities brought about by structuralist semiotics and narratology, (Russian) formalism, and New Criticism, theoretical movements born in the early decades of the twentieth century, continued and developed for most of the century. Although they faced increasing challenges in Britain and the United States from the 1970s, they remain mainstream in Europe and other nations influenced by European theory today. While there are differences between and within modernist formal theories, they share in common a disregard not only for past traditions but also for historical and cultural study of the arts, creating a hierarchy in which cultural theorization is subordinated to formal theorization, a hierarchy literalized in critical footnoting practices. This has been particularly problematic for theorizing adaptation: defined as change to suit a new environment, adaptation cannot be theorized adequately without attention to its historical and cultural environments. Adaptation does not simply adapt from prior texts; it also adapts to new contexts.

The formalist turn further diminished the theoretical fortunes of adaptation by dismissing the cultural theories that had valorized it in earlier centuries. Make-it-new modernism not only downgraded adaptation as a hand-me-down aesthetic form, it further eradicated adaptation's role in bringing about aesthetic and cultural progress. Following the Great War of 1914–1918, faith in the ability of art to bring about cultural progress collapsed. At best, it was an illusion; at worst, it was philosophically deceptive, culturally pernicious, and socially destructive. According to Randall Stevenson, "it was the First World War itself which made the destructive aspects of modernity inescapable and the need for new artistic forms unavoidable" (2016, n.p.).

Formalism's focus on form thus not only theorized adaptation as an inferior aesthetic formal product because it was not new, it also eviscerated its previous value as a progressive, salutary, cultural process. As it delimited the new environments to which adaptation adapts to art forms alone, medium specificity, a key tenet of aesthetic formalism, delimited these formal environments still further by prohibiting intermedial adaptation. This powerful theoretical alliance adapted and intensified the earlier alliance between Romantic originality and neoclassical medium specificity theory, threatening to all but extinguish adaptation as a subject of theorization, limiting adaptation to works within the same medium, scattering its remains to translation theories in literature, transposition and arrangement theories in music, performance theories in theater, and influence studies in many media.

The aesthetic hybridities and pan-adaptation of the Victorian period were also atomized by modernists; Pound used Egyptian hieroglyphs and Chinese ideograms in his poetry, the poets of the Harlem Renaissance composed their poetry to the rhythms of jazz, and John Dos Passos infused his writing with cinematic techniques. However, the early twentieth century also witnessed a resurgence of medium specificity theory. In 1910, the American academic and literary critic Irving Babbitt (1865–1933) worked as arduously to hierarchize the arts and to keep them from mixing as the eugenic scientists of his day worked to codify and hierarchize ethnic and class differences. Babbitt's *The New Laokoön: An Essay on the Confusion of the Arts* seeks to restore Gotthold Lessing's "true" theory to redress the nineteenth century's "general confusion of the arts," targeting interart adaptations such as "Rossetti's attempts to paint his sonnets and write his pictures" (1910, ix). Insisting that the Romantic theories of organic unity that had allowed such inexcusable "confusions" must be corrected by the categorical systematicity of pseudo-scientific theories adapted by Lessing from pre-evolutionary Linnaean botany and biology, *The New Laocoön* rejects the novel as the "confusion of all the other literary forms, the visible embodiment of [the] chaos of human nature" (204–25).[4] (It does not stoop to mention film.)

Modernist film scholars were, however, keenly concerned with medium specificity theory, to which film had to conform in order to qualify as an art in its own right and avoid being classified as a technological recording device for other arts, a craft, or a compilation of other arts. When American poet and film critic Vachel Lindsay (1879–1931) set out in 1915 to prove that "THE MOTION PICTURE ART IS A GREAT HIGH ART, NOT A PROCESS OF COMMERCIAL MANUFACTURE" (1, capitals in original), he had to demonstrate that film adhered to medium specificity theory. Pledging allegiance to medium specificity's cardinal tenet that "what is adapted to complete expression in one art generally secures but half expression in another" ([1915] 1922, 169), Lindsay condemned adaptations as representationally untrue and phenomenologically dissonant, nominating an Italian film of Dante's poetry "a false thing" and its consumption like "trying to see a perfume or listen to a taste" (272).

Even so, Lindsay's conflicted argument was consistent in using literary adaptation to elevate film. Many of the films he engaged to champion film as the seventh art are literary adaptations. When a film adapts canonical literature, it is elevated by the association:

The most successful motion picture drama of the intimate type ever placed before mine eyes was *Enoch Arden*, produced by [Christy] Cabanne.... The

mood of the original poem is approximated . . . it is a photographic rendering in many ways as fastidious as Tennyson's versification. (24)

The adaptation here first approximates, then equals poetry by the most
revered English poet of the nineteenth century; it subsequently exceeds it: "it
fills my eye-imagination and eye-memory *more than* that particular piece
of Tennyson's fills my word-imagination and word-memory" (25, emphasis
added). Here, the eye is set not against the ear, as it is in Lessing's discussion
of painting and poetry ([1766] 1962); rather, it is set against the imagination
and deemed fuller than it phenomenologically.

When the adapted literature was not canonical, Lindsay equally used it
to elevate film above its sources. For example, reviewing D. W. Griffith's
film *The Birth of a Nation* (1915), he assessed, "Wherever the scenario
shows traces of *The Clansman*, the original book, by Thomas Dixon, it is
bad. Wherever it is unadulterated Griffith, which is half the time, it is good"
(47). Beyond supporting medium specificity's tenets that intermedial adaptation inevitably produces bad art, the statement challenges Romanticism's
valorization of "the original book" with the "unadulterated" film, intimating that adaptation is never good under any circumstances, and that
film is only good when it ceases to be an adaptation. Yet as much as adaptation in both case studies serves to valorize film, it does so only by valorizing prevailing *theories*. Indeed, Lindsay confessed that *Enoch Arden*
"is pleasing to me as a theorist" because it offers "a sound example" of the
theory he promoted (24).

Even film theorists of the 1910s who theorized film as a hybrid form incorporating many arts drew the line at interart adaptation. In 1916, German-
American psychologist and media critic Hugo Münsterberg (1863–1916)
conceded, "Nobody denies that the photoplay shares the characteristic
features of drama," but he argued that making adaptations on the basis of
shared features stood in the way of film's emergence as an art in its own
right: "As long as the photoplays are fed by the literature of the stage, the
new art can never come into its own." His conclusion has been reiterated
by countless critics, educators, artists, reviewers, and the public to the present day: "Wherever we examine without prejudice the mental effects of true
works of art in literature or music, in painting or sculpture, in decorative arts
or architecture, we find that the central aesthetic value is directly opposed to
the spirit of imitation" ([1916] 2002, 114). Romantic theories of originality
remained alive and well in the early twentieth century, as claims to originality

(whether based in Romantic genius or difference from other art forms) remained essential to the valorization of art.

In 1924, Hungarian poet, film critic, and scholar Béla Balázs (1884–1949) dealt a redoubled blow to adaptation, arguing that adaptation from one medium to another was not only aesthetically misguided and practically difficult but also theoretically incorrect. While Lessing had pressed the bond between form and content as aesthetically *desirable*, structuralist linguistics rendered its rupture semiotically *impossible*. First, Balázs divorced film from literature using Lessing's word/image medium specificity divide: "A writer's success depends on the power and subtlety of his writing. The artistic nature of film resides in the power and subtlety of its images and its gestural language. This explains why film has nothing in common with literature" ([1924] 2010, 19). Balázs here advanced the oft-reiterated maxim, "You can't make a good film from a good book," using adaptation as a bad theoretical object lesson: "The essential difference between film and literature can be seen most clearly when a good novel or a good play is adapted for film (23); "films that have been conceived in literary terms . . . are bad since they contain nothing that could be expressed only in film" (21).

This rhetoric was not new to film: Balázs built on nineteenth-century theories of prose fiction and theatrical writing so prevalent that they pervaded practitioner discourses. In 1872, dramatist and opera librettist James Robinson Planché (1796–1880) had argued that "the greater the novelist[,] the less able has he proved himself to fulfil the requirements and exigencies of the theatre" (48). Annie Nissen's study of canonical British authors writing across media in the context of early film documents that both film and literary camps responded unenthusiastically to H. G. Wells's hybrid film-novel and that J. M. Barrie's innovative and highly cinematic screenplay for *Peter Pan* was rejected and replaced by an inferior, hack studio screenplay. Nissen has found as much unproductive territoriality in the film and literary industries as in literary and film theories of the day, a territoriality shored up by medium specificity theory in both domains (Nissen 2018, Chapter 5). Indeed, the territoriality maintained by medium specificity theory is not merely formal, but also institutional, economic, and industrial.

Drawing on structuralist semiotic theory, Balázs went further to argue that adaptation is impossible, because content and form are inextricable: "A good film does not have 'content' as such. It is a 'kernel and shell in one.' It no more has content than does a painting, a piece of music or indeed a facial expression" ([1924] 2010, 19). The marriage of structuralist semiotics and

medium specificity rendered the adaptation of form and content aesthetically undesirable and representationally impossible: even adaptation within
the same medium was decreed theoretically incorrect.

The coming of synchronized sound to cinema in the late 1920s sent
German film theorist Rudolph Arnheim (1904–2007) scurrying to police new technologies with medium specificity theory, engaging the formalist theories shoring up Balázs's assault on adaptation. Arnheim's "A New
Laocoön: Artistic Composites and the Talking Film" acknowledges Lessing
and, amazingly, argues that talking pictures are "productions which, because of intrinsic contradictions of principle, are incapable of true existence" ([1932] 1971, 199). According to Arnheim, hybrid media not only fail
aesthetically but also fail to *exist at all* in the domain of theoretical truth.
And yet, in spite of being denied "true existence," talking pictures not only
existed but also flourished, gesturing to the growing gulf between academic
theory and cultural practice. As formalist theories became incapable of explicating hybrid and adapted media forms, they became increasingly irrelevant
to modern media. Paradoxically, having exiled cultural study, they became
themselves culturally defunct.

What is more pertinent to this study of theorization's relationship to adaptation is that, rather than entertain the possibility that a theoretical principle might itself be untrue, hybrid media and adaptations were denied "true
existence." For all the theoretical complaints about the pretensions, failures,
badness, absurdity, and impossibility of adaptation, using neoclassical medium specificity theory to deny the existence of ancient, ongoing cultural
practices such as adaptation and new hybrid media forms and technologies
such as sound film represents the height of theoretical arrogance, absurdity,
and failure. The formalist turn allowed theorists to remain blind to their theoretical failures, while their cloistered formal seclusion rendered their theories immune from cultural challenges.

During the 1930s and 1940s, New Criticism rose to prominence in the
United States,[5] holding near hegemonic sway in literary studies until the
late 1960s. New Criticism theorizes texts as self-contained, organically unified, autonomous wholes, carrying Romantic theories of organic unity away
from the sister arts and intermedial discourses into isolationist studies of individual art works sealed off from their cultural contexts, other works, and
other art forms. New Critical hermeneutic close reading sets parts of a work
in dialogue with other parts, rather than texts in dialogue with other texts or

contexts, while marginalizing or excluding historical, cultural, sociological, and biographical explanations of literature.

Medium specificity theories were often joined to New Critical organic unity in practitioner discourse. Reviewing a stage adaptation of Thomas Hardy's *Tess of the D'Urbervilles* in 1925, English playwright Henry Arthur Jones (1851–1929) insisted: "There can be no true or quite satisfactory adaptation of a novel to the stage. To the extent that a play is a consistent organic whole it must differ widely from the novel from which it is quarried" (Jones 1930, 315). Here, instead of militating against adaptation theory, adaptation practice cedes to it.

When adaptation was considered, it was charged with violating medium specificity theory. Filmmaker and film journal editor and British Film Institute and British Film Academy member Karel Reisz accused adaptation of deserting formal theoretical values in pursuit of cultural commercial ones: "One of the less fortunate effects of the commercialization of the popular arts is to be found in the number of works of art which are exploited by transposing them into another medium" (1950, 188). As James Brander Matthews had done in the nineteenth century, Reisz critiqued adaptations of literature, painting, music, and ice skating as "bastard creations," lacking "aesthetic unity because they have been illegitimately conceived outside their medium" (1950, 188). Here we find evidence for Stam's claim that adaptation has been discussed using a rhetoric of bastardization (2005, 3), but the bastardy here and elsewhere is not based in infidelity to source texts: rather, it is predicated on adaptation's *infidelity to medium specificity theory*, a theory that decrees the impossibility and undesirability of *fidelity between different media*. Prefiguring Geoffrey Wagner's praise of unfaithful adaptations in 1975, Reisz, who pioneered new realism in British cinema after World War II, insisted that only adaptations which "treat the novelist's subject as . . . raw material and interpret it afresh" are "legitimate," because they are "comparable to the novelist's approach to life itself" (189). The only legitimate adaptation is one that does not aspire to fidelity to another aesthetic form but seeks fidelity to "life." Yet this mode of fidelity to "life" is also defined and policed by theorization. The "relative success and failure of adaptations" depend on their fidelity not to sources but to theories; for Reisz and so many others, theoretically faithful adaptations are "the only kind of adaptation worth attempting" (205). The theories may change, but the relationship between theorization and adaptation remains the same.

Blaming both "the incompetence (or unscrupulousness) of most adaptors rather than the impossibility of adaptation itself" (189) for the failure of adaptation, Reisz expressed dismay that adaptation serves other agendas besides theoretical ones and that adaptation's commercial value accords it formidable social, cultural, and economic power (205), threatening theoretical authority over cultural practice.

Modernism, Mass Culture, and Adaptation

In contrast to Reisz's championing of realism in art, the high modernist rejection of realism articulated by Wyndham Lewis in favor of abstract art, stream-of-consciousness writing, atonal music, absurdist theater, minimalist architecture, and cubist, surrealist, and expressionist visual art was inseparable from modernist fears of and opposition to mass culture:

> Popular art does not mean the art of the poor people, as it is usually supposed to. It means the art of the individuals. . . . The "Poor" are detestable animals! . . . BLAST years 1837 to 1900[.] Curse abysmal inexcusable middle-class (also Aristocracy and Proletariat)! (W. Lewis 1914, 7)

Turning from realism's democratizing theories of shared perception to a radical, countercultural, aesthetic individualism undermined the theories of adaptation as a process of shared phenomenological realization that had valorized popular, mass culture adaptation theoretically in the nineteenth century. Modernism also assaulted the sister arts theories that underpinned theories of realization: under high modernism, "English poetry was being freed from painting, English music from 'literature,' painting from anecdote, sculpture from sentiment" (Kenner 1972, 245). Modernist discourses of aesthetic purity were furthermore shot through with the rhetoric of xenophobia gripping Europe as it contended with rising immigration, declining colonial power, and racist political movements; modernist existentialism burgeoned in political climates where capitalist, bourgeois individualism warred with socialism and communism. As in prior centuries, aesthetic classifications were inseparable from national, class, economic, political, and territorial ones; fear of the lower classes, unionizing and radicalizing at home, intensified debates over high and low art, while modernist theorists used medium specificity theory to carve up media and academic disciplinary territory as surely as Europe did geographical territory after the Great War, subsequently working as assiduously to protect high art from the incursions of mass culture as Cold War capitalists worked to root out communist populism.

While many critics have emphasized high modernism's opposition to Americanization and capitalism, Paul Poplawski has highlighted that "high culture's scorn for the indisputably popular range of literature character-ized as low-brow was a pale thing compared with its fear of mass culture in the shape of tabloid newspapers and, later, Hollywood-dominated cinema" (2003, 262). Although theorists of early cinema hoped that film's universal language would promote "egalitarianism, internationalism, and the prog-ress of civilization through technology" by combining technological, egal-itarian downward mobility with adaptive, uplifting educative functions (Hansen 1991, 77), modernist critics adopted a rhetoric of recidivism to attack it. For all modernism's celebration of aesthetic primitivism in other forms, Virginia Woolf scornfully perceived "the savages of the twentieth century watching the pictures" to be, "for all the clothes on their backs and the carpets at their feet," at "no great distance . . . from those bright-eyed, naked men who knocked two bars of iron together and heard in that clangor a foretaste of the music of Mozart" ([1926] 1966, 268).[6] For all their embrace of new art forms, leading modernist critics rejected the new art of film and adapted elitist eighteenth-century aesthetic theories to attack it. Contrasting the modernist avant-garde, which he commended, and kitsch (popular cul-ture), which he did not, art critic Clement Greenberg (1909–1994) replicated Lord Kames's classed divide between the "elegant pleasures" of the elite and "grosser amusements" of the working classes ([1762] 1785, 2.492) and con-tinued Wilkie Collins's diatribes against the lower classes for art, blaming kitsch on the classes beneath his own, "peasants who settled in cities as pro-letariat and petty bourgeois," lacking "the leisure and comfort necessary for the enjoyment of traditional culture" ([1939] 1961, 10). Incongruously, even as Greenberg championed a progressivist avant garde in art, he returned to eighteenth-century theories of culture and class to do so. While his ideas that art should be anti-capitalist, intellectual, innovative, and difficult produced critiques of capitalist culture that fed into Marxist aesthetic criticism by Walter Benjamin, Theodor Adorno, Max Horkheimer, Dwight Macdonald, Jean-François Lyotard, Jean Baudrillard, and many others, he nevertheless denigrated the masses. Where Woolf cast them as primitive savages at a lower stage of evolution from herself, Greenberg figured them as the mind-less dupes of capitalist propaganda fed to them in popular culture.

Adaptation was central to such denigration. Greenberg defined kitsch as low art adapting high art: "using for raw material the debased and academicized simulacra of genuine culture" (10). In contrast to the originality and artistry of the modern avant-garde, kitsch, "mechanical and operat[ing] by formulas" (10), lay outside the domain of art along with the machines and formulae of the sciences that Greenberg figured as antagonists to the humanities. As nineteenth-century critics had done, Greenberg and others exiled adaptation from the domain of art and from their theoretical discourses because it did not conform to or obey their theories.

Others, however, continued nineteenth-century discourses in which adaptation was to be used by the ruling classes to conform the masses to their theories and values. The educational value of adaptation propounded throughout the nineteenth century (Lamb and Lamb 1807; Godwin 1824; Ireland Commissioners of National Education 1835; Graham 1837) came into renewed focus with the advent of motion pictures (Uricchio and Pearson 1993). In 1907, an article in the *Elmira Star-Gazette* commended "the trend the moving picture shows towards the goal of enlightenment and education," claiming that the "real value and usefulness" of film is to "enter the ranks of the educators and work to uplift the minds of the people at large" ("Trade Notes" 1907, 664). In this formulation, it is not through observing medium specificity that "the picture machines are coming to their own" but through adapting high, moral literature for pedagogical purposes. While Münsterberg argued that it was only apart from adaptation that the cinema would "come into its own," for the author of this news article, "coming to [its] own" depended on adaptation. In spite of their differences, what both views share in common is the contradictory claim that coming into one's own depends on conformity to theoretical and cultural values.

Even dissenting critics who celebrated film as a popular art opposed adaptation. In 1924, American author, editor, and drama and cultural critic Gilbert Seldes (1893–1970) daringly hijacked cinema from aspirations to become the seventh high art, locating it instead among seven low-brow arts, which he nominated *The Seven Lively Arts*—the movies, musical comedy, vaudeville, radio, comic strips, popular music, and popular dance. Attacking the sterility of elite art forms, Seldes argued that popular mass arts should be treated just as seriously as elite arts. Charging high-art aesthetes with vulgarity and derivation, as well as arrogance, he declared: "I consider vulgar the thing which offends against the canons of taste accepted by honest people, not by imitative people, not by snobs" (1924, 21). Seldes here upended Collins's insistence that high art, hallmarked by originality, belongs to the higher classes, while imitation defines low art, the province of the lower classes.

Seldes's populist aesthetic theory prefigured late twentieth-century cultural studies challenges to high art and valorizations of popular culture, yet it did not champion adaptation or rescue it from the opprobrium of neoclassical, Romantic, and modernist aesthetic theories. Subscribing to the theories of the high-art critics he otherwise opposed, Seldes praised the original, "inimitable" genius of Charlie Chaplin, while criticizing filmmaker D. W. Griffith's dependence on the stage and the novel for his subject matter and aesthetic principles (1924, 334). If anything, his tirade against literary film adaptation exceeds those levied by the proponents of high art:

> The degree of vandalism passes words; and what completed the ruin was that good novels were spoiled not to make good films, but to make bad ones. *Victory* was a vile film in addition to being a vulgar betrayal of Conrad; even the good Molnar with his exciting second-rate play, *The Devil*, found himself so foully, so disgustingly changed on the screen that . . . nothing remained but a sentimental vulgarity which had no meaning of its own, quite apart from any meaning of his. (337)

While this passage supports Stam's argument that infidelity to sources has been characterized as betrayal (2005, 3), Seldes's critique focuses on the bad *aesthetics* of these adaptations: the betrayal is one of aesthetic vulgarity; the "disgusting change" is one of sentimental vulgarity, not of failure to transcribe the source literally. Beyond failing to convey the meaning of the adapted text, the adaptation is charged with having no meaning of its own. Once again, adaptation becomes a theoretical nonentity. Thus, even as Seldes challenged the elitist theoretical mainstream, he adhered to their elitism when it came to adaptation.

In addition to being a rare academic champion for popular art, Seldes was one of few scholars in the period to address other modes of adaptation besides literary film adaptation. These fared no better: he denounced the "cinema novel" (novelization) as a "burlesque of the films—an adaptation requiring and receiving very little intelligence" (1924, 383). He found adaptation most offensive when the lively arts aspired to elite arts and least offensive when they adapted another popular art: "The fact that ragtime can without offense adapt the folk song of nearly every nation—and is only absurd with Puccini and Verdi's worst when it takes them seriously—indicates how essentially decent an art ragtime is" (72). What most offended Seldes was when adaptation crossed the lines dividing high and low art—whether it stooped from high-art literature to popular film or whether it allowed low-art music to aspire to high-art music. Thus, in spite of his revolutionary contributions to aesthetic theory, Seldes joined the critical mainstream in attacking adaptation for crossing class boundaries.

Mainstream modernist theories also infiltrated industry discourses, in defiance of modernist dichotomies between art and industry and aesthetic and economic values. In a 1917 interview for *Photoplay*, celebrity film scenarist Anthony P. Kelly credited his success to observing medium specificity theory: "the picture instinct . . . is as different from the fiction, or novel instinct, as the novel instinct is different from the dramatic. The three viewpoints are absolutely separate" (Bartlett 1917, 152). Following Lessing, Kelly's rhetoric figures the ability to observe medium specificity in essentialist terms as a biological "instinct."

Far from being invoked to separate high art from commercialism, medium specificity was used to sell film adaptations. An advertisement for Sol Lesser's film of *The Ne'er-Do-Well* (1916), adapted from the 1911 novel by Rex Beach, announced: "Millions have read this unusual tale . . . and every one of them will want to see this great screen adaptation . . . with a big theatrical production" (Universal Film Manufacturing Company 1916). The advertisement contrasts reading to seeing in order to promote consumption: people need to see the film precisely because it is *not* the same experience as reading the book. Conversely, medium specificity sold books that had been adapted to film. Ernest A. Dench's *Advertising by Motion Pictures* contains a chapter entitled, "How the Book Dealer Can Take Advantage of the Movie Adaptation Mania." It attests that "Many movie fans, after seeing the photoplay version of a popular book, and finding it to their liking, have a desire for reading the story" (1916, 230–31). In 1957, George Bluestone cited statistics of how substantially literary film adaptations increased book sales (4); more recently, Liam Burke has noted that film adaptations increase sales of the comic books they adapt (2015, 120).

Capitalizing on the commercial potential of adaptation, film companies in the 1910s produced book adaptations of their films, invoking medium specificity to urge consumption of both: "The latest move of the film producer is to produce an original serial play, have the scenario author write it up in book shape, add some photographs from the film, together with a signed one of the leading actor" (Dench 1916, 129). Despite being mixed media adaptations, these works were marketed *on the basis of medium specificity theory*: consumers were urged to experience a story across different media to stimulate different senses. Today, global franchise entertainment corporations use similar marketing techniques, calling consumers to re-consume stories and characters across multiple media formats (Elliott 2014a).

These practices also preceded the birth of film. Late nineteenth-century publishers exploited popular theatrical adaptations to sell books by replacing their illustrations with photographs of the stage adaptations (Elliott 2003a, 55–56). Recounting the success of his first opera *Maid Marian* in 1822, Planché claimed that his adaptation of Thomas Love Peacock's book to opera not only increased sales of the novel but also sales of other books by its neglected author, reviving his career and reputation. These sales concomitantly fostered Planché's career as an adapter: he was subsequently besieged with requests to adapt novels by other authors: "They knew it was the finest advertisement for a book in the world" (1872, 48).

Evolutionary Medium Specificity Theory

Some film theorists, concerned with fostering both the art and industry of film, recognized the limitations of formalist medium specificity theory for this and therefore modified it, moving it from the domain of universal, essentialist truth into the domain of history, creating a narrative of film's evolutionary progress from derivative aesthetic hybridity toward aesthetic uniqueness. Nominating films "photoplays," "moving pictures," or "motion pictures," as Lindsay, Münsterberg, and early film periodical writers had done, defined them as and by other media forms, threatening their claim to the seventh art (Elliott 2003a, 119–21).

In the first part of the twentieth century, it was theater that most threatened film's claim to medium specificity (Elliott 2003a, Chapter 4). Allardyce Nicoll's *Film and Theatre* (1936) casts off film's theatrical titles to define it by its technologies. Yet Nicoll understood that he could not explain away theater and film's many affinities. He therefore explicated them—and theatrical film adaptation—as a developmental phase through which film had to pass in its progress toward becoming an art in its own right: "Amid the turmoil attending the birth of this new form of expression, it was but natural that men should turn for assistance to the comfortable security of the stage, adapting to the two-dimensional sphere what had already been proved in the three-dimensional" (1936, 62–63). The task now was to identify "the essential features in the cinema's proper and individual manner of expression" (64).

Like others before him, Nicoll addressed adaptation only to reject and denigrate it as a "parasitic" aesthetic confusion and failure. Yet, like his predecessors, he was himself a *theoretical* adapter, adapting Lessing's arguments about poetry and painting to theater and film and making the only valorized adaptive relationship the one between a particular art work and its art form: "The masterpieces in any art will necessarily be based on an *adaptation* to the particular requirements of their own peculiar medium of expression" (189, emphasis added). Once again, film is called to be faithful to medium specificity theory. Only then will it warrant theoretical attention and affirmation.

While in film's early years the primary focus lay on differentiating film from theater, film also had to be distinguished from the novel in order to emerge as an art according to medium specificity theory. In 1931, Sergei Eisenstein advanced a historical, evolutionary account of film's progress toward aesthetic uniqueness, ingeniously differentiating cinema from theater, with which it shares the most palpable similarities, by arguing for its greater affinities with the Victorian novel. In "Dickens, Griffith, and the Film Today," he argued that "from Dickens, from the Victorian novel, stem the first shoots of American film esthetic [*sic*]" ([1931] 1949, 195) and that montage (editing), gleaned from the shifting viewpoints and scenes of the nineteenth-century novel, constitutes film's claim to aesthetic uniqueness, allowing it to lay claim to art. Yet even as Eisenstein made Charles Dickens's "The Cricket on the Hearth" (1845) a proof text for his theory of film's evolution toward medium specificity, he did not address Griffith's film adaptation of that story, *The Cricket on the Hearth* (1909). He ignored Griffith's actual adaptation of Dickens in order to promote a narrative in which film adapts, not to literature, but to *theory* in order to qualify as an art worthy of being theorized. Obsessions with theoretical fidelity, I have argued, have falsified not only the history of adaptation but also histories of film aesthetics (Elliott 2003a, Chapter 3).

Dissenting Voices

In *The Movies Come from America* ([1937] 1978), Seldes continued to oppose the theoretical formalist mainstream by focusing on historical, cultural, and industry explanations for the prevalence and persistence of adaptations in culture, in spite of theoretical attempts to eliminate them. Seeking to understand the conditions that "made the Victorian novel an ideal source book for the pictures," he reasoned that, since these reasons could not possibly be aesthetic, they had to be social and cultural: the Victorian novel's morality appealed to film censors; its cultural prestige elevated the fledgling industry; and its focus on character, empirical point of view, plots, and dialogue were readily transferable to film, especially following the introduction of synchronized sound. He also identified commercial motivations in contemporary literature "written with the movies in mind" ([1937] 1978, 56–70).

In the late 1940s and early 1950s, American librarian and university lecturer on popular culture and mass media Lester Asheim (1914–1997) attacked idealistic, subjective, aesthetic theories for their lack of ability to explicate actual adaptation practices, contending, as Simone Murray would do decades later (2008; 2012a), that adaptation requires sociological, audience- and industry-based study. He did not, however, challenge prevailing humanities theories with new ones: rather, he challenged them with theories from the social sciences, as Murray would also do. In four journal articles derived from his 1949 PhD thesis, Asheim pitted empirical, sociological methodologies against the idealist methodologies of modernist aesthetics, claiming: "That these findings are based upon carefully collected facts rather than upon emotionally charged impressions gives them—whether they be obvious or expected—an objective authenticity which merits more than passing attention" (1952, 258). While acknowledging the limits of his sample of twenty-four Hollywood films adapting canonical and successful popular novels between 1935 and 1946, he nevertheless contended that his "controlled method of analysis," "objective data," and "quantitative comparison" allowed for "a more reliable set of generalizations [to] be built" than theoretical generalizations based on subjective, idealistic, aesthetic tastes (1951a, 289–90). In the 1990s, structuralist narratologist Brian McFarlane would make similar methodological proposals to counter ongoing aesthetic formalist and New Critical approaches to adaptation.

Asheim's methodology was a comparative one that began by documenting omissions, additions, and alterations between adapted novels and adapting films; continued by grouping and taxonomizing them, before developing theoretical principles to explicate the data. Turning from top-down, pseudo-religious, aesthetic theories to bottom-up, pseudo-scientific, sociological ones, he explained adaptation through the historical, ideological, and local exigencies of its industries and the cultural and political affiliations of its audiences. It is audience taste, expressed in economic action, rather than aesthetic theories championed by scholars, he argued, that determines the form and content of adaptations. For the film industry, "the major question is not, 'Is it art?' but 'Will it sell?'" Like Collins a century prior, Asheim concluded that economic forces mean that "the *ultimate* influence is really the audience" (1951a, 292, emphasis in original), while qualifying that film studios "exert an influence over the audience which educates it to willing acceptance of the kind of product with which it is familiar" (1952, 273). His most radical argument against medium specificity was that change in adaptation "does not arise out of the inner necessity of the material but is superimposed from without as a matter of practical policy" (1952, 273).

Although Asheim challenged mainstream theories of adaptation, ousting aesthetics from its presiding position, he nevertheless joined aesthetic formalists in *reading* adaptations to uphold classed media hierarchies. Classic literature, he asserted, is superior to film because it spurs readers to think critically and to challenge social and cultural institutions, whereas in Hollywood film adaptations of that literature, "What really matters is that nothing be retained in the film which will disturb the audience, and challenge it to think . . . [or] call into question the certainties and assurance with which the audience sustains itself" (1951c, 63). Asheim also continued high-art humanist theories of art's moral and pedagogical functions: "If the film is ever to become a true art form, its creators must accept the responsibility of the artist—not merely to reflect what his audience wants—but to teach him to want something better" (1952, 273). Thus, while Asheim joined Seldes in paving the way to pit popular art against high art in late twentieth-century cultural studies, neither rescued adaptation from elitist theoretical opprobrium. Indeed, by finding adaptation intellectually, culturally, and sociologically lacking, both contributed to it, while neither defended adaptation from the formal and aesthetic lack with which other modernist theorists charged it.

There were no sociological studies in this period explicating the persistence of medium specificity theory against the evidence of historical, political, economic, cultural, industry, and institutional practices. Maintained as a universal, essentialist principle, it remained exempt from the cultural and historical scrutiny by which scholars such as Asheim explicated adaptation's resistance to mainstream humanities theorization. Scholars did not consider that the categorical divisions created by medium specificity theory were integrally interconnected with social categorizations of class, race, nationality, religion, gender, sexuality, age, disability, criminality, and education or that they were institutionally vested in the division of the humanities into academic disciplines.

There was, however, one scholar in this period who valorized adaptation using formal theories: French film theorist André Bazin (1918–1958). Rather than demanding that adaptation conform to theory, Bazin *adapted* medium specificity theory to affirm both hybrid media and adaptation *as art*. In "Adaptation, or the Cinema as Digest" ([1948] 2000), he dismissed the high modernist rejection of realism, celebrated film's realist capacities, and praised the hybridity of sound film precisely for its heightened realism, recalling Victorian theories that valued adaptation as a process of phenomenological realization (see Chapter 2 of this book). Reminding readers that adaptation was not some new-fangled travesty of the arts by cinema and radio but characteristic of classical arts from at least the Middle Ages, Bazin rejected the New Critical "idolatry of form" ([1948] 2000, 19) while remaining committed to New Critical organic unity: great art, he argued, is "a unique synthesis whose molecular equilibrium is automatically affected when you tamper with its form" (22). Radically, he maintained that organic unity does not preclude adaptation: in adaptation, "what matters is the equivalence in *meaning* of the forms" (20, emphasis added). Reviving Romantic theories of genius in film auteur theory, Bazin also insisted that "the artistic soul" *can* manifest in another medium (23), even if the forms do not translate precisely, and that "the adapted work . . . exists apart from what is wrongly called its 'style,' in a confusion of this term with the word *form*" (25, emphasis in original). Against claims that adaptation is always an aesthetic failure and can be justified solely by its social and educational value, he insisted that adaptation "is aesthetically justified, independent of its pedagogical and social value" (25).

Bazin also took issue with high-art aestheticism and the elitist intellectualism of scholars such as Greenberg, insisting that that "the difficulty of audience assimilation is not an *a priori* criterion for cultural value" (26, emphasis in original). The true father of (film) adaptation studies, Bazin not only understood that humanities theories "no longer fit with an aesthetic sociology of the masses in which the cinema runs a relay race with drama and the novel and does not eliminate them" (25) but also acknowledged the challenges intermedial adaptations made to medium specificity theory and to New Critical organic unity: "We are moving toward a reign of the adaptation in which the notion of the unity of the work of art, if not the very notion of the author himself, will be destroyed" (26). He envisioned that, a century on, scholars would not view a novel adapted first to a play and subsequently to a film as three different works, but as "a single work reflected through three art forms, an artistic pyramid with three sides, all equal in the eyes of the critic" (26). While poststructuralism and postmodernism would soon challenge New Critical organic unity and Roland Barthes ([1967] 1977) would shortly announce the death of the author, we have not yet arrived at "the reign of adaptation"; we are still in the reign of theorization.

While Deborah Cartmell and Imelda Whelehan rightly declared Bazin "a champion of adaptation in the 1950s" (2010, 34), the reach of his championing was significantly delayed. Although his essay "In Defense of Mixed Cinema" (1952) was included in the first English translation of *What Is Cinema?* (1967), "Adaptation, or the Cinema as Digest" (1948) was not translated into English *until 1997*, an astonishing (and yet also telling) delay of nearly fifty years. If Asheim complained that film adaptations of the 1930s and 1940s silenced literature's radical critiques in order to protect the social institutions and ideologies upon which the film industry rested, it is equally the case that Anglophone academics and publishers of the twentieth century silenced many dissenting voices that critiqued their theories by refusing to translate them. Claude-Edmonde Magny's 1948 work challenging New Critical and evolutionary theories of film's relationship to literature was not translated until the 1970s. Against medium specificity theory, Magny posited a convergence theory of literature and film that was decades ahead of its time, entering the Anglophone critical mainstream only through Keith Cohen's appropriation and adaptation of her ideas in 1979. A history of what is and what is not reprinted in literature/film/adaptation readers and edited collections attests to a similar silencing of nonconformist English language voices, as I demonstrate later in this chapter. Thankfully, Bazin's theories did not have to wait a century, or even half a century, to enter Anglophone studies; from 1980, they were recuperated and adapted to new theoretical contexts, most notably and extensively by Dudley Andrew, as well as by other scholars, including Cartmell and Whelehan (2010), James Naremore (2000b), Timothy Corrigan (1999; 2011), and Colin MacCabe, Kathleen Murray, and Rick Warner (2011).

In France, François Truffaut challenged Bazin's account of celebrated directors who had "rehabilitated adaptation by upsetting old preconceptions of being faithful to the letter and substituting for it the contrary idea of being faithful to the spirit" or style of the novel, arguing instead for the priority of the unique, signature style of the filmic auteur-director ([1954] 1976, 224). Displacing both formalist emphasis on the uniqueness of film as a medium and New Critical focus on the organic uniqueness of individual films, Truffaut drew on Romantic theories of authorship to develop film auteur theory, opposing deferent adaptation and insisting upon originality and distinctive authorial style rather than realism as the way to valorize film adaptation. Countering Bazin's recommendation that the only way to get around medium specificity is for adapters to "invent *equivalent* scenes" for what is "unfilmable" under medium specificity theory, he contended that, in the hands of a great filmic auteur, nothing is unfilmable (226). While other directors and critics touted originality as the only way to free film from dependence on literature and other arts, Truffaut turned to adaptation to vie not only with other filmmakers but also with high-art literature for aesthetic superiority.

George Bluestone and the Abortive Birth
of Adaptation Studies

I have nominated Bazin the father of adaptation studies: however, a majority of critics have conferred that title on George Bluestone, including me in prior critical work. Bluestone was generous, supportive, and immensely helpful to my doctoral study of literary film adaptation and my *Rethinking the Novel/Film Debate* (2003a) is dedicated to him. Yet in *Novels into Film* (1957), George Bluestone joined prior theorists in returning to Lessing and advocating for a separation of aesthetic spheres that would allow film to develop independently as an art form. His opening chapter, "The Limits of the Novel and the Limits of the Film," adapts the subtitle to Lessing's *Laocoön*. That oft-reprinted chapter applies Lessing's distinctions between poetry and painting to novels and films wholesale, without *adaptation* to the new media it addresses. Acknowledging the pictorial illustrations of novels and the words of film, it nevertheless defines novels as "words" and films as "images" on grounds that each features one more prominently and proceeds to categorize them accordingly, just as Lessing had categorized pure word and pure image arts.

Bluestone did not himself accept the title of father of adaptation studies: he told me that he wrote his book to *rid* film of literary adaptation. The so-called birth of the field, then, was actually an attempted abortion of it. That what Bluestone intended as an obituary for adaptation studies has instead become the founding document of many a student course reader and many an introductory lecture on adaptation is an irony keener than any ever located by New Critics. The irony extends from adaptation theory to adaptation practice, as books advising would-be screenwriters how to adapt novels to films also engage his principles as a how-to, rather than the don't-do he intended (Seger 1992; Brady 1994; McKee 1997).

It is little wonder that adaptation studies has struggled theoretically if this infanticidal theory is figured as its "birth." Yet rather than challenging his infanticidal paternity, critics have hailed Bluestone as field patriarch. As a result, Bluestone is one of the most misread and misrepresented scholars in ours (or any) field, viewed as a champion of fidelity in adaptation when he argued that medium specificity makes fidelity impossible and undesirable, and didactically opposed the view that "the novel is a norm and the film deviates at its peril" (1957, 5). Insisting that "cinematic and literary forms resist conversion"—or adaptation, he recommended that "the film and the novel remain separate institutions, each achieving its best results by exploring unique and specific properties" (218). Bluestone's comparative case studies in the chapters were *not* written to call for fidelity in adaptation or to showcase the superiority of literature over film, as so many have argued, but to demonstrate the undesirability of literary film adaptation *in any form* and to persuade scholars to join him in rejecting adaptation altogether.

Like Seldes and Asheim, Bluestone turned to cultural, industry, sociological, and economic domains to explicate the persistence of adaptation in culture when medium specificity failed to do so. His book attends to film industries and technologies, copyright law, film censorship, studio output, book sales, filmmaker practices, genre, audience response, and comments made by novelists, filmmakers, and reviewers on adaptation. Although it engages many of the sociological purviews that Murray championed six decades later, she and others have, unaccountably, cast Bluestone as a purely formal critic (Murray 2008, 5). Nor was he the high-art humanist that so many have charged him with being: beyond industry studies, Bluestone considered "political and social attitudes" (1957, 42 and passim), "American folklore" and cultural mythology (44), "society's shaping power" (44), "conventional myth[s] which distinguish novel from cinema" (45), and psychology and phenomenology.

In spite of his adherence to medium specificity theory, he was theoretically radical in other ways, far ahead of the 1950s mainstream, questioning fixed notions of truth (calling for a shift "from elucidating a fixed and unchanging reality to arresting a transient one" 12), opposing binarisms ("familiar polarities"10), and challenging "obsolete ideals and false ideologies" (10). He furthermore supported André Gide's quasi-constructivist argument that language "not only "*contains* intellectual and moral implications, but . . . [also] *discovers* them" (11, emphasis added), and he rejected Asheim's empirical objectivism on philosophical as well as aesthetic grounds: "Quantitative analyses have very little to do with qualitative changes. They tell us nothing about the mutational process, let alone how to judge it" (5), prefiguring later distinctions between adaptation as process and product by Brian McFarlane (1996), Sarah Cardwell (2002), and Hutcheon (2006). Against charges that film cannot convey thought, Bluestone cited French novelist and playwright Honoré de Balzac's work on the human face and applied it to film (1957, 47). These were progressive views in 1950s academia. And yet Bluestone could not or would not challenge medium specificity theory—nor did subsequent leading theorists and film directors of the 1960s such as Siegfried Kracauer (1960) and Ingmar Berman (1966). Even in the increasingly radicalized 1960s, film auteur theorists continued to champion an "anti-literary brand of cinema" (Leitch 2003b, 2) that was also anti-adaptation.

What this skeletal history of theorizing adaptation in the first part of the twentieth century reveals is that it was medium specificity theory, combined with the high-art, elitist formalist turn in the humanities and the structuralist insistence that form and content cannot and do not separate to allow for adaptation, that crippled adaptation studies—not translation theories mandating literal fidelity of adapting to adapting work. Alliances between these theoretically separate species theorized adaptation as both monstrous progeny *and* theoretical impossibility—a theoretical hybrid that is itself a theoretical impossibility. Even as some scholars produced genuinely progressive theories of film and other popular media, theorization continued to fail adaptation, refusing to adapt to adaptation in order to theorize it better. Moreover, it continued to castigate adaptation for its failure of theory. Even as the persistence of adaptation in industry and culture induced some scholars to adapt theorization to adaptation—to step off the formalist bandwagon and consider cultural and economic factors in adaptation—most did so with only one foot, maintaining aesthetic formalist theories in order to return their findings to the mother ship.

Successful defenses of adaptation resisted the mainstream by looking back as well as forward: Bazin's defense of adaptation both revived Victorian theories of adaptation as realization and prefigured postmodern theories of hybridity and pastiche; Truffaut's apologia for adaptation recalled nineteenth-century defenses of "original" adaptations by geniuses and Augustan uses of adaptation, as well as being a means by which film could claim superiority over literature (and vice versa), a discourse that intensified in the second half of the twentieth century.

Structuralist Narratology and Adaptation

The year 1957 was a hybrid and transitional one for theorizing adaptation. Roland Barthes's *Mythologies* was published in that year, along with George Bluestone's *Novels into Film*. Over time, Barthes mitigated the dire effects of the formalist turn and medium specificity theory on adaptation by reintegrating formal and cultural study in his theory of cultural mythologies and by engaging structuralist *narratology* to theorize the arts across media, circumventing the prohibitions that structuralist *semiotics* and New Critical organic unity placed on adaptation. Although *Mythologies* does not address adaptation directly, it ingeniously overcame formalist objections to cultural studies by theorizing works of art as narrative structures containing and adapting cultural mythologies worthy of study. Its focus on structures pays sufficient attention to form to satisfy formalists; its location of deeper, symbolic meanings beneath surface representations calls scholars away from self-appointed posts as cultural police, patronizing educators of the masses, and saviors of the public from mass media propaganda to excavate popular culture in deep, complex, and serious intellectual ways. Although Barthes did not name it as such, his theory of metalanguage gave adaptation a potentially vital role in repeating and varying ancient mythologies in new cultural contexts (Elliott 2003a, 144–50). Equally salutary for intermedial adaptation, Barthes promoted interdisciplinary study via structuralism, already operative in linguistics (Ferdinand de Saussure; Noam Chomsky), literary theory (Roman Jakobson), philosophy (Henri Poincaré; Bertrand Russell), sociology (Louis Althusser), anthropology (Claude Lévi-Strauss), and psychology (Jacques Lacan; Jean Piaget). Barthes thus paved the way for both the postmodern cultural and structuralist narratological theories that would forge one prong of a forked turning point for adaptation studies in 1996.

The more immediate effect of Barthesean structuralism on 1960s and 1970s adaptation studies was structuralist narratology's mitigation of media divides accentuated by medium specificity theory. Barthesean theory allowed Robert D. Richardson to disagree with Bluestone that literature and film did, or should, occupy separate spheres and to argue that they share formal features, cultural contexts, and influence each other, and to conclude that studying the two together enriches the scholarship of each individually (1969, 3–4). While he did not abandon medium specificity theory, he weakened it: "Granting that the means or mediums of film and literature are different—though perhaps not so radically different as might be supposed . . . there does seem to be enough fairly clear common ground between the two" (1969, 13). Yet for all the inheritances, affinities, influences, and exchanges that Richardson traced between literature and film, he paid scant attention to adaptations, engaging them solely as cautionary tales to support medium specificity and film auteur theories. Thus, even as he broke down dividing lines between media, he maintained medium specificity's borders when it came to adaptation on aesthetic grounds, agreeing with prior theorists that "what makes a good novel rarely makes a good film" (13).

Richardson turned to structuralist narratology to argue that narrative is the linchpin that allows literature and film to be discussed together: "The overarching likeness that makes it possible to consider most films and much of literature together is [that] . . . they have narrative in common" (4). Narrative remains central to adaptation studies today (Mittell and McGowan 2017), a focus that has both enriched and delimited the field. On the one hand, structuralist narratology is a democratizing theory, forging equalities and equivalences across media. On the other, it represents a colonizing move by linguistics and literature to theorize other media according to their principles, rhetoric, and theories. Many film scholars have complained of this, most notably David Bordwell: "Linguistics presumed to offer a way of subsuming film under a general category of signification" (1985, 23). And yet the colonizing dynamics have not been unidirectional. Filmmakers and theorists first used literary rhetoric to aspire to language and literature, then subsequently to usurp and negate *actual* verbal language in film. Truffaut first used literary rhetoric to lay claim to high art for film. Shored up by structuralist theory, Alexandre Astruc, Christian Metz, Marie-Claire Ropars-Wuilleumier, and others subsequently developed a rhetoric of écriture and auteurism in film studies that elevated the image and montage and rendered the word "uncinematic" (Elliott 2005).

These disciplinary wars influenced theories of adaptation. In *Signs and Meaning in the Cinema*, Peter Wollen rejected the middle ground of Augustan and translation theories of adaptation, in which adapted and adapting works compromise and merge, following Truffaut in insisting on the higher priority of adapting literature to the "dispositions" of film auteurs (1972, 108). Like Richardson, he resurrected and reiterated the maxim that you can't make a good film from a good book, going beyond Bluestone's diplomatic recommendation of separate spheres to insist that only "ruthlessly altered and adapted" literature makes viable films (111). In this period, a rhetoric of aggression permeated adaptation discourses, in which filmmakers inflict violence upon literary works in order to produce "good" films. Conversely, Ingmar Bergman argued that the chief "reason why we ought to avoid filming existing literature" is that literary adaptation "kills the special dimension of film" (1966, 97). Film theory became anti-literature and anti-adaptation:

> Like those film adaptations that begin with dissolving shots of their founding novels, films in general base their creative process on a visual dissolution of their words. The process of filmmaking is one of de-verbalizing, de-literarizing, and de-wording verbal language to make film "language." This is not translation but evisceration into images. Indeed, one could argue that the destruction and dominance of the word constitutes a principal aesthetic of film theory. (Elliott 2003a, 83)

The violence of filmmaking rhetoric in the second half of the twentieth century makes clear that, even as scholars sought to democratize literature and film and university campuses resounded with anti-war protests, literature and film were fiercely at war, with adaptation serving as chief weapon and chief casualty.

Literature–Film Wars and the Disciplinary Cold War on Adaptation

Sister-arts discourses in the 1970s and 1980s did not unfold as an interdisciplinary love-in, in part because literature-and-film studies were locked in battles over where film studies should reside in academic institutions, especially in the United States. As film theorists and practitioners had battled to extricate film from literature in order to establish it as an art, all the while *depending* on literature and literary adaptation to establish film as an art, academics now battled for control over film, seeking simultaneously to separate film from literature and to usher it into academia through literature departments.

These battles are epitomized by the prepositions and conjunctions in titles of university textbooks and readers in the 1970s and 1980s. Titles such as *Film and Literature* (Marcus 1971; Beja 1979), *Film and/as Literature* (Harrington 1977), *Film as Literature, Literature as Film* (Ross 1987), *Film as Film* (Perkins 1972), and "Literature vs. Cinema" (Poague 1976) articulate film's contested relationship to literature variously: "and" conjoins them; "vs." opposes them; "as" connotes resemblance, substitution, and performance. Harrington's title first conjoins film and literature, then subsumes film *as* literature, epitomizing bids by literature departments to subsume film via narrative theories. Yet film is more than narrative, and film scholars have vociferously protested against its colonization by literature via narrative theory. V. F. Perkins's title, the earliest and contemporaneous with Wollen's objection to literary adaptation, exiles literature to insist that film be studied on its own terms as film. Ross's title, published last, suggests that film studies' literary phobias were relaxing slightly by the late 1980s now that film was firmly established in academia under the auspices of Lacanian theories that emphasized the visual over the verbal: the reciprocal and inverse structure of Ross's title articulates a more equal relation between the two. Even so, that film is first allied to and then subsumed as literature *before* affirming their inverse relation suggests the ongoing priority of literature over film and film's dependence upon literature to establish itself as a viable academic subject.[7]

Relations between film and literature in the 1970s remained hotly contested. William Jinks's undergraduate introduction to film, *The Celluloid Literature: Film in the Humanities*, makes film a subcategory of literature, a modifying adjective of literature's more substantive noun. While maintaining lip service to medium specificity ("Film and literature are, of course, two very different kinds of experience"), Jinks's study foregrounds their resemblances: "I want in this book . . . to emphasize how close, both in form and in content, literature and the narrative film are to one another" (1971, xiv). However, it does so chiefly to claim film for literature and to insist that "much of the methodology of literary analysis is equally applicable to the study of film" (xiv). Here, equality and equivalence justify the colonizing imposition of literary theories and methodologies upon film. If nominating film "the celluloid literature" categorically subordinates film to literature as a sub-category of literature, then claiming film as "a continuation of the traditional narrative arts" renders it subsequent and subject to literature on a historical continuum (xiv). Conversely, Morris Beja's undergraduate textbook turns to speculative, anachronistic history to claim film for literature: "Had movies somehow existed in ancient Greece—or during the Renaissance—we would surely now be studying them as works of literature" (1979, 53).

And yet literary academics feared as well as desired the incursions of film on literature. The rise of youth culture and the changes in media consumption that accompanied it threatened literature's cultural priority and aged it. Jinks therefore reassured literati that "the study of film can in no way diminish the important values of the more traditional literary genres; it can only serve to augment and perhaps even reinvigorate them" (xiv).

The battle over film studies was fought in scholarly journals as well as pedagogical books. Leland A. Poague's "*Literature vs. Cinema: The Politics of Aesthetic Definition*" (1976) argued that film can be taught as literature and fulfill the same cultural function as literature, going further to claim that the two are *identical*. Poague's essay is also valuable in documenting strident opposition to film's assimilation by literature from film scholars Peter Wollen, Ben Brewster, Stephen Heath, and others.

Amid these contests, adaptation was made a subcategory of literature-and-film studies, relegated to chapters and sections of books on relations between literature and film (Wagner 1975; Andrew 1980; Marcus 1971; Harrington 1977). Twenty-first-century scholars, myself included, have also figured adaptation as an aspect of literature-and-film studies (Elliott 2003a; Corrigan 2011). Yet adaptation has worked variably to subjugate film to literature and literature to film.

Even so, Welch's annotated bibliographies of literature and film studies (1981; 1993) offer evidence for Ray's assessment that twentieth-century literary film adaptation studies privileged literature over film (2000, 44) and aesthetics over fidelity in adaptation. The prolific Gene D. Phillips, who has authored monographs and edited essay collections on film adaptations of literature by Graham Greene (1974), Ernest Hemingway (1980), F. Scott Fitzgerald (1986), and William Faulkner (1988), introduced each with a declaration that "the primary purpose of [each] study is to determine to what degree the films of [their] fiction . . . are *worthy* renditions of the stories from which they were derived" (Phillips 1986, 6; 1988, 2, emphasis added). What makes an adaptation inferior to what it adapts in these studies is its *aesthetics*, not its degree of fidelity to the source text. For Phillips, the task of the adaptation critic work is to determine if filmmakers have attained aesthetic worthiness equivalent to that of the novels they adapt, not whether they have produced a literal translation. Since medium specificity theory figures literal fidelity as aesthetically catastrophic, the process requires infidelity to the novel and fidelity to the medium of film.

However, Welch's bibliographies make clear that such studies were neither the only story in adaptation theorization of the 1970s and 1980s: scholars were as likely to take a neutral or objectivist view of adaptation as to pass aesthetic judgment upon it and, if they did judge it, they were as likely to praise as to criticize film adaptations (see, e.g., Welch's entries for the year 1972; see also Welch 1981). It may be the case that *literary scholars* treating adaptations more often privileged literature, but Welch's bibliography goes beyond literary publications to present a more varied and balanced view of literary film adaptation studies in the period.

Under medium specificity theory, films foregrounding their status as adaptations automatically indicate their failure as films and become unworthy of serious study—a catch-22 for adaptation studies. Adaptation thus became both the skeleton in the closet and the empty closet for film studies. However, introducing *Modern European Filmmakers and the Art of Adaptation*, Andrew Horton and Joan Magretta countered these views, as well as the violent rhetoric of film adaptation: "The study of adaptation is clearly a form of source study and thus we should trace the genesis (not the destruction) of works deemed worthy of close examination in and of themselves"; "attention to this art will enhance our understanding of film" (1981, 1). Challenging film auteur theories of originality, they argued (against Seldes) that "adaptation *can* be a lively and creative art" (1, emphasis added). They also made a significant democratizing move in prioritizing canonical films and filmmakers over canonical literature and authors in their case studies. Similarly, even as Wendell Aycock and Michael Schoenecke's edited collection *Film and Literature: A Comparative Approach to Adaptation*, written by "both literary scholars and film experts," adhered to high-art, aesthetic formalism, "focusing on notable literary works and superior films adapted therefrom" (1988, preface, n.p.), it reversed the trajectory of studying canonical literature adapted to lackluster cinema, instead treating celebrated films, many adapted from lackluster literature. In these and other publications, adaptation was studied to create a more equal balance of power and value between film and literature, and aesthetic theories were engaged to valorize rather than to condemn adaptation. Even so, overall, adaptation remained more opprobriously theorized than literature-and-film relations more generally.

The Theoretical Cold War on Adaptation

While some literature-and-film scholars alternated between co-opting the two media in their battles for disciplinary supremacy, other scholars waged a cold war on adaptation. In the battle of titular prepositions and conjunctions, the absence of literature *on* film or literature *into* film is striking. In spite of attempts to render film and literature the same species, film adaptation (in which literature goes further to *become* film) continued to suffer theoretical neglect and opprobrium. Even as Jinks subjected film to literary nomenclature, terminology, theories, and methodologies, he did not address literary film adaptation as a literalization of his key term, "the celluloid literature"; adaptation was excluded from his discussion, remaining untheorized.

Scholarly monographs on literature and film written or translated in the 1970s and 1980s also ignored adaptation. Marie-Claire Ropars-Wuilleumier's *De la littérature au cinema: Genese d'une écriture* (1970), which uses auteur theory and structuralist analogies to study cinema as a mode of writing, ignores literary adaptation; Claude-Edmonde Magny's *The Age of the American Novel: The Film Aesthetic of Fiction between the Two Wars* ([1948] 1972) treats many intersections of film and literary forms, but not adaptation; Bruce Morrissette's *Novel and Film* (1985) and Robert Stam's *Reflexivity in Film and Literature* ([1985] 1922) do not address adaptation. David Bordwell's *Narration in the Fiction Film* (1985) too ignores the role of adaptation in the development of film fiction. Seymour Chatman's *Story and Discourse: Narrative Structure in Fiction and Film* (1978) equally occludes adaptation; his essay "What Novels Can Do that Films Can't and Vice Versa" (1980) is a homage to medium specificity theory, figuring intermedial adaptation as a domain of aesthetic and academic disability. Chatman's essay, often reprinted in course readers and assigned on course syllabi, has been cited 529 times (Google Scholar, December 23, 2019) and continues to accrue citations. In 2012, neo-narratologist Garrett Stewart continued the long-standing protest against adaptation in "Literature and Film—Not Literature on Film." That this essay is the only one treating adaptation in Lucy Fischer and Patrice Petro's edited collection, *Teaching Film* (2012), demonstrates the ongoing anti-adaptation sentiment in film studies and structuralist theory's preference for parallel studies of media and disciplines.

If adaptation suffers as a subcategory of literature-and-film studies, it is almost nowhere in film studies. Today, film-studies publications more commonly ignore than oppose adaptation. At a time when film studies is working to restore neglected areas (overlooked nations, minority filmmakers, and more), it continues to neglect adaptation. Likewise in literary studies, even as scholars seek in every nook and cranny for what has previously overlooked and forge ever new interdisciplinary connections, the field is largely blind to how adaptation has been overlooked.

As structuralism gained momentum in the 1970s, adaptation studies declined. Prior to the 1970s, publications addressing adaptation outnumbered general discourses of literature and film. Increasing in the 1950s and 1960s, general literature-and-film studies overtook adaptation studies for the first time in the 1970s, peaking in the 1980s. The two volumes of Jeffrey Egan Welch's *Literature and Film: An Annotated Bibliography* spanning the years 1909–1977 and 1978–1988 list 493 publications treating adaptation between 1909 and 1969, 609 from 1970 to 1977, and 1,225 between 1978 and 1988. While the ratio of general literature-and-film studies to adaptation studies has since diminished, the former continue to outnumber adaptation studies to the present day, attesting to the ongoing problems of reconciling adaptation to mainstream humanities theorization. (See the *MLA International Bibliography* for more recent statistics.)

At times, structuralist theorists addressed adaptations as useful focal points through which to compare the structures of literature to the structures of film, since adaptations reduce the number of narrative variables. In *Made into Movies: From Literature to Film* (1985), Stuart Y. McDougal continued Bluestone's attention to film production methods, costs, censorship, casting, and box office, though his main focus rests on the narratological and formal aspects of the two media (plot, character, point of view, inner experience, figurative discourse, symbol and allegory, and time). The book conjoins the two theories that constitute the basis of adaptation studies' compare-and-contrast methodologies: structuralist narratology and medium specificity theory.[8] Structuralist narratology compares them; medium specificity theory contrasts them; adaptations are read to affirm both theories: "By examining some of the principal elements shared by literature and narrative films, we can understand better the unique characteristics of each" (McDougal 1985, 3–4). However, constraining comparison to the auspices of one theory and contrast to those of another delimits the far more complex ways in which literature and film interpenetrate and exchange narratives. Moreover, adaptation involves much more than media forms and narrative.

McDougal's book, like others addressing adaptation in the 1970s (Marcus; Beja; Harrington), is an undergraduate textbook. Scholars citing these works do not always indicate this; as a result, the introductory level of their scholarship has contributed to the low status of adaptation studies, while doing little to redress the low status of adaptation under the theories they propound. Fred H. Marcus's student reader *Film and Literature: Contrasts in Media* divides in half: the first reprints essays that "add up to a mosaic of film theory" (1971, xiv); the second reprints essays on adaptation.[9] Yet Marcus does not identify these essays as a mosaic *of adaptation theory*; instead, they too "contain a substantial body of current *film* theory" (xv, emphasis added). Adaptation here is not seen as something requiring theorization itself but, intriguingly, as a subcategory of film theory, which has subsumed it. There is no third section on literary theory, suggesting that such theory is either a self-evident truth or irrelevant to literary film adaptation.

Adaptation Studies and the Theoretical Turn in the Humanities

The so-called theoretical turn in the humanities took place in the 1960s and 1970s, becoming mainstream by the 1980s, although it has never ceased to be challenged by the theories from which it turned. The term "theoretical turn" describes a shift from humanist, formalist, aesthetic theories focused on identifying and valorizing high-art, canonical works, and their civilizing cultural properties to scholarship informed by radical Marxist, feminist, queer, ethnic, and postcolonial studies locating theories of high art not in transcendent, universal, aesthetic, intellectual, or moral values but in the mercenary, culturally situated, politically oppressive, elitist, hierarchical values of the (usually middle- or upper-class, patriarchal, heterosexual, white) ruling classes. Far from being universal and transcendent, proponents of the cultural theoretical turn argued that humanities theorization is determined by particular, cultural agendas and power structures, is disputed by different social groups, rendering theorization contested, fragmented, and diverse.

The political revolution in humanities theorization was accompanied by a philosophical revolution that rejected not only the politically suspect metaphysics of high-art aestheticism but also the rational, logical, phenomenological, empirical, objectivist, and quantitative methodologies that some branches of the humanities had borrowed from the sciences and social sciences in favor of a philosophical skepticism that found more truth in negation than affirmation, absence than presence, indeterminacy than positivism, and endless deferral than chronological progress. Even so, philosophical and formal theories of the turn, in spite of their skepticism, continued to claim universality for their theoretical principles.

While adaptation studies has been charged with being a bastion of resistance to the theoretical turn, there were reasons for this besides the theoretical conservatism of its scholars—reasons having to do with adaptation itself. An overemphasis on hierarchical binarisms (high art/low art, word/image, etc.) before the turn led to an overemphasis on unilateral theories such as poststructuralist intertextuality and the inversions of hierarchies by left-wing political theories. Poststructuralist semiotics flattened out not only the binaries of literature and film but also the subtleties of adaptation's particular semiotic processes, while the radical political theories shifting adaptation's value away from the aesthetics championed by high-art humanism to democratic popular culture obscured adaptation's promiscuous politics. An over-emphasis on positivism before the turn produced an over-emphasis on negation and indeterminacy after it, dissolving adaptation into generic principles of poststructuralist intertextuality and postmodern pastiche that do not differentiate it from other modes of representation. Similarly, an over-emphasis on deliberate, conscious, individual agency in the production of art prior to the turn led to an over-emphasis on cultural constructivism and on unconscious, unintentional, random, arbitrary aesthetic processes after it, which sidelined adaptation studies' focus on individual adapters, particular adaptations, deliberate agency in adaptation, and adaptation as a material, cultural, and industrial production. Adaptation does not cede to either set of extremes: as a result, it has remained understudied by both.

As a process of repetition with variation, adaptation engages in constant change, while resisting total revolution: it is thus too revolutionary for conservative theories and too conservative for radical theories. As a "both/and" rather than an "either/or" or "neither/nor" process, it resists both the either/or of structuralist binaries and the neither/nor of poststructuralism. It is both hierarchical and democratic, both material and indeterminate, both individual and collective, engaging both conscious and unconscious processes. Too gauche and obvious for philosophical abstraction, too crude and populist for high-art humanism, too implicated in corporate capitalism and politically promiscuous for postmodern cultural studies, too deliberate for psychoanalysis, too derivative for the avant garde, too individualistic for cultural constructivism, too industrial and collective for high-art aesthetics, and too implicated in replication and resemblance for theories championing difference over similarity, adaptation does not conform to any theoretical camp, but, irritatingly for many scholars, straddles them all. More than adaptation's refusal to adhere consistently to one side or the other of the turn, its *simultaneous occupation of both sides* has been profoundly threatening to humanities theorization. To offer an analogy, I have been struck by how often the first (and sometimes the only) martyr protesting racism in any given protest in the United States has been a white person killed by whites. It is as though white supremacists are much more threatened by the suggestion that a white person might oppose racism than by protesting members of the races they seek to dominate. I also recall a story where a feuding parishioner shot a clergyman seeking to reconcile his dispute, even though the man with whom he was feuding was standing right in front of him. A call to occupy a middle ground can be more threatening than being defeated by the opposition because it requires a change of mind. Adaptation is not for aesthetic purists, political ideologues, or systematic cataloguers: it violates and exceeds their principles; it takes both sides of their theoretical debates and no side at all; it crosses boundaries, resists containment, resides outside borders, occupies middle grounds and no-man's land. As I argue later in this book, adaptation thrives most under hybrid—often incongruous—theorization.

It was some time before the debates over the theoretical turn entered adaptation studies with any force. Publications treating literary film adaptation lagged considerably behind the theoretically turning times. In film studies, even as theorists were challenging the structuralist semiotics and narratology that governed adaptation studies, turning to Lacanian psychoanalysis, with its focus on a pre-linguistic, unconscious gaze, and to cognitive theory to oust the dominance of linguistic and literary theory brought by structuralist semiotics and narratology to the field, they turned to these theories to police adaptation. Stephen Heath, for example, pronounced structuralist semiotics "mistaken" (1981, 93), charging it with avoiding cultural ideology and discursive constructions of the psychoanalytic subject. Yet he equally attested that film critics, aestheticians, and historians were still clinging to auteur and medium specificity theories to forefend against literary incursions on filmic territory.

As mainstream film studies moved with Heath away from semiotics and toward Lacanian psychoanalysis, from humanism toward Althusserian Marxism, and from aesthetic formalism toward politicized cultural studies, the wars between old and new theories led some scholars to turn from disciplinary wars to theoretical wars, forging theoretical alliances across disciplines. What had been predominantly a disciplinary war fought over adaptation now became a theoretical war, in which adaptation served as fodder. In 1973, film scholars James M. Welsh and Tom Erskine founded the *Literature/Film Quarterly* (*LFQ*). Thomas Leitch's "Where Are We Going, Where Have We Been?" characterizes the journal and its affiliated Literature/ Film Association at the time as valuing a "belletristic focus, lucid prose, Kantian aesthetics, [and] Arnoldian ideas about the place of art in society" and offering "a haven from prevailing theoretical and political trends in contemporary film studies" (2003b, 2). By contrast to other literature-and-film studies, the journal was almost exclusively concerned with literary film adaptation in its early years: its founding issue treats D. H. Lawrence novels adapted to film.

Welsh's own history of *LFQ* makes clear that the theoretical wars became far more prominent than the disciplinary wars for him and that his main opponents were not literary scholars but "Cinema Studies snobs" and "Francophile zombie theorists" (2003, 4). As adaptation became a weapon in the theoretical wars rather than territory over which literature and film fought, what is most astonishing for this history is that scholars now defended adaptation *using the very theories that had hitherto diminished, oppressed, and castigated it.*

Yet, even as Welch's annotated bibliographies of literature-and-film studies attest to theoretical entrenchment in the 1970s and 1980s, they equally attest to theoretical variety, radicalism, and vibrancy in literary film adaptation studies. While aesthetic formalism, auteur theory, narratology, and one-to-one comparative and translation methodologies still predominated, radical theories were applied to adaptations from the 1970s, including Marxism, queer theory, postcolonialism, and feminist Lacanian psychoanalysis, along with new formal theories: dialogics, poststructuralism, discursive constructionism, postmodern self-reflexivity, and reader response theory (Welch 1981; 1993). In 1978, more critics were complaining about films changing the *ideologies* of novels than their aesthetics, style, or narrative structures; in the same year, films were more often castigated for being too politically conservative than for aesthetic, semiotic, narrative, or intellectual lack.

These entries, gathered from many types of publications, including scholarship, textbooks, student readers, reviews, interviews, biographies, surveys, histories, fan magazines, publisher and library journals, and writing and filmmaking manuals, attest to widespread interest in adaptation; they equally attest to the dispersion of the field and to how little articles and essays on adaptation dialogued with each other. That these radical voices have been largely ignored by field historians is due in part to the fact that their work is scattered across disciplines and publications. Even so, Welch's bibliographies have been available to scholars since the late 1980s, and it is perplexing that they have not been engaged more often to construct histories of theorizing adaptation.

That these bibliographies only address literature and film, when adaptation was studied in other fields, means that they offer only a partial view of a larger field. That said, the *MLA International Bibliography* confirms the dominance of literature and film in adaptation studies of the period. Between 1957 and 1990, of a total of 1,906 results for the subject search term "adaptation," there are 942 entries for the subject term "film adaptation," 175 for "television adaptation," 163 for "dramatic adaptation," 101 for "musical adaptation," 99 for "operatic adaptation," 26 for "radio adaptation," 6 for "poetic adaptation," and 3 for "ballet adaptation"—and many entries treating other media address film adaptation as well.[10]

Since I have already discussed the problem of missing and inaccurate citation, partial field histories, and lack of dialogue in adaptation studies (Elliott 2017), my concern here lies less with underscoring the hitherto largely unrecognized influx of the theoretical turn into adaptation studies from the 1970s than with how adaptation scholars in this period were fighting back against theoretical abuse. If *LFQ* was theoretically conservative by comparison to most single-discipline film and literary journals, it was theoretically progressive in terms of adaptation studies. The journal did much to place film on an equal footing with literature and to protest the literature–film apartheid. An essay in its founding issue, "Film: The 'Literary' Approach," challenges both "judgments about the general superiority of literature" to film and assertions that "literariness" in film is "unimaginative" (Ruhe 1973, 76–7). In another *LFQ* article, "Soft Edges: The Art of Literature, the Medium of Film," Charles Eidsvik challenged medium specificity theory: "Literature is an art comprised of more than one medium and . . . film is a medium for more than one art. . . . [E]ach [is] capable of encompassing part of the other"; the essay also denies that film is a branch of literature (1974, 16). In "The Writing on the Screen," Martin S. Dworkin radically decreed medium specificity theory to be "a matter of conventional attitudes, or of limited abstraction of philosophical analysis, [rather] than of essential differentiations" (1974, ix), decades in advance of Noël Carroll's similar critique in film studies (1996). In 1975, Geoffrey Wagner raised the status of film adaptations when he insisted that they can function as *criticism* of the works they adapt, freeing them from derivative secondariness as translations and aesthetic fallings off from sources through their violations of medium specificity theory. Placing adaptations on a par with academic criticism pressed adaptation studies beyond comparative formal, aesthetic, and narrative studies into ideological critical discourse akin to—and threatening to—academic criticism. Keith Cohen argued further that adaptation's critical power can go beyond interpretation to subversion: "adaptation is a truly artistic feat only when the new version carries with it a hidden criticism of its model or at least renders implicit (through a process we should call 'deconstruction') certain key contradictions implanted or glossed over in the original" (1979, 245). This claim for the deconstructive potential of adaptation carried it away from emulative, appreciative criticism to undermining, negating exposés of the works it adapts.

While Wagner and Cohen continued to draw on auteur theory to elevate film adaptation according to more traditional aesthetics, Eidsvik's trenchant "Toward a 'Politique des Adaptations'" made the radical—and accurate—claim that "adaptation is as or more important in film history than the *film d'auteur*" (1975, 262). Challenging film historians for unaccountably neglecting adaptations, he demonstrated that adaptations have fulfilled many historical and economic functions: they are good for literature, increasing book sales and disseminating their narratives more widely; they restore older forms of narrative in the wake of modernist literature; and they encourage writers to be experimental. Concomitantly, adaptations are good for film, bringing verbal intellect and narratives to them, shaking up middle-brow cultural conformity, presenting filmmakers with technical challenges that press film to develop in ways it might not have done otherwise, and keeping filmmakers aspiring to art, not solely to profit. Critiquing the "cult of the original script with its attendant imposition of Romantic Genius," Eidsvik offered evidence that "adaptations frequently provide advances in the art of film" (1975, 255), recalling Augustan theories of adaptation in the late seventeenth century. He did not stop there, going on to critique adaptation theorization, arguing that theories levying aesthetic judgments on adaptations lose sight of their vital cultural and industry functions and can only be partial in explicating adaptation. Moreover, they are unfair, as expectations are unreasonably higher for adaptations than for other films when critics posit "an exalted, absolute, and ideal vision of the novel and then judge [the] film by that vision" (257). The article concludes by wondering "how much of our sniffing at adaptations stems from our desire to keep movies at a *kitsch* level . . . in their place" to "reinforce our literary snobbery" (258)—a dig at Greenberg and other modernists scornful of popular culture. It is perplexing to me that, instead of reprinting Eidsvik's essay as Harrington did in 1977, student readers since then have reprinted anti-adaptation essays, most commonly Bluestone's adaptation of Lessing (1957), Wagner's taxonomy of adaptation (1975), and Chatman's 1980 homage to medium specificity theory. This is akin to publishing essays championing white supremacy in an African American studies reader. No wonder our field has struggled theoretically.

By contrast, Dudley Andrew's essay "Adaptation" (1984b), which follows Bazin in being pro-adaptation, *has* been widely reprinted. Republished in Leo Braudy and Marshall Cohen's film theory reader (first edition, 1999, and in subsequent editions), Corrigan's literature and film readers (1999 and 2011, and Naremore's edited collection (2000a), as well as countless distributions of the essay in print and electronic versions to university students, Andrew told me in 2010 that it was then his most-cited publication. His chapter's affinity with more positive and nuanced Augustan theories of adaptation was discussed in Chapter 2. The essay looks forward as well as back, prefiguring Hutcheon's expansion of adaptation studies beyond literature and film (2006) when it discusses medieval paintings of biblical stories and literary adaptations in music, opera, and art, as well as Hutcheon's arguments about adaptation's contribution to the survival of forms and archetypes in culture. Looking back to Asheim and ahead to Murray's studies of the adaptation industry (2008; 2012a; 2012b), Andrew's essay calls adaptation studies to take a "sociological turn" away from medium specificity theory: "Let us use [adaptation] not to fight battles over the essence of the media or the inviolability of individual art works. Let us use it as we use all cultural practices: to understand the world from which it comes and the one toward which it points" (1984b, 106). Andrew thus called for a fundamental change in scholarly priorities, a shift in the critical and theoretical questions being asked of adaptations, and the *raison d'être* for studying them.

Other scholars of the 1980s pressed for a cultural turn in adaptation studies. In 1982, Donald F. Larsson argued that local historical and specific cultural matrices are essential to understanding adaptations, which are not only interpretations of their source texts but also of their cultural contexts, ideologies, and values, which should not be and cannot be reduced to transcendental universals. While the emphasis on narrative remained, the essay marked an important shift from formal and textual adaptation studies to attend to historical, political, and cultural contexts that are essential to theorizing adaptation as change made to suit a new environment.

Also in 1982, John Ellis brought Barthes's influential essay announcing "The Death of the Author" (1967) into adaptation studies. Barthes declared an end to author intent as the chief determinant of meaning, shifting the authority of interpretation to readers. Ellis called similarly for a theoretical turn away from medium specificity, auteur, and phenomenological theories to engage localized economic, collective, cultural, consumer-based theories of adaptation:

The adaptation trades upon the memory of the novel, a memory that can derive from actual reading, or, as is more likely with a classic of literature, a generally circulated cultural memory. The adaptation consumes this memory, aiming to efface it with the presence of its own images. The successful adaptation is one that is able to replace the memory of the novel with the process of a filmic or televisual representation. (Ellis 1982, 3)

Transferring the determination of an adaptation's success from scholars and theories to the collective judgment of consumers, the battle between literature and film was located not solely within academia but also in the minds of consumers.

In 1984, Christopher Orr combined and extended these challenges to prior adaptation theorization. Joining Cohen in recommending that intertextual theories replace one-to-one translation methodologies, he followed Ellis in carrying the death of the author into adaptation studies, shifting the focus from studying adaptations as realizations of author intent or evidence of film auteur genius to the interpretive authority of audience response. Like others before him, he argued that the chief value of adaptations for academic study lies not in their aesthetics or formal structures, or in how they illuminate formal and structural relations within and between media, but in their cultural ideologies, urging scholars to track shifts and relations between cultural ideologies within and across media. Turning from universal values and theories to discursive constructionism, Orr's essay established a new role for academics: while it continued to be one of identifying and promoting cultural values, the values were no longer aesthetic or formal ones; they were cultural and ideological: specifically, those of the political left. Orr's essay has been unaccountably neglected as a radical scholarly voice in 1980s adaptation studies—perhaps because Welch omits it from his annotated bibliography. However, that Greg Jenkins includes his and other radical voices from the 1970s and 1980s in his history of adaptation studies (1997) suggests that other factors have been operative in Orr's neglect.

Joy Gould Boyum's *Double Exposure: Fiction into Film*, the first monograph since Bluestone's devoted entirely to adaptation, has also been neglected by later scholars. As both English professor and film reviewer, she was well situated to address both sides of the disciplinary divide and the divide between theory and practice and to explicate why adaptations occupy "a no-man's land, caught somewhere between a series of conflicting aesthetic claims and rivalries" (1985, 15). Observing that "Nobody loves an adaptation," her study was one of the first to identify the double threat that adaptation presents to *both* disciplines—"if film threatens literature, literature threatens film, and nowhere so powerfully, in either instance, as in the form of adaptation" (15)—and to explicate adaptation's low academic status in terms of media and disciplinary rivalries. My 2003 book, *Rethinking the Novel/Film Debate*, is indebted to her methodology of looking at adaptation from both sides of the disciplinary divide.

Like Hutcheon's *A Theory of Adaptation* (2006), Boyum's book is theoretically ecumenical, engaging a pastiche of aesthetic, cultural, rhetorical, and reader response theories. The book is also theoretically Janus-faced, subjecting adaptations to both new and old theories in an effort to prove their aesthetic, cultural, political, and philosophical worth—that is, their multifaceted worth across multiple theories. Half of her book defends adaptation using new theories and cultural discourses; the other half does so engaging the rhetorical and narratological theories that were becoming outmoded in the separate disciplines of literature and film studies. And yet since these theories had not yet been widely marshalled in defense of adaptations but had been used chiefly to abuse or dismiss them, even as they were becoming outmoded elsewhere, within the field of adaptation studies, hers was cutting-edge, necessary work.

Adaptation Studies in the 1990s

Welch's annotated bibliographies of literature and film end with the year 1988; Harris Ross's bibliography ends in 1985. However, the *MLA International Bibliography* makes clear that studies of adaptation continued to grow and to redress prior imbalances favoring literature over film. Phebe Davidson's *Film and Literature: Points of Intersection* (1997) turned from narratological studies of film and literature in parallel play to focus exclusively on adaptations. It also changed the relative weighting of canonical literature and canonical film to prioritize recent and quality films over adaptations of historical, canonical literature. In *Cinema and Fiction: New Modes of Adapting, 1950–1990* (1992), editors John Orr, Colin Nicholson, and other contributors also turned from venerating historical canons and the past to focus on the role of arts and media in recent and current political and cultural contexts.

Scholars who did excavate the past in the 1990s focused as much on the past of film history as on the past of literary history. *MLA International Bibliography* entries for the 1990s include articles on adaptations by filmmakers John Huston, Tony Richardson, Luis Bunuel, Otto Preminger, David Mamet, Steven Spielberg, Alexander Korda, Kenneth Branagh, Laurence Olivier, Henrich Böll, Merchant Ivory, Peter Weir, Akira Kurosawa, David Lean, Andrzej Wajda, Francis Ford Coppola, Jean-Claude Carrière, Alfred Hitchcock, and David Lean, as well as adaptations of works by literary authors Samuel Beckett, Harold Pinter, Jane Austen, William Shakespeare, Henry James, Stephen Crane, Charles Dickens, Honoré de Balzac, Joseph Conrad, James Joyce, Lewis Carroll, Philip K. Dick, Mark Twain, Emily Dickinson, Georges Sand, Alfred Camus, John Fletcher, Angela Carter, Johann Wolfgang von Goethe, Graham Greene, Nathaniel Hawthorne, Edgar Allan Poe, and the Brontës.

The 1990s also witnessed increasing attention to adaptation in media beyond literature and film. My own research into adaptation theorization after Welch's and Harris Ross's bibliographies conclude extends beyond literature-and-film studies, finding academic essays on adaptation in the journals of numerous disciplines: literary journals, comparative literature journals, film journals, television journals, mass communications journals, art journals, theater journals, music journals, dance journals, medical journals, legal journals, education journals, philology journals, psychological journals, historical journals, and national and regional journals. It also finds articles on adaptation in journals organized by genre (children's literature, science fiction, Gothic, etc.) and theoretical approaches (gender studies, cultural studies, postcolonialism, etc.). Adaptation discourses also unfold in newsletters, screenwriting journals and books, practitioner interviews, advertising, professional reviews, and consumer reviews.

The 1990s saw rising scholarly interest in canonical literature adapted to television. The *MLA International Bibliography* lists only 13 publications treating television adaptation (searched for as a subject term) prior to 1980; the years 1980–1989 produced 152 publications, and 1990–1999 saw 186 publications, including the first book-length study of the subject (Giddings et al., 1990). Radio adaptation studies grew from 6 publications prior to 1980 to 21 in the 1980s and 25 in the 1990s. The BBC had been dramatizing canonical literature in radio and/or television format since the 1920s; academic interest was triggered by the tandem rise of cultural and political theories of arts and media and the growing cultural prominence and consumer popularity of these adaptations, peaking with the BBC's *Pride and Prejudice* (1995). From the 1990s, left-wing scholars forged a sharp political critique of British heritage adaptations (most notably, Higson 2003; 2004; 2006; see also Caughie 1998). The timing was unfortunate for adaptation studies: at the very moment when the high production values of these heritage adaptations promised to liberate adaptations from high-art aesthetic scorn, their aestheticism became grounds for their theoretical denigration under radical political theories, as their high-quality aesthetics were viewed as agents of reactionary politics and cultural elitism.

At the same time, scholars worked to liberate low-art and popular adaptations from theoretical scorn, democratizing adaptation studies by addressing mass media and modernizing the field by treating new media. In 1995, Randall D. Larson published the first book-length work on film novelizations and movie and television tie-ins.[11] In 1999, Cartmell, Whelehan, and their contributors set up a politically inflected dialectic between film adaptation and novelization in *Adaptations: From Text to Screen, Screen to Text* aimed at redressing prior disciplinary hierarchies, in which literature took priority and only book-to-film adaptations were studied.

The 1990s also saw the dominance of Anglophone adaptation studies partially redressed, with studies of adaptation in other nations, including Iran, Ireland, Australia, South America, France, Germany, Spain, Italy, Japan, Egypt, Taiwan, Greece, and Canada. In such contexts, translation theory emerged as both close relation and theoretical model for adaptation studies

(Cattrysse 1992; Helman and Osadnik 1996), and cross-cultural, cross-media adaptation studies worked to reunite formal with cultural adaptation studies.

Beyond literature, film, theater, radio, and television, the *MLA International Bibliography* indicates that in the 1990s there were critical writings on the adaptation of folk songs, film music, animation, fairy tales, opera, radio, TV serials, poetry to art and theater, short story to play, the Bible, melodrama, comics, literature to music, painting, photography, British Gothic plays, literature-to-literature adaptation, screenplays, Greek Orthodox hymns, and adaptation in various film genres (horror, comedy, science fiction, animation, children's fiction, detective fiction, and more).

Adaptation scholarship in the 1990s, then, was diverse; yet its very diversity, scattered across so many different media, disciplines, nations, periods, and publication formats, meant that scholars did not often dialogue with each other and were unaware of the diversity and range of the field. Indeed, one of the reasons that film and literature dominate twentieth-century adaptation studies is that they forge one of the few intersections over which scholars have engaged in longstanding debate.

Joining disciplinary diversity, new theories were levied on adaptation in the 1990s: Gilles Deleuze and Félix Guattari were invoked; imperialism, a male gaze, and regionality were addressed; adaptation featured prominently (and negatively) in heritage criticism, while traditional studies of rhetoric, endings, narrative voice, aesthetic success, perspective, and hermeneutics continued unabated. From the mid-1990s, adaptations were being scrutinized in terms of identity politics: political conservatism (e.g., North 1999)—especially politically conservative historical nostalgia (e.g., Rice and Saunders 1996)—patriarchy, colonialism (e.g., Gelder 1999), racism, nationalism, sexism (e.g., Kaye 1996), and heterosexism (e.g., Shaughnessy 1996).

Yet a publication count indicates that these were pioneering beginnings rather than sweeping movements, awaiting fuller development in the twenty-first century. For example, the *MLA International Bibliography* yields 8 hits for the subject terms "adaptation" and "feminism" in the 1990s, rising to 19 in the 2000s and 39 in the 2010s (to 2018). There are 8 hits for the subject terms "adaptation" and "queer theory" in the 1990s, 19 in the 2000s, and 39 in the 2010s (to 2018). There are 19 hits for "adaptation" and "race" as subject terms in the 1990s, increasing to 33 in the 2000s and 50 in the 2010s (to 2018). A subject term search for "adaptation" and "nationalism" reveals a similar rise, with 10 hits in the 1990s, 19 in the 2000s, and 28 in the 2010s.

Similarly, "adaptation" and "postmodernism" yields 13 hits for the 1990s, 28 for the 2000s, before dropping to 23 in the 2010s, a drop mirroring that of the humanities more generally.[12] A special issue of the *Canadian Review of Comparative Literature* treating literature, film, and adaptation in 1996, freely available online, includes a select bibliography of 380 publications between 1985 and 1996, offering a wider, more internationally balanced focus than the largely Anglophone *MLA International Bibliography* provides, in spite of the "International" claims of its title (Deltcheva 1996b).

There were also attempts to theorize adaptation systematically in the 1990s using cutting-edge polysystems approaches (Cattrysse 1992; Helman and Osadnik 1996). Polysystems theories study adaptation in relation to multiple rather than single sources, set adaptation in dialogue with other terminologies (remake, pastiche, and parody), and attend to the adaptation industry, where it defines and studies adaptation via reception. Decades later, Hutcheon (2006) and Murray (2008; 2012a) would make similar arguments, without citing this pioneering work; Cattrysse's return to promote his neglected ideas in 2014 is discussed in Chapter 4.

1996: A Landmark Year

The year 1996 was a landmark year for adaptation studies: following piecemeal applications of new theories to adaptation studies, two publications in that year, Brian McFarlane's *Novel to Film: An Introduction to the Theory of Adaptation* and *Pulping Fictions: Consuming Culture across the Literature/ Media Divide*, co-edited by Deborah Cartmell, Ian Q. Hunter, Heidi Kaye, and Imelda Whelehan, carried them into book-length studies. Drawing on the narrative theories of Barthes and the structuralist narratology of Chatman, McFarlane's theory of novel-to-film adaptation rejects translation theories for their "near-fixation with the issue of fidelity" and the impressionistic value judgments of aesthetic formalism, pitting a unifying structuralist narratology against adaptation's uses in the literature-and-film wars (1996, 194). Sidestepping comparative studies focused on adaptation as *product*, McFarlane theorized adaptation as a *process*, seeking to do so systematically. He circumvented, but did not directly oppose, medium specificity and semiotic structuralist theories that form cannot be separated from content by engaging structuralist theories of deep structures which, he argued, can and do pass between media forms. In his conclusion, McFarlane conceded that adaptation cannot be understood apart from contextual and cultural factors, and he posited that Barthesean structuralist theory might indicate how to integrate them. However, he acknowledged that, unlike grammar and narrative structures, contextual factors cannot be studied in any systematic or totalizing way (210).

By contrast, *Pulping Fictions'* editors and contributors focused predominantly on cultural factors in adaptation, treating pulp fiction, popular film, and trash culture as well as canonical works, declaring their aim "to scrutinize . . . an abiding hostility to mass culture and a reluctance to engage with a wider postmodern field of cultural production" manifested by aesthetic formalists and high-art humanists (1996, 2–3). Opposing systematic, objective, categorical methodologies and universal theoretical principles, declaring the arbitrariness of systematicity, the illusory nature of objectivism, the oppression and occlusion of categorization, and the philosophical impossibility and political undesirability of theoretical master narratives, they charged aesthetic formalism, high-art humanism, and systematic theorization with maintaining oppressive, elitist, conservative, white, patriarchal, and western hierarchies and institutions, against these theories' official claims to be apolitical and concerned with only formal and universal affairs. These two publications marked a divide between primarily formal and primarily cultural adaptation studies, which continued into the twenty-first century.

Adaptation theorization lives not only by what lies within the pages of its publications but also by its industries and their hierarchies in the forms of academic and publishing institutions. McFarlane's single-author monograph, published by Oxford University Press's prestigious Clarendon Press, propounds a single ("the") theory of adaptation and treats only canonical novels and films. *Pulping Fictions*, a collaboratively edited, multi-author collection published by the left-wing Pluto Press, established in 1969, pursues postmodern pluralism and treats mass, popular media. According to Google Scholar, as of December 23, 2019, McFarlane's book had been cited 1,318 times; *Pulping Fictions* had been cited only 39 times.

Yet the tide was turning. Between 1997 and 2001, the editors of *Pulping Fictions* produced six more essay collections, all published by Pluto Press; by contrast, only one formalist monograph appeared in the same period, James Griffith's *Adaptations as Imitations* (1997). Commendably, in light of this history, Griffith sought to revive Augustan theories of adaptation, recuperating adaptation following its modernist castigation. Against prevailing theories focused on what adaptations could not or should not do according to the laws of Romantic originality, aesthetic formalism, and medium specificity, he argued that "adaptations can do many of the things they are too commonly thought to be incapable of doing—that is, imitate, in a fashion equal to the achievement of the original novel, various narrative techniques, forms, and effects" (69). It was not until I researched the longer history of adaptation theorization that I fully appreciated the book's historical attempts to recuperate adaptation as a good theoretical object. However, although Leitch revisited Griffith's neoclassical theory of imitation briefly in his twenty-first-century monograph (2007, 103–6), Griffith's work has not been continued. For all his efforts to recuperate adaptation according to high-art, aesthetic, humanist theories, these were the very theories being rejected by the 1990s academic mainstream. Although McFarlane has had more of an afterlife in adaptation studies than Griffith, he too arrived too late to rescue adaptation from the abuses of aesthetic formalism and the denials of structuralist semiotics. As the next chapter details, these theories were already under attack by dialogic and (post)structuralist theories of intertextuality. While systematic theorization remains prominent in European and Latin American media studies today (e.g., Gambier and Gottlieb 2001; Rajewsky 2002; Cattrysse 2014; Verevis 2016), they have found little support from the twenty-first-century Anglo-American theoretical mainstream.

The postmodern cultural and radical political theories that Cartmell and Whelehan brought to the field have had more of an afterlife in Anglophone adaptation studies. For Sarah Cardwell, the theoretical turn "[nudged] adaptation studies further away from literary/film/television studies and [embedded] it more deeply within cultural studies . . . [precipitating] conceptual and methodological disruption at the heart of adaptation studies" (2018, 9; see also Cardwell 2002, 69).

The year 1996 was also a landmark year in terms of adaptation metacriticism and surveys of adaptation theorization, indicating the field's growing self-reflexivity, which helped to develop adaptation studies as a field. In 1996, the *Canadian Review of Comparative Literature* published a special issue, *Literature and Film: Models of Adaptation*. It announced its concern with the "problem" of theorizing adaptation in its preface: "The purpose of this special issue is to discuss the wide variety of problems" in the field. It dared to challenge medium specificity theory, calling literature-and-film studies to move away from "autonomous fields of inquiry . . . in favor of one vast interrelated plane." As a product and process that had already done this, literary film adaptation was given a leading role in this initiative: "One of the most productive areas for investigation has become that of the adaptation" (Deltcheva, Osadnik, and Vlasov 1996, 637). In a separate introduction, Roumiana Deltcheva championed "inter- and multidisciplinarity and cross-media approaches" (Deltcheva 1996a, 639). In lieu of medium specificity theory, the articles in the issue engaged André Lefevere's theory of translation as refraction, Mikhail Bakhtin's theory of the chronotype, Michel Foucault's theory of discursive constructionism, Gérard Genette's structuralist narratology, Gideon Toury's cultural intersemiotic theories, Itamar Even-Zohar's theory of polysystems, and various cultural studies theories, including Theodor Adorno's neo-Marxist theory of popular culture, feminism, and discussion of film adaptation's role in creating literary bestsellers. Two articles in this special issue challenged medium specificity theory directly via case studies of silent film intertitles and "film prosaics."

The year 1996 also produced a metatheoretical survey by Karen E. Kline, who proposed four theoretical paradigms under which literary film adaptation studies was operating at the time, each focused on the field as a locus for disciplinary wars. Two waged them; one sought to navigate them diplomatically; the last sidestepped them in favor of theoretical wars. The first, translation, privileges literature over film: "Critics adopting the translation paradigm . . . privilege traditionally literary elements while minimizing specifically cinematic elements, and they value similarities rather than differences between the written and cinematic texts" (71). The third, transformation, "inverts the classic hierarchy asserted by the translation paradigm. . . . [T]he film occupies a privileged position as an original," so that "critics adopting this paradigm often end up privileging the cinematic text over its literary source" (74). The second, pluralism, propounds an analogical, equivalency model of adaptation to equalize the two media, following structuralist theories of media relations. The fourth paradigm moves away from disciplinary to theoretical wars, "encouraging critics toward a neo-Marxist critique of the commercial systems supporting book publication and film production" (75). In rejecting this theoretical model, Kline revealed her own theoretical position: "The resulting analysis has the potential to become formulaic" (75). Yet the polemical political theories of the day were no more formulaic than the formalist and structuralist ones she favored.

Although I have some quibbles with Kline's field summary, as she may have with mine, there is a larger metacritical point to make—one that I rescued from a footnote, since it warrants equal attention with other metacritical arguments: the extent to which female adaptation scholars have been ignored, plagiarized, and displaced in adaptation studies. Kline's summary of the field is fuller, more accurate, and more nuanced than those of prior and contemporaneous male scholars whose work is more cited and reprinted than hers.

Indeed, male scholars at times obscure female scholars in their citations. In his summary of prior adaptation studies, Stam (2005) credits Boyum's arguments about reader response to Stanley Fish, while Boyum herself cites a female theorist as her source. Claude-Edmonde Magny's remarkable *The Film Aesthetic of Fiction between the Two Wars*, published in 1948 and translated into English in 1972, was heavily cannibalized by Chatman (1978) and Cohen (1979), neither of whom cites her, and who were subsequently credited with her ideas, while she is largely forgotten.

Returning to the late 1990s, in spite of ongoing theoretical rifts, some scholars envisioned a more integrated, less theoretically polarized field. Praising McFarlane and Griffith "for reinvigorating a still largely underdeveloped field," Lloyd Michaels looked forward in 1998 to future adaptation scholarship that would span a range from formalism to industry studies to consumer response criticism and from generic to political to cognitive studies. Even so, Michaels's theoretically expansive vision called for taxonomical, categorical methodologies to order it:

> Several possibilities suggest themselves: a taxonomy of transformative strategies, either derived from Propp (expansion, simplification, substitution) or Wagner (transposition, commentary, analogy); a catalogue of various tropes (irony, symbolism, metaphor, synecdoche, flashback); a generic categorization (short story, drama, poetry, diary, biography, autobiography, reportage); a survey of television serial adaptation (commercial networks compared with public broadcasting); a spectrum of "properties" and spectator knowledge (classic, bestseller, potboiler, cult book). Each of these prospective books might be informed by theories of authorship, capitalist production, spectatorship, and cognition. All in good time. For now, we need to be patient. (1998, 432)

Some adaptation scholars would follow some of his recommendations in the twenty-first century; others would ignore or oppose them; still others would go far beyond them, as the final chapter of this history attests.

4

Theorizing Adaptation in the Twenty-First Century

The Rise of Adaptation Studies

While literature-and-film studies predominated in the 1970s, with adaptation typically featuring as its most denigrated sub-category, interest in adaptation increased in the 1980s and 1990s. By 2006, the ratio of general literature-and-film studies to literary film adaptation studies had changed decisively. In that year, Andrew Higson announced: "It is adaptations . . . that dominate the literature/film relationship" (62). More broadly, my introduction to this book indicates that, of the 25,241 hits produced by entering "adaptation" as a subject term (including fields beyond literature and film), 13,903 were published after 1990 and 11,145 after 2000 (to 2018).[1]

The titles of twenty-first-century literature-and-film studies publications also indicate the rise of adaptation. Robert Stam and Alessandra Raengo's edited collection *Literature and Film* (2005a) bears the subtitle *A Guide to the Theory and Practice of Film Adaptation*; James M. Welsh and Peter Lev's pedagogical work, *The Literature/Film Reader* (2007), is similarly subtitled *Issues of Adaptation*; John M. Desmond and Peter Hawkes's pedagogical essay collection inverts the terms in its title, *Adaptation: Studying Film and Literature* (2006, reprinted 2015). The three terms unite in the main title of Deborah Cartmell's edited collection, *A Companion to Literature, Film, and Adaptation* (2012).

In the twenty-first century, adaptation publications have expanded beyond literature and film to consider other media. While my history attests that adaptation in other media has been studied for centuries, what changed in the twenty-first century was that adaptation studies began to be a diasporic field encompassing many media and disciplines, rather than a sub-field discussed separately within disciplines. The two 2005 essay collections co-edited by Stam and Raengo extend adaptation scholarship to new media, including the internet, CDs, DVDs, electronic games,

Theorizing Adaptation. Kamilla Elliott, Oxford University Press (2020). © Oxford University Press.
DOI: 10.1093/oso/9780197511176.001.0001

interactive installations, and virtual environments, while also expanding adaptation studies of older media, including adaptation and the oral tradition, the Bible, history, photography, portraiture, early cinema, and musicals, and carrying adaptation studies beyond Anglophone works to Italy, France, China, India, and Africa. Although other scholars had treated other media and non-Anglophone adaptations for centuries, bringing the adaptations of many media and nations together in a single volume announced adaptation studies as an interdisciplinary, international field. Structuralism and cultural studies had prepared the way for such expansion and integration theoretically.

A year later, Linda Hutcheon's *A Theory of Adaptation* authoritatively declared adaptation studies open to

> not just films and stage productions but also musical arrangements and song covers, visual art revisitations of prior works and comic book versions of history, poems put to music and remakes of films, and video games and interactive art. (2006, 9)

More pertinent to the arguments of my book, Hutcheon insisted:

> Videogames, theme park rides, Web sites, graphic novels song covers, operas, musicals, ballets, and radio and stage plays are . . . as important to . . . theorizing as . . . the more commonly discussed movies and novels. (2006, xiv)

Since then, entire books have been devoted to adaptation in new media (e.g., Constandinides 2010; Urrows 2008; Gratch 2017), and the intermedial and multimedial adaptations of global franchise entertainment industries have been studied (Parody 2011; Elliott 2014a; Meikle 2019a). New media platforms that allow non-professionals to disseminate their adaptations widely (e.g., fan fiction, online videos, and music remixes) have carried the production of adaptation beyond mainstream adaptation industries (Martin 2009; Marlow 2009; Horwatt 2009; Moore 2010; O'Flynn 2013; Gratch 2017; Blackwell 2018). While scholars have continued to broaden adaptation studies nationally (e.g., Dovey 2009; Gordon 2009; Deppman 2010; Rentschler [1986] 2015; Gelder and Whelehan 2016) and to consider cross-cultural adaptation (e.g., Zhen 2005; O'Thomas 2010; Della Coletta 2012; Smith 2016; Stam 2017), studies of global adaptation have also emerged (Davison and Mulvey-Roberts 2018; Krasilovsky 2018; Yang and Xiaotian 2019).

By the late 2010s, major adaptation studies were dropping literature and film from their titles, most notably *The Oxford Handbook of Adaptation Studies* (Leitch 2017a) and *The Routledge Companion to Adaptation* (Cutchins, Krebs, and Voigts 2018). These edited collections contain chapters on theatrical adaptation, adaptation and illustration, adaptation and opera, popular song and adaptation, radio adaptation, comic-book adaptation, videogame adaptation, adaptation and social media, adaptation and new media, and adaptation and remix culture, as well as chapters studying the relationship between adaptation and history and adaptation and politics. However, literature and film continue to feature prominently in their tables of contents and remain central to adaptation studies today, as the titles and tables of contents of the field's three journals, *Literature/Film Quarterly, Adaptation: The Journal of Literature on Screen*, and the *Journal of Adaptation in Film & Performance* also attest.[2]

The Theoretical Turn in Adaptation Studies

Although the theories of the theoretical turn were applied to adaptation from the 1970s, the theoretical turn did not enter the adaptation studies mainstream until the turn of the twentieth century (1996–2005). It did so in a bifurcated way: there was a postmodern cultural, radical political theoretical turn in Britain and a quasi-poststructuralist formal and semiotic theoretical turn in the United States. In spite of their division along cultural and formal lines, poststructuralist and postmodern theorists allied in rejecting aesthetic formalism, New Criticism, and high-art humanism, while positions on structuralist semiotics and narratology varied.

In Britain, Deborah Cartmell, Imelda Whelehan, Ian Q. Hunter, Heidi Kaye, and contributors to their seven essay collections (1996—2001) championed postmodern cultural studies. In addition to *Pulping Fictions* (1996), discussed at the end of Chapter 3, they published:

Trash Aesthetics: Popular Culture and Its Audience (Pluto, 1997)
   Sisterhoods across the Literature/Media Divide (Pluto, 1998)
   Alien Identities: Exploring Differences in Film and Fiction (Pluto, 1999)
   Classics in Film and Fiction (Pluto, 2000)
   Adaptations: From Text to Screen, Screen to Text (Routledge, 1999)
   Retrovisions: Reinventing the Past in Film and Fiction (Pluto, 2001)[3]

Both *Pulping Fictions* and *Trash Culture* engage postmodern and left-wing political theories to challenge divisions between high and low culture in literature, film, and adaptation. The introduction to *Classics in Film and Fiction* draws on Pierre Bourdieu's political theory of cultural capital to argue that "a belief in 'classics' superior to other works reproduces . . . hierarchical society and its power," and that what constitutes a classic is not a merely a matter of aesthetic formalism "but rather a highly politicized issue," with "both classroom and social class . . . implied in . . . the term 'classic' " (2000, 3).

The introduction to *Retrovisions* establishes the collection's postmodern view of history as nonlinear, subjective, relative, and constructed, often as a coercive discourse of power, requiring postmodern skepticism and radical political critique to challenge and dismantle its authority (2001, 1–2). In these marriages of postmodern philosophy and radical politics, left-wing ideologies and values predominate over philosophical skepticism and ecumenical pluralism. *Pulping Fictions* attacks high culture and valorizes low culture; *Classics in Film and Fiction* challenges the canon and high-art humanism; *Trash Culture* analyzes low adaptations of high culture to subvert the canon; *Sisterhoods* reads literature, film, and adaptation via feminist and queer theories; *Aliens* engages the extra-terrestrial and non-human to probe the politics of "class, race, gender, nationality, and sexual orientation" (1999, 3).

Formal adaptation studies also underwent a theoretical turn, led by American film scholars James Naremore, Robert B. Ray, Robert Stam, and Thomas Leitch. At the turn of the millennium, Ray mounted an influential theoretical critique of "the field of literature and film," then still synonymous with adaptation studies,[4] contending that the field floundered and was marginalized by literary studies and film studies alike because it lacked "a presiding poetics" (2000, 44), because it used adaptation studies "to shore up literature's crumbling walls" against the rising tide of film and popular culture (46), and because it functioned as a bastion of resistance to the theoretical turn in the humanities. The belatedness of the theoretical turn in adaptation studies led Ray to describe the field as "ultimately antitheoretical," "thoroughly discredited," and "irrelevant" (45–46), and Leitch to charge that "adaptation theory [had] remained tangential to the thrust of film study because it [had] never been undertaken with conviction and theoretical rigor" but had been "practiced in a theoretical vacuum" (2003a, 168).

Even so, Ray acknowledged that "the field of literature and film was not without paradigm. . . . [I]t inherited the assumptions of the dominant New

Criticism" (44–45). For Ray, "the New Criticism proved ultimately antitheoretical" (2000, 45); for Leitch in 2003, central tenets of medium specificity theory, Romanticism, aesthetic formalism, and New Criticism constituted "fallacies in contemporary adaptation theory" (2003a, essay title).[5] Leitch argued for institutional as well as theoretical change, advocating the establishment of "Textual Studies, a discipline incorporating adaptation study, cinema studies in general, and literary studies" (2003a, 42), a reorganization that would simultaneously affirm the intertextual theories that he recommended for retheorizing the field and diminish uses of adaptation studies to foster disciplinary rivalries by housing media under a single discipline.

Also in the 2000s, Stam recommended that Bakhtinian dialogics replace New Critical organic unity, word and image divides, Marxist dialectics, and structuralist binaries and that scholars engage poststructuralist theory to deconstruct notions of originals and copies and to challenge one-way translation methodologies in adaptation studies, as well as to subvert linear, progressive, evolutionary histories of media forms and adaptation. He further contested Romantic and modernist auteur theories with Barthes's death of the author and Foucault's discursive constructionism (2000; 2005). My own *Rethinking the Novel/Film Debate* (2003a) is also indebted to Foucault's theories of discourse. Its attempts to re-historicize and retheorize literature–film relations (including adaptation) combined linear historical study with New Historicism and metacritical discourse analysis with cognitive linguistics to rethink adaptation studies, as well as novel-and-film studies more generally.

In contrast to Ray, Cartmell, Whelehan, and their co-editors and contributors did not view high-art humanism, aesthetic formalism, and New Criticism to be "irrelevant" but to exert formidable cultural, social, political clout in academia and culture, fostering unjust and oppressive social, media, political, cultural, and academic hierarchies that required dismantling by postmodern theories and revolutionizing by radical political ones. Despite their differences, both groups shared a progressivist view of theorization: although they disagreed on which new theories and methodologies were needed for the field to progress, they agreed that using the "right" new theories would resolve the problems of theorizing adaptation brought about by the "wrong" old theories. Straddling as it does so many media, disciplines, and cultures, and, being itself antithetical to humanities theorization, adaptation served as an incisive and powerful case study for these revolutionary theoretical endeavors. What we did not see then was that the problem of theorizing adaptation was a systemic one based in dissonance between adaptation and theorization as cultural processes in the humanities that could not be resolved by changing old theories for new: we needed a revolution in what theorization is and does in the humanities and in its relationship to adaptation, as well as to what it theorizes more generally.

By 2005, most of the theories pioneered by turn-of-the-century scholars had been applied to adaptation substantially in works published by mainstream academic presses. In that year, Robert Stam wrote and co-edited three volumes expanding and synthesizing the field of adaptation. The monograph *Literature through Film: Realism, Magic, and the Art of Adaptation* (Stam 2004) offers a theoretical history of literary film adaptation departed from prior histories by following the history of the novel rather than the history of film. Reading film adaptations as interpretations of the works they adapt, it puts film adaptation on a par with literary criticism. Stam's authoritative and polemical introduction to the second work, an edited collection titled *Literature and Film: A Guide to the Theory and Practice of Film Adaptation* (Stam and Raengo 2005a), benefits from his expansive knowledge of film, media, and literary theories, providing an incisive metacritical analysis of adaptation's relationship to other field histories and theories, diagnosing and recommending ways to redress adaptation's theoretical problems, and deftly integrating formal and cultural aspects of the theoretical turn, as well as adaptation theory and adaptation practice. The third volume, *A Companion to Literature and Film* (Stam and Raengo 2005b) expands adaptation studies still further. Beyond their role in expanding and rendering adaptation's disciplines, nations, and media, the three volumes are *theoretically* pluralistic, engaging theories of comparative narratology, intertextuality, adaptive phenomenology, psychology, transécriture and narrative mediatics, theologies of adaptation, social discourse theory, sociology, cultural materialism, queer theory, and of nation and race.

In *Adaptation and Appropriation* (2006), Julie Sanders too engages both formal and cultural aspects of the theoretical turn, bringing "structuralism, post-structuralism, postcolonialism, postmodernism, feminism and gender studies" to bear upon adaptation (publisher's blurb), while in 2005, contributors to Mireia Aragay's edited collection *Books in Motion: Adaptation, Intertextuality, Authorship* (2005a) applied poststructuralist intertextuality, postcolonialism, feminism, postmodernism, and dialogics blended with psychoanalysis to adaptation, along with essays rethinking fidelity and auteur theories. The field was becoming theoretically pluralistic, a product of postmodern theory; the following year would witness the publication of a formidably pluralistic theoretical monograph. But it would also demonstrate staunch resistance to the theoretical turn in adaptation studies.

Formal and Cultural Theoretical Wars in Adaptation Studies

Adaptation scholars were by no means agreed on the theoretical turn. The year 2006 was not only the year in which Higson affirmed the predominance of adaptation in literature-and-film studies; it also witnessed the publication of two monographs indicating ongoing theoretical divides between form and cultural adaptation studies and between pre- and post-theoretical turn theories: Linda Costanzo Cahir's *Literature into Film: Theory and Practical Approaches* and Linda Hutcheon's *A Theory of Adaptation*. While in 1996 the incipient cultural studies collective had been more oppositional and the established formal scholar more ecumenical, these roles reversed in 2006 as the theoretical turn became more established and older theories became less mainstream. Cahir's study is more hostile to and exclusive of cultural studies than McFarlane's was in 1996, opening with a virulent polemic against the theoretical turn by James M. Welsh, co-founder of *LFQ* and the Literature/Film Association. In 1996, Cahir worked as hard to carve out separate spheres for older formal and newer cultural adaptation studies as prior scholars had done to separate literature from film. Against poststructuralist and postmodern cultural attacks on comparative translation methodologies, Cahir advocated restoring "translation" as the primary field terminology, displacing "adaptation":

> "To adapt" means to alter the structure or function of an entity so that it is better fitted to survive and to multiply in its new environment. . . . "To translate," in contrast to "to adapt," is to move a text from one language to another. It is a *process of language*, not a process of survival and generation. (2006, 14, emphasis in original)

Understanding that adaptation, as a process of changing something to suit a new environment, requires attention to cultural contexts, Cahir sought to redefine the field as a purely formal field of intermedial translation. This argument threatened the survival of adaptation as a field of study.

By contrast, Hutcheon argued that translation approaches are inadequate for theorizing adaptation (16–18). Building on the theories of Roland Barthes, Hutcheon argued that narratives are both cultural and formal constructs and that the two cannot be separated. She also understood that other media forms are just as much contexts for adaptation as the cultural contexts that we more commonly nominate as such. Hutcheon extended postmodern diversity and pluralism from subject matter to *theories*, granting space in her monograph for theories that other postmodern cultural scholars would later advocate discarding (Cartmell and Whelehan 2010). Even so, her expansion of adaptation studies to all manner of media and her inclusion of popular culture implicitly, and decisively, rejected the high-art aesthetic theories that exclude such works from scholarship. Ecumenism, then, can refute theoretical principles as well as support them. Additionally, her insistence that adaptation must be defined in terms of reception as well as production (15–16) challenged the priority of author intent and adapter agency in formal studies, priorities that were the main focus of aesthetic formalist adaptation studies. Five years on, Colin MacCabe insisted that "how and why filmmakers adapt books and what they did to adapt them" remained central to adaptation studies (2011, 7). As Cahir opposed cultural theories of adaptation at the level of field definition, MacCabe opposed them at the level of methodological taxonomies. Contracting the chapter titles ordering Hutcheon's theoretical work—Who? What? How? Why? When? Where?—to "how," "why," and "what" eradicates the "where" and "when" that are the main focus of cultural and contextual studies.

While Cahir's work garnered respect, Hutcheon's *A Theory of Adaptation* became the most cited tome in adaptation studies, cited 4024 times by comparison to 155 citations of Cahir's book.[6] However, Amazon sales rankings reveal a resounding reversal in the economies of the academic adaptation industry: Hutcheon's book ranks 11,640,936 and Cahir's 914,326,[7] suggesting that Cahir's book has been used more in adaptation pedagogy by scholars who teach, while Hutcheon's has been used more by scholars who publish.[8] Pricing must play a role in sales (Cahir's is more affordable than Hutcheon's across all platforms), and sales rankings change over time, so that it is impossible to know whether Hutcheon's sold better at other times. Both books have been reprinted: Hutcheon's 2012 second edition stands at 3,408,133 in Amazon's sales rankings; Cahir's 2014 reprint has not been differentiated from the first print run. The wider total circulation of Cahir's book helps to explain why older theories persist in adaptation studies, proliferate in media industries, and among the general public.

Tensions between formal and cultural theories of adaptation continued, with variations, culminating in another pair of books published one year apart: Cartmell and Whelehan's *Screen Adaptation: Impure Cinema* (2010) and MacCabe, Warner, and Murray's *True to the Spirit: Film Adaptation and the Question of Fidelity* (2011). Both books share an interest in defending adaptation from charges of secondariness: Cartmell and Whelehan continued their longstanding commitment to rescuing adaptation from high-art, humanist contempt in their book, while MacCabe resisted the prioritization of literature over film in adaptation, calling for equality between adapted literature and adapting films, in his introduction to the edited collection (MacCabe 2011, 8). Yet they disagreed theoretically. In 1999, Whelehan had been confident that "a cultural studies approach foregrounds the activities of reception and consumption, and shelves—forever perhaps—considerations of the aesthetic or cultural worthiness of the object of study" (18). Yet, finding that such considerations had not been shelved over a decade on, she and co-author Cartmell expressed perplexity at their persistence, describing them as "a small body of work moving against the main tide of theory . . . an attitude to adaptations . . . that refuses to go away" (2010, 11). It may have been small body of work when Cartmell and Whelehan's book went to press; however, in the year their book was published it was outnumbered by aesthetic formalist publications.[9]

The following year, MacCabe responded in print: "The fact is that people are still interested in how and why filmmakers adapt books and what they did to adapt them. So these issues and questions are not going to *go away* and perhaps it is time to ask why it is that we refuse to address them" (2011, 7, emphasis added). MacCabe not only defended his interest in aesthetic and practitioner adaptation studies, he also attacked theoretical rejections of them: "academic abandonment of questions of value is not simply theoretically ignorant but also practically disastrous" (9). To be fair, Cartmell and Whelehan have manifested longstanding interest in adaptation practitioners, most notably television adapter Andrew Davies, hosting him and others at conferences, and publishing articles by practitioners in the journal they edit, *Adaptation*. The opposition is not one between theory and practice, nor between maintaining and abandoning values generally, but between the values of high-art humanism and left-wing cultural studies.

Puzzlingly, given that his theories are older than theirs, MacCabe charged his opponents with theoretical superannuation: "Adaptation studies, rather like Don Quixote, continue to fight the day before yesterday's battles" (7). Yet the charge is not that cultural studies adaptation scholars adhere to theories older than his own, but that they continue to fight theoretical battles in the 2010s that were fought in other fields in the 1980s and 1990s. MacCabe's view is that older theories survived the theoretical turn, and will continue to survive, so that these battles are no longer worth fighting because he will never concede to the turn. Yet battles over cultural values are not only yesterday's battles, they are also today's and tomorrow's battles: as in politics, they will continue to be fought by scholars as long as there is one opponent left standing.

Although Cartmell and Whelehan's co-authored book was published by a well-regarded academic press, Palgrave, and although they edit the Oxford journal *Adaptation*, MacCabe's co-edited collection was published by Oxford University Press, its prestige heightened by essays from internationally re-nowned scholars Dudley Andrew, Laura Mulvey, Tom Gunning, and Fredric Jameson. Once again, the reception of the two books divides: as of December 23, 2019, MacCabe's book had been cited 80 times to 158 for Cartmell and Whelehan's book (Google Scholar), while it ranked above theirs in sales (1,657,007 in Amazon sales rankings to their 1,930,308 ranking).[10] However, the gap in sales is narrower than a decade before, indicating the ascendancy of cultural adaptation studies.

Cartmell and Whelehan's theories were under attack from within the contextual adaptation studies camp as well. In 2008, and again in 2012, Simone Murray forged a wider rift than the longstanding ones running between literature and film and between modernist formal and postmodern cultural theories, opposing humanities methodologies and theories with those of the social sciences. Objecting to textual studies of all kinds, including radical political and poststructuralist textual studies, Murray too sought to "shelve" prior theories: "Adaptation studies urgently needs . . . to *move out from under* the aegis of long-dominant formalist and textual analysis traditions . . . and *instead* begin to understand adaptation sociologically" (2008, 10, emphasis added). The argument is not for the theoretical and methodological supplementation or expansion advocated by Hutcheon, but one of removal and usurpation. Placing textual studies of all kinds into one group, Murray asserted that poststructuralist advocate and dialogician Robert Stam had "merely closed the circle" on more than 50 years of textual adaptation studies inaugurated by aesthetic formalist George Bluestone (2008, 5). Few would agree with this view; Stam engaged dialogics, reader response theory, and poststructuralism to open up textual studies from New Critical analyses of closed organic wholes and binary, chronological comparisons of two media forms.

The social sciences methodologies recommended by Murray have indubitably informed, developed, and supplemented adaptation studies. Even so, annihilating textual studies seems too much like a "final solution" from the social sciences for humanities adaptation studies. Moreover, it excludes essential aspects of humanities adaptation from study. As a process by which texts adapt or are adapted to new contexts, humanities adaptation studies requires consideration of both texts and contexts. Texts and contexts are not antonyms: texts are embedded in the word "contexts," indicating their inextricability, and the etymology of "con" here hails from "connect," meaning "with," not "contrary," meaning "against."

One of the many reasons that Cartmell and Whelehan have been recognized as field leaders is that, for all their protests against high-art formalism, their writings maintain focus on both textual *and* contextual factors in adaptation. Indeed, far from being offended by Murray's critique of textual cultural studies, Cartmell responded positively with an industry-based study of *Adaptations in the Sound Era, 1927–37* (2015), and went further to argue that "New scholars . . . should . . . reflect on the commercial and material conditions (rather than a single literary text) as what *really* underpins the field" (2017, n.p., emphasis added). Concomitantly, Leitch has observed that Murray herself undertakes textual readings in her monograph (2018, 700).

Stepping back from the adaptation industry to ponder the academic industry, championing industry studies as the only valid or "real" form of adaptation scholarship does not take sufficiently into account the economic and class hierarchies within academia. The archival research required to produce Murray's and Cartmell's impressive case studies requires substantial funding and ample leave from teaching and administration duties, as the acknowledgments to both books attest: only a handful of fortunate scholars have access to such resources.[11] Textual study, by contrast, is available to every scholar.

Championing one theoretical position and opposing others is endemic to theorization and academic study; yet in the multidisciplinary field of adaptation studies, seeking to do away with theories has indubitably occluded vital aspects of adaptation. Such a diverse field as adaptation studies benefits from diversity not only in its subject matter but also in its theories and methodologies. The preface to *A Theory of Adaptation* underscores Hutcheon's remarkable theoretical ecumenism, one that extends to theories that other postmodern scholars oppose: "At various times . . . I take on the roles of formalist semiotician, poststructuralist deconstructor, or feminist and postcolonial demythifier" (2006, xii). Inevitably, her work has been castigated by scholars who want her to take sides in the theoretical wars or to produce a definitive theory that refutes all the rest. Fellow postmodernists Cartmell and Whelehan view her book as a failed attempt at Grand Theory, criticizing her for making the attempt: "the attempt to answer what, who, why, how,[12] and where coupled with the dizzying number of examples provided in the book point to the conclusion that there cannot be, as the title promises, *a* theory of adaptation" (2010, 56, emphasis in original). Yet Hutcheon's preface cautions against such interpretations of her book: "*A Theory of Adaptation* is quite simply what its title says it is: one single attempt to think through some of the theoretical issues surrounding the ubiquitous phenomenon of adaptation *as adaptation*" (2006, xvi, emphasis in original). It is *a* theory, not *the* theory of adaptation—a postmodern pastiche of many theories.

Other scholars have been disappointed by Hutcheon's refusal to offer *the* definitive theory of adaptation. Heidi Peeters lauds Hutcheon as "one of the most prolific thinkers of our time . . . active and successful within various domains of the humanities," but adds: "somewhat disappointingly, *A Theory of Adaptation* does not offer the Grand Theory we might have been hoping for"; "there are no great answers in this publication, no paradigm shifts in conceptualizing adaptations," only "hundreds of lively examples" and "energetically scattered insights mixed with pieces of an overview of what has been said within the adaptational field so far" (2007, n.p.). Hutcheon's commitment to postmodern philosophy means that she has also disappointed systematic, empirical scholars for whom her subheadings (Who? What? Why? When? Where?) should have created a totalizing, factual, empirically verifiable, reproducible theory of adaptation. Instead, her book pursues a localized, pluralistic empiricism, offering many answers to the Who? What? Why? When? Where? questions from many theoretical purviews. Rather than imposing theory upon her investigations, her book seeks to "derive theory from practice" (cf. Elliott 2003a, 6) by "teas[ing] out the theoretical implications from multiple textual examples" (2006, xii). Hutcheon's book resists top-down theorization: "at no time do I (at least consciously) try to impose any of these theories on my examination of the texts or the general issues surrounding adaptation" (2006, xii).

Although Hutcheon is more theoretically ecumenical than any other adaptation scholar I have read, she has been critiqued for short-changing theoretical approaches that she considers to be overdone. Suzanne Diamond finds that "the most provocative and generative questions that one might pose in a film course are matters Hutcheon leaves untheorized: whether a differently told story is, in fact, 'the same' story; where 'difference' and 'sameness' inhere among stories; and who is authorized to establish these distinctions" (2010, 96). Hutcheon intended this: "What I do want to get away from is just comparing the source text to the adaptation—doing 'this' is like 'that'—going back and forth. I think that's not useful and yet most of the work done on adaptation" does this (Zaiontz 2009, 1). Even so, her interest lay more in moving "away from" theories and methodologies that she considered to have been overdone than in returning to resolve their unresolved theoretical problems and answer their unanswered theoretical questions, an undertaking that my book can only make a small start upon.

Leitch has nominated Hutcheon's A Theory of Adaptation "a theory of theories" (2013a, 159). Yet Hutcheon does not grant all theories equal space and time or present them as they have been presented by their proponents. The very act of placing theories claiming to be universal in a theoretical pastiche along with other theories undermines their totalizing claims and positions them within a larger master narrative of postmodern pluralist theory, which the proponents of universal theory ardently oppose. A Theory of Adaptation is not a theory that weaves theories into a coherent whole, or one that attempts to adjudicate or resolve their debates, or one that knits them into a complex metacritical nexus: the postmodern philosophy that governs the book allows theories to coexist without integration, congruity, debate, or rational cohesion. However, for those who believe that reasoning, consistency, and logic are essential for any theory to attain the status of theory, for those who believe that some theories are right (correct, true, ethical, salutary) and others are wrong (incorrect, fallacious, unethical, pernicious) and that it is the task of scholars to adjudicate these differences, Hutcheon's theory of theories is unsatisfying. For many, placing empiricism (Who? What? Why? When? Where?) in the service of postmodern skepticism is philosophically jarring. Yet as much as they may seem philosophically and methodologically opposed, postmodern indeterminacy and empirical objectivism share a rejection of didactic, a priori value judgments in favor of open-ended questions and the free play of ideas and, as I argue subsequently, incongruously hybrid theorization has been more successful in theorizing adaptation than unified, rational, logical theorization. Angelique Chettiparamb has argued that "innovation is most likely to happen in the hybrid zone; academics working [in interdisciplinary fields] can easily become 'hybrid critics' as they look back with fresh insights at their parent discipline and identify lacunae and gaps" (2007, 7). Indeed, one of the reasons that postmodernism has been invaluable for adaptation studies is that it reveals connections that were invisible to logical, chronological, systematic structures.

Where my study departs from Hutcheon's is in considering theoretical relationships—their debates, wars, and alliances. As I do, I engage theoretical methodologies developed by others: aspects of dialectics and dialogics, traditional and New Historicism, discourse analysis, and rhetorical study. My study finds that the late twentieth and early twenty-first centuries witnessed ongoing *alliances* forged between ideologically *opposed* theories, as well as conceptual continuities traversing otherwise differing theories. Systematic formalist theorists joined leftist cultural scholars to combat aesthetic formalism on different—even opposed—ideological grounds: systematic theorists such as McFarlane rejected theories of aesthetic value for lacking objectivity and empirical evidence, while postmodern cultural scholars such as Cartmell and Whelehan rejected them because of their implications in conservative politics. Conversely, cultural scholars, for all their ideological disagreements with aesthetic formalists, allied with them against objectivist, empirical, and systematic theories, declaring their inadequacy for explicating the "higher" values that have been, whether political or aesthetic, the *raison d'être* of most humanities studies. In a third crossover alliance that protests against making political value the focus of academic study, aesthetic formalists such as MacCabe allied with systematic theorists such as Patrick Cattrysse to argue that the focus of adaptation studies should rest on aesthetic value, not political ideologies. In a fourth transtheoretical coalition, polysystems theorist Cattrysse joined with postmodern theorists against purist formalism in demanding attention to contextual factors; both rejected unilateral attention to a single adaptation's reworking of a single source text in favor of studying multiple textual sources and multiple contextual influences, including legal, industry, economic, pedagogical, and reception factors. In a fifth allied opposition, formalist translation scholars and postcolonial theorists expanded intercultural adaptation studies, with publications treating adaptation in Ireland, Australia, Canada, South America, France,

Germany, Spain, Italy, Greece, Canada, Japan, Egypt, Taiwan, Iran, and other Arabic-speaking nations (see the *MLA International Bibliography*). These continue in twenty-first-century publications seeking to forge connections between adaptation studies and translation studies (Gambier and Gottlieb 2001; Zatlin 2005; Milton 2009; O'Thomas 2010; Raw 2012; Krebs 2012; 2013; Minier 2013; Cattrysse 2014; Raw 2017). Clearly, divisions between theoretical camps do not run along decisive, consistent philosophical or ideological lines, but intertangle. This is also the case in negotiations between theoretical progressivism and theoretical return within adaptation studies.

Theoretical Progressivism and Theoretical Return

In 2018, Sarah Cardwell reflected:

> Adaptation studies appears to be flourishing. International academic interest in the field is lively. Yet, although it is tempting to press ever onwards in the current path, it is often valuable briefly to pause and reflect. (14)

Since the incipient influx of the theoretical turn into adaptation studies in the 1970s, the field has been marked by tensions between theoretical progressivism and theoretical return. These tensions are only partially explicated by conservative resistance to the theoretical turn. There are other factors, including the failure of newer theories to resolve the problems of older ones for adaptation, tensions between neo-theorization and post-theorization, and changes in individual theorists over time. More fundamentally, since adaptation is a process of both progress and return, it has *itself* encouraged alternations between looking forward and back, adapting theory to itself.

Wars between theoretical conservatives and theoretical progressives go some way toward explicating tensions between theoretical progress and return in adaptation studies, but they do not tell the whole story. When the theoretical turn entered the humanities, hitherto dominant theories experienced a marginalization similar to that which they had formerly levied upon adaptation. Previously, they had marginalized adaptation for violating their theories; now, scholars who did not wish to adapt to new theoretical environments embraced adaptation as theoretical kin, at odds with mainstream humanities theorization. These scholars understood that, just as adaptation enables older narratives to survive (Hutcheon 2006, 32), it also enables older *theories* to survive. Adaptation itself answers Cartmell and Whelehan's question as to why older theories have not "gone away": as adaptation infuses theorization, theoretical return persists along with theoretical progressivism within adaptation studies. These dynamics also answer MacCabe's question as to why radical scholars continue to engage in older theoretical debates.

Table 4.1, generated by a subject term search of the *MLA International Bibliography* for "adaptation" combined with a subject term search by theorist name, indicates the presence of both older and newer theorists in adaptation studies.[13]

Older theorists feature prominently. Classical theorists (Aristotle; Plato) appear on the table, along with neoclassicist Dryden and the nineteenth-century philosopher Kant. Modernists (Bazin; Bluestone; Sartre; Warren) outnumber postmodernists (Hutcheon). Classical psychological theorists (Freud; Jung) feature more than twice as often as poststructuralist psychoanalysts (Lacan; Mulvey); classical cultural and political theorists (Lévi-Strauss; Marx; Benjamin; Durkheim; Adorno) similarly eclipse newer ones (Bourdieu; Said); poststructuralist theorists feature in 20 entries (Kristeva; Derrida), while structuralist theorists (Barthes; Genette; Levi-Strauss; McFarlane; Peirce) appear in nearly double that number. While Mikhail Bakhtin and Gilles Deleuze top the table, their major works were published in the 1970s–1990s. The essays comprising Bakhtin's *The Dialogic Imagination* (1981) were written in the 1930s and 1940s and brought into adaptation studies by Robert Stam in 2000. Deleuze's second spot arises more from his prominence in film studies than in adaptation studies: only 1 of the 36 publications makes adaptation its main focus, by contrast to 9 of the 38 publications in which Bakhtin features. Bakhtin remains resonant in adaptation studies because of his focus on the hybridity of language (polyglossia), the primacy of context (heteroglossia), relations between texts (intertextuality), and the cultural politics of representation, all of which remain central in adaptation studies today. Postmodern theorist Linda Hutcheon is the most prominent specifically adaptation theorist on the list.

Table 4.2, a representation of the most cited monographs in adaptation studies, shows that Hutcheon's *A Theory of Adaptation* is the most cited by a long way, in part the result of her global reputation, its title and subject matter, and its accessibility to undergraduate students. But this is also due to her theoretical hybridity and ecumenism, which answer the needs of adaptation's own hybridity and the hybridities of our diasporic field.

Table 4.1 Subject term search of the *MLA International Bibliography* for "adaptation" and theorist names

Theorist Name	No. of Citations with the Subject Term "Adaptation"
Mikhail Bakhtin	40
Gilles Deleuze	38
John Dryden	36
Walter Benjamin	27
Sigmund Freud	27
Michel Foucault	18
Linda Hutcheon	17
Gérard Genette	16
Roland Barthes	14
André Bazin	14
Carl Jung	14
Jean-Paul Sartre	14
Robert Penn Warren	13
Jacques Lacan	12
Julia Kristeva	11
Theodor Adorno	11
Judith Butler	10
Jacques Derrida	9
Edward Said	8
Aristotle	6
Plato	6
Karl Marx	5
Laura Mulvey	4
Immanuel Kant	4
George Bluestone	3
Pierre Bourdieu	3
Claude Lévi-Strauss	3
C. S. Peirce	3
Jean-François Lyotard	2
Thomas Leitch	2
Brian McFarlane	2
Julie Sanders	2
Robert Stam	2
Simone Murray	1

Note: Search date December 23, 2019.

Table 4.2 Most-cited monographs in adaptation studies

Author, Title, Date	No. of Citations
Linda Hutcheon, *A Theory of Adaptation* (2006/2012)	4024
Julie Sanders, *Adaptation and Appropriation* (2006/2017)	1658
Brian McFarlane, *Novel to Film* (1996)	1318
George Bluestone, *Novels into Film* (1957)	1202
Dudley Andrew, *Concepts in Film Theory** (1984)	1187
Thomas Leitch, *Film Adaptation and Its Discontents* (2007)	704
Kamilla Elliott, *Rethinking the Novel/Film Debate* (2003)	541
Robert Stam, *Literature through Film* (2004)	468
Sarah Cardwell, *Adaptation Revisited* (2002)	372
Joy Boyum, *Double Exposure: Fiction into Film* (1985)	242
Simone Murray, *The Adaptation Industry* (2012a)	241
Phyllis Zatlin, *Theatrical Translation and Film Adaptation* (2005)	234
Christine Geraghty, *Now a Major Motion Picture* (2008)	230
Cartmell and Whelehan, *Screen Adaptation* (2010)	158
Linda Cahir, *Literature into Film* (2006)	155

Note: Data from Google Scholar, accessed December 23, 2019. The list of single-authored works makes an exception to include Cartmell and Whelehan's co-authored work (2010). The list excludes more specialized adaptation studies treating the adaptations of artists, nations, periods, and topics. Some of these monographs are not exclusively devoted to adaptation, but they all treat it substantially.

*This monograph contains Andrew's oft-cited chapter on adaptation; there are no separate citation counts on Google Scholar for this chapter.

It also indicates that monographs engaging the theories of the theoretical turn are more frequently cited by scholars than those pursuing pre-turn theories. That older works have had more time to be cited renders this finding all the more resonant. Table 4.3's list of adaptation studies' most cited essay collections presents a similar theoretical landscape.

However, Table 4.4's list of adaptation studies' most frequently cited articles and chapters shows that formal adaptation publications predominate over cultural ones; even so, most of these works engage the progressive formal theories of the theoretical turn rather than older formal theories. (Chatman's structuralist narratological essay is an exception.)

In spite of the preference for theoretical progress over theoretical return in scholarly citations, my introduction to this book documents an ongoing rhetoric of theoretical failure, lack, and disappointment in surveys of field theorization, even in the wake of progressive theorization. The theoretical

Table 4.3 Adaptation studies most cited edited collections

Editor(s), Title, Date	No. of Citations
Stam and Raengo, *Literature and Film* (2005)	448
James Naremore, *Film Adaptation* (2000)	454
Cartmell and Whelehan, *Adaptations* (1999)	373
Timothy Corrigan, *Literature and Film Reader* (2011)	256
Robert Richardson, *Literature and Film* (1969)	212
Cartmell and Whelehan, *Cambridge Companion to Literature on Screen* (2007)	187
Stam and Raengo, *A Companion to Literature and Film* (2005b)	171
Mireia Aragay, *Books in Motion* (2005)	146

Note: Data from Google Scholar, accessed December 23, 2019.

Table 4.4 Adaptation studies most cited essays

Author, Title, Date	No. of Citations
Robert Stam, "Beyond Fidelity: The Dialogics of Adaptation" (2000)	947
Seymour Chatman, "What Novels Can Do that Films Can't" (1980)	529
Thomas Leitch, "Twelve Fallacies in Contemporary Adaptation Theory" (2003a)	365
François Truffaut, "A Certain Tendency in French Cinema" ([1954] 1976)	337
André Bazin, "Adaptation, or the Cinema as Digest" ([1948] 2000)	229
Thomas Leitch, "Adaptation Studies at a Crossroads" (2008b)	211
James Naremore, "Film and the Reign of Adaptation" (1999)	191
Patrick Cattrysse, "Film (Adaptation) as Translation" (1992)	187
Robert B. Ray, "The Field of 'Literature and Film'" (2000)	187
John Ellis, "The Literary Adaptation" (1982)	141
Laurence Venuti, "Adaptation, Translation, Critique" (2007)	138
Brian McFarlane, "Reading Film and Literature" (2007)	111
André Bazin, "In Defense of Mixed Cinema" ([1952] 1967)	110

Note: Data from Google Scholar, accessed December 23, 2019.

turn has enriched the field, but it has not resolved adaptation's theoretical problems, nor has it ended adaptation's marginalization by single disciplines or silenced critiques of adaptation scholarship from without or within. As Ray found adaptation studies to lack "a presiding poetics" (2000, 44) and Leitch decreed the first and founding fallacy of adaptation studies to be that "there is such a thing as contemporary adaptation theory" (2003a, 149), in 2010, Brett Westbrook continued the critique, articulating it as a rupture between theorization and adaptation: "lack of theory about adaptation studies stands in direct contrast to the rise of theory in and of itself" (25). Westbrook made this claim in spite of the panoply of new theories informing adaptation before 2010 and those introduced subsequently. In 2011, Clare Parody theorized adaptation in light of franchise entertainment and new media theories. Between 2011 and 2013, Jennifer Jeffers (2011), Cristina Della Coletta (2012), and Anne-Marie Scholz (2013) theorized adaptations as cross-cultural, transnational, and historico-cultural events. In 2013, John Hodgkins brought affect theory into the field, while Kyle Meikle developed an archaeological approach to adaptation theory. In 2014, Gordon E. Slethaug raised aspects of postmodern philosophy and theory neglected by earlier postmodern political scholars, while Christophe Collard applied Bonnie Marranca's theory of mediaturgy and simultaneity to adaptation.

The year 2015 brought biopolitics (Nicklas) and new perspectives on transmediality (Straumann) and intermediality (Constantinescu) into the field, as well as a study of "History as Adaptation" (Leitch). The following year, 2016, welcomed a theory of "tradaption" (Fortier); in 2017, Cartmell theorized adaptation as exploitation; Meikle delineated a theory of adaptation audiences; and Pascal Nicklas and Arthur M. Jacobs wedded neurocognitive science to the aesthetics of adaptation. In 2018, Nicklas and Sibylle Baumbach co-edited a special issue of the journal *Adaptation* linking adaptation to perception, treating the subject with a range of theoretical perspectives from phenomenology through cognitive science to interactivity. In 2019, Kyle Meikle published a monograph treating *Adaptations in the Franchise Era: 2001–16* (2019a); Werner Schäfke and Johannes Fehle edited an essay collection examining *Adaptation in the Age of Media Convergence*; Jeremy Strong edited a special issue of the journal *Adaptation* theorizing adaptation in terms of history (2019); Eckart Voigts presented a conference paper on posthuman adaptation and digimodernism (2019); and Meikle linked film adaptation to climate adaptation through a rubric of recycling (2019b). These theories and studies are illustrative rather than exhaustive: there is no doubt that adaptation studies has manifested theoretical and disciplinary diversity and intelligent attention to recent and current theoretical trends and issues. As I have argued, and will argue further in Part II of this book, discourses of theoretical lack continue not because adaptation studies lacks theories, or because adaptation scholars are theoretically lacking, but because *theorization* is lacking in explicating adaptation and because adaptation and theorization in the humanities continue to engage in a dysfunctional relationship. In 2015, Rainer Emig argued that adaptation studies had not yet adequately or fully engaged the canonical radical theorists of the 1960s–1990s (Derrida; Foucault; Lyotard; Kristeva; Baudrillard; Bhabba; and Butler). Emig was right. Scholars have applied these theories slimly, slightly, and loosely in isolated case studies or momentarily in pastiches of many theories.[14] Although adaptation studies engages a wide range of theories, its diversity has been scattershot rather than sustained. Adaptation studies has no equivalents of film studies' extensive attention to Lacanian psychoanalytic theory or Deleuzian philosophy, nor does it have counterparts to or literary studies' sophisticated developments of deconstructive postcolonial or feminist theorization. In 2018, Sarah Cardwell assessed:

Today's apparent eclecticism and openness constitute a breadth that belies a lack of depth. There are many oversights in this new age of adaptation studies: topics that lie neglected, questions that remain buried and unanswered, and alternative approaches not yet adopted. These are the unforeseen drawbacks of the particular nature of expansion the field has undergone since the late 1990s. (7)

But another reason we have not applied theories extensively or deeply may be the failure of these theories to explicate adaptation. The theoretical turn did not resolve modernism's problems with theorizing adaptation largely because both post- and neo-theories were far more interested in adapting theorization than in theorizing adaptation. That one of the greatest theorists and thinkers of our day, Linda Hutcheon, has not theorized adaptation to the satisfaction of many scholars, including fellow postmodernists, supports my argument that there are impasses between theorization and adaptation in the humanities that progressivism in the form of new theories and theoretical pluralism have not resolved and cannot resolve. While Hutcheon's theory of postmodernism (1988) and theory of parody (1985) are highly regarded, we have seen that her theory of adaptation received mixed reviews. Scholars may *debate* Hutcheon's theories of postmodernism and parody, including Fredric Jameson, but that discourse of *disagreement* over her other theories differs markedly from the rhetoric of *disappointment* that has characterized reviews of her theory of adaptation. Hutcheon did not theorize adaptation as satisfactorily for other scholars as she had theorized postmodernism, I argue, not because of any theoretical failure or scholarly lack on her part—indeed, her book manifests a wider range of research than any other in the field and is brimming with dazzling insights—but because adaptation as a process resists the processes of humanities theorization, as Part II of this book details. As long as that impasse remains, introducing new theories does not, therefore, resolve the problem of theorizing adaptation: indeed, creating a pastiche of many theories may even exacerbate it. What we need are not new theories of adaptation but new theories of theorization.

There are also specific theoretical reasons why the problem of theorizing adaptation has not been resolved by newer theories. Even as poststructuralism challenged structuralism and aesthetic formalism, it did not answer their unresolved questions concerning what passes in the process of adaptation or rescue adaptation from formalist and aesthetic theoretical abuse. Rather, poststructuralism exacerbated these problems. This history traces an increasing assault on adaptation by formal theories: aesthetic formalism renders separating form from content unaesthetic; structuralist semiotics renders it impossible; and poststructuralist semiotics evaporates the notion of content altogether (Elliott 2004)—so much so, that for Cardwell, (post)structuralist intertextuality "challenge[s] the very existence of the category of adaptation" (2018, 9). In so doing, it fails to explain adaptation's processes of change to suit new environments and, in its hostility to similarity, it does not theorize adaptation's repetitions. Moreover, poststructuralism *displaces* the processes of adaptation with those of deconstruction. Deconstruction and adaptation may have points in common and inform each other, but adaptation does not reduce to deconstruction. Nor did adaptation need poststructuralism to problematize its relations between originals and copies or to theorize its disruptions of hierarchical binarisms: adaptation had been doing both for centuries.

For these reasons, there have been few poststructuralist studies of adaptation; most have drawn on poststructuralism suggestively and generically (e.g., John O. Thompson 1996; Naremore 2000b; Stam 2000; Sanders [2006] 2017; Hurst 2008; Vartan 2014; Geal 2019) to dismantle adaptation's cultural and media hierarchical binarisms. Neo-translation and neo-structuralist theories feature far more prominently in adaptation studies than post-structuralist theories, as chapters in the 2017 Oxford *Handbook* (Bal; Boozer; Elleström; Raw; M.-L. Ryan; Stam) and 2018 Routledge *Companion* (Gaudreault and Marion; Geal) attest. That one of the field's most respected scholars, Stam, made a theoretical return to structuralist and dialogical theories of intertextuality in his contribution to the 2017 *Oxford Handbook* rather than developing the poststructuralist theories he propounded more than a decade earlier supports the argument that poststructuralism has been less fruitful for explicating adaptation than structuralism. Theoretical return, then, can represent a return to theories that are more hospitable to adaptation from those that are less so.

Another reason why adaptation theorization has struggled is that, while leading twenty-first-century adaptation scholars have been ready to challenge Romantic originality with poststructuralism and postmodernism, most have not substantially challenged medium specificity theory.[15] Although Hutcheon acknowledged that medium specificity is a discourse rather than a scientific fact, she presented no counterarguments to it, instead valuing it as a useful tool for studying intermedial adaptation (2006, 33 ff.). Similarly, while Stam challenged the hierarchical binarisms levied on literature and film, he subscribed to medium specificity as "The Automatic Difference" (2005, 16–24). In 2010, Christa Albrecht-Crane and Dennis R. Cutchins recommended a *return* to medium specificity theory as remedy for field marginalization:

> In order to move from the fringe of critical studies and assume the more central role we believe adaptation studies can and should fulfil, a number of important ideas must be adopted. Perhaps the most significant of these is the notion that literature and cinema are radically different from each other ... *fundamentally* different[t]. .... [W]e are arguing for a revised approach to adaptation studies that takes into account the ways in which different media contain structures and constraints unique to a particular medium. (2010b, 13–14; 21, emphasis in original)

Since the single disciplines marginalizing adaptation studies had mostly rejected medium specificity theory by this time, the recourse to it here may be an attempt to reassure single disciplines that adaptation will not transgress their disciplinary lines.

Why medium specificity persists has more to do with institutional territoriality than with theoretical difficulties. Medium specificity theories are not difficult to refute theoretically and have been refuted in adaptation studies via many epistemologies many times: logical reasoning (Leitch 2003a), empiricism and cognitive theory (Elliott 2003a), radical politics (Cartmell, Hunter, Kaye, and Whelehan 1996; 1997; 1998; 1998; 2000) postmodern and poststructuralist critiques (Sanders [2006] 2017; Hurst 2008), and cultural constructivism (Rajewsky 2002). But medium specificity persists, fueled by the economic interests of academic and media industries, as my history has shown.

Janus-Faced Adaptation Studies: Post-Theorization and Neo-Theorization

I have argued that a blend of theoretical progress and return may be generated in part by the exigencies of theorizing adaptation as a process of variation and return. As a result, adaptation requires what Leitch has nominated as a Janus-faced looking both back and forward (2005, 234). Adaptation's split temporality both resists and fosters theoretical progress and theoretical return, pulling away from and toward both.

But there are other reasons. When new theories fail to resolve old questions and debates, scholars return to discarded theories to determine what theoretical babies might have been thrown out with old theoretical bathwater. While most field histories and overviews construct a narrative of theoretical progress (Whelehan 1999; Ray 2000; Stam 2000; 2005; Aragay 2005b; Murray 2012a; Leitch 2017b), some have advocated theoretical return to retrieve and recuperate theories discarded by progressivists (Cahir 2006; Welsh 2007; Corrigan 2010; Andrew 2011; MacCabe 2011; Cattrysse 2014; Richard 2018). Leitch's history of adaptation studies, which moves through a pre-(film) history, 0.0, and versions 1.0, 2.0, and 3.0 spanning the late 1950s to the present, takes a progressivist path (2017b). By contrast, Timothy Corrigan, who joined Cartmell and Whelehan in calling for theoretical progress in the editorial introduction to the first issue of 2008, later advanced the value of engaging older and newer theories in tandem for contemporary adaptation studies:

> We need to encourage the refractive spread of adaptation studies where evolutionary progress can also be a return to positions that we may have archived too quickly—from Vachel Lindsay and Bela Balázs to Bazin and Bellour and well beyond. (2010, n.p.)

For Corrigan, modernity spans the sixteenth to the late twentieth centuries and is "the gateway to the emerging centrality of adaptation as a cultural and epistemological perspective"; following modernism, postmodernism brought about even "more fluid and pronounced versions of adaptation" (2017, 23). Even as Corrigan's chapter traces a theoretical progress, it considers how "earlier terms and perspectives have resurfaced within contemporary debates and changing directions" (2017, 33) and his student readers reprint essays by older as well as newer scholars (1999; 2011). Cardwell, discussing Corrigan, concurs with him:

> Adaptation studies would benefit from hitting "replay" and re-instituting a vital, energetic and ongoing engagement with its key terms and concepts. . . . Old definitions and debates will no longer do, but we must avoid throwing the baby out with the bathwater. (2018, 15–16)

Even progressive scholars understand the need for theoretical return in adaptation studies: Naremore's *Film Adaptation* (2000a) contains not only cutting-edge progressive studies by Ray and Stam but also a 1948 essay by Bazin as well as Andrew's 1984 essay on adaptation. In spite of their theoretical differences, Cartmell and Whelehan (2010) and MacCabe (2011) too have affirmed Bazin's contributions to adaptation studies. For all the criticisms levied against heritage adaptations (Higson 2003; 2004; Voigts-Virchow 2004, and more), adaptation scholars remain interested in heritage *theories*, as do publishers, evidenced in Routledge's 2013 five-volume series of "adaptation classics," which reprints adaptation scholarship published from the 1940s to the 1990s.

"Post-" theories have not necessarily or unilaterally produced progress for theorizing adaptation; concomitantly, returning to earlier theories has not always been a regressive or reactionary move. Even the newer theories of the theoretical *turn* engage in theoretical *return*. These dynamics are articulated in the proliferation of post- and neo- prefixes attached to theoretical stem words, as in poststructuralism, postmodernism, posthumanism, postfeminism, and postcolonialism and neo-narratology, neo-Marxism, and neo-feminism. Both prefixes undertake operations akin to adaptation: both repeat aspects of the theories they vary to suit new academic and cultural environments. Undoubtedly, the theoretical adaptations of neo- and posttheorization have helped theories that might otherwise have become extinct to survive. Progress and return and repetition and variation, then, have been essential not just to the survival of fictional stories but also to the survival of theoretical stories.

The 2000s and 2010s produced robust and expansive neo-theorization, which has often been neglected in progressivist histories that focus on posttheorization. Neo-theorization has tended to be less radical than posttheorization. When poststructuralism proved too formally radical for many structuralists, neo-structuralists were nevertheless persuaded that political and cultural issues need to be theorized, not just formal ones (Nünning 2003). Neo-formalists have also revisited and updated translation theories, pressing them beyond dyadic, comparative textual studies into multifarious con(text)ual, cross-cultural, intermedial, and/or polysystems analyses (Zatlin 2005; Chan 2012; Raw 2012; Krebs 2012; 2013; Cattrysse 2014; Smith 2016; Lee, Tan, and Stephens 2017). More specific to adaptation, the twenty-first century also produced neo-ekphrastic (Clüver 2017), neo-canonical (Szwydky 2018), neo-fidelity, neo-originality, and neo-medium specificity theories of adaptation that similarly complicated, nuanced, and sharpened prior theories. Kranz and Mellerski's *In/fidelity: Essays on Film Adaptation* (2008) rejects the binary in favor of a spectrum of essays on the subject ranging from traditional translation to radical poststructuralist approaches. The contributors to *True to the Spirit: Film Adaptation and the Question of Fidelity* (MacCabe et al. 2011) also span a theoretical spectrum. Casie Hermansson (2015), David T. Johnson (2017), and Dennis Cutchins and Kathryn Meeks (2018) have offered incisive metacritical discussions of fidelity debates that are a far cry from the simplistic "fidelity myth" discussed in Chapter 1 of this book. Similarly, scholars continue to ponder and retheorize complexly (rather than simply affirm or dismiss) originality in adaptation (Emig 2018; Jellenik 2018). Neo-medium specificity studies have also become more complex and nuanced. Arguing that if a particular formal feature can appear in two media, it cannot be specific to either, Lars Elleström devised new modes of media categorization that redress the essentialism of older theories via flexible material models that straddle many media and account for multimedial forms combining different media modalities untheorized by Lessing's binaries (Ellestöm 2010). Shannon Brownlee (2018) has pondered the challenges that digital media and identity politics present to medium specificity theory. Arguing that so-called essentialist media differences are culturally and technologically constructed just as so-called essentialist race, gender, age, and sexual differences are performed, Brownlee's chapter that "the modernist emphasis on ontology can give way to a postmodern emphasis on discourse without requiring us to abandon the concept of medium altogether" (165). Following Mary Anne Doane in resisting poststructuralist deconstructions of media differences on political grounds, Brownlee's argument is that such universal flattenings are culturally oppressive in failing to recognize and respect media and cultural differences (166). These and other twenty-first-century adaptation studies indicate that scholars still return to address the unresolved problems of older theories for adaptation—problems that post-theories have failed to resolve.

Individual scholars have also returned to reconsider prior theoretical positions. In a field that is itself continually adapting, adaptation scholars understand the necessity of both repeating and varying prior theoretical positions. In 2012, Leitch engaged in theoretical return, retracting his 2003 argument that intertextual theories would resolve the problems of adaptation studies under older formal theories, delineating their limitations for theorizing adaptation (2012a). Similarly, after Christine Geraghty championed contextual over formal adaptation study in 2007, in 2012 she returned to consider formal issues in her study of Charles Dickens's *Bleak House* adapted to television.

Such hybrid temporality often allies to hybrid theoretical methodologies and principles, as in Hutcheon's strange brew of postmodern indeterminacy and empirical methodologies. Leitch has straddled structuralist and poststructuralist theories productively, refusing both systematicity of the former and the dissipation of the latter. In 2018, he described his methodology as "empirical, particularistic, moving from observations about particular adapted and adapting texts to more general theories and back again, and ultimately unsystematic (perhaps even anti-systematic), intuitive, and playful" (Leitch and Cattrysse 2018, n.p.). Fredric Jameson has theorized adaptation using a blend of modernist medium specificity theory, high-art aestheticism, and poststructuralist Marxism (2011). Other adaptation scholars have moved productively between historicism, New Historicism, and postmodern ahistoricism. In 2017, Cartmell turned from her earlier interest in postmodern ahistoricity to a more traditional historical study: "Seventeen years later, it is apparent to me that the time of the adaptation is what we are interested in and that the context in which we place the adaptation should be within other adaptations (and other works) produced in the same period" (n.p.). For these and other scholars, myself included, theorizing *adaptively* means moving between older and newer theories that may not cohere logically, epistemologically, or methodologically with each other but may explicate adaptation more satisfactorily than adherence to single theories or logically congruous ones.

Theoretical Lack, Theoretical Pluralism, Theoretical Abandonment

For Andrew, "adaptation feeds cultural studies, a discipline born for this era of proliferation, where textual contagion counts more than does interpretation" (2011, 28). Joining the postmodern expansion of adaptation studies to ever-widening media, disciplines, nations, and cultures, the twenty-first century witnessed a drive for widening participation in the *theories* applied to adaptation. This was the product not only of theoretical trends in the humanities but also of scholarly awareness that, because adaptation is itself pluralistic, it requires pluralistic theorization: "adaptation cannot and must not rely on one theory or even one clearly prescribed set of theories only. . . . [I]ts multi- and interdisciplinary status also determines its multi-, inter-, and transtheoretical attachments" (Emig 2012, 14).

For Westbrook, theoretical lack in adaptation studies is the result of adaptation's vast macroscopic historical and temporal expanse and of its microscopic multiplicities. For this reason, "a grand unifying theory for adaptation studies is not, in fact, possible; the sheer volume of everything involved in a discussion of film adaptation is virtually immeasurable, which means that no one single theory has the capacity to encompass every aspect of an adaptation" (Westbrook 2010, 42). The best that scholars can do, his chapter argues, is to engage a postmodern theoretical pluralism, which has no hope of being able to account fully for the vast process that is adaptation, but will theorize it better than any other option.

Yet other scholars have objected to postmodern pluralism. Andrew's epigraph to this section suggests that the theoretical pluralism of postmodern cultural studies lacks interpretive depth, pursuing proliferating expanse instead, and that it lacks cohesion, proceeding by a process of contagion rather than healthy growth. In 2010, Cartmell and Whelehan discussed the pleasures of postmodern pluralism in a rhetoric of theoretical promiscuity, celebrating "the excitement of encountering in every site of adaptation an entirely new set of relations which allows us to draw promiscuously on theoretical tendencies in film and literary studies" (22).

Even so, postmodern pluralism has introduced particular challenges for adaptation studies that do not appear in single disciplines. Whereas postmodern pluralism shattered hegemonic theories in established disciplines, rendered their centripetal forces centrifugal, toppling their monolithic canons, when postmodernism entered adaptation studies the field was already piecemeal, patchy, and sharded. Nor was postmodernism the only pluralist or interdisciplinary theory seeking to theorize adaptation. Scholars have worked to connect the field's shards and patches via structuralist narratology (McFarlane 1996), postmodern pastiche (Hutcheon 2006), dialogics (Stam 2000), intertextuality Leitch 2003a), intermediality (Constantinescu 2015), and polysystems theories (Cattrysse 1992; 2014).

Pluralist theories do not agree. Although Cattrysse called adaptation studies to turn from individual to corpus studies, from single sources to multiple ones, and from author/auteur studies of particular adaptations to wider reception and industry studies through polysystems theory, commendably reintegrating textual and contextual adaptation studies rent asunder by both modernism and the theoretical turn, and calling the field to break from comparative case studies of paired works into methodological pluralism, his epistemologies and methodologies remain diametrically opposed to those of postmodern cultural studies. Katja Krebs has commended his theory of pluralism as a progress from postmodern pluralism:

> While Hutcheon, Sanders, and Leitch, to name but a few, laid the groundwork which allowed Adaptation Studies to establish itself as a field of inquiry in its own right, Cattrysse moves the field into the next necessary stage: that of developing conceptual tools which stand the test of critical investigation. (Krebs, book jacket endorsement of Cattrysse 2014)

Both Cattrysse and Krebs were trained in Europe countries where theorization—in order to qualify as theorization—must engage systematic methodologies, empirical epistemologies, and logical critical thinking.

Recalling Welsh's critiques of the theoretical turn, albeit from an entirely different theoretical tradition, in 2014, Cattrysse attacked "high" theory as theory that "only dogs can hear" (32), pitting descriptive, empirical, corpus-based methodologies against philosophical, aesthetic, and political theories, arguing that "Knowledge is reliable if one can verify it empirically . . . if a statement of fact can be demonstrated as accurate, it can be accepted as true by everyone equally" (35). However, the facts that "everyone equally" can accept as true (as universal truths) are not limited to empirical observations: in his scholarship, they include the value judgments of aesthetic and humanist theories. Continuing to promote "descriptive-explanatory" adaptation studies four years later, Cattrysse defended aesthetic "quality" as a valid criterion of judgment contiguous with and predicated on scientific evolutionary theory (2018, 52). Thus, even as he valuably opened adaptation studies to corpus *methodologies*, he closed down the corpus of *theories* and *epistemologies* permitted to theorize adaptation.

Postmodern pluralism recommends the opposite: engaging many theories, it refuses to systematize them logically, chronologically, or hierarchically, arguing that empiricism is neither objective nor factual, but is the subjective cultural construction of dominant groups, all the more deceptive and pernicious because it lays claim to fact and universality. Far from universal, shared truth, Westbrook called for a postmodern "glorious plurality" of theories that would allow critics to "choose from a candy store of available approaches: semiotics, feminist criticism, Russian Formalism, media studies—the whole menu" (2010, 43). His inclusion of Russian Formalism and invocation of "the whole menu" aligns him more with Hutcheon than with Cartmell and Whelehan in his theoretical ecumenism. However, the candy store metaphor implies that no theory is essential to a nutritionally balanced field and that all theories are dispensable. Moreover, such ecumenical optionality remains problematic not only for those whose theories of theorization require logic, empiricism, and systematicity to qualify as theorization but also for those whose theories are predicated upon opposing other theories deemed to be politically, ethically, and culturally pernicious. If for Cattrysse postmodern pluralist candy is frivolous and inessential, for Cartmell and Whelehan, some of the candy is decidedly bad for the field.

Developing adaptation studies as an interdisciplinary field cannot take the form of mandating universal agreement on epistemologies, values, ideologies, and methodologies or even agreement on what theorization is and should do: other fields do not require this to exist as fields, while the disciplinary, historical, and geographical range of adaptation studies renders universal agreement even more of an impossibility than in single disciplines. Yet development as a field does require *dialogue* between disciplines and theories, including dialogue between contesting forms of theoretical pluralism. Leitch and Cattrysse engaged in just such a debate, published by *Literature/ Film Quarterly* in 2018. Concluding his remarks, Leitch recommended theoretical pluralism as a way to navigate theoretical differences:

In the absence of a single consensual theory, we [should] work toward a theory of theories . . . a grammar of theories seems like a less impossible goal than the dream of a common theory, and one that's likely to engage a wider array of scholars who don't necessarily agree about anything else. (Leitch 2018b, n.p.)

Leitch understood that the free-for-all advanced by postmodernism pluralism is not really free for scholars pursuing other kinds of pluralism. Positing a middle ground between postmodern arbitrariness and structuralist systematicity, "a theory of theories" requires a degree of metacritical analysis, while a "a grammar of theories" requires a degree of systematicity; even so, a system akin to grammar is more malleable and variable, more hospitable to change over time than the universally agreed-upon facts to which empirical systematicity lays claim. It allows for diversity and freedom at the same time as it creates structures that set theories in relation to each other like parts of speech in a sentence.

Joining theoretical pluralism, theoretical wars, and theoretical compromise, the 2010s have witnessed a movement toward theoretical abandonment. This is also a theoretical position—or rather, a range of theoretical positions. In 2011, MacCabe agreed with Westbrook that "the number of variables involved in any adaptation from the linguistic form of the novel or short story to a film's matters of expression approach infinity" (2011, 8). However, while Westbrook recommended postmodern theoretical pluralism as a response, MacCabe opted for theoretical abandonment: "There are thus no models of how to adapt in this volume" (2011, 8). The reference to "models" indicates that MacCabe's theory of theorization is prescriptive and practitioner-based ("how to adapt"), which he deems impossible in a field as microscopically and macroscopically vast as adaptation studies. However, he readily embraces auteur theories in his own adaptation study, and his opposition to prescriptive models of adaptation is partly predicated on the theories of originality and genius to which he subscribes.

In his conclusion to *The Oxford Handbook of Adaptation Studies*, wittily titled, "Against Conclusions: Petit Theories and Adaptation Studies," Leitch too has called adaptation studies to abandon its quest for "dogmas," "organizing principles," or "a set of solutions to consensual problems" to pursue "petit Theory," defined as "a series of working hypotheses . . . that might be true and might not . . . but help us think better" (2017c, 703–4). Like Hutcheon, Leitch has tied analytical methodologies to indeterminate philosophies to oppose large-scale, synthetic theorization in favor small-scale, piecemeal theorization based in questions. Both have rejected fixed, final, definitive, or satisfying answers; in so doing, both promote an adaptive theory of theorization. But there are differences between the two. While for Hutcheon the questions Who? What? Why? How? Where? remain constant, with the variable, eclectic answers providing the variation, for Leitch the chief value of answers is as springboards to new questions. Both Hutcheon's repetition of the same questions in varied environments and Leitch's incremental adaptation of theorization via Q&A produce adaptive theorization that adapts theorization to and through adaptation. Yet Hutcheon's methodology is more concerned with answers, while Leitch's is more concerned with questions.

Conclusion to the History

In 2014, Patrick Cattrysse referred readers to prior field histories rather than write one himself, while critiquing prior histories as incomplete: "No one can claim . . . to have studied all publications ever published in the field" (2014, 21–22). All histories must be partial, in both senses of the word—incomplete and reflecting the partialities of their authors. The actual history of theorizing adaptation reaches much farther back than mine and will continue after it; it is spread more widely across nations, cultures, disciplines, and media than mine, and extends beyond the particular research questions that have informed it. But the partial nature of all histories should not be grounds for refusing to write histories. All fields benefit from multiple, constantly rewritten, *adapting* histories. New histories not only keep a field up to date but also redress the omissions, distortions, and errors of prior histories. In fact, the worst outcome of my history of theorizing adaptation would be if it were to be treated as a final, definitive history. More histories of theorizing adaptation are needed—multiple histories that debate with and build on prior ones.

History is essential to understanding adaptation's relationship to theorization for many reasons, not the least of which is that it shows theorization to be historically contingent rather than universal. A history of theorizing adaptation underscores how much particular, local political, cultural, economic, industrial, and academic institutions affect and employ theorization for their agendas; concomitantly, it identifies transhistorical dynamics that do not emerge in localized historical studies. It also identifies theoretical changes and theoretical alliances for adaptation that do not emerge in studies governed by a single theory.

This history has challenged humanities histories of theorizing adaptation that chart a march of theoretical progress: it tells a story of theoretical return—of theories that have refused to die, of theories that seemed to be extinct but reappeared like recessive genes decades or centuries on. It locates these processes not to complain of the failure of scholars to progress but to highlight the ways in which theorization has failed adaptation and in which scholars have adapted theorization to the returns and progresses of adaptation itself. Similarly, this history suggests that adaptation's own pluralism has attracted pluralist theorization (Andrew 2011, 28), and that even calls for theoretical abandonment may express adaptation's own blithe abandonment of theoretical principles.

This history of theorizing adaptation has also focused on the rising and falling theoretical fortunes of adaptation. A history of theorizing adaptation in earlier centuries, when adaptation was theorized as a good theoretical object, is illuminating for theorizing adaptation more positively now; even a history of how adaptation became a bad theoretical object reveals ways to theorize adaptation more constructively, serving as a cautionary tale for scholars today.

The transhistorical resistances of adaptation and theorization in this history suggest that there are larger systemic problems between the processes of adaptation and theorization in the humanities. This conclusion to the history therefore calls for another perspective, another mode of discourse to probe them further. The title of this history, "Theorizing Adaptation," articulates a one-way, top-down process in which adaptation is "-ized" by theories, a hierarchy that has not been sufficiently redressed by the philosophical skepticism and cultural revolutions of the theoretical turn. Part II of this book, therefore, works to invert the hierarchy that is "Theorizing Adaptation" with a reciprocal, inverse discourse of "Adapting Theorization" that calls humanities theorization to adapt to and through adaptation.

PART II
ADAPTING THEORIZATION

SECTION I
RETHEORIZING THEORIZATION: INTRODUCTION

It is customary to conclude histories of adaptation studies by valorizing particular theories or methodologies over or against others. To cite just a few examples from my history, in 1996, Brian McFarlane urged adaptation studies to turn away from the impressionism of aesthetic formalism to the rigors of structuralist narratology; in 1999, Imelda Whelehan called the field to take a theoretical turn away from aesthetic formalism toward radical politics and postmodern pluralism; Simone Murray concluded her history of theorizing adaptation in *The Adaptation Industry* (2012a) with an appeal to move away from textually based humanities theories to sociological ones; in 2014, Patrick Cattrysse pitted polysystems theories against postmodern pluralism. Yet in 2017, Thomas Leitch bookended *The Oxford Handbook of Adaptation Studies* with an introduction surveying prior field theorization and a conclusion calling for the replacement of master theories with a methodology of asking questions, positing answers, asking questions of those answers to generate new answers, ad infinitum. For Leitch, "what adaptation scholars most need is not new theories, but new attitudes towards theories" (2017c, 702). Following their histories of theorizing adaptation, these scholars, and many more, have advocated field retheorization: some by revolution, others by incremental change; some by a shift in epistemologies, others by a change in methodologies.

I too transition from Part I's history to call for field retheorization in Part II, "Adapting Theorization." As the title suggests, I do so not by valorizing some theories over others or by devising a new theory to supersede prior theories, but by working to adapt theorization. Instead of asking, "What's wrong with humanities adaptation studies and how can theorization fix it?" I ask, "What's wrong with humanities theorization and how can adaptation fix it?" The first half of Part II, "Retheorizing Theorization," takes a metatheoretical purview, pondering how theories of theorization in the humanities have situated it in relation to what it theorizes generally and to adaptation particularly. Its central argument is that humanities theorization has failed to theorize adaptation satisfactorily for most scholars not because the field has been using the "wrong" theories, or because adaptation's innumerable variables and vast cultural and disciplinary sprawl make it impossible to theorize, or because theorization cannot ever definitively explicate anything that it theorizes, or because adaptation falls between disciplines, cultures, and media and becomes fodder in their wars. These may be factors exacerbating "the problem of theorizing adaptation" raised in the Introduction to this book, but the more fundamental problem arises from tensions between what adaptation is and does as a process and what theorization is and does as a process. Theirs is a mutual resistance: if adaptation fails theorization, it is equally the case that theorization fails adaptation. Adaptation refuses to cede to the subservient role accorded it by theories of what theorization is and should do in the humanities; theorization, in turn, resists adaptation when it fails to conform to its tenets, denigrating, opposing, and ignoring it; even so, adaptation continues to resist theorization, blithely surviving and thriving in culture and practice, even when theorization pronounces it to be a theoretical impossibility, offending theorists as it promiscuously shifts theoretical allegiances, never fully aligning itself to any.

Humanities theorization has failed to recognize adaptation as a rival process vying with theorization to adapt other things and processes to itself, including theorization. Humanities theorization, then, has not only failed to theorize adaptation, it has also failed to theorize its own troubled relationship to adaptation. Instead, it has continued to theorize its relationship to adaptation, as it does whatever it theorizes, as a largely one-way, top-down process. Whether theories are positivist or indeterminate, whether they are radical or conservative, whether they are cultural or formal, whether they are abstract or material, whether they engage logical, empirical, hermeneutic, aesthetic, ethical, political, cultural, formal, or any other kind of epistemologies and methodologies, adaptation resists them all, not because they are theoretically incorrect but because of what adaptation is and does, in opposition to what humanities theorization is and does. The task of "Retheorizing Theorization" is to diagnose and retheorize their problematic relationship.

I owe the structure of "Retheorizing Theorization" to Paul de Man, via Brett Westbrook. Westbrook pondered adaptation's resistance to theory by adapting de Man's "The Resistance to Theory" (1986) to an essay titled,

"Being Adaptation: The Resistance to Theory" (2010). In contrast to de Man and adaptation scholars at the turn of the twenty-first century, Westbrook did not focus on adaptation studies' resistance to the theories of the theoretical turn but on the resistance of adaptation to theorization *generally*. While de Man proposed one theory to rule all others (poststructuralism), Westbrook recommended postmodern theoretical pluralism (Chapter 4). However, as I argued there, if the problem of theorizing adaptation in the humanities is theorization's *relationship* to adaptation, applying more theories to adaptation will not resolve it. Replacing one tyrannical master with many masters, however weak, benevolent, or variegated, continues and may even exacerbate the hierarchy. Theories may mitigate each other's power via pluralism, like feuding tribes, and their ongoing feuds may tarnish humanities theorization's claims to truth, but they do not mitigate the problems of those over whom they feud, and pluralism does not redress the relationship between theorization and what it theorizes.

"Retheorizing Theorization," therefore, takes a metatheoretical approach, setting theories of theorization in dialogue with theories of adaptation. Following the three stages of theorization discussed in de Man's and Westbrook's essays—definition, taxonomization, and theoretical principles—it goes beyond subjecting adaptation to the three stages of theorization: it equally subjects theorization to its own three stages. Indeed, one of the most surprising and welcome findings of this research has been that theorization also resists its own processes and stages.

5

Redefining Definitions

Theorization typically begins with definitions. Before a subject can be theorized, it must be defined: even poststructuralist theorist Paul de Man, who challenged the possibility of definition, conceded that all theorists, including himself, must begin with "the most elementary task of scholarship, the delimitation of the corpus" (1986, 5). In spite of his theoretical radicalism, de Man did not dispute theorization's right to dominate what it theorizes. Right from its first stage, the top-down operations of theorization are apparent: theorization decides the nature and identity of what it theorizes.

This chapter challenges that view through metatheoretical discussion of how the *processes* of definition, as well as specific definitions of adaptation, have situated adaptation in relation to theorization. It begins by defining "definition," continues by considering some problems of defining "adaptation," and ends with recommendations for redefining the relationship between theorization and adaptation.

Defining Definition

Definition is a relational process: defining a word requires establishing relations between it and other words. These relations are epitomized by dictionary definitions, which define words through synonyms and syntactic contexts. Although the main argument of this chapter is that adaptation resists theoretical definition, definition is akin to adaptation: both establish relations by navigating similarities and differences between entities and related others and by relations of entities to their contexts. Definition, then, shares conceptual and processual features in common with adaptation that should render them compatible. In humanities theorization, however, they are not, because of how theorization defines definition and what it charges definition with doing to what it theorizes via definition.

The *Oxford English Dictionary* defines "definition" as "a precise statement of the essential nature of a thing" (*OED*, 2nd rev. ed., s.v. "definition,"

Theorizing Adaptation. Kamilla Elliott, Oxford University Press (2020). © Oxford University Press.
DOI: 10.1093/oso/9780197511176.001.0001

definition 4, accessed March 19, 2018, http://www-oed-com/view/Entry/ 48886); "the action of making definite" (*OED*, "definition," definition 5); "stating exactly what a thing is" (*OED*, "definition," definition 3); and "the setting of bounds or limits; limitation, restriction" (*OED*, "definition," definition 1). It defines "adaptation" as "the action or process of adapting one thing to fit with another, or suit specified conditions, esp. a new or changed environment" (*OED*, "adaptation," definition 2.a). Although this definition may qualify as "a precise statement of the essential nature of [adaptation]," "stating exactly what [adaptation] is," defining adaptation fails to fix it or make it definite in the way that humanities theorization requires. Corinne Lhermitte (2004) documents that adaptation has connoted transformation, adjustment, and appropriation from its first appearance in the thirteenth century. Thus, although adaptation can be defined verbally, *its definition* resists the definition of "definition" as a process of fixing, exactness, precision, and essentialism. As a process of ongoing change, adaptation's dictionary definition fails to set bounds, limits, and restrictions on it. Mark Fortier has therefore advocated an open-ended definition of "adaptation," since adaptation's only certainty is "change . . . with origin and constancy adrift and always at risk" (2014, 374–75). Fortier's argument is in part the product of post-theoretical resistance to fixed definition, which argues for the impossibility of definition generally; however, adaptation is *etymologically* resistant to definition and was so long before the theoretical turn in the humanities. Refusing synonymity with definition's definitions, adaptation presents itself as an antonym to definition. It equally resists post-theoretical concepts of the resistance to definition: their resistance is based in philosophical skepticism and indeterminacy; adaptation's derives from change to suit new environments. Although Stephen Price considers that "Adaptation offers the most familiar illustration of the play of presence, absence, and ghostliness" (2010, 53), Timothy Corrigan's "historical survey" of "Defining Adaptation" "demonstrates the scope of adaptation as different practices and evolving definitions" (2017, 28). Like Fortier, Corrigan concludes that, "because its activities and perspectives continue to evolve rapidly, there cannot be any single or stable definition of adaptation" (2017, 34). Jillian Saint Jacques makes the astute observation that

> there will always be something about adaptation—both in theory and praxis—that we cannot know, that we will never know, as the presence of

adaptation at any cultural interstices indicates the interplay between disparate bodies of work emerging in a process of change. (2011b, 40–41)

Contrary to poststructuralist theories that *différance* lies in the gaps, adaptation fills those gaps with processes of change forged through differential similarities that construct new relations between entities and contexts, resisting
not only the fixed essentialism of definition but also poststructuralist theories of resistance to definition.

Defining Adaptation

When the *Oxford English Dictionary* defines adaptation as modifying something to suit new conditions, it presents adaptation as product, process, and a
combination of the two:

> 3 a. The quality or state of being adapted or suitable for a particular use,
> purpose, or function, or to a particular environment; adaptedness.
>   6. A result of a process of adapting or being adapted; an adapted or mod-
> ified version or form. (*OED*, 2nd. ed., s.v. "adaptation," accessed June 5,
> 2017, http://www-oed-com/view/Entry/2115)

Brian McFarlane defined adaptation as both product and process in 199, as
did Sarah Cardwell in 2002; Hutcheon built on their work, adding a third definition to render adaptation a product, a process of production, and a process
of consumption (2006). In 2015, Nico Dicecco suggested a functional definition of adaptation that defines it by what it *does* rather than what it *is* (162).
   In contrast to these variegated definitions, the *Oxford English Dictionary*
narrows its definition of humanities adaptation to a product:

> 4. An altered or amended version of a text, musical composition, etc., (now
> esp.) one adapted for filming, broadcasting, or production on the stage
> from a novel or similar literary source. (*OED*, 2nd. ed., s.v. "adaptation,"
> accessed June 5, 2017, http://www-oed-com/view/Entry/2115)

This definition reflects the predominant focus of humanities adaptation studies on adaptation as aesthetic product; the "now esp." further

indicates adaptation studies' primary focus on literature in performance, especially film.

A Rose by Any Other Name...

My history of theorizing adaptation demonstrates that adaptation has been a rose by many other names, multiplying rather than narrowing or fixing its definition for theorization. Because adaptation is implicated in almost everything, its many manifestations, as well as its many near relations, have generated a panoply of synonyms and alternative terminologies for adaptation. Compounding historical terminological changes discussed in Chapter 2, the pluralism of twenty-first-century adaptation studies has produced an explosion of words synonymically defining and metonymically substituting for adaptation. In 2006, Julie Sanders and Robert Stam located alternative terminologies for adaptation in prior scholarship and generated more of their own. These included *borrowing, stealing, inheriting, assimilating, influence, inspiration, dependency, indebtedness, haunting, possession, homage, mimicry, travesty, echo, allusion*, and *intertextuality* (Sanders [2006] 2017, citing Poole 2004); *variation, version, interpretation, imitation, proximation, supplement, increment, improvisation, prequel, sequel, continuation, addition, paratext, hypertext, palimpsest, graft, rewriting, reworking, refashioning, re-visioning, re-evaluation, bricolage*, and *pastiche* (Sanders [2006] 2017, 3–4); *reading, rewriting, critique, translation, transmutation, metamorphosis, recreation, transvocalization, resuscitation, transfiguration, actualization, transmodalization, signifying, performance, dialogization, cannibalization, re-envisioning, incarnation*, and *re-accentuation* (Stam 2005, 25). In 2013, Eckart Voigts-Virchow added *protocol* (Moore 2010), *murder* (Marsh 2011), *phantom* (S. Murray 2008), *vampire* (Leitch 2011), *theatre* (Ley 2009), and *mimicry* (Emig 2012), recommending two more: *citability* (Benjamin [1936] 1968) and *iterability* (Balkin 1987). These lists do not exhaust the terminology that has defined or glossed adaptation, nor do scholars consider them to be definitive of adaptation in toto: "No single term has so far captured the essence of the field"; "terminological multiplicity should be a welcome effect of researching Adaptation Studies, as it is a field without an essence" (Voigts-Virchow 2013, 63).

Joining adaptation's resistance to essentialist definition and its multiple definitions across fields, disciplines, media, cultures, and eras are the definitions levied on adaptation by theorization. Voigts-Virchow's conclusion is the product of postmodern philosophy, as are the alternative terminologies *pastiche, palimpsest,* and *bricolage. Dialogization* derives from Mikhail Bakhtin's theory of dialogics; *imitation* invokes Augustan theories of adaptation; *intertextuality* and *supplement* articulate poststructuralist theories; *mimicry* and *assimilation* are postcolonial paradigms; *paratext, hypertext, prequel, sequel,* and *transmodalization* derive from structuralist narratology; *inspiration, transformation, transfiguration, incarnation, recreation,* and *metamorphosis* articulate the pseudo-religious philosophies underpinning humanist, Romantic, and metaphysical theories of art. Gothic motifs of *vampirism, haunting,* and *possession* are often infused with the psychoanalytic theories that have recently dominated Gothic studies, while *actualization, revocalization,* and *realization* draw on cognitive and phenomenological media theories. *Homage, inheriting, influence, echo, allusion, indebtedness,* and *travesty* are central to canonical aesthetic theories, while *appropriation, plagiarism, cannibalization, mutation,* and *travesty* (again) are regularly invoked in political challenges to high art. Such synonyms make clear that the definition of adaptation does not necessarily (or even often) precede the formulation of theoretical principles, as the three stages of theorization prescribe: rather, adaptation's definition often *derives from and is already subjected to theoretical principles.* Theorization, then, has not only failed to define adaptation definitively, it has also created closed circles, in which definitions do not pre-exist theoretical principles but are defined and predetermined by them. Here, humanities theorization's refusal to subject its own processes to its own stages of theorization may well inspire laughter or outrage.

Alternative terminologies for adaptation also derive from the second stage of theorization—from those taxonomies we call academic disciplines. Each discipline engages different terminologies prioritizing its subject matter: language scholars have focused on adaptation as translation; literary academics have defined adaptation as a form of reading, (re)writing, and literary criticism; theater scholars have defined adaptation as performance; music critics engage a rhetoric of transposition. Cross-disciplinary humanities studies such as semiotics, narrative studies, media studies, and cultural studies also define adaptation in their interdisciplinary images: as a mode of semiotic, narrative, media, cultural, or ideological transfer, subsumed by interdisciplinary terminologies such as intertextuality, remediation, transmodalization, and multimodality.

When theories and disciplines define adaptation with their synonyms, they theorize and discipline it on their terms. Often, this has been expressed in a rhetoric of an actor cast in a role where it performs *as* something other. The following twenty-first-century titles and sub-titles illustrate:

"Adaptation as Rewriting" (Lhermitte 2004)

"Adaptation as Writerly Praxis" (Messier 2014)

"Adaptation as Translation" (Koff 2018)

"Adaptation as In-Depth Dialogue" (Geerts 2017)

"Adaptation as (Re)Interpretation and (Re)Creation" (Deutelbaum 2016)

"Adaptation as Textuality, Intertextuality, and Metatextuality" (Bolton 2017)

"Adaptation as Critique" (Rizk 2015)

"Adaptation as Critic" (Elliott 2014c)

"Adaptation as Analysis" (Smol 2018)

"Adaptation as a Philosophical Problem" (Jameson 2011)

"Adaptation as an Undecidable" (Hurst 2008)

"Adaptation as Connection" (Schober 2013)

"Adaptation as the Art Form of Democracy" (Cartmell 2012b)

"Adaptation as Compendium" (Elliott 2010)

"Adaptation as Reception" (Scholz 2009)

"Adaptation as Cultural Production" (Hutcheon 2007)

"Adaptation[...] as Cultural Event[...]" (Scholz 2013)

"Adaptation as City Branding" (Herrmann 2018)

"Adaptation as Exploration" (Krämer 2015)

"Adaptation as Exploitation" (Cartmell 2017)

"Adaptation as Hospitality" (Chun 2014)

"Adaptation as Salvage" (Conroy 2018)

"Adaptation as Dissimulation" (Dicecco 2011)

The question arises, do these other words define, approximate, or displace adaptation? On the one hand, adaptation is undeniably implicated in many of the things that gloss it and is capable of performing as many things, so that such definitions illumine aspects of adaptation. On the other hand, such rhetoric makes adaptation recede from view, just as the focus on the actor-as-character is not often one of mutual and reciprocal exchange but one in which the task of the actor is to recede from view to foreground the performed character. In the process, adaptation takes a back seat to its alternative terminologies. Thus, even as such rhetoric demonstrates the vitality and relevance of adaptation to an ever-growing array of media, industries, technologies, disciplines, theories, nations, eras, and related processes, it equally indicates how adaptation is more often than not studied as instrumental to and a performer of other things, rather than as a process in its own right.

I illustrate this argument with what may be adaptation's closest relation, translation. Chapter 2 of this book documents that the terms "adaptation" and "translation" have been used interchangeably (see also Krebs 2013). While defining adaptation as a type of translation is a perfectly legitimate enterprise, illuminating both terms, such definition generally serves as a prelude to theorizing adaptation under translation theories. While change to suit a new environment does encompass linguistic change to suit a new linguistic environment, George L. Bastin has observed that "the study of adaptation encourages the theorist to look beyond purely linguistic issues"; it is "both a local and global procedure"; it goes beyond translation to engage in "a creative process" (1998, 6).

If adaptation can be defined as a type of translation, so too translation can be defined as a type of adaptation. More often than not, adaptation is held up as a bad type among better types: a bad kind of aesthetic production, a wrong kind of semiotics, a pernicious manifestation of cultural politics, a bad translation (Elliott 2018). Thus, while adaptation and translation have shared theoretical fortunes to a degree—for example, translation studies has also been denigrated and charged with a fixation on fidelity criticism (Minier 2013; see Chapter 1 of this book), for many translation scholars, adaptation is the name given to the worst kind of translation, a type that does not even qualify as translation. *The Routledge Encyclopedia of Translation Studies* opens its entry on adaptation with this (anti)definition: "Adaptation may be understood as a set of translative interventions which result in a text that is not generally accepted as a translation." It continues: "the term may embrace numerous vague notions such as appropriation, domestication, imitation, rewriting, and so on"; it concludes that "the concept of adaptation requires recognition of translation as non-adaptation" (1998, 3). Surveying adaptation's history in translation studies, the article attests: "Generally speaking, many historians and scholars continue to take a negative view of adaptation, dismissing the phenomenon as a distortion" (1998, 3).

Conversely, translation has been figured as a bad type of adaptation within adaptation studies. As Katja Krebs has observed, adaptation is associated with creative freedom and translation with confinement (2013, 3). At the turn of the twenty-first century, James Naremore criticized translation both as "a metaphor for adaptation" that distorts its definition and for subjecting adaptation to "dominant critical approaches" from translation studies (2000b, 7–9), preferring the auteuristic, anti-translation theory propounded by Wagner. Pitting translation against adaptation also fueled theoretical wars within adaptation studies at the baseline of definition when Linda Cahir (2006) and Patrick Cattrysse (2014) advocated defining and theorizing adaptation as translation in order to exile postmodern cultural theories from adaptation studies. Moving beyond these antagonist relations, other recent scholars have shown that the two processes share many things in common and often occur concurrently (Venuti 2007; Milton 2009; Raw 2012; Krebs 2012; Minier 2013).

Some scholars have recommended that alternative terminologies *replace* adaptation. We have seen that Cahir sought to replace it with translation; other potential substitute definitions have included the structuralist narratological terms discussed by Hutcheon (2006, 15), as well as *imitation* (Griffith 1997), *remediation* (Bolter and Grusin 1999), *intertextuality* (Moeller and Lellis 2002, 6; Leitch 2003a), *appropriation* (Sanders 2006), *transformation* (Frus and Williams 2010), *intermediality* (Sisley qtd. by Punzi 2007, 16; Constantinescu 2015), and *intership* (Bal 2017b). Catalin Constantinescu has argued that "the term intermediality should be preferred over transmediality, intertextuality, bricolage, Verfilmung, adaptation or Ekphrasis, as it covers better and more adequately the complexity of relationships between film and literature" (2015, abstract). However, his argument that "adaptation cannot be conceived in the absence of intermediality" (2015, 174) does not take into account adaptations within the same medium, which are prominent in the history of adaptation. In 2007, Christine Geraghty assessed that "intertextuality is the beginning not the end" of adaptation study, expressing concern that the term, for all its democratizing impulses, continues to give priority to source texts (193–34). Responding to longstanding suggestions that intertextuality should displace or contain adaptation as a subcategory, Cardwell objected astutely that intertextuality gives "a somewhat misleading impression of breadth and openness while actually dominating and constraining our remit" (2018, 15). Clearly, defining adaptation can be an act of theoretical and disciplinary colonization that obscures adaptation as a subject, field, and interdiscipline. Defining adaptation as other things at worst displaces it as the subject of discourse and at best renders it secondary to another primary subject of discourse.

In some cases, calls to displace adaptation with other terminologies have been the product of theoretical progressivism. For Cardwell, theoretical progressivism prematurely rejected older definitions of adaptation:

> Thoughtful challenges to key concepts which once served to define and delimit adaptation (e.g., original/source/ur-text, interpretation/translation) too often lead to the words being summarily cast aside; alternative, looser, and more fashionable terms (e.g., meta- and inter-textuality and inter- and trans-mediality) proliferate; potentially valuable distinctions between adaptation and related practices become blurred; and adaptation becomes harder and harder to pin down. (2018, 8)

In other cases, alternative terminologies have been proposed to overcome adaptation's bad theoretical rap. In the twentieth and twenty-first centuries, Walter Benjamin's theory of mechanical reproduction ([1936] 1968), Roland Barthes's of mythologies ([1957] 1972), Gérard Genette's of literature in the second degree ([1982] 1997), Bolter and Grusin's of remediation (1999), and Henry Jenkins's of convergence culture (2006) all address adaptation without naming it as such, as do many other intertextual, intersemiotic, intermedial, and intercultural studies (Rajewsky 2005; Chan 2012). Films of Shakespeare's plays have more frequently been nominated performances than adaptations (Worthen 2014). Mieke Bal has written: "Although we don't want to call our film Madame B an adaptation of *Madame Bovary*, it can be considered as one. We just so dislike the premises of most adaptations of that novel that we refrain from calling it so" (personal communication, March 30, 2014). In a later essay, Bal went further to recommend a change in adaptation's terminology to rehabilitate adaptation:

> I propose to suspend the term "adaptation" and replace it with "intership." That noun brings together all activities qualified with the preposition inter- , from interdisciplinary to intertextual, international, intermedial, intercultural to interdiscursive. Inter- means between. It denotes a willingness to exchange on an equal basis. (2017b, 179)

While I am in sympathy with Bal's efforts to democratize the relationship between adapted and adapting entities, "intership" does not democratize the relationship between adaptation and theorization, which is the central concern of this book. Until we redress that relationship, changing the name will not do away with adaptation's status as a bad theoretical object any more than changing what white Americans nominate the descendants of African slaves has redressed racism in the United States. Each time a new name is proposed with a view to eliminating racism, the name gradually becomes as racist as prior names, because racist ideas about African Americans persist. Similarly, until adaptation is respected by humanities theorization as an equal, changing the name will do nothing to redress its opprobrious treatment by "theorism." When theorization fails adaptation at its first stage of definition, it is little wonder that scholars have had so much difficulty theorizing adaptation.

Everything Is an Adaptation . . .

In contrast to the *Oxford English Dictionary*'s narrow definition of adaptation in the humanities, adaptation is not limited to texts and media adapting to each other formally under translation or media theories: as many adaptation scholars attest, it extends to contexts—media industries and technologies, cultures and societies, historical eras and geographical locations, economic and legal structures, psychological processes, and more. It also spills out from the media disciplines in which it has been studied into other humanities and social sciences disciplines, a process epitomized by publications such as *The Adaptation of History* (Raw and Tutan 2012), *Adaptation Studies and Learning* (Raw and Gurr 2013), and "Psychology and Adaptation" (Raw 2014). Beyond the humanities, adaptation is studied in biology (Darwin [1859] 2009; [1871] 2004; Mendel [1865] 1866; Watson and Crick 1953), sociology (Dawkins 2006), psychology (Buss 1999), technology (Kauffman 1993), migration (Bettini 2017), and climate change (Pelling 2011).

Daniel Fischlin and Mark Fortier have assessed that, "writ large, adaptation includes almost any act of alteration performed upon specific cultural works of the past and dovetails with a general process of cultural creation" (2000, 4). Their "almost" reminds that not everything is an adaptation, even in biology (Le Page 2008). Moreover, what adapts or is adapted cannot be defined solely by its adaptive properties and processes. Yet even narrowed to Fischlin and Fortier's definition of altering "specific cultural works of the past," adaptation spans a broad representational continuum ranging from allusions to generic intertextuality, from outright plagiarism to unconscious reference, from multimedia global franchises (Krasilovsky 2018) to single works adapting themselves internally, as in illustrated literature and worded films (Elliott 2003a, Chapters 2–3). Beyond such specifics, "adaptation writ large" is an amorphous, connective entity that precedes and exceeds any entities, contexts, and systems, encompassing not only all adaptation processes and products but also those who adapt and those who study it. It is a larger process, older than us, that also adapts us and will outlive us.[1]

Within the humanities, Hans-Bernhard Moeller and George Lellis have argued that "all creation can be considered adaptation" (2002, 6). The notion that everything is an adaptation is not a new one. In "The Perambulatory Movement" (1856), Leigh Ritchie admired "this remarkable invention—or adaptation, since it is ruled that everything is an adaptation now-a-days," the passive voice indicating that this notion was then a common idiom (116). Similar ideas were advanced a century prior in *The Monthly Review*: "Never was invention at a lower ebb. One would think that every thing [*sic*] has been said" ("Review of *Giphantia*" 1761, 223). The question arises, if every cultural creation is an adaptation, how do we define adaptation in a way that sets it apart from the many things it inhabits, of which it is only a part? The *Oxford English Dictionary* itself cedes the impossibility of defining "everything": "the subst. element has usually no definable meaning. . . . The distributive sense etymologically belonging to the word is often absent" (*OED*, 2nd rev. ed., s.v. "everything," definition 1.a, accessed April 12, 2018, http://www-oed-com/ view/Entry/65347). Here, adaptation not only extends to "everything," it further shares "everything's" problematic relationship to definition. And yet in spite of its semantic elusiveness, the *Oxford English Dictionary* defines "everything" as characterizing something "of supreme importance" (*OED*, "everything," definition 1.c). It is thus astonishing—and telling—that adaptation has been deemed *unimportant* and unworthy of study by so many humanities theories. Yet when we define adaptation as a rival cultural process to theorization, it becomes clear that adaptation is threatening to theorization not only in its resistance to it but also in its far greater reach.

Leading adaptation scholars, recognizing the breadth of adaptation, even when limited to aesthetic productions, have sought to narrow its definition. Worrying that since "[e]very representational film adapts a prior conception . . . [this] may encourage a hopelessly broad view of adaptation," Andrew defined "adaptation in the narrow sense" as "the restricted view of adaptation from known texts in other art forms," " works . . . announcing themselves as versions of some standard whole" (1984b, 97). Intriguingly, in spite of her commitment to postmodern pluralism, Hutcheon joined Andrew in limiting her definition of "adaptation proper" to "an extended, deliberate, announced revisitation of a particular work of art" (2006, 170), departing from Andrew only in not requiring a change in medium. Hutcheon's narrowed definition was both produced by and at odds with her postmodern widening of the field. Having opened the field to so many new media, she explained: "From a pragmatic point of view, such vast definition would clearly make adaptation rather difficult to theorize" (2006, 9).

Hutcheon's narrowed definition has been challenged for excluding modes that others consider to be adaptation: allusion and quotation (Brinch 2013, 235); fan fiction, fan films, remakes, sequels, and spin-offs (Verevis 2006; Jess-Cooke 2009; Loock and Verevis 2012), and unconscious and unintentional adaptations (Cartmell and Whelehan, 2010; Hayton 2011; L. Burke 2015). Similarly, although Leitch commended Hutcheon's distinction between adaptation and intertextuality, he remained unconvinced that adaptation's definition should lie as much in the mind of consumers as she indicated (2012a, 95).

Poststructuralist intertextuality, postmodern pluralism, and dialogics also expanded adaptation beyond translation binaries, individual works, and political dialectics into multiplicities, pressing adaptation toward infinity. Unlike biological adaptation, to which intermedial adaptation has been compared (Elliott 2003a; 2012a; Hutcheon 2006; Voigts-Virchow 2006; Bortolotti and Hutcheon 2007; Boyd 2009; 2017), humanities adaptation studies has no mathematical formulae to order its processes, no chemical tests to track its minutiae. For Westbrook (2010) and MacCabe (2011), humanities adaptation's microscopic immensity may be more infinite than its large-scale sprawl.

Yet despite these dynamics and critiques, adaptation as defined by Andrew and Hutcheon prevails: indeed, Andrew's 1984 definition was ratified by the *Oxford English Dictionary* in 1989: "An altered or amended version of a text, musical composition, etc., (now esp.) one adapted for filming, broadcasting, or production on the stage from a novel or similar literary source" (*OED*, "adaptation," definition 4). More recently, Cardwell too defined adaptation as "the purposeful refitting of material from one artistic context to another" (2018, 13).

A narrowed definition of adaptation persists in part because it serves the adaptation industry as well as academic paradigms. It too defines adaptation narrowly in marketing, crediting, financial, and legal practices: for example, my history of theorizing adaptation shows how Romantic and modernist theories of individual artist agency shaped copyright laws and how medium specificity theory increases sales by differentiating adaptations in different media. These and other similar dynamics go some way toward explaining why, in the adaptation industry, adaptation supersedes the alternative terminologies recommended by the academic industry: there are "best adapted screenplay" awards, but no awards for best translation or intertextuality; one must purchase the rights to adapt a whole work, but not to allude to it. Practitioner interviews, how-to manuals, and professional and consumer reviews of adaptation (more accessible now than ever online in blogs, vlogs, tweets, and status updates) have also retained adaptation as their dominant terminology.

Tellingly, adaptations defined in the narrow sense—deliberate, announced, whole works from one form to another—have been the most disciplined and punished by humanities theorization. By contrast, allusion, quotation, pastiche, palimpsest, intertextuality, and intermediality, which are deemed to occur casually, slightly, inevitably, randomly and/or unconsciously, have been far more hospitably received, in part, I believe, because they hail from and conform to humanities theorization, while adaptation does not.

Adaptation, defined against itself and for disciplines and theories, remains at odds with theoretical definitions, in spite of—and because of—so many efforts to define it. A plurality of terms and definitions may illuminate many aspects of adaptation, but it equally presses adaptation away from study as a process of its own. Theoretical and disciplinary rivalries exacerbate these dynamics when they war over adaptation's definitional custody.

Defining Theorization

If we are to set adaptation and theorization in reciprocal rather than one-way dialogue, theorization too requires definition. Like adaptation, theorization is both product (theory) and process (theorization). Intriguingly, theory too resists definition as a precise statement of its essence, spanning a continuum of variable and diametrically opposed definitions ranging from "a mental view" (*OED*, 2nd rev. ed., s.v. "theory," definition 4, accessed March 23, 2018, http://www-oed-com/view/Entry/200431) to "a systematic statement of rules or principles to be followed" (*OED*, "theory," definition 3) to "a hypothesis that has been confirmed or established by observation or experiment, and is propounded or accepted as accounting for the known facts" (*OED*, "theory," definition 6). In June 2015, the *Oxford English Dictionary* added another definition of theory articulating definitions of theory produced by the late twentieth-century theoretical turn:

> An approach to the study of literature, the arts, and culture that incorporates concepts from disciplines such as philosophy, psychoanalysis, and the social sciences; esp. such an approach intended to challenge or provide an alternative to critical methods and interpretations that are established, traditional, and seen as arising from particular metaphysical or ideological assumptions. (*OED*, "theory," definition 1.c)

Humanities theory is hybrid and pluralistic: there is no consensus on definitions of what theorization is, does, or should do in the humanities. Some scholars define it as conceptualization: standing back and forming "second-order judgments about the world and our own behavior in it" (Waugh 2006, 10; see also Pollock 2007, xiv). Others define it metatheoretically as "thinking about thinking" (Culler 1997, 15). For most, however, theory must have explanatory power (Rimmon-Kenan 2002). For some, explanatory power requires systematicity, objectivism, and empiricism; for others, abstraction is the highest form of theorization; many seek a middle ground between the two. David Strang and John W. Mayer, for example, define theorization as the "self-conscious development and specification of abstract categories and the formulation of patterned relationships such as chains of cause and effect" (1993, 492). Here, abstraction is predicated on categorization, patterns, and logic.

Theorization, then, is no more fixed by definition than adaptation; indeed, its dictionary definitions vary so widely that scholars do not always recognize what others define and practice as theorization as being theorization at all. To illustrate this from my own experience, midway through an international symposium on theorizing adaptation, I asked a professor which papers he liked best; he replied, "The theoretical ones." Since all of the papers addressed theoretical approaches to adaptation, I was puzzled. I learned that he only recognized systematic, descriptive, empirical, objectivist studies as "theoretical"; political, philosophical, aesthetic, and cultural theories were, for him, not "theoretical." Conversely, other scholars at the symposium considered his definition of theorization to have been theoretically disproven by the theoretical turn and to be untheoretical or antitheoretical. These differences extend to contesting theories of definition: empirical, analytical, and logical theories require clear, unambiguous, positivist definitions, as defined by the dictionary (which is not yet up to date with theoretical changes in defining definition); poststructuralist and postmodern theories decree the impossibility, undesirability, and instability of essential, definite, exact definitions.

Defining "theorize," the *Oxford English Dictionary* distinguishes the intransitive verb, "To construct or develop theories" (*OED*, 2nd rev. ed., s.v. "theorize," definition 3, accessed June 9, 2018, http://www-oed-com/view/Entry/200430), from the transitive verb, "To construct a theory of or about" (*OED*, "theorize," definition 2.a) or "to assert a theory" (*OED*, "theorize," definition 2.c). To theorize is to "make or constitute in theory; to bring into or out of some condition theoretically" (*OED*, "theorize," definition 3.c.); to make something in theory is to *adapt* it to theory: to make what it theorizes in its image.

The *Oxford Dictionary of English*, an edition that "focuses on English as it is used today" (book jacket), renders the *opposition* of theory to what it theorizes one of theorization's main definitions:

> That department of an art or technical subject which consists in the knowledge or statement of the facts on which it depends, or of its principles or methods, as distinguished from the *practice* of it. (*Oxford Dictionary of English*, 3rd ed., s.v. "theory," emphasis in original)

Beyond the particular ways in which adaptations have been chastised for being untheoretical or antitheoretical by particular theories, this definition of theory sets theory and practice at odds *generally*, allocating them to separate spheres. The dictionary reinscribes the binary opposition and renders it hierarchical when it sets "practice" in opposition to "theory" and places it in theory's service:

> The actual *application* or *use* of an idea, belief, or method, as *opposed* to the theory or principles of it; performance, execution, achievement; working, operation; (*Philos.*) activity or action considered as being the realization of or *in contrast to* theory. (*Oxford Dictionary of English*, 3rd ed., s.v. "practice," emphasis added)

In this formulation, practice is the application, operation, realization, or use of theoretical ideas, beliefs, and methodologies. It does not exist or function in its own right. Rather than defining adaptation as a process akin to itself and in competition with it, theorization has defined it as a practice to be subjected to itself and placed in its service. This hierarchical relationship is reinforced by other binary relations included in this definition, most prominently, the authority of mind over matter. Theory is attached to and defined as mind and truth, concerned solely with "knowledge," "facts," "principles," and "methods," avoiding manual labor, while practice is cast and defined as matter and laboring body, "performing," "executing," "achieving," "working," and "operating" for theory, with no other reason for existence. Theory rules and practice is governed; theory decrees and practice obeys; theory hypothesizes and practice provides evidence; theory pronounces and practice illustrates. As I will argue in subsequent chapters, adaptation too manifests mind; it too generates principles and methodologies. Concomitantly, theorization is the practice of theory, a practice that is itself subject to the principles of adaptation.

De Man's "The Resistance to Theory" champions deductive theorization, where "success depends on the power of a system (philosophical, religious or ideological)...that determines an a priori conception of what is...by starting out from the premises of the system rather than from the ... thing itself—if such a 'thing' indeed exists" (1986, 5). Here, theorization overshadows what it theorizes to the point of *questioning its existence apart from theorization*. This is totalitarian theorization indeed. This tendency is not limited to de Man: the *Oxford English Dictionary*'s examples of theory in use show it theorizing religion, facts, experience, logic, danger, and suffering "away" or "out of existence." My history of theorizing adaptation too attests to strenuous efforts by deductive theorists to theorize adaptation out of existence.

Andrew has critiqued deductive theorization in adaptation studies: "It will no longer do to let theorists settle things with a priori arguments.... Let us use [adaptation] not to fight battles over the essence of the media or the inviolability of individual art works." Instead, "let us use [adaptation] as we use all cultural practices, to understand the world from which it comes and the one toward which it points" (1984b, 106). In a bid to free adaptation from a priori theorization, Andrew redefined it: "We need to study [adaptations] themselves as acts of discourse" (1984b, 106). Redefining adaptation as discourse, as a speaking cultural practice, empowers it to talk back to the discourses of theorization.

Humanities theorization may have undergone political, cultural, and philosophical revolutions, but the relationship between theory and what it theorizes has changed surprisingly little. Although the theoretical turn rejected master narrative theories of theorization in favor of piecemeal, local, pluralist, indeterminate theorization, the hierarchical relationship between theory and what it theorizes remains: what is theorized must still conform to theoretical principles (of indeterminacy, of pluralism, of diversity, of absence, etc.). By contrast to scientific and social scientific theorization, humanities theories cede only to other theories; rarely, if ever, do they allow their subject matter to bring about a theoretical revolution. When practice does controvert, disprove, or overthrow theory, it is allowed to do so only in the service of another theory. Following the theoretical turn and its assault on hierarchies of all kinds, it is perplexing that the hierarchical binarism between theory and practice has been so little challenged, based as it is in a classical dualist metaphysics that has been deconstructed (almost) everywhere else. It is particularly unaccountable that it persists in such a field as adaptation studies, which has in recent decades prioritized mutual exchange over one-way transfer and worked to dismantle media and disciplinary hierarchies.

The failure to deconstruct the hierarchical relationship between theory and practice is no intellectual conundrum: it can be as swiftly and readily challenged and dismantled as any other, right at the baseline level of definition. To begin with, theory and practice are profoundly interdependent: theories depend upon practices to prove them—whether the sensorially perceptible practices that serve as evidence for empirical theories, or the logical rhetorical practices that establish philosophical theories, or the cultural practices that support aesthetic, historical, social, and political theories. As scholars have noted, theorization is itself a practice: it is theory applied. Theoretical practices are, like adaptation, acts of "repetition with variation," as theorization applies the *same* principles, processes, and methodologies to *varied* subject matter. These are only some of the ways to deconstruct their oppositions.

Given how easy it is to deconstruct the opposition between theory and practice *in theory*, the failure to do so *in practice* must derive from other factors. The ancient hierarchy of mind over matter, theory over practice, remains because it is essential to scholarly identities and the cultural authority of academic institutions. The inequitable relationship between theory and practice brings economic rewards and cultural prestige within the academic industry. Our scholarly identities depend on a circular, yet hierarchical, nomenclature and rhetoric that renders us theorists of practice and practitioners of theory. Our careers and credibility depend on the dominance of our minds over our subject matter, as well as the perceived superiority of our minds over those of the general public, who pay us to teach them and to serve as experts for governments, media, and other industries. The task of redressing "the problem of theorizing adaptation" at the level of definition, then, is not simply one of agreeing on or multiplying theoretical definitions of adaptation: it is also a task of redefining what theorization is and does in the humanities and of redefining its relationship to adaptation.

Definitions in Dialogue

Adaptation not only resists theoretical definitions of itself and hierarchies of theorization over it as "practice," it further presents itself as a rival process that seeks to adapt theorization to and through itself—to remake it in *its* image. Setting definitions of adaptation and theorization in dialogue reveals many points of overlap and opposition and similarity and difference in the two processes dismantling their hierarchical opposition from both sides. Theorization adapts cultural materials to itself; Rainer Emig has argued that theory "is itself an ongoing adaptation (2012, 23). Conversely, adaptation has been theorized as a form of criticism (e.g., by Wagner 1975; Andrew 1980; 1984b; Sinyard 1986; Marsden 1995; Snyder 2017; Sabey and Lawrence 2018), theorization (Sanders [2006] 2017), and philosophy (Constable 2009). As Emig has posited: "It is not only adaptation that must be positioned in theory, but adaptation is also always already a component of theory" (2012, 23). Fischlin and Fortier conflate adaptation with critical editions: "any modern or historical production of Shakespeare, whether theatrical, critical, or editorial, is an adaptation" (2000, 17). Thus, adaptation has not been defined solely as subject matter for theorization but also as a process akin to theorization.

Adaptation and theorization share other features in common: they are both transdisciplinary and interdisciplinary:

"Theory" is born out of this moment. It is an unstable fusion of literary studies, linguistics, psychoanalysis, anthropology, Marxism, philosophy, gender studies, poststructuralism, new historicisms, postcolonial and ethnic studies, an open-ended postmodern assemblage that displaces the modernist formalism dominant from the 1930s to the 1960s in the US. . . . [T]here is no department of theory, nor a separate discipline. It piggybacks on existing disciplines and interdisciplines. It keeps changing shape, having multiple strands and configurations. (Vincent B. Leitch 2005, n.p.)

Similarly, there is no department or discipline of adaptation: it too is an unstable fusion of multiple strands and configurations piggybacking on existing disciplines, sub-disciplines, and interdisciplines.

The opposition between theorization and adaptation, then, is not so much one of theory rightfully lording it over practice as of rival, overlapping, inassimilable cultural processes vying with each other. And yet because academia prioritizes theorization over adaptation, theorization is accepted, touted, taught, and promoted throughout academia, while adaptation is rejected, discredited, and ignored for its failure to conform to theorization.

Redefining Defining Adaptation

If adaptation studies is to be a field, not simply a sub-category of many fields, it cannot be defined solely by definitions of other things patched together from other fields: it needs to be defined first and foremost *as adaptation*. Even though Hutcheon championed theorizing adaptations as adaptations, she immediately shifted to defining adaptation by another term: "To deal with adaptations as adaptations is to think of them as . . . inherently 'palimpsestuous' works, haunted at all times by their adapted texts" (2006, 6). Two pages later, "as adaptations" lies in brackets and "as palimpsests" prevails as an unbracketed definition: "we experience adaptations (*as adaptations*) as palimpsests" (8, emphasis in original). Similarly, although Cattrysse set out to theorize "adaptation as adaptation" (2014, 15), he argued that it should be theorized "as translation" (47–51).

There is an alternative to defining adaptation by words that fail to differentiate it from other subject matter. It is the way of tautology: defining *adaptation as adaptation*. Tautology, in spite of its identical repetition of terms, has various definitions itself: in formal logic, it is defined as a self-evident, universal truth; more often, it is derided as rhetorical redundancy. The tautology "adaptation as adaptation," however, precludes both identicality and redundancy: the two adaptations on either side of the "as" conjunction are not identical; the conjunction separates them in time and space, resisting their conflation and configuring them relationally rather than essentially and singly. The interplay between the two precludes essentialist definition, as the conjunction places a performative gap between the repeated terms. Here, adaptation finally performs as itself and defines itself.

Defining adaptation as adaptation allows it to participate in and shape its own definition, rather than being defined solely by other entities, theories, and fields. Corrigan has argued that "definitions of adaptation tend to survive as they are continually readapted" (2017, 33). He is right, not just in terms of definitional survival but also in the sense that any viable definition of adaptation must be itself *adaptive and adapting*. Defining adaptation as adaptation by way of tautological simile, rather than by theorization's definition of definition, constitutes a vital first step toward retheorizing theorization and adapting it to adaptation.

Adapting Definitions of Adaptation

I hesitate to offer a definition of adaptation by way of conclusion, fearing that it will be both cited as definitive and critiqued for definitive lack by scholars who remain committed to defining adaptation definitively, as theorization dictates. And yet, not to offer an adaptive definition of adaptation would leave the arguments of this chapter too much in the domains of speculation and abstraction. I therefore ask every scholar who cites the following definitions to also cite this proviso: "This adaptive definition of adaptation has been adapted from prior scholarship and is subject to further adaptation."[2]

Adaptation is an interactive, relational process that changes entities to suit new environments; it is also a term describing an entity thus changed. Adaptation is therefore double-faceted in several ways: it is both process and product (Cardwell 2002); it adapts both from and to (Leitch 2005); it encompasses both entities and environments, texts and contexts (Geraghty 2008).

Adaptation's adaptive mechanisms prioritize repetition with variation and continuity with discontinuity. Adaptation is not purely differential, but incorporates sameness; it is not purely progressive, but also engages in return (Corrigan 2017).

Adaptations incorporate multiple texts and inhabit multiple environments (Hutcheon 2006). These include not only historical, geographical, social, cultural, ideological, political, aesthetic, economic, industrial, media, and technological environments but also academic, disciplinary, and *theoretical* environments.

Adaptations are determined not only by artists but also by critics and theorists (Marsden 1995), politics and other cultural ideologies (Hassler-Forrest and Nicklas 2015), censorship (Berger 2010) and copyright laws (Nissen 2018), technologies (Sanders [2006] 2017, 32), industries and economics (Murray 2012a; 2012b).

Adaptation adapts the textual and contextual borders that it crosses as well as the texts and contexts it adapts.

Adaptation extends from processes of production and products to processes of consumption and consumers (Hutcheon 2006). Different consumers respond to adaptations differently across time, nations, classes, genders, and ideologies. Individuals change perceptions of an adaptation over time as we ourselves change.

Joining multiple processes of production and consumption, humanities adaptation occurs on all levels from the macroscopic to the microscopic. The adaptation of a novel to a film is not simply a matter of narratological and ideological transfer—of plots, characters, points of view, and themes from page to screen. It is also at work in the tiniest pieces of lines on surfaces, which may have no narrative, ideological, or symbolic significance in themselves (Elliott 2003a, 72–73); it resides in the smallest bytes of digital technologies. In the midrange, it inhabits nonverbal modes of representation which may inform, but do not reduce to linguistic analyses.

Adaptation can be deliberate (as in the selective breeding of animals or an acknowledged adaptation of a prior aesthetic work) or unintentional and unconscious (Hayton 2011); that said, even intentional adaptations involve processes and outcomes that exceed and elude intentionality.

Adaptation cannot be traced to an origin, nor will it ever reach a final destination.

Adaptation adapts the industries and individuals who produce and consume it, including the scholars who study it and the theories that we use.

There is no place outside of adaptation to survey adaptation transcendently or objectively.

The process of adaptation itself adapts over time.

So too do definitions of adaptation.

The following two chapters continue the task of retheorizing theorization in a discussion of taxonomies and theoretical principles.

6

Resetting Taxonomies

Dudley Andrew has written, "The job of theory in all this is to keep the questions clear and in order" (1984, 106). The second stage of theorization is taxonomization: following baseline definitions, taxonomies nuance, order, subdivide, and hierarchize a field's subject matter in preparation for the third stage, the application of theoretical principles. Taxonomical systems need not be hierarchical; they may be conventional, as in the Library of Congress's alphabetical classification system, or web-like, as in a thesaurus. As with definition, although taxonomization officially precedes the development of theoretical principles, it may derive from them, as the definition of "taxonomy" suggests: "Classification, esp. in relation to its general laws or principles" (*OED*, 2nd rev. ed., s.v. "taxonomy," definition 1, accessed November 23, 2018, http://www-oed-com/view/Entry/198305). This chapter considers how adaptation has been taxonomized by disciplines and theories, how it has resisted taxonomization, and debates over taxonomization within adaptation studies.

Taxonomizing Adaptation

Deborah Cartmell and Imelda Whelehan have affirmed that "using taxonomies . . . is as old as the field itself" (2010, 6). Laurent Mellet has observed a "progressive shift . . . from definition (of word, image, and adaptation) to a new vogue of categories and labels"—or taxonomies—in twentieth- and early twenty-first-century adaptation theory (2011, 99). Even so, taxonomizing adaptation is problematic for reasons similar to those problematizing its definition. We have seen that adaptation's resistance to definition is not simply that adaptation's definitions are contested, as definitions are in all fields, or because post-theories declare the impossibility of definition, or because adaptation is dispersed across so many fields and subjects; adaptation resists definition because it is itself defined as anti-definition. Similarly, as a process characterized by crossing taxonomical borders between media,

Theorizing Adaptation. Kamilla Elliott, Oxford University Press (2020). © Oxford University Press.
DOI: 10.1093/oso/9780197511176.001.0001

historical periods, geographical locations, languages, cultures, industries and technologies, production and consumption, and more, adaptation is itself anti-taxonomical. Adaptation exposes the permeability and instability of theoretical taxonomies by crossing their lines and occupying the spaces between them. Beyond crossing them, adaptation is at work on taxonomical lines, adapting them, as well as the ways in which it crosses them. Hence, even though adaptation is anti-taxonomical and taxonomies are often anti-adaptation, there is a place for taxonomical discourse in adaptation studies. A study of taxonomies illuminates how adaptation has been boxed in, contained, and (mis)classified by disciplines as well as theories, and how adaptation has resisted these constraints. Adaptation has violated theoretical taxonomies between high and low art (Cartmell, Hunter, Kaye, and Whelehan 1996; 1997; 1998; 1999; 2000) and crossed boundaries forged by medium specificity theories (Leitch 2003a), while rupturing bonds between form and content deemed to be inviolable (Elliott 2004). When adaptation crosses theoretical and disciplinary borders, it is condemned as trespasser, illegal immigrant, miscegenator, and bastard. Even when it is granted a disciplinary or theoretical green card, its participation in multiple disciplines and theoretical promiscuity has led to taxonomical custody battles, as theories, disciplines, and interdisciplines vie to taxonomize it according to their categories.

Joining adaptation's violation of taxonomies and battles over its taxonomization, the wide ranging of adaptation across so many borders has led scholars to ask, as with definition, how can we possibly taxonomize it? Twenty-first-century scholars divide over whether adaptation studies needs more robust taxonomization, whether adaptation taxonomization is impossible, or whether it is undesirable. All three positions are governed by theories. For Margot Blankier, the remedy to "The Limits of Existing Adaptation Theory" (article title) is to taxonomize adaptation more rigorously: "What is missing is a cohesive grammar to describe the ways in which adapted texts are linked and interact" (2014, 111). Calling scholars to "integrate existing taxonomies and theories into real-world practices and audience reception" (121), her position is that the humanities already has all the taxonomies that it needs to taxonomize adaptation.

Seven years prior, Thomas Leitch created just such "a grammar," spanning a wide range "of hypertextual relations as they shade off to the intertextual" (2007, 95)[1]; yet doing so led him to conclude the impossibility of taxonomizing adaptation because scholars are unable to separate particular adaptations into categories because even apparently straightforward adaptations typically make uses of many different intertextual strategies. The slippery slope between adaptation and allusion cannot be divided into discrete stages . . . there is no normative model of adaptation. (2007, 126)

Three years on, Cartmell and Whelehan agreed with Leitch:

In the attempt to anticipate every possible permutation of the relationship between one narrative form and another we attempt a list that will never be exhaustive but is, frankly, exhausting and does not produce the holy grail of the definitive critical model which will help us further analyze the process of adaptation. (2010, 21)

Cartmell and Whelehan went further than Leitch to disparage taxonomization as a theoretical enterprise, denying its claims to factuality and objectivity, arguing that taxonomies reveal nothing except "the prejudices and partialities of their inventor" and charging taxonomizers with producing only derivative "taxonomies laid out previously by another commentator" (2010, 21). While the last two claims seem contradictory—Can a taxonomy be both idiosyncratic and derivative?—they are congruent with the postmodern cultural theories informing Cartmell and Whelehan's critique. Postmodernism maintains that theorization is both subjective *and* derivative. Indeed, Cartmell and Whelehan have celebrated such theoretical recycling in their own work: "Good bricoleurs, we repurpose perspectives and strategies that have served other critics well in quite other environments" (2010, 22). In so doing, they have theorized adaptively: repeating and varying prior theories and methodologies brings the process of theorization closer to the process of adaptation.

Just as Cartmell and Whelehan's critique of taxonomies reflects their theoretical principles, the adaptation taxonomies that they oppose reflect other theoretical tenets. Cartmell and Whelehan focused their taxonomical critique on Geoffrey Wagner's widely imitated tripartite taxonomy of adaptation (1975), discussed in Chapters 2 and 3, a taxonomy that measures "degrees of separation between original text and adaptation." While Cartmell and Whelehan have claimed that adaptation taxonomies privilege " 'closeness to origin' as the key business of adaptation studies" (2010, 6), Wagner did the reverse, privileging *distance* from origin as the key business of adaptation studies.

Like Wagner, Gordon E. Slethaug proposed adaptation taxonomies as a way of moving the field away "from rigid faithfulness to see the new possibilities in adaptation" (2014, 3). In the same year, Blankier blamed insistence on fidelity between adapting and adapted works for the limits of adaptation theory and the rift between adaptation theory and practice, recommending taxonomization as a remedy. As I have argued, if there is a recurring fidelity problem with adaptation taxonomization, it is not one of fidelity between adapting and adapted works but of *fidelity to theories*. Wagner is far more concerned with the fidelity of his taxonomies to the *theories* of medium specificity and neo-Romantic originality revived by mid-century theories of film auteurism than with the fidelity of a film adaptation to its source text: indeed, fidelity to his theories mandates *in*fidelity between adapting and adapted works. That he does not celebrate a film's adaptation of literature to a new environment, but rather vaunts the originality of film auteur genius in unfaithful adaptations, reinforces the anti-adaptation focus of his taxonomy. Similarly, Cartmell and Whelehan's resistance to taxonomies and Blankier's and Slethaug's support of them derive from fidelity to their espoused theories.

Wagner's taxonomy of adaptation values *most* adaptations that adapt source texts the *least*. The two extremes of his tripartite taxonomy—maximal fidelity to a source text and maximal infidelity to it—each diminish adaptation: the most unfaithful adaptation adapts the source text the least, while the most faithful adaptation does little adapting to the new environment. Dudley Andrew's taxonomy of adaptation (1984) favors the middle way of partial fidelity to both source text and new environment: making room for both types of adaptation valorizes adaptation from both sides.

Adaptation scholars have been largely focused on adaptation taxonomies derived from translation studies and narrative studies. When Andrew called adaptation studies to take "a sociological turn" beyond "tiresome" translation-based taxonomies, he invited the field to consider taxonomies beyond media forms and signs—"eras, styles, nations, and subjects"—and the "complex interchanges" that adaptation generates by crossing their taxonomical lines (1984, 104). For all their opposition to translation-based taxonomies, Cartmell and Whelehan have engaged other kinds of formal and cultural taxonomies to organize their edited collections. Recommending genre as a way of taxonomizing adaptations in "a 'discursive cluster' that confers a group or community identity" across media and disciplines (2010, 6), genre taxonomies enable other taxonomical lines to be crossed: the genre of comedy, for example, traverses media forms, nations, and eras. In addition to generic taxonomies, their co-edited *Cambridge Companion to Literature on Screen* (2007a) divides into taxonomies of theories, historical periods, cultural contexts, media types, industries, and modes of production and consumption. Cartmell's *Companion to Literature, Film, and Adaptation* (2012) is organized similarly. Other adaptation publications have been taxonomized by nation, language, theme, technology, industry, particular authors and works, and by the taxonomies of identity politics: race, nation, gender, sexuality, disability, age, and their many sub-taxonomies.[2] These disciplinary taxonomies and sub-taxonomies hail from similar taxonomies in other disciplines and from theoretical taxonomies that cross disciplines.

Cartmell and Whelehan's objection to taxonomizing adaptation, then, is not absolute: rather, they reject the taxonomies generated by the theories they oppose and support the taxonomies of the theories they support. Taxonomies are endemic even to theories that oppose taxonomization. For example, feminist theorization may object to gender taxonomies, but it has itself been taxonomized theoretically (psychoanalytic feminism, poststructuralist feminism, ecofeminism, semiotic feminism, Marxist feminism, queer feminism, and more) and historically (first-wave, second-wave, third-wave feminism, and post-feminism). Similarly, poststructuralism, which opposes taxonomies and breaks down boundaries between words and pieces of words, has itself been taxonomized as Derridean, Barthesean, de Manian, Lacanian, Kristevan, and more.

Disciplining Adaptation

Patricia Waugh has written: "'Theory,' forged in the crucible of literary studies with ingredients [from many disciplines], now exports its processed goods back to all those disciplinary markets from whence it received its raw materials" (2006, 31). Theoretical and disciplinary taxonomies interpenetrate: theorization derives from and returns to disciplines, and disciplines are shaped by theories of taxonomization. J. D. Aram has defined disciplines as "thought domains—quasi-stable, partially integrated, semi-autonomous intellectual conveniences—consisting of problems, theories, and methods of investigation," assessing that their position within institutions of higher education gives them "a heightened sense of autonomy, definitiveness, and stability" (2004, 380–81). For B. R. Clark, disciplines "shape the ways in which knowledge is bundled" (1983, 26), while for J. Parker, "to be engaged in a discipline is to shape, and be shaped by, the subject, to be part of a scholarly community, to engage with fellow students—to become 'disciplined' " (2002, 374). Like adaptation, disciplines are not categorically discrete; they further-more engage in processes of adaptation to and through their subject matter in collaboration with other scholars.

Even so, theories governing the formation and maintenance of disciplines have had negative repercussions for adaptation, and adaptation has been threatening to their theories. As so many adaptation scholars attest, adapta-tion sits uneasily within and between disciplines. Before Hutcheon's *A Theory of Adaptation* (2006) opened adaptation studies to all manner of media, "ad-aptation study was largely confined to cinematic versions of classic novels"; "the classic status of the films' avowed sources provided a center for the field, or at least the illusion of a center" (Leitch 2010, 244). My history has shown that even this center was troubled by disciplinary trespasses on both sides of the border and disciplinary contests over adaptation.

Adaptation's disciplinary crossings have destabilized its definitions. Being neither definitively books nor films, literary film adaptations reside in no discipline's land. Even when disciplines welcome interdisciplinary adap-tation, they disagree on how to study it, each subjecting adaptation to the taxonomies of its own discipline, which is itself part of a larger discipli-nary taxonomy. In literary studies, a literary film adaptation is defined and taxonomized as a type of translation, interpretation, or remediation of lit-erature. Harris Ross's annotated bibliography of literature and film is struc-tured according to literary taxonomies: "language and film"; "prose fiction and film"; "drama and film"; "poetry and film"; "adaptation, writers and the film industry"; and "literary figures and film" (1987, table of contents). Here, film repeats as a single, undifferentiated, untaxonomized category, while lit-erature is sub-taxonomized variably.[3]

Chapter 5 indicates that when adaptation is defined as translation, it is usually defined and taxonomized as the worst kind of literary translation or interpretation. Literary scholars resent film adaptations for impinging on their territory as literary and cultural critics—all the more so when these adaptations find a wider, more enthusiastic audience than we do, encour-aging us to denigrate it theoretically in order to render it aesthetically, intel-lectually, and ideologically inferior to our interpretation and theorization of literature.[4]

Film scholars too have resented literature's trespasses on filmic territory via adaptation, which they theorize as threats to film's aesthetic prowess and disciplinary autonomy. William Luhr and Peter Lehman expressed a widely held view that any critical attention to literary sources denotes a failure in film art: "if [a film] makes no sense without recourse to a prior text, then it is not aesthetically realized. If it is aesthetically realized, then its use of source material is of historical, not of aesthetic interest" (1977, 223).[5] Taxonomizing adaptation as film-in-its-own-right annihilates adaptation as a cinema studies taxonomy.[6] Instead, adaptation is scattered among other filmic taxonomies such as genre, director oeuvre, historical period, and nation. Garrett Stewart (2012) has gone further to didactically oppose adaptation as a viable category of literature-and-film studies.

As adaptation studies expanded beyond literature and film, adaptations continued to be taxonomized along disciplinary lines: theater, television, visual art, music, dance, new media, and more. Within disciplines, they were additionally sub-taxonomized according to genre, historical period, nation, language, makers, consumers, technologies, industries, politics, economics, and individual artists and their oeuvres. Beyond media disciplines, adaptation has been taxonomized by history (Stam 2005; Leitch 2015), philosophy (Constable 2009), psychology (Mitry 1971), politics (Jameson 2011; Hassler-Forrest and Nicklas 2015), and the interdisciplines of translation studies (Cahir 2006; Venuti 2007), narratology (McFarlane1996; Bal 2017b), cognitive linguistics (Elliott 2003a), and gender studies (Whelehan 2000). These lists are not exhaustive: adaptation studies, if not quite a disciplinary Tower of Babel, is a field in which many disciplines taxonomize adaptation both similarly and variably. Even within a discipline, theorists do not agree on taxonomies. Moreover, as Angelique Chettiparamb reminds, any taxonomies we may construct "are quasi-stable because they are continually changing and evolving, partially integrated, because they are internally fragmented and specialized, [and] semi-autonomous, because the boundary of each discipline cannot be clearly defined" (2007, 3). That disciplines cannot clearly ascertain where their boundaries lie renders their strenuous efforts to police adaptation's crossings of them ludicrous as well as futile. Moreover, disciplines are themselves adapting; so are their boundaries: adaptation is already inside and at work upon the border walls erected to keep it out.

Adaptation is just one mode of interdisciplinarity traversing disciplinary boundaries. Other interdisciplines have also forged taxonomies to constrain adaptation to their parameters and theories. Chettiparamb summarizes the arguments for interdisciplinary study: to create a unity of knowledge across disciplines; to foster creativity and academic freedom; to develop "conceptual links using a perspective in one discipline to modify a perspective in another"; "to solve unresolved problems in an existing field"; to integrate fields; to fill "the gaps that disciplinarity leaves vacant"; to transcend and surpass the limits of disciplinarity (2007, 13–16). In an interview with Nicholas Ruiz III, Vincent B. Leitch, however, attested to the limits of interdisciplinarity in academic practice:

> Whereas modern interdisciplinarity dreams of the end of disciplines with their awful jargon and fallacious divisions of knowledge, the newer post-modern interdisciplinarity respects difference and heterogeneity, proliferating several dozen new interdisciplines such as black studies, women's studies, media studies, cultural studies, postcolonial studies, science studies, disability studies, body studies, queer studies, etc. Significantly, these fields . . . struggle against the hegemonic order. . . . Yet, still and all, they submit to modern disciplinarity, its requirements, standards, certifications as well as its methods (exercises, exams, rankings, supervision, norms). (V. Leitch and Ruiz, 2005, n.p.)

Moreover, for all the aspirations of interdisciplinarity to break down disciplinary divisions and hierarchies, interdisciplinarity has often taken the form of imposing the principles, methodologies, theories, and values of one discipline on another, as Chapter 3 makes clear.

Beyond the literature and film wars of the 1970s and 1980s, titles such as *The Language of New Media* (Manovich 2001), *The Politics of the Media* (Whale 1977), *The Psychology of Media and Politics* (Comstock and Scharrer 2005), *The Science of Digital Media* (Burg 2009), and *Economics of Information Technology and the Media* (Low 2000) illustrate and epitomize acts of [inter]disciplinary possession. However, "of" in these titles is ambivalently proprietary, connoting that language, politics, history, philosophy, psychology, science, and economics both possess and belong to media. While reversing "the history of philosophy" to "the philosophy of history" inverts the dominant discipline, such reversals do not redress the colonizing aspects of interdisciplinarity when it comes to media or adaptation studies, since these are not allowed theorizing power over other disciplines but are viewed as subjects to be theorized and disciplined by the disciplines accorded theorizing power.

Currently, philosophy is the discipline deemed to be most theoretical, the most synonymous with humanities theorization—so much so that the two terms have been used interchangeably many times. Before Google limited the number of hits produced by a search, a Google Books search for the exact phrase "theorizing or philosophizing" produced thousands of hits; a search for "theorize or philosophize," many thousands more.[7] In the twenty-first century alone, we find books in which philosophy disciplines psychology (Thagard 2007), art (Stecker 2005), religion (M. Murray and Rea 2008), language (Morris 2006), science (Rescher 2006), history (Little 2010), economics (Hausman 2008), law (Pound 1954), mathematics (J. Brown 2008), social sciences (Fay 1996), biology (Grene and Depew 2004), language (Morris 2006), literature (Hagberg and Jost 2010), film (N. Carroll and Choi 2005), music (Davies 2003; Sanders 2007), technology (Kaplan 2009), and education (Winch and Gingell 1999). It even disciplines itself in "the philosophy of philosophy" (Williamson 2007).

While history has been classified as a social science, today it more commonly resides in humanities academia. There, it constitutes philosophy's main rival and runner up as the humanities' theoretical master discipline: it too has "-ized" almost every other discipline, as twenty-first-century books on the history of philosophy (Erdmann [1890] 2002), psychology (Wertheimer 2012), art (Janson [1981] 2001), religion (Lentz 2002), language (S. Fischer 2004), science (Chemla 2005), economics (Canterbery 2010), law (Grossi 2010), mathematics (Boyer and Merzbach 2011), the social sciences (Backhouse and Fontaine 2010), literature (Carter and McRae 1997), film (Dixon and Foster 2008), music (Burney 1782), technology (Inkster 2004–2012), education (Amala, Anupama, and Rao 2004), and the auto-disciplining "history of history" (Munslow 2012) attest. There is also a Bloomsbury Press series, *The History of World Literatures on Film* (Hasenfratz and Semenza, 2015–2019).

Adaptation not only challenges taxonomies within and between theories and disciplines, it further challenges theories of which disciplines are allowed to be theorizing disciplines in the humanities. There is a hierarchy of theorizing disciplines at present: certain disciplines are unilaterally and unquestioningly granted theorizing power: runners up to philosophy and history are politics and linguistics. Social sciences disciplines, including psychology, sociology, anthropology, and economics, have lately been accorded theorizing power in the humanities, and Simone Murray's work has carried them into adaptation studies. Gilles Deleuze has made film studies a theorizing discipline, arguing influentially that film generates philosophical concepts (Deleuze [1983] 1986; [1986] 1989), while Catherine Constable (2009) has examined ways in which particular films adapt philosophy.

By contrast, adaptation inhabits all disciplines and its theorization requires input from them all. However, many humanities disciplines have been denied theorizing power: they are theorized as subjects to be theorized by the theorizing humanities disciplines. And yet, as critics have argued for centuries, theorization has failed the arts: they cannot be fully explicated by or conformed to rational, logical, ideological, verbal theories and constructs. Dennis Cutchins, Laurence Raw, and James M. Welsh have declared the impossibility of

> teach[ing] students a particular approach to adaptations or a heuristic that they could apply equally well in any situation. . . . [T]he more we study the issue, the more we find ourselves believing that the only legitimate response to art is more art. (2010b, xiv)

They have therefore encouraged their students to engage in the *practice* of adaptation, "making the kinds of decisions and creating the sorts of interpretations filmmakers do when they approach a text to adapt it" (xvi) to better understand adaptation.

Following the theoretical turn in the humanities, when aesthetic criticism was rejected as too impressionistic by empirical scholars and too politically conservative by radical ones, adaptations were increasingly read not as art forms but as empirically systematic narrative structures, historical and industrial productions, economic commodities, mental constructs, or manifestations of political and cultural ideologies. The question arises, do aesthetic forms have theorizing properties that do not reduce to philosophy, history, psychology, narratology, or any of the other usual theorizing disciplines? Deleuze and Félix Guattari have addressed this question:

> the question arises not only of what a concept is as philosophical Idea but also of the nature of the other creative Ideas that are not concepts and that are due to the arts and sciences, which have their own history and becoming. . . . The exclusive right of concept creation secures a function for philosophy, but it does not give it any preeminence of privilege since there are other ways of thinking and creating, other modes of creation that . . . do not have to pass through concepts. (Deleuze and Guattari [1991] 1994, 8)

Deleuze and Guattari's protest against Hegel's subsumption of the arts by philosophy, which "left scarcely any independent movement of the arts or sciences remaining" ([1991] 1994, 12), informs my critique of humanities theorization's hierarchical subjugation of what it theorizes. Yet my position differs from theirs: they deny conceptual agency to the arts; I do not. In 2014, I argued that the so-called non-theorizing disciplines do engage in conceptual acts akin to theorization and that the multimedia engagements of adaptation call for greater inclusivity in the disciplines that we allow to theorize it:

> Martin Mull coined a widely reiterated saying, "Writing about music is like dancing about architecture."[8] Echoed and extended by Elvis Costello in 1983 ("It's a really stupid thing to want to do"),[9] the expression mocks rather than explores the idea that nonverbal, nonrational disciplines can be "about" each other. It implies the impossibility and ludicrousness of explicating a nonverbal art with a verbal art by analogy to a more impossible, more ludicrous interdisciplinary relation in which one nonverbal art becomes "about" another one. But in a fully interdisciplinary, intermedial field of adaptation, every movement between forms and media is an act of criticism or theorization "about" intermedial relations. (Elliott 2014c, 75–76)

Arguing that the aesthetic shifts of adaptation undertake critical and theoretical work, I supported that argument with the creative-critical work of my undergraduate students. Dancing about William Shakespeare's *Romeo and Juliet* in one project illuminated relations between the rhythms of his poetry and the rhythms of ballet in the critical essay accompanying the creative project; casting only the female characters in that dance, including the Nurse's dead daughter, revealed gender dynamics that do not emerge when the men are present, making a new contribution to feminist scholarship of the play. Adapting *Romeo and Juliet* to a rugby game enabled an incisive critical commentary on the intermedial dynamics of competition and play in theater and sport. Adapting Bram Stoker's *Dracula* to Shironuri makeup carried Judith Butler's theories of gender performativity (1993) across representational forms; using text from the novel to create tears pasted onto a live woman's face broke down taxonomies between word and referent, text and image, body and artefact. The project's simultaneous adaptation of text to tears and tears to text additionally illustrated ways in which adaptation breaks down divisions within and between adapted and adapting forms; text-tears simultaneously maintain and rupture the signifier/signified across media boundaries; they *are* each other's form and content, further blurring boundaries between word and image and between adapted and adapting entities. Painting Robert Louis Stevenson's visually ambiguous and elusive Mr. Hyde in nineteenth-century realist, impressionist, and cubist styles led to insightful analyses of representations of evil across the taxonomies of art movements, as well as between the disciplinary taxonomies of literature and art. Adapting Lewis Carroll's Alice books to a three-layer cake combining ingredients that were individually delicious but disturbing when combined (caramelized mushrooms, poppy seed cake, and gummy worms representing Alice's encounter with the Caterpillar) led to reflections on the adaptation of linguistic nonsense to gustatory nonsense. All of these projects engaged in aesthetic practice that *theorized* adaptation. Creative-critical acts of adaptation cross media and disciplinary taxonomical lines, as well as divisions between adaptation theory and adaptation practice, retheorizing their relations. Creative practice makes adaptation more like theorization, and creative-critical practice adapts theorization to adaptation.

Methodological Taxonomization: Adaptation and the Case Study

There have been other taxonomical obstacles to redressing the hierarchical relationship between theorization and adaptation. Surveying literary film adaptation studies at the turn of the twenty-first century, Robert B. Ray argued that the field's lack of a "presiding poetics" and "cumulative knowledge" arose in part from its prevailing case study methodology (2000, 44–45). Thomas Leitch agreed and expanded:

> There is . . . such a thing as adaptation studies. It is pursued in dozens of books and hundreds of articles. . . . But this flood of study of individual adaptations proceeds on the whole without the support of any more general theoretical account. . . . [S]tudies of particular literary texts and their cinematic adaptations greatly outnumber more general considerations of what is at stake in adapting a text from one medium to another. (2003a, 149)

As my brief discussion of case studies in this book's introduction attests, most adaptation monographs also unfold as essay collections: Thomas Van Parys's review of Leitch's monograph (2007) assesses that "the twelve chapters are pretty much stand-alone analyses and discussions of various topics" (2007, n.p.). Van Parys himself subsequently contributed to an edited book, *Adaptation Theory* (2011), which is also a collection disparate studies.

Publishers' blurbs affirm the eclecticism and scatter within the field's book-length works, whether they are essay collections or monographs:

> ... explores the vast terrain of contemporary adaptation studies and offers a wide variety of answers to the title question. ... (Hermansson and Zepernick 2018)
>
> ... explores the varieties of methodologies and debates within the field, [d]rawing on approaches from genre studies to transtexuality to cultural materialism. ... (Cartmell and Whelehan 2010)
>
> Fifteen essays investigate a variety of texts that rework everything from literary classics to popular children's books. (Frus and Williams 2010)
>
> This collection of essays offers a sustained, theoretically rigorous rethinking of various issues at work in film and other media adaptations. (Albrecht-Crane and Cutchins 2010a)
>
> Writers are drawn from different backgrounds to consider broad topics. ... There are also case studies ... which allow the reader to place adaptations of the work of writers within a wider context. ... (Cartmell and Whelehan 2007a)
>
> ... explores multiple definitions and practices of adaptation and appropriation ... [r]anging across genres and harnessing concepts from fields as diverse as musicology and the natural sciences. ... (Sanders [2006] 2017)
>
> The thirteen especially composed essays that follow. . . variously illustrate. ... (Aragay 2005b)
>
> Twenty-five essays by international experts cover the most important topics in the study of literature and film adaptations ... a cornucopia of vibrant essays ... a wide and international spectrum of novels and adaptations (Stam and Raengo 2005b)
>
> ... wide-ranging. ... (Cartmell and Whelehan 1999)

Monographs focused on retheorizing the field tend to open with an introductory theoretical chapter, with the remaining chapters serving as case studies supporting the recommended theory or theories (Bluestone 1957; McFarlane 1996; Griffith 1997; S. Murray 2012a; Slethaug 2014). Reviewing monographs by James Griffith and Brian McFarlane, Lloyd Michaels assessed that the case study format limits authors' ability and his own as reviewer to clarify their contributions to the field, since they "reside precisely in the details" of the case studies (1998, 431). Michaels called for "the *next* study of adaptation . . . to adopt a new principle of organization, and a more synthetic methodology, so as to extend the primary interest of the book beyond the specific texts receiving treatment" (1998, 432, emphasis in original). Jason Mittell and Todd McGowan's *Narrative Theory and Adaptation* (2017) uses the film *Adaptation* (Jonze 2002) as an extended case study spanning the whole book.

Ray blamed the prevalence of case studies on "the exigencies of publication" (2000, 44–45). Yet since all fields have similar "exigencies," there must be other reasons. Some are pragmatic. Leitch observed in 2010 that the field "is getting too big for its current supply of centripetal energy to prevent it from exploding in a shower of brilliant sparks" (244). As a result, few scholars have time to trace its trans-taxonomical ventures across nations, eras, media, disciplines, or theories. Instead, most scholars study adaptation as a sub-taxonomy of their home discipline.

There are also theoretical reasons. The two main theoretical collectives being applied to adaptation in 2000 were a constellation of aesthetic formalism, high-art humanism, New Criticism, Romantic originality, translation theory, and medium specificity theory and a variegated collection of postmodern, (post)structuralist, and radical political theories. Both found individual case studies of paired adapting and adapted works to be adequate prooftexts for their aesthetic, philosophical, and political theories. Case studies are sufficient to establish the value judgments of aesthetic formalism and radical politics; they can equally illustrate theoretical indeterminacy, pluralism, and social injustice.

Responding to Ray's critique, Cartmell and Whelehan defended the case study on pragmatic grounds:

> Ray is undoubtedly right in his assertion that the field of adaptation studies is dominated by the case study, but his conclusion that this allows for no metacritical perspective . . . may be misguided. Adaptations critics know only too well how much easier it is to work through a critical position by the use of a key example. (2010, 55)

They too are "undoubtedly right": it *is* easier to theorize through case study examples.

Mieke Bal cautioned against taking the easy path, even as she defended the case study:

To cast out the case study would be throwing away the baby with the bath-water[;] . . . however, the method has acquired a dubious reputation as a facile entrance into theoretical generalization and speculation, as well as judgment, especially for adaptation studies. (2017b, 183)

While general principles can be *illustrated* by a single case study, Bal doubts that they can be *generated* by one. As a narratologist, Bal remains interested in "theoretical generalization" and judgment: however, some postmodern cultural and aesthetic formalist theorists resist larger theoretical arcs as themselves facile and consider case studies to be the only theoretically sound methodology. In 1975, film critic Richard Corliss rejected theoretical generalization as itself "facile," pitting case studies against it: "My aim has been to avoid facile generalizations by confronting specific films" (Corliss 1975, xxvii).

Hutcheon addressed the theoretical limitations of case studies in the preface to *A Theory of Adaptation*: "Such individual readings . . . rarely offer the kind of generalizable insights into theoretical issues that this book seeks to explore" (2006, xiii). The New Critical Idiom series preface to the second edition of Sanders's *Adaptation and Appropriation* states similarly: "The present need is for individual volumes on terms which combine clarity of expression with an adventurousness of perspective and a breadth of application" ([2006] 2017, p. xi). In illustrating their larger theoretical purviews with multiple case studies, Hutcheon and Sanders departed from the usual essay-length case study of a single adaptation. Hutcheon explained: "My method has been to identify a text-based issue that extends across a variety of media, find ways to study it comparatively, and then tease out the theoretical implications from multiple textual examples" (2006, xii).

Scholars have queried their methodologies. Reviewing Hutcheon's book, William Whittington assessed:

Hutcheon avoids extended case studies, opting instead for examples drawn from many sources in a form of meta-analysis. This approach is simultaneously a strength and weakness. Overall, the author demonstrates an extensive command of examples from novels, the stage, film, and even radio and theme parks, but an extended examination of one or two of these areas might have served as a model for future analysis by students and scholars. (2008, 406)

Jillian Saint Jacques went further to express himself "fundamentally skeptical" of Hutcheon's and Sanders's scholarship, charging that "they do not adequately analyze the cultural objects they use to 'illustrate' their larger theories," concluding that: "Neglecting to accord cultural objects due diligence in favor of producing larger organizational theories to account for the same cultural objects is a sure sign of theoretical languor" (2011b, 17–18).

To me, neglecting to examine how adaptations have been and might be theorized both via larger and more microscopic arcs is also a sign of theoretical languor. Hutcheon's scintillating micro case studies and Sanders's wide-ranging, multiwork case studies manifest extensive research, as well as valuable theoretical insights. Adaptation studies needs multiple angles and distances of view as much as it needs multiple disciplines and theories. It especially needs larger arcs of research to offset the ways in which small-scale adaptation case studies have enabled large-scale theories to dominate the field.

In 2015, Greg M. Colón Semenza and Bob Hasenfratz expressed concern that "The case study approach has resulted not only in too much ungeneralizable data but also so much data that we have no way of analyzing it all, no way of using it to speak to one another, especially across disciplinary boundaries" (9). Adaptation studies needs collective action across disciplines to challenge big-boss theories that begin their oppression and occlusion of adaptation at the first two stages of theorization: definition and taxonomization. While our field's taxonomical disciplinary and theoretical fragmentation have indubitably enriched and diversified adaptation studies, they have also prevented adaptation studies from gathering *collective* power through which to talk back to the theories that have defined, taxonomized, and theorized it not only as *other* than itself but also *against* itself.

Taxonomizing Adaptations as Adaptations

We need to taxonomize adaptations as adaptations as well as define them as adaptations. Why would I advocate taxonomizing adaptations as adaptations when I have argued that it is the nature of adaptations to resist taxonomization? Is that not a contradiction? We need to taxonomize adaptations as adaptations because taxonophobia of taxonomizing adaptations as adaptations—according to types of adaptations and degrees of adaptedness—has scattered adaptation to the winds of othering taxonomies based in other subjects and disciplines. Not only have othering taxonomies prevented field development, cohesion, and dialogue across disciplines, they have further reinforced the one-way, top-down occlusion and oppression of adaptation by theorization. The even more urgent dialogue needed in adaptation studies is one that allows it to taxonomize back to the theories and disciplines that have taxonomized it.

I am not the first scholar to recommend taxonomizing adaptations as adaptations. In 2002, Sarah Cardwell recommended that adaptation be studied across media as a genre—the genre of adaptation (67). Although her study is limited to "classic-novel adaptations," it encourages scholars to "draw upon a whole range of generic features in order to establish their identity: features of content (lavish costumes and sets, long shots of country houses and landscapes, restrained action, large amounts of dialogue), and features of style and mood" (2002, 67). Cardwell's recommendation that scholars taxonomize and study adaptation as a genre with shared features and conventions, rather than taxonomizing it according to the media and genres of various disciplines, allows it to enter the taxonomy of genres as a subject in its own right.

Following Cardwell's call to taxonomize adaptation as a genre across media, Cartmell recommended the development of sub-genres within adaptation studies, calling for

> less general work on film adaptation and more genuinely focused and adventurous studies in areas such as popular adaptations, screenwriting "auteurs," the script, specific ideological approaches to adaptations, teen adaptations, adaptations of graphic novels, adaptations of history, novelizations, video game adaptations, television-to-film adaptations, film-to-theatre adaptations, or adaptations before sound. Each of these deserves a book-length study of its own rather than being fleetingly glanced at in studies that try to do too much. (2009, 463–64)

In 2007, Christine Geraghty cut across medium specificity theory when she traced adaptation taxonomies running across media and disciplines, including sound, music, costumes, and casting. In "Adaptation, the Genre" (2008a), Leitch examined masculine adventure adaptations as a genre; his conclusion that adaptation can be a model for all Hollywood genres underscores the theoretical potential of taxonomizing adaptations as a genre, granting them theorizing power through taxonomization, rather than taxonomizing them as a prelude to subjecting them to theoretical principles.

We need not fear that taxonomizing adaptations as adaptations will constrain them in the same way that othering taxonomies have done. Any taxonomy of adaptation as adaptation requires consideration of how adaptation crosses taxonomical lines. Adaptation's border crossings can be themselves taxonomized, crossed, and re-taxonomized to illuminate the processes by which adaptations simultaneously resist and inhabit taxonomies and how they adapt taxonomical borders by crossing them.

Such an adaptive process of taxonomization requires me to adapt the arguments I made earlier in this book about adaptation taxonomies that categorize degrees of (in)fidelity between adapted and adapting works. Previously, I argued that taxonomical categories valorizing Romantic originality and medium specificity theories militate against adaptation's identity *as* adaptation in relation to sources, while taxonomical categories valorizing fidelity to sources militate against adaptation to new contexts, and I joined Dryden and Andrew in favoring the middle taxonomy that valorizes both modes of adaptation. Yet Wagner does taxonomize adaptations as adaptations, because he considers degrees of adaptation and adaptedness, and he does valorize a high degree of adaptation *to* a new context, even as he rejects too much adaptation *from* a source.

Taxonomies measuring degrees of adaptation are not the only way to taxonomize adaptation as adaptation. If adaptation studies is to taxonomize back to othering disciplinary taxonomizations, it needs an interdiscipline of its own. We have seen that both single disciplines and interdisciplines such as translation, intertextual, intermedial, and cultural studies all taxonomize adaptation as other things or sub-taxonomize adaptation as a part of their whole. While in 2003, Leitch advocated the establishment of "Textual Studies, a discipline incorporating adaptation study, cinema studies in general, and literary studies" (2003a, 42) in an effort to diminish the distorting effects of literature and film rivalries on adaptation studies by housing them under a single discipline, by 2012 he had reconsidered his position, concluding that adaptation does not reduce to intertextuality and thus cannot be adequately defined, taxonomized, and theorized by it (2012a). In 2018, Cardwell also worried that intertextual and intermedial theories were subsuming adaptation as a distinct subject, advocating "separate and complementary" spheres for intertextual and adaptation studies.

My history attests that many scholars have worked to develop adaptation studies as a field, founding associations, conferences, journals, book series, and producing teaching guides that have brought adaptation scholars together in person and in print. The proliferation of edited collections, companions, and handbooks by comparison to monographs in our field attests further to both its diasporic nature and attempts to bring the field together. In their inaugural editorial to the Oxford journal *Adaptation*, Cartmell, Corrigan, and Whelehan maintained that the journal's "very presence is testimony to the fact that adaptation studies has an important place in serious academic debate and is a discipline in its own right," one poised "to reset, contest, and expose the existing boundaries" between disciplines" (2008, 4). Yet questions continue to be raised regarding the disciplinary status of adaptation studies. In 2011, David T. Johnson asked, "[Is] adaptation studies . . . a discipline or a subspecialty that crosses traditional disciplinal boundaries"? His conclusion was that "this field is still in the process of being defined" (2011, abstract). The following year, in "Is Adaptation Studies a Discipline?" (2012b), Leitch continued to contemplate the likelihood, advantages, and disadvantages of it being established as one. In 2015, Rainer Emig pondered "how to unite the different disciplinary methods and traditions that inform Adaptation Studies" in a way that would show "the added value of our results if we approach them not from the angles of existing disciplines but from the intersectionality of a new one that now can fully claim to be an Academic Discipline worth the title 'Adaptation Studies,'" one that brings some "kind of unity" to the "the potentially unlimited scope of our objects of study" (n.p.). In his introduction to *The Oxford Handbook of Adaptation Studies* (2017a), which itself functions to bring together adaptation scholarship. across fields, periods, theories, and disciplines, Leitch discusses adaptation studies as a field. Yet in 2018, discussing Jillian Saint Jacques's characterization of adaptation as an anti-discipline (Saint Jacques 2011b), he concluded that, as "a force field more powerful in its ability to challenge established disciplines than its aspiration for a place at their table," that it might be "better to be Robin Hood than Prince John" (Leitch and Cattrysse 2018, n.p.).

These are pertinent discussions. If adaptation resists disciplinary and field borders, how can it be or become a discipline or field itself? If it is an active process akin to theorization, how can it be studied as an "object of study"? Joining journals, edited collections, associations, and conferences devoted to adaptation, postmodern theorization has helped to develop adaptation studies as a diasporic field, united by shared processes and functions across divergent disciplines, theories, cultures, and epochs. Hutcheon's opening of adaptation studies beyond literature, theater, film, and television to other media in the same monograph indubitably helped to taxonomize adaptations as adaptations: reading adaptation across so many disciplines paradoxically maintained a sharper focus on adaptation as the object of study, by contrast to the dyadic tussling over adaptation between literature and film that so often obscured it (Chapter 3). Postmodern disciplinary and theoretical ecumenism has also forfended against adaptation being delimited to service as weapon and fodder in taxonomical disciplinary wars, even as it has been involved in theoretical wars over adaptation (Chapters 3and 4).

Developing Adaptation Taxonomies

Rather than constructing a list of all possible adaptation taxonomies (an impossible task), here I suggest strategies and rationales for taxonomizing adaptation. Rather than banishing taxonomical discourse from adaptation studies on postmodern theoretical grounds or despairing of it on pragmatic grounds, it is vitally needed to understand what adaptation is and does. Taxonomizing adaptation need not be divisive, categorical, or fixed: like adaptation itself, we can engage some taxonomies to break down others and to create dialogues between taxonomies. My aim is not to divide the field via taxonomies but to create connections between its disparate parts that can garner collective power against the hierarchical and divisive taxonomies levied on adaptation by theorization deriving from other subjects and disciplines.

Taxonomies that taxonomize adaptation as a sub-category of other disciplines foreground those disciplines, their theories, and their agendas. Given all the othering taxonomies that adaptation scholars, myself included, have so readily imposed upon adaptation, surely there is room—if not an urgent need—for taxonomies that situate adaptations in relationship to each other as adaptations. Unless we discuss adaptation practices and discourses in terms of each other, adaptation studies will continue to be taxonomized instead as a sub-category of other fields and (inter)disciplines. Emig has argued that we should carry adaptation from its sub-taxonomization as a sub-field of other disciplines to a discipline of its own, in which other disciplines constitute *its* sub-fields and sub-taxonomies (2015, n.p.). In the same year, Leitch did just this. In "History as Adaptation" (2015), he reversed the usual direction of scholarship in which adaptation performs as history, rendering history the performer of adaptation and maintaining adaptation as the focus of study. In the process, historical adaptation moved away from being a sub-category of history genres to become a sub-category of adaptation genres, along with literary adaptation, film adaptation, musical adaptation, dance adaptation, new media adaptation, and many more. Setting adaptation within disciplines in dialogue with each other across disciplines builds adaptation studies as a field informed by its own subcategories. For all their opposition to some kinds of adaptation taxonomies, Cartmell and Whelehan understand that "the will to taxonomize" in adaptation studies is "symptomatic of how the field has tried to mark out its own territory" (2007, 2), reflecting "more than anything its need to establish a critical perspective of its own" (2010, 6).

The paradox of how adaptation studies can cross other taxonomical lines while maintaining its own warrants further reflection. When I began this study, I was interested solely in opposing the tyranny of humanities theorization over adaptation. As the project developed, that goal adapted. My interest now lies in developing more reciprocal and equal relations between adaptation and theorization, including dialogue between theoretical, disciplinary, and adaptation taxonomies. The field needs more integrated dialogues rather than a binary revolution. Setting othering taxonomies in dialogue with adaptation's own and pondering their relationships to each other will inform adaptation studies as a field more acutely than exiling othering taxonomies from the field. The more adaptation scholars taxonomize back to the things that have taxonomized adaptation as something other, the more adaptation will emerge as a field or interdiscipline in its own right, on a par with the fields that have taxonomized it. Theories too can be rendered sub-categories of adaptation studies: setting aesthetic formalist adaptation studies, postmodern adaptation studies, feminist adaptation studies, post-humanist adaptation studies (etc.) in dialogue with each other will also develop adaptation studies and redress theorization's hierarchical relationship to adaptation.

For those who remain taxonophobic on theoretical grounds, adaptation taxonomies need not be (nor can they be) systematic or categorical: they can take the form of postmodern pastiches or dissipate along chains of poststructuralist difference. Nor need they be chronological: they can take the form of palimpsests. Neither need they be hierarchical or linear: they can sprawl like rhizomes or webs. Disciplinary and theoretical taxonomies have grouped, compartmentalized, ordered, and systematized other fields. Adaptation has kept them from calcifying and stagnating for centuries, and can certainly do likewise within its own field.

Theories have done little to illuminate adaptation's border crossings. Those that maintain and champion taxonomies attack them; those that reject taxonomization do little to illuminate adaptation's taxonomical violations, explaining them only in terms of theoretical principles that apply equally to everything, with adaptation serving as undifferentiated exemplum of them. By contrast, setting adaptation taxonomies in dialogue with adaptation's violation of those taxonomies will develop understanding of adaptation's complex and contradictory relationship to taxonomies. We might even taxonomize adaptation's different *kinds* of border crossings as a prelude to setting them in dialogue to understand their interrelations.

Adaptation also has internal taxonomies and taxonomy crossings. My adaptive definition of adaptation at the end of Chapter 5 attests that adaptation is never single: it is always relational, always a relationship of process and product, texts and contexts, repetitions and variations, adaptation from and adaptation to, production and consumption, and many other relationships. Adaptation adapts the taxonomical borders it crosses, adapting them, making possible paradoxical—even oxymoronic—theories of "original adaptations" (see Chapter 2), requiring scholars to express relations between conventionally opposed pairs with diacritical marks: *Literature/Film Quarterly*; "adaptation and/as/or" (Leitch 2010); "textual-contextual" (Elliott 2014b), since they elude semantics. The second half of Part II, "Refiguring Theorization," ponders these and other dynamics in the rhetoric of theorizing adaptation. Before that, Chapter 7 attends to some ways in which the third and final stage of theorization—the development of theoretical principles—can be retheorized.

7

Rethinking Theoretical Principles

Following definition and taxonomization, the third stage of theorization is the development of theoretical principles, which aim to govern, explicate, and even predict what has been defined and taxonomized. It seems odd to me that fixed definitions and segregated taxonomies should be deemed an adequate foundation for universal principles—akin to incarceration as a prelude to totalitarianism. However, objections to universal principles have generally been made on other grounds: some have argued that disagreements over theories, ideologies, epistemologies, and methodologies have rendered even scientific disciplines "unknown and unknowable," so that "no theory or conceptual framework can continue to encompass the entire field" (Dogan and Pahre 1990, 58). Even so, many humanities theorists continue to perceive the highest attainment of theorization to be one of formulating universal theoretical principles. These universal principles may be generated by pseudo-scientific theories or by pseudo-religious ones; they may lay claim to objective factuality or abstract, higher truths; they may be universal principles decreed to be certain and inviolable or universal principles of indeterminacy and unknowability (everything is indeterminate; everything is unknowable).

The purpose of this chapter is not to adjudicate which principles of theorization are truest or to generate new principles to govern adaptation but to probe their general relationships to the principles of adaptation. The principles of what theorization is and should do in the humanities have been extensively canvassed and debated; the principles of adaptation have been rarely addressed. This chapter makes a small start on redressing that imbalance. It begins by considering humanities' theorization's preoccupation with truth by contrast to how little adaptation has been concerned with truth. It continues by pondering why the humanities have struggled more than the social sciences and sciences to theorize adaptation and what we can learn from their less problematic relations to adaptation. It concludes by proposing what principles of adaptation might look like and concludes by pondering how these principles might talk back to theoretical principles and how they

Theorizing Adaptation. Kamilla Elliott, Oxford University Press (2020). © Oxford University Press.
DOI: 10.1093/oso/9780197511176.001.0001

might reach across the diasporic field that is adaptation studies to develop it through dialogue and debate over what the principles of adaptation are and how they challenge the theoretical principles that have been levied on adaptation.

Initially, when I conceived my project as a revolution rather than an adaptation of humanities theorization, I hypothesized that the principles of adaptation might *displace* those of theorization; now my view is that they need to be set in *dialogue* with the principles of theorization. I am not the first scholar to recommend or attempt this: in "Adaptation and/as/or Postmodernism" (2010) and "Adaptation and Intertextuality, or What Isn't an Adaptation, and Does It Matter?" (2012a), Thomas Leitch sets the principles of adaptation in dialogue with the principles of postmodernism and (post)structuralist intertextuality. Such dialogues are essential for establishing a more mutual relationship between adaptation and theorization, in which theoretical principles not only dialogue with but also adapt to the principles of adaptation. Beyond adaptation studies, such dialogues hold potential for humanities theorization to adapt to and through its subject matter more generally.

Theorization, Adaptation, and Truth

Researching this book, I was struck by how much theorization has been concerned with truth and how little truth has been the focus of adaptation. Pursuing truth first and foremost, it is theorization that has prioritized fidelity—far more so than adaptation. Indeed, the *Oxford English Dictionary*'s first and foremost definition of "truth" makes fidelity a synonym for it, piling up further synonyms for fidelity to define truth as "steadfast allegiance; faithfulness, fidelity, loyalty, constancy" (*OED*, 2nd rev. ed., s.v. "truth," definition A.I.1, accessed May 24, 2018, http://www-oed-com/view/Entry/207026). Theorization in the humanities has often been an exercise in coercive fidelity, in which theorization conforms what it theorizes to its principles or truths: indeed, truth's second definition is "Something that conforms with fact or reality" (*OED*, "truth," definition II.5), yet as so many post-theorists have argued, "fact" and "reality" are theoretical constructs. The *Oxford English Dictionary* defines truth in "art or literature" as "conformity with the reality of what is being represented; accuracy of representation or depiction; the quality of being true to life" (*OED*, "truth," definition 12.a.). Humanities academia's roots in theology, both theoretically and institutionally, have pressed "reality" and "life" beyond empirical and phe-nomenological domains to the "higher" truths of aesthetic, political, eth-ical, social, and cultural values and ideologies that have been and remain the *raison d'être* of most humanities scholarship.

Part I of the book attests that adaptation has been subjected to various truth-based epistemologies: studied as an empirical object, scrutinized by logic and rationality, analyzed chronologically in terms of cause and effect, investigated as a process of deliberate and agentless intertextual produc-tion, and of conscious and unconscious consumption, it has been assessed according to aesthetic, cultural, and political values deemed to be not only true but also ethically right and socially salutary. It has also been subjected to revolutions against and deconstructions of all of these epistemologies. Even theorists contesting prior theories of what truth is equally assert that their anti-truth or post-truth theories are *truer* than other theories of truth—truer truths *about* truth.

I have argued that adaptation resists all of these epistemologies, partially or wholly. Like humanities productions generally, adaptation undertakes il-logical, emotive, aesthetic, imaginative, visceral, and abstract processes that elude rational and empirical theorization. Recent theories of affect, embod-iment, materialism, intuition, and speculative realism have joined older theories of the unconscious and aesthetic pleasure (*jouissance*) to move beyond the logical, actual, and factual to study nonverbal, non-empirical other aspects of humanities subjects, as well as to decenter the human with the non-human (Grusin 2015; Ruud 2018). These theories too present their principles as truths.

The question for this study is: What does humanities theorization's em-phasis on truth obscure or omit about adaptation? If not everything is an adaptation, neither is everything a claim or a challenge to truth. Concepts such as imagination, possibility, envisioning, creativity, emotions, and aes-thetics have been subjects of humanities scholarship for centuries. These do not reduce to truth as it is understood by philosophy or empiricism. More specific to this study, if we ask, "To what does an adaptation refer?" the answer would not be truth, to which theorization aspires; it would be to adaptation's own adaptive relations. Adaptation is much more concerned with adaptive relations than with epistemological relations—with the adap-tive relationships of entities to their environments via repetition and varia-tion. These relationships have been delimited by the truth/not-truth binary of humanities theorization.

Another problem with theorizing imaginative works in terms of "conformity with . . . reality" or being "true to life" is that they didactically announce themselves as *not* being representations of real life; indeed, many aesthetic works aim to elude, escape, go beyond, or offer alternatives to "real" life. Even when they aspire to realism, they present themselves at a remove from the real. Although theorists have argued that all discourses are fictional (Schmidt 1980), some fictions are more fictional than others: imaginative works are didactically announced and studied as fictions; moreover, any theory of the fictionality of all discourses depends on theories of these announced fictions.

As fictions of fictions, as representations of representations, adaptations redouble departures from truth, going in the opposite direction from the essentializing, abstracting impulses that have been the aim of much humanities theorization, piling form upon form and refusing to distill to essentialist or abstract theoretical principles. How can we understand adaptation's complexly layered processes if we evaporate, abstract, or conflate them? In the case of theoretical principles propounding cultural values as aesthetic, ethical, or political truths, adaptation is theoretically promiscuous, as prone to challenge as to support values and to change allegiances without warning; even a single adaptation may adopt contradictory and incongruous relations to theoretical truths (Elliott 2008; 2018).

Principles of Theorization

My history of theorizing adaptation has shown how specific theoretical principles have affected the theoretical fortunes of adaptation; this metatheoretical discussion ponders the functions of theoretical principles more generally. The *Oxford English Dictionary* defines "principle" diversely as origin, source, motive, explanation, fundamental truth, widely applicable general law, and rule of conduct or practice (*OED*, 2nd rev. ed., s.v. "principle," accessed February 9, 2018, http://www-oed-com/view/Entry/151459). These variations articulate different theories of what theoretical principles are and should do: those investigating origins, sources, and motives manifest faith in chronology, logic, and cause and effect; those seeking fundamental truths strip away layers to locate cores and essences; even anti-essentialists develop "widely applicable general" laws or truths about anti-essentialism; those concerned with aesthetic, ethical, or political cultural values construct theoretical principles as rules to be observed and practices to be adopted. Even after the theoretical turn, we have seen that adaptation remains the illustrative or exemplary prooftext for new theoretical principles just as it did for prior ones.

The humanities have struggled to theorize adaptation more than the sciences and social sciences largely because of humanities' theo-rization's inheritance from theo-logy. From Matthew Arnold's championing of high culture (1869) as the successor to Christianity to Jacques Derrida's negative theology (1989b) and beyond, scholars have forged continuities between humanities theo-rization and theo-logy. Like theo-logy, theo-rization in the humanities has more often than not unfolded as a top-down, god-like, authoritative proclamation of truths, beliefs, values, judgments, and laws levied upon subject-ed matter. Like theology, much humanities theorization has been didactically and centrally devoted to the promulgation and inculcation of pre-determined, improving, higher ethical, aesthetic, political, cultural, and philosophical truths and values.

Although the theoretical turn in the humanities generated political, philosophical, and cultural revolutions in the *content* of theoretical principles, it did not adequately redress the hierarchy between theoretical principles and what they theorize. Even scholars engaging theories devoted to theoretical skepticism have maintained the hierarchy of theorization over adaptation: for example, in *Adaptation Theory and Criticism*, Gordon E. Slethaug accepts "the governing principles . . . of modernism and postmodernism" over adaptation (2014, 7), claiming that "all instances of adaptation are governed by principles of [Derridean] supplementation" (31).

Bruno Latour has argued, "In theory, theories exist. In practice, they do not" (1988, 178). Given all of the hierarchical binarisms dismantled in recent decades, it is perplexing that the one between theory and practice should remain: indeed, one single, undeconstructed binarism has all the more power after other binarisms have been dismantled. Even self-reflexive theories of theorization mandating that theorists acknowledge their historical situatedness, biases, and the impossibility of seeing anything objectively or impartially do not subvert the authority of theorization over its subject matter: rather, they intensify it by subjecting the theorist to the authority of theoretical principles. Such top-down imposition of theoretical principles figures adaptation as subject matter to be theorized rather than as a process whose own principles are at work upon theoretical principles and are more prone to resist than to support them.

The relationship between theorization and what it theorizes is more equitable in the sciences. The sciences theorize theories and theoretical principles as provisional and temporary; they are not immutable, God-given truths; when they fail to explicate their subject matter, they are discarded. Scientific theorists accept that their principles need to adapt to what they theorize. As Thomas S. Kuhn's history of scientific theorization attests:

> In the course of any spell of normal science anomalies accumulate, problems and difficulties which only arise because of the attempt to fit nature into the pattern defined by the existing orthodoxy.... Eventually practice rearranges itself around new procedures and new concepts which are thought to deal more adequately with the anomalies.... [A] scientific revolution occurs. (1962, 11)

In this account, subject matter matters to mind and has been allowed to change minds. Evidence of biological evolution brought about one of the greatest revolutions in scientific theory, severing it from theology. We need a similar revolution in the humanities—adaptation may well be the mechanism for it.

Even as Kuhn acknowledged that cultural, political, and social factors inflect scientific paradigms, he critiqued the social sciences and humanities for discouraging divergent thinking: "We have attempted to teach students how to arrive at 'correct' answers that our civilization has taught us as correct" (1962, 141). By contrast, "Confronted with anomaly or with crisis, scientists take a different attitude toward existing paradigms, and the nature of their research changes accordingly" (90). Even more than the social sciences, humanities theorization has advanced theoretical principles that, like gods or totalitarian dictators, are not subject to challenges from what they theorize, what they govern, or even to their own laws.

Against these tendencies, two twenty-first-century adaptation theorists have engaged methodologies that bring the field closer to Kuhn's account of scientific theoretical revolutions based in a Q&A dialogue between what theorizes and what is theorized. As we have seen, Leitch's "Against Conclusions" (2017c) figures theorization as a process of asking questions, positing answers, questioning those answers, finding them lacking, asking new questions, locating new provisional answers, without ever settling finally on any. Leitch's essay recalls Jonathan Culler's view of theorization as a continual questioning of attitudes and positions, including one's own, a methodology that "offers not a set of solutions but the prospect of further thought," rendering theorization "endless" (1981, 15; 120). This theory of theorization grants scholars eternal life in the realm of questions, without requiring any decisive findings or answers—indeed, decisive and final answers are eschewed, as answers are merely stepping stones to further questions. Linda Hutcheon's methodology in *A Theory of Adaptation* (2006) is also based on questions—the empirically focused questions, Who adapts? What is adapted? Where is it adapted? How is it adapted? When is it adapted? Governed by postmodern theoretical principles, the answers to these questions are variable and open-ended. Like Leitch's ongoing questions that militate "Against Conclusions" (2017c), Hutcheon too raised "new questions" at the end of *A Theory of Adaptation* (2006, 170). Leitch's and Hutcheon's Q&A methodologies have been productive and have established them as field leaders, I believe, because their methodologies are theoretically *adaptive*, as questions and answers *adapt to each other* to produce theorization. However, their methodologies differ. Leitch's Q&A theory of theorization is one of incremental progress, resembling Augustan theories of how the arts incrementally progress through adaptation, in which each answer is, for a season, deemed to be the best answer so far, arrived at via discarded answers on which it improves. Just as there is no end to the process of adaptation, so too there is no end to Leitch's Q&A—no possibility of ever reaching a final answer. By contrast, apart from a few points in *A Theory of Adaptation* when Hutcheon allows the reader to glimpse her own theoretical allegiances and preferences, Hutcheon allows multiple, often contradictory, answers to her questions to co-exist in an indeterminate, pluralist pastiche. Her questions do not produce answers that must be discarded in a quest for better ones; rather, answers accumulate, conflict, and coexist without resolving into a unified whole. Despite her personal adherence to postmodern pluralist theoretical principles, Hutcheon's hybrid methodology in *A Theory of Adaptation* challenges the hierarchy of theorization over adaptation through postmodern pastiche, which disempowers theories through their unresolved disputes with other theories, and through empiricism, which seeks a more reciprocal relationship between theory and what it theorizes: "I have tried to derive theory from practice" (2006, xiv).

Joining a more democratic and adaptive relationship between theory and practice, humanities theorization can learn from the sciences to be more open to theoretical experimentation that may result initially in theoretical failure and trials that may produce errors. Our obsession with truth as it is defined by theology and philosophy has rendered us fearful of experiments and trials that may fail truth and result in theoretical incorrectness. However, adhering to theoretical principles that refuse to recognize error has, to my mind, produced greater inaccuracy and entrenched theoretical failure in adaptation studies. Adaptation is itself a process of trial and error: some adaptations succeed, survive, and thrive; others fail and die. Scientists have learned a great deal about the principles of adaptation from failed adaptations and mutations—so too can humanities scholars. Thomas Henry Huxley wrote: "For the notion that every organism has been created as it is . . . Mr Darwin substitutes . . . a method of trial and error" (quoted in Leitch 2009, 95). Humanities experimentation need not undertake scientific methodologies nor subscribe to empirical epistemologies—indeed, my history suggests that much pseudo-scientific theorization, particularly the anti-adaptation theory of medium specificity, has done occluded understanding of adaptation more than it has illuminated it. By contrast, the creative-critical, practical-theoretical modes of studying adaptation discussed in Chapter 6 and in "Doing Adaptation: The Adaptation as Critic" (Elliott 2014c) have illuminated adaptation theorization with adaptation practice. Creative-critical practices are experimental and exploratory, aimed at discovering new information about the processes and products of adaptation rather than focused on subjecting adaptation to the principles of theorization. Although scholars reading my book to locate authoritative, universal principles of theo-rization to impart to students will be disappointed, they will find richly productive ways of researching and teaching through creative-critical practices that, in my experience, have illuminated the processes of adaptation and their relationship to theorization. As I argue in the second half of Part II, "Refiguring Theorization," theoretical experimentation can be undertaken at the microscopic level of rhetoric in ways that adapt theorization and adaptation to each other. More than revolutions from one theory to another, adaptation studies needs a revolution in the *relationship* between adaptation and theorization; more than new theoretical principles to subject adaptation, adaptation studies needs its own principles, based in its own adaptive processes.

Theorizing Adaptations as Adaptations

Addressing the resistance of scholars to his theory of deconstruction, Paul de Man argued that "The resistance to theory is a resistance to the use of language about language" (1986, 12). I argue similarly that the resistance to adaptation is a resistance to the use of adaptation in ways that are "about" adaptation. Just as de Man claimed that "Literary theory can be said to come into being when the approach to literary texts is no longer based on non-linguistic . . . considerations" (1986, 10), so too adaptation theory can be said to come into being when the approach to adaptations is no longer based on non-adaptive considerations. This is another reason why creative-critical practice is so effective in theorizing adaptation, because it works to adapt creative practice to critical theory, and vice versa.

We need to stay with adaptation, pondering it on its own terms, in its own right, according to its own (anti)definitions, (anti)taxonomies, and (anti)theoretical principles, rather than fleeing to the familiarity of theoretical principles devised to explicate other things. No matter how much theories devised to explicate other things may illuminate adaptations, they do not theorize adaptation as adaptation or produce principles of adaptation. Indeed, the more we theorize adaptation in terms of other things, the further we stray from theorizing adaptation. We have been too focused on theoretical specificities—medium specificity in particular—and insufficiently on adaptation specificities. Since we will inevitably continue to theorize adaptations as other things, at least for now, what we need is a reciprocal discourse, in which other things are theorized as adaptations, as well as a dialogue between the two discourses.

Although some scholars have claimed to theorize adaptations as adaptations (Cattrysse 2014; Hutcheon 2006), we have seen how swiftly after that declaration they subjected adaptation to theoretical principles from translation studies and postmodern philosophy. Indeed, it is postmodern principles focused on consumer response that define what theorizing adaptation *as* adaptation means for Hutcheon: "It is only as inherently double- or multilaminated works that [adaptation] can be theorized as adaptation" (2006, 6). She later explained:

> In [*A Theory of Adaptation*], I thought I had to treat adaptations as adaptations. The reality is that as readers or moviegoers, if we don't know it's an adaptation, or we know it is but don't know the adapted text, then it doesn't matter, we simply experience it the way we would any other work of art. (Zaiontz 2009, 1)

Thus, even as she theorized adaptations as adaptations, she did so according to particular theoretical principles. Moreover, she maintained that if consumers do not recognize adaptation as such, "it doesn't matter." Yet for adaptation studies, theorizing adaptation as adaptation does matter.

Hutcheon also argued that "adaptations disrupt elements like priority and authority" (2006, 174). This includes the priority and authority of theorization over adaptation, which Hutcheon challenged via an empirical methodology aiming to disrupt the priority of theory over practice. In ancient Greece and Rome, an empiric was a physician who relied on practical experience to treat patients rather than theoretical writings. Empiricism mandates that theories be tested against observations of practice rather than on intuition, revelation, or a priori reasoning. Even poststructuralists, who reject empiricism as a path to theoretical truth, have conceded that any theory "has to start out from empirical considerations" (de Man 1986, 5). Defined as "Primary reliance on evidence derived from observation, investigation, or experiment rather than on abstract reasoning, theoretical analysis, or speculation" (OED, 2nd rev. ed., s.v. "empiricism," definition 6, accessed May 15, 2017, https://www-oed-com/view/Entry/61344?), empiricism goes some way toward challenging the priority of humanities theorization over what it theorizes and encouraging experimentation. Even so, empiricizing adaptation is not identical to theorizing adaptation as adaptation. This is not only because empiricism is so easily conscripted to serve pre-existing theoretical principles but also because the principles of empiricism are not the principles of adaptation.

Eckart Voigts-Virchow comes closer than any scholar I have read to identifying what it means to study adaptation as adaptation, according to its own principles: "The study of meta-adaptation, namely the observation of adaptational observation, or the dialogue with adaptational dialogue, or the attempt to see *adaptations as adaptations*, is the best way to make adaptational processes explicit" (2013, 66, emphasis added; see also Voigts-Virchow 2009). Not only does "meta" articulate a methodology that considers adaptation in terms of adaptation's own principles but also, as a prefix denoting change, transformation, permutation, and substitution, it articulates principles of adaptation. Voigts-Virchow here proposes that we observe, dialogue, and write about adaptations as adaptational objects and processes. A commitment to meta-methodologies has also shaped my decision to write a metacritical history, a metatheoretical theory, and a meta-rhetorical rhetoric of adaptation in this book. This is because it is only at the level of meta-analyses that I have been able to discover and partially redress "the problem of theorizing adaptation" in the humanities.

Principles of Adaptation

The principles of adaptation resist definition: the dictionary tells us *what* adaptation is (change/changing) and *why* it happens (to suit a new environment), but not *how* it happens, indicating the elusiveness of studying the principles of adaptation as a process. Theorization has rushed to fill that gap, explicating the "how" of adaptation via theoretical principles of individual agency, industrial production, economics, politics, semiotics and narratology, consumption, phenomenology, psychology, and more. Most prior discussions of "the principles of adaptation" are limited to principles of adaptation *practice*, set apart from and subjected to theoretical principles.[1] Whether in how-to-adapt manuals for practitioners such as Ben Brady's *Principles of Adaptation for Film and Television* (1994) or academic writings, "the principles of adaptation" usually refer to principles that must be followed by practitioners in order to make "successful" adaptations— whether that success is defined in commercial, aesthetic, narratological, psychological, political, ethical, ideological, or philosophical terms. This is what Colin MacCabe meant when he described theorizing adaptation as providing "models of how to adapt" (2011, 8).

The relegation of adaptation's principles to the domain of practice places them below theoretical principles in a hierarchical binary. Reinforcing the hierarchy, the principles of producing adaptation are subordinated to theoretical principles. How-to books such as Brady's recommend the theoretical principles of Aristotelian drama; other practitioner guides subject the principles of adaptation to the theoretical principles of medium specificity, aesthetic formalism, and structuralist narratology (Seger 1992; Field 2003; McKee 1997).

In a rare departure from these tendencies, in his chapter "The Principles of Adaptation" (1979), Morris Beja did consider how the principles of adaptation resist theoretical principles in a study of adaptation practices. Even as Beja adhered to the theoretical principles of his day, dubbing fidelity mandates "wrong-headed," he pronounced them "fully understandable and not especially depressing" (88). Against medium specificity principles decreeing that a good film cannot be made from a good book because of their essentialist, irreducible formal differences, he identified adapters who had done just that (86). Against the determinacy and categoricity of formal theoretical principles, he demonstrated the complexity and fluidity of actual adaptation practice; like Leitch 42 years later (2017c), he raised numerous questions without arriving at "definitive answers" (81), concluding that the principles of adaptation must remain "general" rather than "categorical" (86), in contrast to mainstream narratological theories of the day.

However, Beja did not allow the possibility that prevailing theoretical principles might be *themselves* inadequate for theorizing adaptation: instead, like other scholars discussed in my history, he turned from humanities to social sciences theories to explicate adaptation's resistance to humanities theorization, faulting the pragmatics of production, tensions between artistry and economics, industry conventions, and audience expectations for adaptation's failures to live up to the humanities' aesthetic ideals.

De Man has argued that a "method that cannot be made to suit the 'truth' of its object can only teach delusion" (1986, 4); Mieke Bal concurs that "no concept is meaningful for cultural analysis unless it helps us to understand the object better on its—the object's—own terms" (2007, 8). It seems to me that too much energy has gone into debates over which theoretical principles, developed to theorize other things, should govern adaptation studies, and not enough into locating and debating principles of adaptation. Enough of my own time has been spent writing metacriticism of theorization's problematic relationship to adaptation. It is time to turn from critiquing the principles of theorization to ponder and develop the principles of adaptation.

Principles of adaptation will not do away with principles of theorization, but can enter into dialogue with them, holding them accountable to adaptation. Principles of adaptation will provide a much-needed discursive juncture for adaptation scholars, enabling dialogue and debate across disciplines and theories. In a conference paper presented in 2015, Rainer Emig asked "whether Adaptation Studies wish[es] to be a multidisciplinary enterprise looking at widely diverging manifestations of Adaptation in all areas of culture—and perhaps even beyond—or whether Adaptation Studies aim[s] at being (or becoming) a discipline of its own" (n.p.). If we extract, develop, debate, and disseminate whatever principles of adaptation have emerged from our research, this can provide a common ground on which we come together to discuss adaptation as adaptation, even when we disagree on what these principles are. The principles will inevitably differ according to the disciplinary, historical, cultural, and theoretical situatedness of their devisors; even so, a shared focus on principles of adaptation will provide a centrifugal force to offset the centripetal effect of so many media forms, disciplines, periods, cultures, and theoretical principles, creating a common discursive ground for scholars. It will allow us to ponder and debate whether and how the principles of adaptation vary across media, fields, technologies, industries, eras, cultures, and more.

Debating principles of adaptation should also help to bridge some of the impasses in our field created by theoretical principles, which have all too often sent embattled scholars into dismissive, reductive, and hostile separate spheres. Even as we debate the principles of adaptation, we can relax in our theoretical disagreements, understanding that the principles of adaptation are themselves adapting (Elliott 2012a) and can help us adapt to each other.

I make a small start on this task here, hoping that other scholars will debate, build on, and develop their own principles of adaptation. The principles that follow represent my own ideas, developed over many years; at the same time, they are very much the principles of this moment, shaped by this study of adaptation and theorization. I expect them to adapt as I continue to research, as I revisit prior research, and as new processes, products, and types of adaptation emerge. I also expect them to adapt to and through principles of adaptation developed by others.

The principles of adaptation are pervasive, but not universal.

They stretch across time and space, but do not transcend them.

The principles of adaptation are more concerned with the successful survival of what adaptation adapts than with authority over it.

The principles of adaptation are not top-down affairs, but work horizontally and interactively within and between entities and environments to adapt them to each other in multiple ways, since each entity has multiple environments, adapts to other entities within those environments as well as to those environments, and as environments also adapt to what inhabits them.

Always relational, the principles of adaptation also adapt these multifarious *relationships* between entities and environments.

The principles of adaptation are more fluid, hybrid, and mobile than they are categorical, unitary, and stationary.

They principles of adaptation adapt the borders that adaptation crosses as well as what resides on either side.

The principles of adaptation are experimental; they do not always succeed in helping what they inhabit to survive. Indeed, the principles of adaptation decree that some things must die in order for other things to survive.

The principles of adaptation repeat and vary simultaneously. They cannot, therefore, produce the same results over repeated experiments, nor can they be predicted based on how they have functioned in the past.

The principles of adaptation return and move forward simultaneously. They cannot, therefore, be explicated solely within a present moment or a local context.

The principles of adaptation are at work in the production and consumption of adaptations on all levels from the macroscopic to the microscopic.

The principles of adaptation do not conform to the principles of logic, rationality, objectivism, and empiricism, nor do they conform to illogical, irrational, subjective, and metaphysical epistemologies that have challenged them.

The principles of adaptation are ideologically promiscuous, uninterested in the pursuit of truth or in fealty to any particular ethics, aesthetics, politics, or ideology.

The principles of adaptation themselves adapt.

While the principles of adaptation cannot themselves be predicted, they can have prescriptive functions by suggesting adaptive *methodologies* for adaptation studies. The following list makes a small start on this. It includes some methodologies already operative in adaptation studies; I invite other scholars to add to them, debate them, and *adapt* them.

Develop methodologies that study adaptation as adaptation—as an adaptive relational process running between entities and environments in multifarious ways.

Study adaptation simultaneously as process and product, as repetition and variation; do not separate these categorically or privilege one over the other: adaptation does not do so.

Do not separate entities and their environments: against theoretical divisions of formal and cultural or textual and contextual adaptation studies, develop "a formal culturalism, a cultural formalism, a textual contextualism . . . a contextual textualism" (Elliott 2014b, 585–86).

Study the adaptation of environments to the adaptations within them, as well as the adaptation of entities to environments. Set these studies in dialogue with each other.

Consider the adaptation of a single entity in the context of its multiple environments; conversely, consider multiple entities adapting to each other and to each other's adaptations within a single environment. Set these studies in dialogue with each other.

Set aspects of adaptation in dialogue with each other to generate discourses in which adaptation becomes "about" adaptation. Set many aspects of adaptation in dialogue within a single adaptation; conversely, set a single aspect of adaptation in dialogue with its manifestations across many adaptations.

Study adaptations of a single work over a long period of time to create longer genealogies of adaptation.

Set multiple adaptations of a single work in dialogue with each other to learn more about the adaptation *of* adaptation.

Find other ways to study the adaptation of adaptation itself—its adapting definitions, taxonomies, principles, functions, practices (Elliott 2012a).

Rather than judge an adaptation's failure or success according to a priori theoretical principles (aesthetics, narrative, politics, etc.), judge it by how *adaptive* it is.

Consider what aspects of adaptation humanities theories have caused us to overlook; study them.

Step away from the case studies to undertake microscopic and macroscopic studies of adaptation in order to bring greater variety and new angles of view to the field and to connect the field across media and disciplines.[2] Build studies of micro-adaptations across media (e.g., the adaptation of rhythm or clothing or a cultural ideology across media). Be willing to spend years or even decades on a macro-adaptation study.

Do not limit adaptation study to logical, empirical, or rational epistemologies—adaptation is not limited to these. Conversely, do not limit adaptation to their theoretical binaries (illogical, abstract, affective, psychoanalytic epistemologies): adaptation is not limited to these and is not fully explicated by them. Instead, let adaptation talk back to theories and epistemologies of all kinds.

Develop hybrid and relational methodologies that cut across theoretical and disciplinary divides as adaptation does.

Rather than asking solely, "How does my field theorize adaptation?" ask, "How does adaptation retheorize my field and how does it call my scholarship—and me—to adapt to it?"

Be self-reflexive about one's own adaptation scholarship: Why I have chosen these theories and theories of theorization? How have I adapted adaptation to theorization? How have I adapted (or not) my theoretical principles over time? What strange theoretical brews has adaptation called me to engage? Why have I opposed or disregarded certain kinds of adaptation and championed others? How has adaptation positioned me as a scholar? What sacrifices have I made to be an adaptation scholar? What benefits has studying adaptation brought me?

Dare to challenge academic institutional environments when they are inhospitable to adaptation.

Dare to challenge mainstream and one's current ways of studying adaptation and to experiment with new ways. Dare to err. Dare to fail. Dare to adapt.

Adapting Adaptation Theorization

The principles of adaptation and the methodologies generated by them also contain possibilities for adapting how we theorize adaptation and the relationship between adaptation and theorization. As before, the following list is under development and open to debate, refutation, supplementation, and adaptation.

Treat theorization not as a discourse that governs and explicates adaptation but as one of its many environments. Consider how it tries to adapt adaptation and how adaptation adapts (or does not) to it.

Do not allow theoretical environments to override attention to adaptation's other environments.

Set theorization in dialogue with adaptation and adaptation's other environments.

Ponder how and why adaptation has thrived in some theoretical environments and struggled to survive in others. Challenge the theoretical environments that have given adaptation a failing grade: ask how *they* have failed adaptation.

Treat theorization as a process that is itself subject to adaptation by what it theorizes, not just to adaptation by other theories.

Let the principles of adaptation talk back to the principles of theorization.

What these lists, I hope, make clear is that our discourses of adaptation need to extend from the adaptation of fictional stories to the adaptation of theoretical stories. While Robin Sims attests that theory not only adapts but also "continues to mutate" (2016 246), the central argument of "Retheorizing Theorization" is that theorization needs to adapt not solely to other theories but also to what it theorizes, and that adaptation is the subject, vehicle, and process par excellence for this enterprise.

Beyond adaptation studies, the adaptation of theorization is a particularly pertinent issue in a wider context where many scholars perceive the theoretical turn in the humanities to be threatened, stale, or superannuated. Valentine Cunningham, rejoicing over what he perceived to be the long-awaited come-uppance of the theoretical turn, articulated the view of those adhering defiantly to the theories rejected by that turn, declaring their comeback and triumph (2002). Supporters of the theoretical turn, however, have argued that the turn only became stale and diluted when it entered the academic mainstream, and that it now requires revivification (Docherty 1996). Others have worked, conversely, to render the theoretical turn more accessible to the mainstream and more relevant to society (Payne and Schad 2003). Some have seized on the perceived crisis to promote one theory over the rest (Eagleton 1996) or to defend one post-theory from attacks by others (C. Davis 2004). These theorists take seriously the adage "adapt or die."

Subsequently, scholars have declared the crisis to be over, claiming that the theoretical turn *has been* revivified, made relevant to new issues and contexts, and that scholars can rest assured of its survival and vitality (Attridge and J. Elliott 2011). In *Literary Criticism in the 21st Century: Theory Renaissance*, Vincent B. Leitch agreed with Derek Attridge and Jane Elliott that humanities theorization has undergone a renaissance that is firmly established, even as it is "fractalized," disorganized, and divided into "many subdisciplines, fields, and topics" (2014, vi) that proliferate and fuse.[3,4] Yet theories continue to adapt to other theories rather than to what they theorize. David N. Rodowick has affirmed that theoretical change occurs when "theory takes itself as its own object, examines and reconfigures its genealogy, conceptual structure, and terminology, and posits for itself a new identity and cultural standing" (2007, xv). As a result, the top-down rhetoric of "theorizing adaptation" pervades adaptation studies, while a reciprocal, inverse rhetoric of "adapting theorization" remains underdeveloped.

Adaptation scholars have taken steps toward redressing this imbalance. Cardwell has objected to the dominance of theorization over adaptation: "Adaptations are rarely studied for themselves—rarely is interpretation valued as much as theorizing," as adaptations are read "to illuminate theories of narrative or medium specificity; to engage in a debate about the cultural values and statuses of literature, film and television; or to investigate continuities and change in cultural production" (2002, 69). Building on earlier perceptions that adaptations function as critical "commentaries" on the forms they adapt (Wagner 1975; Andrew 1984b; Sinyard 1986) in new theoretical contexts, Julie Sanders has argued for their mutual influence: "Impacted upon by movements in, and readings produced by, the theoretical and intellectual arena as much as by their so-called sources," adaptations create "potent theoretical intertexts of their own" (2006 13; 18). In 2006, Hutcheon asserted the importance of adaptation practice to adaptation theory, arguing that "[v]ideogames, theme park rides, Web sites, graphic novels, song covers, operas, musicals, ballets, and radio and stage plays are . . . as important to . . . theorizing [adaptation] as are the more commonly discussed movies and novels" (xiv). In 2009, Catherine Constable demonstrated how film adaptations have adapted philosophy. My study builds on these to propose, in place of totalizing theory or piecemeal theory, *adaptive theorization*, in which theorization is adapted through its encounter with adaptation. Adaptation is not simply a cultural practice: it is also a process akin to and at odds with theorization.

Part II, Section I of this book, "Retheorizing Theorization," has argued that the failure to theorize adaptation as adaptation begins at the theoretical baseline of field definition, continues in the second stage of theorization, the development of taxonomies, and culminates in the third stage, the development and application of theoretical principles. It suggests that the main way to redress theoretical failure in adaptation studies is for theorization to define, taxonomize, and theorize adaptation as adaptation. Theorizing adaptations as adaptations is a self-reflexive simile, differentiating adaptation *from itself* through a mirrored exchange of adaptation as vehicle and adaptation as tenor. Such a simile resists both the essentializing and othering effects of humanities theorization by functioning as its own other and its own self. The mediating "as" is neither adjective, noun, nor verb: it is an adverb "expressing a comparison of equivalence" (*OED*, 2nd rev. ed., s.v. "as," definition A, accessed September 12, 2017, https://www-oed-com/view/Entry/11307). Equivalence is neither identity nor the hierarchical, oppositional, binary, random, or arbitrary modes of difference that humanities theorization has imposed on adaptation. Equivalence is theoretically ecumenical, whether in the equivalences of translation, democratic political principles, or philosophical principles that seek equivalences (correspondences) between subject matter, discourse, and truth. Beyond theoretical ecumenism, the asymmetrical equivalences and symmetries of the "as" simile make space for both agreement and disagreement: for the both/and/and/and (etc.) pluralism of postmodernism, for the either/or binaries of structuralism, and the neither/nor/never of poststructuralism. Throughout my career, adaptation has revealed theoretical blind spots, limitations, hypocrisies, abuses, omissions, and contradictions in my own scholarship. Rather than chastise adaptation for revealing them, as theorization has done, we would do better to engage in adaptive theorization. The following are some *principles of adaptive theorization*, in progress and subject to ongoing adaptation:

Adaptive theorization begins with the willing suspension of belief in theoretical principles, including our most cherished beliefs.

Adaptive theorization calls scholars to depart from the usual theoretical suspects, principles, practices, and methodologies and engage with those generated by adaptation itself.

Adaptive theorization applies the principles of adaptation to adaptation and continues to adapt them over time.

Adaptive theorization allows the principles, processes, and products of adaptation to adapt.

Adaptive theorization does not focus on point–counterpoint debates between rival theories, engaging adaptation solely as a prooftext for theoretical contests; rather, it considers how each theory might adapt to adaptation first and foremost, and only then how rival theories might adapt to each other in more mutual, reciprocal interchanges.

Adaptive theorization does not pursue total theoretical revolutions; it adapts rather than refutes or overthrows.

Adaptive theorization theorizes theories as adaptations.

Adaptive theorization joins adaptation in refusing stasis, fixity, and uniformity.

Adaptive theorization, being a relational process involving repetition with variation, does not dissolve into nihilism, anarchy, random arbitrariness, or the totally differential.

Adaptive theorization will be more figurative than didactic.

Adaptive theorization will always be itself adapting.

For all the oppositions and impasses between theorization and adaptation, this study has identified points of confluence between them with potential to generate adaptive theorization. Even as adaptation resists definition, it does so *through* its definition. The second half of Part II, "Refiguring Theorization," demonstrates some ways in which figurative rhetoric can further adapt the relationship between theorization and adaptation in the humanities.

SECTION II
REFIGURING THEORIZATION: INTRODUCTION

"Refiguring Theorization" shifts from macroscopic historical and theoretical metacriticism to microscopic rhetorical analysis. Chapter 8, "The Rhetoric of Theorizing Adaptation," demonstrates that theorizing adaptation has unfolded not only at the level of books, book chapters, journal articles, and reviews but also at the level of sentences, phrases, words, and pieces of words. Moreover, relations between parts of speech incisively inform relations between adaptation and theorization. Such microscopic processes often mirror the macroscopic findings of my metacritical history and my metatheoretical history: for example, the tyranny of "theorizing adaptation" has been exerted by the tiniest pieces of rhetoric. Analyzing relations between parts of speech governed by the laws of grammar makes clear that some problems of theorizing adaptation lie within the systems and structures of rhetoric itself. Even so, microscopic rhetorical analysis takes larger discourses to pieces to understand their workings and as a prelude to constructing new discourses of theorizing adaptation.

The *Oxford English Dictionary*'s primary definition of rhetoric is: "The art of using language effectively so as to persuade or influence others, *esp.* the exploitation of figures of speech and other compositional techniques to this end" (*Oxford English Dictionary*, 2nd rev. ed., s.v. "rhetoric," definition 1.a, accessed July 4, 2018, https://www-oed-com/view/Entry/165178), a definition derived from, but not limited to, Aristotle's *Poetics*. Rhetoric's conjoined persuasive and aesthetic functions render it particularly resonant for pondering the relationship between theoretical discourses and aesthetic practices, with potential for refiguring their relationship.

The first half of Chapter 8, entitled "A Grammar of Theorizing Adaptation," probes how grammatical relations between parts of speech have constructed relations between adaptation and theorization. The second half of Chapter 8,

"Theorization—Adaptation—Figuration," attests to the central and vital role that figurative rhetoric has played in humanities theorization generally and in adaptation studies particularly. Identifying commonalities between these three processes positions figuration as a potential mediator between theorization and adaptation. Like adaptation, rhetorical figures can be defined, but their definitions often resist the definition of definition as fixed; they can be taxonomized, but they cross theoretical taxonomical borders; they can be conscripted by theories but, in so doing, like adaptation, they have often been constrained by theoretical definitions, taxonomies, and principles that militate against their own processes. Like adaptation, figuration has potential to change and *adapt* humanities theorization. It has already done this many times by providing a variegated, adaptive rhetoric that has generated new ways of thinking, speaking, and writing in the humanities, offering a model for how adaptation might do likewise.

Chapter 9, "Refiguring Adaptation Studies," examines how particular rhetorical figures have informed and can further inform particular theoretical problems within adaptation studies and refigure adaptation theorization within adaptation studies.

8

The Rhetoric of Theorizing Adaptation

Although rhetoric is broader than verbal language and has been defined as "The structural elements, compositional techniques, and modes of expression used to produce a desired effect on a viewer, audience, etc., in music, dance, and the visual arts" (*OED*, 2nd rev. ed., s.v. "rhetoric," definition 4.b, accessed August 6, 2017, https://www.oed-com/view/Entry/165178),[1] humanities theorization has unfolded primarily as a verbal rhetorical enterprise. As a metacritical study, this book too focuses primarily on verbal discourses of theorizing adaptation and itself unfolds as verbal discourse. This is not to say that future studies must continue in this vein; indeed, I hope that scholars will consider how other representational modes have theorized and might theorize adaptation: such studies have already enriched our field and will continue to do so.

A Grammar of Theorizing Adaptation

Unlike most grammars, this one does not catalogue and analyze all parts of speech, although my research did consider them all, and the diacritics of theorizing adaptation as well. My initial draft for this chapter exceeded 25,000 words, carrying me far beyond the word limit allowed by the press. Moreover, its findings were variable: some were banal and obvious; others were pedantic, tedious, and mechanical. More fundamentally, the categoricity of such an approach and its aspirations to totality were diametrically opposed to the methodologies and arguments governing this study, creating an illusion of coverage, when adaptation cannot be studied comprehensively in categorical ways, because it is always changing and violating the categorical boundaries that theorization erects to contain it. Moreover, both the longer draft and the following extracts from it make clear that some limitations of theorizing adaptation lie within the structures and systems of rhetoric itself. Therefore, in this chapter I present only the most resonant findings for this

Theorizing Adaptation. Kamilla Elliott, Oxford University Press (2020). © Oxford University Press.
DOI: 10.1093/oso/9780197511176.001.0001

study of adaptation's relationship to theorization, beginning with the suffixes that differentiate adapt-ation from theor-ization.

Suffixes

That adapt-*ation* and theor-*ization* do not function equally is apparent in their suffixes. In the mid-nineteenth century, Charles Dickens mocked "-ization" as a preposterous, pretentious rhetorical construct:

> He was not aware . . . that he was driving at any ization. He had no favorite ization that he knew of. But he certainly was more staggered by these terrible occurrences than he was by names, of howsoever many syllables. (1865, 1: 107)

In the twenty-first century my focus lies on the coercive and oppressive aspects of "-ization." To "-ize" is to "make or conform to, or treat in the way of, the thing expressed by the derivation" (*OED*, 2nd rev. ed., s.v. "-ize," definition 1.a, accessed February 2, 2018, https://www-oed-com/view/Entry/100447); to "-apt" (from the verb "apt"), is to "make fit, adapt (to), prepare suitably (for)" (*OED*, 2nd rev. ed., s.v. "apt," definition 1.a, accessed February 2, 2018, https://www-oed-com/view/Entry/9970); "to incline, dispose to" (*OED*, "apt," definition 3). In other words, to "-ize" is to conform something to the term that precedes it; to "-apt" is to suit or fit something to something *else*. To theorize is to conform something to theory; to adapt is to alter something so that it better fits with its environment, allowing it to survive and thrive in it. Humanities theorization has threatened the survival of adaptation as a theoretical object; for me, adaptation is a better model for humanities study than the modes of theorization we currently engage.

The contrast carries into adapt-ation and theor-ization, nouns of action formed from verbs. The suffix -*ation* is "the condition of being" the word that precedes it, while "-ixation" actively makes, conforms to, and treats in the way of the term that precedes it (*OED*, 2nd rev. ed., s.v. "-ization," accessed February 2, 2018, https://www-oed-com/Entry/100446). Given such etymological contrasts, it is hardly surprising that theorization has dominated adaptation: its coercive and dominating tendencies are embedded in its suffix.

The title of this book, *Theorizing Adaptation*, articulates the relationship between adaptation and theorization as a process in which theorization, operating as a present participle verb, works actively upon adaptation as a noun subject. Pondering how adaptation might vie with theorization rhetorically on an equal footing, I considered the reciprocally inverse terms "adaptization" and "theoration." "Adaptization" exists in computer studies, where it describes the technological processes by which programmers adapt legacy software to new computer environments (Wavresky and Lee 2016). "Theoration" is, however, nowhere. My own values and beliefs favor making theorization more like adaptation rather than the other way around. "Theoration" articulates a less coercive process of studying adaptation, conferring on adaptation (and whatever else it "theorates") the status of "being itself." I do not believe for a moment that theoration will catch on in academia: scholars are too invested in authority and mastery over what we theorize. Still, the term deserves further consideration as a model for humanities theorization generally and for adaptation studies in particular, as I argued in Chapters 5–7 of this book.

Prepositions

Prepositions have played a major role in constructing variable relationships between adaptation and theorization. "On" has figured their relationship as a one-way, top-down process, in which theorization is levied or superimposed on adaptation, as in these titles:

"The Discourse on Adaptation" (C. Orr 1984)
Alternative Perspectives on Adaptation Theory (Verrone 2011)
Critical Perspectives on Film Adaptation (Hudelet and Wells-Lassagne 2013)

"On" overlays rather than reveals; "on" indicates that theorization and adaptation are not set in a horizontal relationship to one another, nor have they been integrated. Tellingly, there is no reciprocal discourse of "adaptation on theorization."

By contrast, "in" has generated reciprocal discourses of adaptation in theorization and theorization in adaptation. "In" positions the first term inside the second, which becomes its container, as the following examples illustrate:

"Adaptation in Theory" (Emig 2012)
"Adaptation in Theory and Practice" (Snyder 2017)

"In" figures theorization as adaptation's container, its environment. My history has shown that theorization has been a variably (in)hospitable environment for adaptation and that adaptation has often refused to adapt to it. Yet these titles and the essays they head do work to situate adaptation more hospitably in theoretical environments, against discourses that have found theory to be lacking in adaptation studies.

"In" has further enabled a reciprocal discourse in which adaptation contains theorization. For all the criticisms that adaptation studies' prevailing case study methodologies delimit field theorization (Chapter 6), they do position adaptation theory "in" adaptation practice. Three of four articles in a recent issue of *Adaptation* (Dec. 2018) do just this:

"Analyzing Adaptation Reception in Reaction Videos" (Rowe 2018)
  "Originality and Imitation in Two Modern Adaptations of *Tristram Shandy*" (Seager 2018)
  "Uncanny Adaptation: Revisionary Narratives in Bryan Fuller's *Hannibal*" (Raines 2018)

Adaptation practice, here and in countless other case studies, is figured as containing theory: the task of the critic is to bring it out from practice into critical discourse. The "in" preposition in such case studies can be seen as creating a more equitable relationship between theory and practice, in which theory is excavated from practice rather than imposed on it, and such case studies commendably seek to inform theorization with adaptation practice.

Other prepositions articulate an ambiguous relationship between adaptation and theorization. "Of" expresses ambivalence as to which of its conjoined entities possesses and which is possessed. Both *Introduction to the Theory of Adaptation* (McFarlane 1996) and *A Theory of Adaptation* (Hutcheon 2006) present theory and adaptation as mutually belonging to each other. While "of" has potential to press adaptation and theorization into more equitable and mutual possession of each other, this potential has not yet been fully realized in the rhetoric and discourse of theorizing adaptation. The reciprocal counterpart to "the theory of adaptation," "the adaptation of theory," is barely present in adaptation studies, a lack that this book, as well as my prior research, seeks to redress. Currently, as my introduction to this book attests, the most common invocation of the "of" preposition in adaptation has been the problem *of* adaptation *for* theorization (Introduction), with very little reciprocal discourse regarding the problem *of* theorization *for* adaptation.

Even so, "of" is a tiny word with expansive conceptual potential for adaptation studies. The *Oxford English Dictionary* accords it sixty numbered definitions, many with lettered subcategories, and uses over 35,000 words to define it, not including the quotations exemplifying its historical usage (*OED*, 2nd rev. ed., s.v. "of," accessed February 20, 2018, https://www-oed-com/view/Entry/130549). Even with all of these words, strikingly, the dictionary is unable to define "of" without using "of" in the definition: "of" remains indispensable to its own definition, refusing to be displaced by other words. In this way, it does better than adaptation, which has tended to disappear into its synonyms and contexts, subsumed by other words (Chapter 5). "Of" has also been used to taxonomize adaptation as other things in other (inter) disciplines (Chapter 6): we study the adaptation *of* narrative, *of* aesthetics, *of* politics, *of* culture, *of* history, *of* location, *of* identity, *of* literature, and many other things and subject adaptation to the principles *of* theorization rather than attending to the principles *of* adaptation (Chapter 7). Adaptation studies needs more self-reflexive definitions, taxonomies, and principles *of* adaptation; it also needs to study the "The Adaptation *of* Adaptation," in which adaptation possesses and is transformatively possessed by itself (Elliott 2012a).

Prefixes

Prepositions and prefixes overlap: indeed, one of prefix's obsolete definitions *is* "preposition." In his conference presentation "Fatal Analogies?" (2015), Rainer Emig's subtitles indicated that he was equally, if not more, concerned with fatal *prefixes*:

> "Meta, Hyper, Inter, Trans: The System of Fashion of Adaptation Studies"
> "To Bring Them All and in the Darkness Bind Them: Adaptation Studies as a Multi- or Transdisciplinary Enterprise"
> "Lost in Trans? Decisions and Homework" (2015, n.p.)

Emig was right: such prefixes carry us away from adaptation to other interdisciplinary processes in which adaptation may participate, but which are not adaptation per se. For Emig, as for Leitch (2012a) and Cardwell (2018), the problem of theorizing adaptation is not simply "the potentially unlimited scope of our objects of study" (Emig 2015, n.p.) but also the limitations of prefixes that do not sufficiently differentiate adaptation studies from other interdisciplines whose interdisciplinarity is articulated by prefixes, as in trans-lation, trans-cultural, inter-textual, inter-medial, inter-disciplinary, and trans-disciplinary studies.

Even so, examining how prefixes have been used in adaptation studies and related fields identifies some striking differences that do set adaptation apart. Translation, transcultural, intertextual, intermedial, transcultural, interdisciplinary, and transdisciplinary studies favor the prefixes *inter-* and *trans-*: indeed, leading structuralist theorists have contested as to which should predominate. For Gérard Genette, *trans-* encompasses and articulates every kind of relationship between texts: "all that sets the text in relationship, whether obvious or concealed, with other texts" and "covers all aspects of a particular text" (1982, 83–84)—it is his one prefix to rule them all. For Genette, other prefixes merely articulate sub-categories of his larger trans-whole: *inter-*, *para-*, *meta-*, *hyper-*, *archi-*, *anti-*, *con-*, *de-*, *epi-*, and *ex-*. *Trans-* also features as a prefix for numerous subcategories within his system. The closest that Genette came to theorizing adaptation was in his categories of hypotext and hypertext, used to describe "literature in the second degree," with *hypo-* referring to the adapted and *hyper-* to the adapting work. Here, adaptation becomes a subcategory of structuralist intertextuality.

By contrast, for neo-narratologist Mieke Bal, *inter-* is the cardinal prefix. That Genette has used *trans-* to describe the same processes to which Bal has applied *inter-* suggests that the two prefixes are, to some extent, interchangeable. For Bal, "'inter-' adds more specificity to what it indicates than alternatives such as 'trans-' and 'multi-'. I have made this argument repetitively since the 1980s, but it is still needed, it seems" (Bal, "Intership," 2017b, accessed September 5, 2019, http://www.miekebal.org/publications/articles/2010s/, n.p.). Recently, Bal has also championed the *inter-* prefix in adaptation studies, recommending that scholars "suspend the term 'adaptation' and replace it with 'intership'" in order to rid the field of its hierarchies" (2017b, 179). For Bal, *inter-* has the added benefit of connecting adaptation to other interdisciplines: it "brings together all activities qualified with the preposition inter-, from interdisciplinary to intertextual, international, intermedial, intercultural to interdiscursive" (2017b, 179). Once again, adaptation studies becomes part of a larger structuralist whole.

By contrast, the most common prefix engaged within adaptation studies has been *re-*. While all three appear in Hutcheon's influential definition of adaptation as "an acknowledged *trans*position of a *re*cognizable work or works; a creative and an *inter*pretive act of appropriation/salvaging; an extended *inter*textual engagement with the adapted work" (2006, 5), the following list

of prefixes used in adaptation indicates the far greater prevalence of *re-* words
(34) by comparison to *trans-* (13) and *inter-* (8) words.

trans- words	inter- words	re- words
translation	intertextuality	repetition
transition	intermediality	remediation
transformation	interculturalism	remake
transmutation	interplay	remodeling
transmediation	interdisciplinary	realization
transcoding	interaction	reading
transmogrification	intersection	reworking
transaction	interpretation	remix
transgression		re-presentation
transnational exchange		rewriting
transfiguration		reimagining
transvocalization		reworking
transmodalization		response
		recycling
		re-remembering
		reframing
		reflection
		refraction
		revision
		reproduction
		reconstruction
		recreation
		recasting
		rebooting
		reformatting
		retelling
		refunctioning
		refashioning
		resuscitation
		re-accentuation
		re-envisioning
		re-evaluation
		return
		replication

The relative lack of *re-* prefixes in structuralist theory may be a product of humanities' theorization's phobia of resemblance and fetishization of difference (Elliott 2012b), identified in Part I of this book and further in Chapter 9. It may equally articulate the eternal present of classical narratology's ahistorical, universal theories, in contrast to the Janus-faced temporality of adaptation (Chapter 4).

The *re-* prefix features prominently in Robert Stam's and Thomas Leitch's taxonomies of adaptation. Stam's list of synonyms for adaptation (2005, 25) includes five *trans-*, five *re-* prefixes, and no *inter-* prefixes.[2] In "Revisionist Adaptation: Transtextuality, Cross-Cultural Dialogism, and Performative Infidelities" (2017), Stam again marshals *re-*, *trans-*, *dia-*, and (implicitly) *inter-* (*cross-*) prefixes to address adaptation in relation to other interdisciplines. *Re-* features three times as often as any other prefix in Leitch's "grammar of *hyper*textual relations as they shade off to the *inter*textual" (2007, 95).[3] In 2014, the *Interdisciplinary Humanities* journal published a special issue on adaptation, "*Re*-Imagining, *Re*-Remembering, and Cultural *Re*cycling: Adaptation across the Humanities" (Neblett), its title brimful of *re-* prefixes.

It may be that in future decades other terms will supersede *inter-* and *trans-*; in the wake of postmodern and new media theories, scholars are increasingly turning to multimodality (Gambier and Gottlieb 2001; Elleström 2010) and plurimediality (Marcsek-Fuchs 2015) studies, while adaptation scholars too are attending to multicultural adaptation (Dix 2018) and multiple adaptation environments (Grossman and Palmer 2017). But adaptation, as a process of repetition with variation, will always re-quire a *re-*, titles in the most recent issue of the journal *Adaptation* at the time of this writing, a special issue on intersemiotic translation as adaptation (Giannakopoulou and Cartmell 2019), include seven trans-words, five inter-words, and four re-words.

Post-Theorization, Neo-Theorization, Meta-Theorization

Chapter 4 considered how Janus-faced alternations between theoretical progress and theoretical return articulate processes of variation and repetition within adaptation itself. This chapter casts a rhetorical lens on how prefixes have worked to adapt theorization to new environments in such movements as postmodernism, poststructuralism, post-feminism, post-Marxism, post-humanism, and post-theory and in neo-formalism, neo-structuralism, neo-narratology, neo-Freudian theory, neo-feminism, neo-Marxism, neo-liberalism, neo-humanism, and New Historicism. Generally, *post-* articulates a more radical adaptation of its stem theory than *neo-*, with some exceptions. More often than not, *neo-* has been positioned between the older theoretical stem word and the more radical aspects of *post-* reworkings of it, while nevertheless adapting the stem word to some aspects of the theoretical turn (Nünning 2003).

Post- and *neo-*engage in both theoretical progress and theoretical return. Before the *post-* prefix became prominent in humanities theorization, Jean Paul Sartre articulated the concepts that would inform its paradoxical position between progress and return: "A so-called 'going beyond' Marxism will be at worst only a return to pre-Marxism; at best, only the rediscovery of a thought already contained in the philosophy which one believes he has gone beyond" (1963, 7). After the theoretical turn, even as Pushkala Prasad defined "The Traditions of the 'Post'" as taking "issue with virtually every major plank of the edifice of Western philosophy and science that came into being after the Enlightenment . . . go[ing] to the heart of Western metaphysics and demolish[ing] it," she emphasized the revolutionary aspects of post-theorization, qualifying that "post traditions" maintain aspects of the critical traditions they oppose ([2005] 2015, 211–12).

The prefix *post-* is temporally equivocal, preceding stem words that it works to post-date. Nicholas Royle has pondered its temporo-spatial ambiguity, since *post-* means after in time, but behind (posterior) in space (1999, 3). While from a chronological purview, these temporal relations forge theoretical impossibilities, from the purview of adaptation, there is nothing impossible about them. As in genetic adaptation, the *post-* of the past reappears in the present and the future through repetition. Whether *post-* is defined as *anti-*, *re-*, or *neo-* (opposing, repeating, or renewing what it prefixes), *post-* theorization involves a return to and *adaptation of* prior theories. Its process of repetition with variation is rhetorical as well as ideological, as stem theories repeat, varied by the prefix *post-*. Thus the prefix *post-* does not so much represent a movement beyond or away from its stem words as a forging of continuities and discontinuities with them, as in processes of adaptation.

These adaptive rhetorical processes continue and extend in lineages of post-post-theorization. Jeffrey Nealon has defined post-post-modernism in a rhetoric of adaptation, as "a mutation within postmodernism" (2012, ix). While for some, *post-* does away with *pre-* and with notions of predecessors, origins, and originals (e.g., Gianni Vattimo [1988] in philosophy and Stam [2005] in adaptation studies), for Nealon, *post-* intensifies the relationship to its stem word, allowing it to be "redeployed" with greater effect in a new context, with "redeployed" signaling a process of varied repetition adapting theories to new environments.

For all their ideological differences, *neo-* and *post-* theorists alike engage in theoretical repetition with variation, adapting theorization to new contexts. Adaptation scholars have done likewise. Mireia Aragay's "Reflection to Refraction: Adaptation Studies Then and Now" (2005b) uses the *re-* prefix to articulate the shift from traditional to *post-* theories in her wide-ranging field history from high-art aestheticism in the 1920s to postmodern cultural studies in the 1980s and from 1950s medium specificity theory to 1990s polysystems and performance theories. While Aragay's introduction does not reflect on its title's *re-* words, their etymology informs her arguments about the adaptation of adaptation theory in the twentieth century. The repeated *re-* prefix (re-flection, re-fraction) indicates connected but divergent theoretical processes. In the humanities, "reflection" refers to thinking that involves recalling or recollecting; "refraction" articulates alteration or distortion through the mediation of expression, personal perspective, or social context (*OED*, 2nd rev. ed., s.v. "reflection" and "refraction," accessed March 9, 2018, https://www-oed-com/view/Entry/160921 and https://www-oed-com/view/Entry/161038).[4] The early and mid-twentieth-century adaptation theorists discussed by Aragay foregrounded adaptation as a process of reflection, in which one medium reflects (or fails to reflect) another; their theorization unfolded mostly as dyadic reflections between two media forms, two cultures, two periods, or two theories. The reflective critic is also a reflective medium, adjudicating between the dyads and assessing their relative aesthetic, philosophical, and cultural values. According to Aragay's field history, as the theoretical turn took hold in the humanities mainstream in the 1980s, adaptation studies turned to refractive methodologies: to poststructuralist intertextuality, which deconstructed structuralist semiotics, metaphysics, reason, and logic; to the polysystems theories that fractured and multiplied, but did not abolish, categorical theorization and empiricism; to the ahistorical, localized, reception-focused theories of postmodern cultural studies; and to the production-based, temporal, local, and cultural constructivism of performance theory. These theoretical adaptations manifested both the outwardly dispersive multiplicities of adaptation and the inward shatterings of post-theoretical self-reflexivities.

While Aragay and others have focused on post-theorization in progressivist histories of adaptation theorization, my history in Chapter 4 attests that neo-theorization has also been prominent and progressive. Dudley Andrew's neo-Bazinian scholarship has made him one of the most widely cited scholars in adaptation studies. The prefixes through which he assesses postmodern cultural adaptation studies suggest his preference for neo-theorization: "adaptation feeds [postmodern] cultural studies, a discipline born for this era of *pro*liferation, where textual *con*tagion counts more than does *inter*pretation" (2011, 28, emphasis added). Here, Malthusian metaphors of overpopulation (proliferation), shortages (of interpretation), and of disease (contagion) express his reservations about such forms of post-theorization.

Throughout my career, prefixes have been integral to my thinking and methodologies. In *Re-thinking the Novel/Film Debate* (2003a), I re-visited, re-historicized, and re-theorized discourses of novels and films in other inter-disciplinary and inter-medial debates (poetry and painting; prose and illustration; worded films). In this book, my methodology has been meta-critical, trans-theoretical, trans-historical, and inter-disciplinary. For some scholars, *meta-* means "about"; others define it as "within" (for Genette, a metanarrative is an embedded one). For me, *meta-* is both about and within: indeed, I am keenly aware that there is no "outside" position from which I can observe my own metacriticism. Nowhere is such situatedness more pronounced, and at the same time more invisible, than in writing about/within rhetoric. Even so, moving from macroscopic transhistorical and transtheoretical discourses to microscopic pieces of rhetoric does enable new metacritical purviews of dynamics between the larger and closer views of the field.

Within the microscopic domain of rhetoric, figuration has been crucial to conceptualizing relations between disciplines, media, sign systems, theories, and theoretical tenets both here and in my prior research. The prefixed terminology of figurative rhetoric (para-dox, ana-logy, meta-phor, and anti-metabole) was essential to the formation of arguments in *Rethinking the Novel/Film Debate* (Elliott 2003a), where I navigated two sides of theoretical paradoxes via analogies, pondered how visual metaphors produce adaptive metamorphoses in film animation, and used antimetabole to develop a theory of word-image relations.

Antimetabole has also been central to *Theorizing Adaptation*: indeed, the titles that divide its two parts, "Theorizing Adaptation" and "Adapting Theorization," constitute an antimetabole. My arguments about theorizing adaptation *as* adaptation in Chapters 5 through 7 are informed by the figure of simile. Chapter 9 considers how other rhetorical figures have figured and can refigure adaptation studies. Before that, the second half of Chapter 8 makes the case for figurative rhetoric (or figuration) as a mediator between theorization and adaptation more generally.

Theorization—Adaptation—Figuration

The value of figuration lies not so much in the way that it references a single thing but in how it constructs *relations* between entities, processes, contexts, concepts, and epistemologies. As James Underhill has argued, "From Aristotle to Ricoeur, metaphor has tended to attract those who build bridges between academic disciplines" (2011, 43). As such, it is a fertile rhetoric for mediating between theorization and adaptation.

This section considers how figuration has functioned within humanities theorization and adaptation studies and how it has figured—and might refigure—relations between theorization and adaptation. Figuration is already central to both, and my study builds upon on a long figurative lineage within each. Figuration holds potential to build bridges between adaptation and theorization not only through its adaptive figurative operations but also because all three processes already share features in common. Like theorization and adaptation, figuration is an ancient practice and process, manifesting diversely across disciplines and representational forms. All three are processes that reshape and remake what they touch, including each other. For centuries, rhetorical figures have been accorded theorizing agency in explicating and revivifying humanities theorization. Figuration is adaptive as well as theoretical, forging new relations through its operations on existing ones. For Percy Bysshe Shelley in *A Defence* [sic] *of Poetry*, the poet, through "vitally metaphorical" writing, "marks the before unapprehended *relations* of things and perpetuates their apprehension" and communicates this to others ([1821] 1840, 5 emphasis added). For Paul Ricoeur in *The Rule of Metaphor: The Creation of Meaning in Language*, metaphorical speaking and writing usher in a second order of meaning that creates new ways of thinking and theorizing: through the adaptive processes of metaphor, "language can extend itself to its very limits, forever discovering new resonances within itself" (Ricoeur 2003, book jacket). Figuration, then, is not limited to describing what is or has been: it can equally envision what is not yet and articulate what might be via adaptive figurative processes.

Theoretical uses of figuration to explain unfamiliar concepts in terms of familiar ones extend to illuminating adaptation's uncanny relation to theorization. Moreover, figuration shares adaptation's problematic relations with theorization and informs them. Like adaptation, figuration has refused to conform consistently to theoretical definitions, taxonomies, and principles; as with adaptation, theorization has often retaliated against that resistance by conscripting and constraining figuration in the service of various theories (Elliott 2003a, 15; 194–95).

After defining figuration, the remainder of this section ponders some roles that figuration has played in humanities theorization generally and in humanities adaptation studies particularly, before considering in more detail how figuration might refigure their relationship to each other.

Defining Figuration

Figuration has been defined variably and its definitions have been contested in ways that would fill many books. Here, two poles introduce and anchor this discussion of figuration's relationship to theorization and adaptation: first, its ancient rhetorical definition as a special kind of language and, second, recent poststructuralist redefinitions of figuration as characteristic of all language—and, therefore, not special at all. In classical rhetoric, a figure (of speech) is a "form of expression, deviating from the normal arrangement or use of words . . . adopted in order to give beauty, variety, or force to a composition" (*OED*, 2nd rev. ed., s.v. "figure," definition 5.21.a, accessed June 17, 2018, https://www-oed-comes/view/Entry/70079). This definition highlights not only figuration's deviation from "the normal" ways of speaking or writing in order to introduce "variety," but also its aesthetic beauty and polemical force, articulating the two main emphases of humanities theorization historically: formal aesthetics and cultural polemics. In 1886, C. B. Bradley harnessed figuration to support high-art aestheticism: "Grammar treats of the normal and commonplace uses of language; Rhetoric, of the uncommon and specially significant. The material is the same in both, but Grammar is the familiar and household Art; Rhetoric, the Fine Art" (140–41). Rhetoric's conscription to support aesthetic theories continued for most of the twentieth century. However, the definition of figurative rhetoric as a special kind of language, different from "normal" language, was challenged in the late twentieth century, along with the theories it supported, forging radical philosophical, cultural, and political polemics. In *Allegories of Reading*, post-structuralist Paul de Man repeated and varied New Critic I. A. Richards's argument ([1936] 2001) that the figure of metaphor is the "omniscient principle of language," countering: "The figurative structure is not one linguistic mode among others, but it characterizes language as such" (1979, 105). However, just as all men are equal, but some are more equal than others, so too while all language can be shown to function figuratively, some rhetoric remains more self-consciously and didactically figurative than others. Indeed, de Man would not have been able to make this argument without an understanding of metaphor as it is classically defined. My analysis of how figuration has mediated, and might mediate, between adaptation and theorization to refigure adaptation theorization depends on both traditional and more recent definitions and theories of figuration.

Figuration in Humanities Theorization

The most common debates over figuration in humanities theorization concern its relationship to truth. Like adaptation, figuration too has its (in)fidelity discourses—it too has been charged with being unfaithful to theorization and its theories of reality, objectivism, empiricism, and truth. Unlike adaptation, however, figuration has also been hailed as a vehicle of higher truth, an avenue to new truths, and an agent of revolutionary truth. For Mark Johnson in "Philosophy's Debt to Metaphor," "The history of western philosophy is, for the most part, one long development of the objectivist dismissal of metaphor, punctuated rarely by bold declarations of the pervasiveness of metaphor in thought" (2008, 39). Ricoeur admonished scholars to approach interpretation as a process of configuration and re-figuration in order to get away from the delimiting trammels of realism and as a way to explicate and connect pre-production, product, and reception: "What is at stake, therefore, is the concrete process by which the textual configuration mediates between the prefiguration of the practical field and its refiguration through the reception of the work" (1990, 1.53). Like adaptation, figuration exceeds the theoretical epistemologies that critique and constrain it and generates new concepts that challenge existing theories.

As with adaptation, categorical, systematic, empirical, and rational theorists have rejected figurative rhetoric as impressionistic, imprecise, subjective, illogical, untheoretical, and untrue because it is not mappable, or

only partially mappable, onto material, literal, objective, and logical epistemologies of truth. Peter Elbow has argued that to make a metaphor is to "call
something by a wrong name," adding: "you are thinking in terms of something else . . . You are seeing one thought or perception in terms of another"
(1973, 53–54). For literal, denotative, empirical, logical, and correspondence
theories of truth, calling something by another name, as metaphor does, is
"wrong," imprecise, and false. Yet for Nelson Goodman, "The oddity is that
metaphorical truth is compatible with literal falsity" (1984, 71). For de Man
this was something to be celebrated, since it proved the *truth* of poststructuralist theory: if all language is figurative, then all language is indeterminate
(de Man 1979, 10).

Figuration has also been denigrated for falling from truths in the form of
cultural and political ideologies and values. Theorists have charged figuration with political abuses of power, all the more pernicious when the figurative lays claim to the literal and becomes authoritatively "binding":

> What therefore is truth? A mobile army of metaphors, metonymies, and
> anthropomorphisms: in short a sum of human relations that became po-
> etically and rhetorically intensified, metamorphosed, adorned, and after
> long usage seem to a nation fixed, canonic, and binding. (Nietzsche [1873]
> 1997, 92)

Just as all language is figurative, but some is more figurative than others,
so too all cultural rhetoric is an operation of power, and for Nietzsche and
others, figurative rhetoric is more powerful than other rhetoric.

Yet in spite of theoretical objections to figuration, figurative devices have
been central to theorization. Figurative rhetoric has been used to explicate
theoretical concepts in various ways: analogies have explained scientific theories to lay readers (genes are the building blocks of the body[5]), similes have
concretized linguistic abstractions (signifier and signified are as inseparable
as two sides of a single sheet of paper[6]), and metaphors have theorized adaptation processes (as in adapting the "spirit" of a text or theories of adaptation
as "the word made flesh"[7]).

Beyond its explanatory functions, figuration has been accorded philosophical, conceptual, and paradigmatic authority in the humanities. In
"White Mythology: Metaphor in the Text of Philosophy," Jacques Derrida
affirmed: "In every rhetorical definition of metaphor is implied not just a
philosophical position, but a conceptual network within which philosophy

as such is constituted" ([1971] 1974, 30). Even in its ancient classical rhetorical sense, figuration was seen as a conceptual activity (Kennedy 1994, 63). Mark Johnson has argued that, "Without metaphor, there would be no philosophy" and that "philosophy's debt [to it] is no greater, nor less, than that of any other significant human intellectual field or discipline" (2008, 39).

In the mid-twentieth century, figuration became not simply an explanatory agent of theoretical principles *but identical to them* when structuralist Roman Jakobson argued that metaphor and metonymy *are* (rather than are metaphors for) the paradigmatic and syntagmatic axes of all symbolic communication: "A competition between both devices, metonymic and metaphoric, is manifest in any symbolic process, be it intrapersonal or social" (1956, 76). Ricoeur subsequently extended figurative structures from representational forms to processes of textual production and consumption: "the concrete process by which the textual configuration mediates between the prefiguration of the practical field and its refiguration through the reception of the work" (1990, 1.53).

Theorists have also carried figuration from verbal rhetoric into the rhetoric of other media. In 1974, Christian Metz brought structuralist linguistics into film theory; in 1977, Roland Barthes extended structuralist theories of writing to other media (*Image—Music—Text*); in 2001, new media theorist Lev Manovich argued that "the World Wide Web hyperlinking has privileged the single figure of metonymy at the expense of all others" (86). Beyond media forms, in *Metahistory* (1973), Hadyn White argued that the deep structures ordering the writing of history are figurative, adding synecdoche and irony to the usual theoretical suspects, metaphor and metonymy. In "Brecht and Discourse," Barthes extended figuration beyond its structural, formal functions to consider its ideological and cultural operations: "political discourse is fundamentally metonymic, for it can only be established by the power of language, and this power is metonymy itself" ([1975] 1989, 219). Other scholars subsequently carried Barthes's critique of the "metonymic fallacy" (1974, 11) into theories of identity politics (Alcoff and Potter 1993, 14) and media industries. Arguing that "figuration and the importation of paradigms are fundamental conceptual processes that define the media industry," John Thornton Caldwell asked "why high theory pays so little attention to the centrality and self-consciousness of industrial figuration" (1995, 136). In 2010, Julie Park applied "what Roman Jakobson has claimed is the mode of the realist novel—metonymy with its contingent, accidental, and alienable connections, as opposed to metaphor's essential ones" to cultural studies, arguing that metonymy "is also the procedure of commodity culture and its fetishism" (xxiv).

Turning inward to thought as well as outward to culture and society, scholars have for decades argued that the mind is structured figuratively and that these mental structures that construct figurative forms of communication, representation, and societies in their image. Richards famously decreed that metaphor is "the essence of thinking" and that "thought is itself metaphoric" ([1936] 2001, 60; 73); Jakobson theorized Freudian dream condensation as synecdochal and dream displacement as metonymic (1956, 76–77); Jacques Lacan developed and debated Freud's theories: "At the level of the unconscious there exists an organization that, as Freud says, is not necessarily that of contradictions or of grammar, but the laws of condensation and displacement, those that I call the laws of metaphor and metonymy" (1992, 61). Metz segued similarly from the figurative operations of film in *Film Language: A Semiotics of the Cinema* ([1974] 1991) to their psychoanalytic functions in *The Imaginary Signifier: Psychoanalysis and the Cinema* ([1975] 1977).

While some theories perceive representational and mental structures to operate both metaphorically and metonymically, poststructuralist theorists have rejected metaphor for generating and articulating a false, metaphysical theory of representation. Yet, as poststructuralists were devaluing metaphor, cognitive theorists were prioritizing it in theories of mind. For George Lakoff and Mark Johnson in *Metaphors We Live By* (1980), "Metaphor is primarily a matter of thought and action and only derivatively a matter of language" (153), "a way of thinking, a way to invent ideas, rather than a way to clearly express thinking" (11). In *Philosophy in the Flesh: The Embodied Mind and Its Challenge to Western Thought* (1999), they asserted the embodied basis of all thought, critiquing disembodied theories of mind as illusory and identifying the use of embodied metaphors in even the most abstract philosophies. Despite their differences, both cognitive theorists and deconstructive thinkers alike affirmed the centrality of figuration to theorization.

Figuration in Adaptation Studies

Figuration has been central to explicating adaptation when categorical theorization failed to do so. It has thus not only informed theorization in our field but has also informed and mitigated its lack. Adaptation studies, with its roots in translation theory, has privileged comparative figures over contiguous ones, an issue that Chapter 9 seeks to redress. Nico Dicecco turned to metaphor to theorize adaptation when he determined that the theories of "medium-specific material differences . . . render literal replication in adaptation impossible": "adaptation is a class of metaphor, depending on a paradoxical relationship that equates unequal terms" (2011, n.p.). In 2003, I pondered how metaphor might theorize adaptation:

> [M]etaphor emerges as an ideal model for literary film adaptation. It allows the original book (the tenor) to be transformed by its film adaptation (the vehicle). It renders adaptation metamorphosis rather than a crude or reductive literalization of interart analogies. . . . [M]etaphor presses . . . toward a less linear, more cyclical, less binary, more multiplicative process of metamorphosis . . . epitomized and illustrated in animated processes that carry metaphor into metamorphosis. . . . The metamorphosis is . . . based on . . . resemblances. . . . Through the incremental changes associated with metaphoric processes and with animation, these resemblances lead gradually to a change in identity, in which the tenor *becomes* the vehicle. (Elliott 2003a, 230–31, emphasis in original)

Although metaphor has featured in adaptation studies, it should come as no surprise that adaptation studies has not followed the humanities' theoretical mainstream in prioritizing either metaphor or metonymy: another figure has taken precedence: that of analogy.

Beyond adaptation studies, analogy has been accorded theorizing properties more generally: in philosophy, it has been made the basis of reasoning and argumentation: the *Oxford English Dictionary* cites a 1750 treatise recounting: "They learnt the art of reasoning by similitudes and analogies" (*OED*, 2nd rev. ed., s.v. "analogy," definition 7.a, accessed April 13, 2017, https://www-oed-com/view/Entry/7030); in logic, it has been defined as a "process of arguing from similarity in known respects to similarity in other respects" (*OED*, "analogy," definition 7.b).

Analogy has dominated adaptation studies for this and other reasons. First, it shares commonalities with adaptation. As I have argued throughout this book, adaptation is best theorized by processes and constructs that resemble it—or at least do not override its identity with their own. Beyond commonalities, just as Jakobson argued that metaphor and metonymy are not simply metaphors for theoretical concepts but *are* the concepts themselves, so too one of analogy's definitions *is* adaptation: "correspondence or adaptation of one thing to another" (*OED*, "analogy," definition 2). Second, analogy has for centuries forged bridges between interart theories and adaptation. Sister-arts theories have engaged interart analogies to speak of one art in terms of another; adaptation fulfills such analogies by *making* one art into another (Elliott 2003a, 12). Third, sister-arts analogies have also been used to oppose categorical theories of adaptation, most notably medium specificity theories, which figure the arts as separate species that cannot mate to produce adaptation and cannot evolve over time into other arts (Chapter 2). Under the theoretical constraints of medium specificity, adaptation depended on analogy *to exist as a theoretical object at all*. Analogy was not so much the *best* way to adapt, as in Geoffrey Wagner's preferred mode of adaptation, analogy (1975, 226–31), under formal and structuralist theories, it became the *only* way to adapt (Chapter 3). For Martin C. Battestin, analogy is essential to adaptation, because medium specificity renders "the two media, visual and verbal, in every essential respect disparate" (Battestin 1998, 503). Countless other literary film adaptation scholars have also invoked analogy as the only way to adapt (Eikhenbaum [1926] 1973, 122; Bluestone 1957, 80; Boyum 1985, 8; Elliott 2003a, 184–244)—so much so that analogy once again becomes synonymous with adaptation.

Analogy has been nominated the key to the practice as well as the theory of adaptation: "The rhetoric of fiction is simply not the rhetoric of film, and it's in finding analogous strategies whereby the one achieves the effects of the other that the greatest challenge of adaptation lies" (Boyum 1985, 81). Beyond adaptation studies, Christophe Collard has theorized analogies as unifying agents "across formal distinctions" in mediaturgy and convergence culture (2014, 265). For all its affinities with adaptation, analogy in these discourses has worked less to theorize adaptation on its own terms than to conform and constrain it to humanities theories. Structuralist theories have constrained interart analogy categorically as scientists have done, delimiting it to a term indicating resemblances of form or function in organisms of different evolutionary origin that have *no substantive or intrinsic* (genetic) *basis* (*OED*, "analogy," definition 8). Here, and in humanities adaptation theories that figure the arts as separate species, analogy is diametrically opposed to adaptation and evolution.

Other theorists have engaged interdisciplinary analogies to theorize adaptation across disciplines (Griffiths 2016). For Sarah Cardwell, "the two processes of adaptation [biological and intermedial] are, to an extent, analogous"

(2002, 13). Yet four years on, Julie Sanders cautioned: "A volume on the literary processes of adaptation and appropriation can only deploy [biological adaptation] at the level of metaphor and suggestion" (2006, 24). Subsequently, however, Gary G. Bortolotti and Linda Hutcheon rebutted Sanders, arguing that the relation "between biological and cultural adaptation" is "not an analogy, not a metaphoric association—but a homology" (2007, 444). Thus, even as Sanders engaged more radical *humanities* theories than they, in terms of adaptation theorization, Bortolotti and Hutcheon were the more radical theorists, challenging medium specificity theory's constraints on analogy across media and disciplines. Here adaptation scholars resist theoretical attempts to segregate adaptation across disciplines and to deny intrinsic relations between analogically related entities.

In conclusion, both humanities theorization and adaptation point to the already formidable power of figuration to reconceptualize both. The next chapter attends to more specific ways in which figuration has done so and to how it might reconceptualize their relations to each other.

9

Refiguring Adaptation Studies

When I turned to analogy to explicate the paradox that figures novels and films as *both* adaptable sister arts *and* unadaptable separate species (2003a, 1), I was so preoccupied with using figures to *resolve* theoretical problems that I failed to observe that paradox is also a rhetorical figure and that theoretical problems too have been represented figuratively. Scholars have been so focused on the problem of adaptation for theorization that few have attended to the problem of theorization for adaptation. Theoretical paradoxes in adaptation studies bear witness to the failure of theorization to explicate adaptation. Joining theoretical paradoxes, the various contradictory theories that have allied against adaptation discussed in Part I of this book constitute theoretical oxymorons. Moreover, the figure of antithesis articulates not only oppositions between adaptation and theorization but also the legion binary oppositions that theorization has imposed on adaptation and that adaptation has resisted and crossed, as well as the theoretical binary forged between binaries and their deconstruction and hierarchical binaries and revolutions against them.

Rhetorical figures furthermore articulate particular theoretical problems within adaptation studies: parallelism describes the separate spheres that medium specificity has sought to impose on adaptation media and that formal and cultural theorists have sought to impose on adaptation studies (Cahir 2006; Elliott 2014c). Chapters 5 through 7 of this book have shown how often theorizing adaptation has taken the form of periphrasis—theorizing *around* adaptation rather than theorizing it *as* adaptation. These chapters recommended the figure of self-reflexive simile—theorizing adaptation *as* adaptation—to redress periphrasis.

Happily, figuration posits many more solutions to theoretical problems than problems. The playful, risk-taking, rhetorical and conceptual experimentation that figuration enables may be as prone to fail as to succeed, but it offers another way for the humanities to engage in theoretical experimentation, a less stentorious alternative to de Man's use of metonymy as a "negative road of exposing an error" (1979, 16), and an invigorating alternative

Theorizing Adaptation. Kamilla Elliott, Oxford University Press (2020). © Oxford University Press.
DOI: 10.1093/oso/9780197511176.001.0001

to the skeptical ennui that permeates our post-theoretical, post-truth age. If we are going to "do" post-truth, let us do so actively, adventurously, and creatively rather than sneeringly, despairingly, and nihilistically. If we are going to pursue aesthetic and political cultural values, let us do so more adventurously than censoriously. This chapter demonstrates some ways in which figuration, as a relational rhetorical process, can also help us to break out of old ways of arguing and into new ways of dialoguing. In spite of all the theoretical constraints imposed upon it, figuration plays breezily, insolently, informatively, and refreshingly across and between theories, methodologies, and disciplines. Whether we believe that there is a pre-existing reality that representation expresses or that representation is constructed, or a combination of the two, figuration offers all of us new ways of approaching our theories. It does not matter whether our interests lie in aesthetics, semiotics, narratology, history, culture, politics, industry, or anything else: figuration can revivify and refigure all theoretical and disciplinary purviews. The following sections discuss just a few ways in which rhetorical experiments, methodologies, and concepts can refigure adaptation studies, in the hope that other scholars will expand, debate, and develop these discussions.

Reconceptualizing Adaptation Studies

Scholars have expressed faith that theorization generally and adaptation studies particularly can be reconceptualized and integrated via rhetoric. Jean-Michel Rabaté has written:

> Up to now philosophers have tried to change the world, and they have failed. Now, it seems, the task is to translate it . . . in the hope that, if we translate better, searching for more precise and exact idioms, respecting all the startling idiosyncrasies of concepts in their original languages, we will bring about a momentous change. (2014, 25)

Sarah Cardwell has argued that, "via the metacriticism of common, shared language, adaptation studies could seek to develop a more precise vocabulary from which new conceptual insights and debate can evolve" (2018, 16).

New concepts for theorizing adaptation can be generated at the level of individual words and pieces of words. Moreover, a shared language can help to develop adaptation studies as a field. A shared language does not require theoretical agreement; for Cardwell, a shared language offers a basis for debate and conceptual innovation. Repeating and varying a shared language enables scholars to theorize adaptively.

Chapter 8 has argued for the potential of figuration to refigure relations between adaptation and theorization. Chapter 9 considers how particular rhetorical figures might refigure particular theoretical problems within adaptation studies. As with Chapter 8, its methodology is suggestive, generative, and experimental: it does not aspire to comprehensive coverage of all figures (although my initial research considered them all), and it prioritizes understudied figures over the usual figurative suspects. It does not appoint particular figures to legislate or rule adaptation studies, nor does it constrain rhetorical figures to theoretical principles, neither does it seek to create a new theory or theoretical school via figuration. Its interest lies in using rhetorical figures to generate concepts, strategies, and methodologies for redressing particular problems that humanities theorization has created for adaptation studies.

Even if we agree with Paul de Man that figuration is an ineluctable feature of all language because language always represents one thing in terms of another, specific rhetorical figures offer specific ways to reconceptualize, refigure, and adapt theorization, even as they remain open to other uses, concepts, and possibilities. Their specificity provides an identifiable rhetoric that can be shared and debated (repetition), while their many interpretations and applications create scope for theoretical diversity (variation). There is nothing to prevent a classically defined rhetorical figure from opening out into countless variations and nuances, informing each scholar's theories, ideologies, fields, contexts, and interests more particularly, while at the same time providing a common ground upon which to dialogue with other scholars. In the absence of a home discipline, an agreed upon adaptation canon, theory, or field definition, figuration can provide a common ground on which diverse and even opposed theories, epistemologies, methodologies, disciplines, and cultures can dialogue with less polarization and scatter than at present, while affording room to experiment, create, and explore new concepts and new relationships between adaptation and theorization. Due to the word limit for this book, I was not able to develop extended theories or case studies even for the few figures addressed in this chapter; I can, therefore, only make a small, suggestive start on what is a vast enterprise.[1] Beyond the paired terms *adaptation* and *theorization*, the following section asks how rhetoric generally and figures particularly might help to navigate some the paired terms embedded in adaptation's definition, pairs that have been problematically theorized by the hierarchical binaries of aesthetic formalism and revolutions against them, the separate spheres of structuralism, the evaporations of deconstruction, and the random, associative pastiches of postmodernism.

Refiguring Adaptation's Paired Terms

Adaptation has been defined at a baseline level as a process which adapts entities to suit new environments via mechanisms of repetition and variation (*OED*; see Chapter 5). This definition generates three paired terms that interact with each other in the process of adaptation: adapted/adapting, entities/environments, and repetition/variation. As my history has shown, the paired terms of adaptation have been attached to, subjected to, and displaced by paired terms generated by particular humanities theories such as good art/bad art, good politics/bad politics, good field/bad field, original/imitation, unique/derivative, unified/hybrid, higher/lower, canonical/popular, abstract truth/empirical truth, formal/cultural, textual/contextual, production/consumption, pre–theoretical turn/post–theoretical turn, and neo-/post-theorization, as well as to the paired terms of humanities theorization more generally such as mind/matter, theory/practice, true/untrue, theory/history, and pseudo-religious/pseudo-scientific theorization. Adaptation's paired terms have been subjected further to media and disciplinary pairs such as lyrics/music, fiction/theater, prose/illustration, literature/film, film/videogames and to larger media paired terms such as old media/new media. Culturally, adaptation has been theorized via social, geographical, and historical paired terms such as upper/lower classes, English/French, Occidental/Oriental, colonial/postcolonial, local/global, classical/neoclassical, neoclassical/Romantic, and modern/postmodern. Methodologically, adaptation scholarship has most commonly been pursued in essay-length case studies of paired adapting/adapted works.

Theorization has also subjected adaptation to theories *about pairs* that may oppose or obscure the operations of adaptation's own pairs—theories that have constructed them as binary oppositions, allocated them to separate spheres, called for revolution in which one side overthrows the other, read them dialectically, dispersed them into pluralities, subjected them to processes of deconstruction, or rejected pairs in favor of unique, original, individual, organically unified units.

Adaptation's paired terms constitute a trinity of sorts, in which the three are one and three at the same time, as inadequately explicated by dyads and binaries as they are by unitary and pluralistic theoretical constructs. Scholars have addressed how adaptation's tripartite relations violate mainstream theories of unity and pairs since at least the 1940s, when André Bazin foresaw that "the critic of the year 2050 would find not a novel out of which a play and a film had been 'made,' but rather a single work reflected through three art forms, an artistic pyramid with three sides, all equal in the eyes of the critic" ([1948] 2000, 26). Even as Bazin magnanimously extended New Critical theories of organic unity to intermedial adaptation, he shrewdly assessed that it would be a century before mainstream humanities theorization caught up to adaptation to theorize it in this way. In the 1980s, Dudley Andrew too conceived of adaptation not as a binary opposition or hierarchy but as a more equitable, mutual process of "intersecting," in which "the uniqueness of the original text is preserved to such an extent that it is intentionally left unassimilated in adaptation," allowing for "a dialectical interplay between the aesthetic forms of one period with the cinematic forms of our own period" (1984b, 99–100). In the 2000s, Linda Hutcheon turned to postmodern theories of pastiche and palimpsest to maintain multiple rather than dialectical points of intersection between adapted and adapting works, theorizing these intersections via a plurality of theories (2006). Two years on, Rochelle Hurst turned to poststructuralist theory to deconstruct the binaries created by medium specificity and structuralist theorists. Yet rather than deconstruct them into absence, indeterminacy, and endless deferral, she constructed a hybrid. Arguing that adaptation "inhabits both sides of the binary," she figured literary film adaptation as "a hybrid, an amalgam of media—at once a cinematized novel and a literary film, confusing, bridging, and rejecting the alleged discordance between page and screen, both insisting upon and occupying the overlap" (2008, 186–87). A book does not become film in adaptation: it becomes *an adaptation*. Each of these theorists has figured the relationship between adapted and adapting works as an ongoing co-existence rather than a before-and-after this-and-that; each has refused to allow one side of the pair to displace the other, or to separate, or to inhabit a hierarchy. This is theorizing adaptation as adaptation.

Biological adaptation too has its base pairs: the chemical base pairs of DNA—cytosine (C) pairs with guanine (G) and adenine (A) pairs with thymine (T)—which replicate and vary the order of pairing (CG/GC and AT/TA) and, by joining to construct inverse double-stranded, spiral helixes construct an immense range of combinations and structures in spite of the constraints on which chemical can pair with which and the constant width maintained by the spiral helixes. These variations, even as they multiply exponentially and are ongoing, are not infinite in any transcendental sense of that word, neither are they utterly random: they are patterned and governed by rules. In the same way, even though the rhetoric of adaptation's paired terms can recombine in multiple ways in adaptation discourses, and even though the microscopic details of any individual adaptation and the vastness of its contexts multiply beyond our capacity to categorize, catalogue, or explicate them, they do not do so infinitely or without constraints: adaptation always involves processes of change to suit new environments and of repetition and variation.

Humanities rhetoric, however, even when it takes on material forms in the visible, audible, tactile technologies of handmade, print, and electronic media, does not have a materiality whereby its adaptation processes can be explicated chemically or mathematically. The closest that we can come in the humanities to atomizing our adaptation processes is via dissecting its representational signs; the closest that we can come to articulating these processes more microscopically in metatheoretical, rhetorical verbal discourse is to analyze pieces of words and parts of speech to understand how rhetoric has constructed adaptation.

The relationship of adapted/adapting entities at the microscopic level of rhetoric is itself one of repetition with variation: the verb stem "adapt" repeats, while the suffixes vary (-ed; -ing). The repeated verb stem articulates the imbrication of adapted and adapting entities in each other and the impossibility of definitively separating them; their varying suffixes represent their relationship as a temporal, one-way process in which the adapted work is passive and the adapting work is active. This is not quite precise: indeed, the rhetoric of adapted and adapting entities, environments, and processes that I have used throughout this book fails to articulate the complexities of their relationships or the processes of adaptation between adapted and adapting works. What is adapted is also adapting; conversely, what is adapting is also adapted. To illustrate with humanities adaptation studies' most commonly discussed mode of adaptation, literary film adaptation: while film crediting practices may describe a book as having been adapted *by* a screenwriter or adapted *to* the screen, they may equally describe a film as having been adapted *from* the book *by* an author. In production, even as the production team focuses on adapting a book to their film, they are also concerned with adapting their film to that book. The process is a mutual one, more accurately represented in a rhetoric of adapting a book and film to each other, with the end product being an adaptation in which the book and film have been mutually adapted to each other. Recalling Andrew's favored mode of adaptation as a process of intersecting, in which "the uniqueness of the original text is persevered to such an extent that it is intentionally left unassimilated in adaptation . . . modulated by the peculiar beam of the cinema (1984b, 99) and Hurst's astute observation that "an adaptation is never simply a film or a novel; rather, it skims across both sides of the binary, refusing to completely align with either" (2008, 188), adaptation studies would benefit from neologisms and rhetorical portmanteaux to describe such adaptations. The rhetoric of "cinematization" and, conversely, "novelization," is more akin to that of theorization in overriding the adapted work with the adapting one. "Bookfilm," "filmbook," and similar rhetorical constructs come closer to articulating the process by removing the space between the words, but they do not integrate them as Andrew's or Hurst's theories do or as they combine in actual production and consumption practices. Indeed, even the rhetoric of adapted/adapting does not describe the process precisely: the process of adaptation does not happen all at once; rather, it is one of adapt-ed-ing-ed-ing-ed-ing (ongoingly) over time. Likewise, adaptation does not happen as a unitary whole: parts of the book are adapt-ing-ed (etc.) to the film, while other parts remain unadapted. Conversely, parts of the film are adapt-ing-ed (etc.) to the book, while other parts are not. Complicating the process further, these parts are also adapt-ed-ing to each other as the adaptation process unfolds. More broadly, they are also adapt-ing-ed (etc.) to the process that *is adaptation*. Thus even the end product that scholars discuss and analyze more confidently than we do the elusive processes of adaptation requires a less binary rhetoric than "bookfilm," one that might be better articulated by alternating the letters of "book" and "film"—"bfoiolkm". Yet this is simultaneously too schematic and lacks the coherence and resonance of successful verbal portmanteaux such as prosumer (which blends producer and consumer). While "cineliterature" may be more pronounceable, it perpetuates discourses in which film features as an adjectival subcategory of literature as noun (see Chapter 3) and also fails to articulate the process as one of *adaptation*. The laws of grammar and ordinary rhetoric, then, may prove inadequate to theorize adaptation.

Consumers of adaptations are also involved in processes of adapt-ed-ing-ed-ing what they consume. For example, one consumer of literary film adaptation may adapt memory of prior reading to a present encounter with a film adaptation, doing so piecemeal and over time as the film unfolds. Another consumer may not read the book until after seeing the film, adapting past memory of watching the film to present reading of the book, also doing so incrementally over the time of reading. Yet another consumer may stop the film midway to read or re-read portions of the book, alternating between consumption of book and film rather than between memory of prior consumption and present consumption. There are as many ways to consume an adaptation as there are consumers, and the same consumer may consume the same adaptation differently over a lifetime. I do not view television adaptations of Charlotte Brontë's *Jane Eyre* today with the same romantic fervor with which I consumed them as a teenager, nor do I read that novel now in the same way as I did then. Consumption processes also vary with new technologies. For example, Lindiwe Dovey's study of postcolonial adaptations of the Anglo-American canon indicates how prosumers of adaptations have blurred the lines between producers and consumers (2013, 170).

The relationship between adapt-ed-ing entities and their environments is similarly complex and interpenetrating. Far from being passive and static backdrops for adapted and adapting entities, environments are also adapt-ed-ing-ed-ing-ed-ing (etc.) to what inhabits them. Moreover, as entities and environments co-adapt, their *relationships* also adapt. In adaptation, entities and environments cannot be carved into separate theoretical territories (Elliott 2014b). This is not only because adaptations are composites of entities and environments but also because media and art forms are just as much environments for other media and art forms as nations, cultures, and industries. Marshall McLuhan has written: "It is now perfectly plain to me that all media are environments, all media have the effects that geographers and biologists have associated with environments in the past" (McLuhan 1970, 11–12). Just as biological organisms inhabiting the same environments adapt to each other as part of their environments (Margulis and Sagan 2002), further adapting to the *adaptations* of other organisms within the same environment (Ryan 2002), so too media adapt to each other within larger media environments (Ropars-Wuilleumier 1970; Metz [1971] 1991; Chatman 1978; Cohen 1979; Foltz 2017). Nor can media environments be separated from other environments: they are themselves adapted-ing-ed (etc.) by and to social, cultural, economic, legal, political, academic, disciplinary, and theoretical environments.

Beyond such contemporaneous interpenetrating adaptations, adaptation is *itself* adapting over time not only in the humanities but also in the sciences, as Timothy Shanahan's *The Evolution of Darwinism: Selection, Adaptation, and Progress in Evolutionary Biology* (2004) makes clear. Biological adaptation is evolving and its theories are evolving along with it. So too adaptation in the humanities is adapting and our theories need to adapt to it (Elliott 2012a).

The third pair, repetition and variation, are also enmeshed: what repeats is adapted by what varies; conversely, what varies is adapted by what repeats, and their relationships to each other also adapt. We have seen that John Dryden's theory of translation and adaptation valued repetition and variation equally, favoring a middle way so that neither repeats nor varies too much, one whose repetitions and variations are as attuned to present environments as to the achievements of past works. Dryden and his contemporaries further theorized adaptation as an incremental progress, in which repetitions and variations of celebrated works improved the arts and their cultural environments gradually over time. Artists too were seen to evolve as artists via adaptation within their lifetimes and to enter genealogies of prior great artists after their deaths via adaptation. Nearly two centuries later, Charles Darwin ([1859] 2009) theorized biological adaptation similarly as a gradual progress toward perfection. Yet his progressive theory is predicated on mechanisms that return to and carry forward parts of the past: repetitions are as vital as variations to surviving and thriving in new environments when other organisms do not; maintaining advantageous characteristics is as essential to successful adaptation as developing new ones. Scholars have argued similarly that the repetitions and variations of adaptation have been central to the survival and thriving of arts, media, and narratives (Dobson 1992; Marsden 1995; Hutcheon 2006); the repetitions and variations of theorization have been similarly central to its survival in the humanities (Chapter 8).

And yet while adaptation and theorization may each survive and thrive through adaptation, my history has shown that theoretical environments became increasingly hostile to adaptation in the humanities and that theorization's refusal to co-adapt with adaptation has inhibited adaptation's ability to survive and thrive in mainstream humanities academia, while also making theorization less robust in adaptation studies than in other fields—so much so that recent scholars have called for theoretical abandonment in adaptation studies, which would render theorization extinct in that environment (Chapter 4).

The problem of ordinary rhetoric and the laws of grammar is that they are too categorical, even when pulled to pieces and reassembled, to theorize adaptation satisfactorily. The remainder of this chapter therefore turns from ordinary rhetoric to ponder how specific rhetorical figures have and can redress the threat of adaptation and theorization's mutual extinction within each other's environments.

Same Difference: Refiguring Theories of Difference and Similarity

My history of theorizing adaptation identifies a transhistorical, transtheoretical dynamic in which humanities theorization has for centuries celebrated difference and castigated similarity across a variety of otherwise opposed theories, from neoclassical medium specificity to Romantic originality to modernist existentialism, from New Critical unique organic unity to structuralist binary opposition to poststructuralist *différance*, from Marxist dialectics to Bakhtinian dialogics to postmodern pluralism, from textual studies to intertextual studies to multimedial studies, from bourgeois individualism to modernist existentialism to postmodern diversity to post-humanist hybridity. The principles and cultural values vary, but the value for difference in opposition to similarity repeats. Similarity has been devalued as aesthetically inferior, perceptually naïve, philosophically false, and politically oppressive, while difference has been valorized as aesthetically superior, perceptually sophisticated, philosophically true, and politically liberating.

This longstanding bipolar, hierarchical binary between similarity and difference has been detrimental to theorizing adaptation, which is ineluctably a process of both repetition and variation. In such contexts, adaptation studies emerges as a field of perpetual disappointment: scholars making comparisons and identifying repetitions—which we must do if we are to study adaptation as adaptation—are charged with being epistemologically naïve, methodologically simplistic, theoretically outmoded, and politically and philosophically incorrect, because similarity *itself* is deemed to be all of these things. Just as adaptation itself has been condemned as a bad theoretical object, so too have similarity and repetition in the humanities. To offer some perspective on this, were anyone to inform evolutionary scientists that any repetitions they perceived in biological adaptation were irrelevant, pernicious, and false, while all variations they noted were important, salutary, and true, they would laugh that suggestion to scorn. Yet when humanities adaptation scholars consider comparison and similarities, theorists tell us just that—and we have ourselves castigated each other for undertaking comparative criticism.

The pervasive, repeated excoriation of fidelity criticism in adaptation studies discussed in Part I of this book derives from a masochistic introjection of humanities' theorization's bipolar assaults on similarity and fetishistic worship of difference. As adaptation scholars charge each other with theoretically incorrect attention to fidelity (repetition) in adaptation, we have been overwhelmingly and disproportionately concerned with valorizing *in*fidelity (variation) in adaptation, out of fidelity to humanities theories that fetishize difference. Paradoxically, the claim that adaptation scholars have been culpably obsessed with repetition and similarity in the form of fidelity and comparative criticism has become the most *repeated* argument of late twentieth- and twenty-first-century adaptation studies.

It is not repetition and similarity that are simplistic and false: it is humanities theories' reductive and repressive theorization of them. Transtheoretical taboos against similarity and fixations on difference have led to the overdevelopment of theories of difference and the underdevelopment of theories of similarity in the humanities, a problem reinscribed in academic industries, which make difference from prior scholarship a prerequisite for funding, publication, hiring, and promotion and a cardinal value in media industries, which depend on difference to sell products.

Histories of theorization offer past perspective and ways to move forward. Resemblance, similarity, and repetition have not always been treated derogatorily and reductively; eighteenth- and nineteenth-century theorists attached repeating resemblances to positive aesthetic and cultural values and forged nuanced theories of similarity.[2] In 1759, Edmund Burke wrote:

> The mind of man has naturally a far greater alacrity and satisfaction in tracing resemblances than in searching for differences; because by making resemblances we produce *new images*, we unite, we create, we enlarge our stock; but in making distinctions we offer no food at all to the imagination; the task itself is more severe and irksome, and what pleasure we derive from it is something of a negative and indirect nature. ([1759] 1761, 18–19, emphasis in original)

Sixty years on, Percy Bysshe Shelley valorized similarity at the very heart of Romanticism, that theoretical shrine to originality: "Reason respects the differences, and imagination the similitudes of things" ([1821] 1845, 1). For Shelley, resemblance belongs to the hallowed sphere of Romantic imagination, while difference resides in the lesser realm of reason.

Victorian philosopher John Stuart Mill demonstrated that resemblance is complex, nuanced, and variable: "resemblance may exist in all conceivable gradations, from perfect undistinguishableness to something very slight indeed" (1846, 47). In the twentieth century, Paul Ricoeur argued that resemblance should not be set in binary opposition to difference, but that "resemblance itself must be understood as a tension between identity and difference" (2003 [1975], 4)—it is not identity: it is itself a process of navigating between repetition and variation, like adaptation.

Even in the heart of deconstruction, similarity emerges as difference's repressed, subjugated, and complicit other: deconstruction depends on processes of adaptation—on rhetorical repetition and variation—to manifest *différance*. Jacques Derrida's best-known deconstruction of a proper name to common nouns—Francis to *françois, franc,* and *français* and Ponge to *éponge*—depends on phonetic and graphic *repetitions* (of *franc* and *ponge*) to demonstrate deconstructive *différance* (1989a, 62–72). These processes of graphic and phonetic repetitions and variations that adapt words into other words undertake a process of rhetorical adaptation. Thus, while I have argued that deconstruction fails to explicate adaptation's processes, it may be that adaptation's processes can illuminate deconstruction in new ways.

Adaptation has far more often been subjected to the categorical theories of the relationship between difference and similarity. Such theories are cyclical, in that categorization is itself predicated on categorical theories of the relationship between similarity and difference. Categorization differentiates them categorically: this is the same as that and therefore belongs in the same category as that; this is different from that and therefore belongs in a different category from that. More succinctly: this is categorically different; that is categorically the same. Categorical theories of similarity and difference disproportionately govern the stages of theorization discussed in Chapters 5 through 7. Definition unfolds by categorical distinctions between synonyms and antonyms; taxonomization determines that *A* is categorially the same as *B* and allocates them to the *same* category; it decrees *C* to be categorically different from *A* and *B* and allocates it to a *different* category. Universal theoretical principles, by contrast, lay claim to theorizing everything alike. Paradoxically, even as universal theoretical principles lay claim to unitary comprehensiveness, in the humanities, most universal theories champion difference as a cardinal theoretical principle.

What has not yet been sufficiently theorized is why the relationship between similarity and difference should be so pervasively constructed as a categorical one and how that categoricity has delimited other relationships that unfold between similarity and difference. To my mind, the most incisive challenge to categorical distinctions between similarity and difference comes not from poststructuralism, which exacerbates hierarchical categorizations of similarity and difference by evaporating similarity altogether (even as it depends on similarity to do so), but from within categorical theorization itself. Cognitive theorist Eleanor Rosch (1978) has shown that differences holding at one level of categorization *become similarities* at other levels. Difference holds most firmly at the "basic level of categorization," defined as the level at which category members are recognized most rapidly, the highest level at which category members share perceived shapes, the highest level at which an image can stand for the category, the level coded earliest in the language, and the level learned first by children. For example, in a categorical chain running from everything to physical objects to biological objects to mammals to cats to the body parts of a cat to a cat's molecular structures, "cats" is the basic level of categorization. In a similar categorical chain running from everything to physical objects to biological objects to mammals to dogs to the body parts of a dog to a dog's molecular structures, "dogs" constitutes the basic level of categorization. At this level, cats appear categorically (pun intended) distinct from dogs; at higher and lower levels of categorization, their differences diminish and disappear. Crucially, Rosch does not dismantle categorization as a theoretical methodology; what she does dismantle are *categorical distinctions between similarity and difference*, doing so categorically.

In adaptation studies, Hutcheon has observed the imbrication of similarity and difference in adaptation: "The adaptive faculty is the ability to repeat without copying, to embed difference in similarity, to be at once both self and Other" (2006, 174), while Andrew turned to Bazin to restore the fortunes of similarity: "Bazin may lead to Derrida and Deleuze, with their proliferation of difference, but . . . he [also] leads to Mondzin and to Jean-Luc

Nancy, who write not of difference but of 'similitude' " (2010, 5). We need to build on this foundation.

Although there is a limit to what humanities adaptation studies can learn from biological adaptation studies, we are already imbricated, sharing a subject and a rhetoric: scientists discuss the adaptive processes of DNA in a rhetoric of transcription, translation, messengers, codes, information, instructions, reading, regulation, suppression, and expression (T. Brown 2012). Scientists even have a rhetoric of "redundant copies" and the chemical nucleobases of DNA and RNA have even been nominated "canonical." Concomitantly, humanities adaptation studies engaged a rhetoric of narrative survival in new cultural environments (Hutcheon 2006, 32; Boyd 2017, 587). Yet there the humanities and sciences part ways: longstanding attention to repetition as well as variation in evolutionary biology has produced sophisticated methodologies for studying the two in relation to each other. The repetitions and variations of genetic adaptation have been theorized not only in chemical imaging and mathematical formulae but also in a rhetoric of doubles, pairs, copies, and inverted repetition (T. Brown 2012). By contrast, humanities adaptation studies has been delimited by categorical theories of similarity's relationship to difference, especially under the categoricity of medium specificity and structuralist theories and the categorical identity politics that have dominated the field. While we cannot turn to chemical and mathematical analyses to develop more complex relations between similarity and difference, we can turn to rhetorical figures that navigate similarity and difference *differently* in order to nuance their relationship generally and repetition's relationship to variation in adaptation particularly.

Categorical theories generated by the categorical nature of ordinary rhetoric and grammar have limited and blunted our ability to conceptualize relations between similarity and difference with nuance and finesse. Rhetorical figures offer other ways to conceptualize that relationship, as well as to forge more complex, multi-faceted theories of similarity that can vie and dialogue with the complex and varied theories of difference already present in the humanities. No one figure can account for all possible relations between similarity and difference, nor can all figures together articulate every possible relationship, but figures do offer ways to break through the hierarchical binarism of similarity's relationship to difference and the categoricity of ordinary rhetoric that has delimited understanding of it.

One Figure to Rule Them All

My move toward engaging multiple comparative figures to retheorize adaptation is at odds with the direction of recent mainstream theories engaging figuration, which have migrated from the binary figures of metaphor and metonymy proposed by Roman Jakobsen in the mid-twentieth century away from comparative figures altogether and toward the single contiguous figure of metonymy, proposed as one figure to rule all others and the theoretical mainstream. The rejection of comparative figures did more than lower the theoretical fortunes of similarity: it annihilated it—at least officially. De Man was one of many poststructuralists in the 1970s and 1980s to reject structuralism's privileging of metaphor over metonymy (Chapter 8), countering that metonymy is more central than metaphor to the production of meaning through difference. De Man went further to call for "the deconstruction of metaphor and of all rhetorical patterns such as mimesis, paronomasia, or personification that use resemblance as a way to disguise differences," demanding their subjugation to "the rigors of grammar," epitomized by the figure of metonymy (1979, 16). Barbara Johnson similarly lauded metonymy and denigrated metaphor, scorning their union in structuralist theory as "the salt and pepper, the Laurel and Hardy, the Yin and Yang, and often the Scylla and Charybdis of literary theory" (1984, 205), while Gilles Deleuze and Félix Guattari pronounced metaphor to be "an unfortunate procedure without real importance" ([1980] 1988, 44).

Metonymy has also overtaken metaphor in its humanities disciplinary affiliations. While structuralists Roman Jakobson and Morris Halle assigned poetry, Romanticism, and surrealism to the domain of metaphor, and prose (especially realist fiction) to the domain of metonymy (1956, 92–96), film theorist Christian Metz allocated *all* film genres to the metonymical camp ([1975] 1977, 197).[3] In the twenty-first century, new media theorist Lev Manovich too restricted digital hyperlinks to the single figure of metonymy (2001). Since most adaptation studies have focused on the adaptation of prose fiction to film, both of which are designated metonymic, metonymy should logically predominate in adaptation studies, but it has not: as Chapter 8 attests, analogy has been the field's predominant figure, bucking the humanities mainstream. Concomitantly, leading humanities theorists valorizing difference over similarity have been hostile to analogy because it is a figure of similarity. In 1963, Michel Foucault blamed analogies for constructing a false "unity of essence" through a "classificatory gaze . . . in which vicinity is defined not by measurable distances but by formal similarities," creating "a flat, homogeneous, non-measurable world" with a single essence manifesting "a plethora of similarities" ([1963] 2003, 5–6). Doing exactly what he criticized comparative figures for doing, Foucault flattened disparate modes of comparison into unity of essence. Deleuze too critiqued analogy for masking and displacing differentials ([1968] 1994).

It is troubling that figuration, celebrated as a *different* way of representing from ordinary rhetoric and a pathway to *different* ways of theorizing, should find some of its figures charged with differential lack and rounded up for elimination from theoretical discourse. Clumping diverse rhetorical figures of similarity into one camp while reducing differential figures to the single (same) figure of metonymy creates a flat, homogenous, simplistic, totalitarian theory of figuration and of similarity's relationship to difference—one that ignores *differences* between different kinds of similarity and *similarities* between different kinds of difference, while manifesting the *same* hostility to similarity and the *same* valorization of difference. Beyond the fact that adaptation cannot be understood without a complex examination of its interplay between repetition and variation, in the multidisciplinary, multicultural, multimedial, multitheoretical, and transhistorical field that is adaptation studies, surely we need more—not fewer—figures to theorize adaptation (and everything else). Rhetoric offers a palette of figures playing variably between similarity and difference that can inform and develop comparative adaptation methodologies beyond the categorical compare-and-contrast methodologies that have delimited their multifarious relations and the blanket deconstructions that have vaporized one-half of the relationship.

Figures of Differential Similarity

The best-known figure of differential similarity in theoretical discourses has been metaphor. From the Greek, to carry across, it is a figure that transfers the characteristics of one thing to another that differs from it and to which those characteristics do not literally apply. In other words, it forges comparisons across differentials. In so doing, metaphor is a threatening figure for categorical theories of similarity and difference and *for modes of theorization based on categorical distinctions between similarity and difference.* Injecting similarity into the epicenter of difference, it refuses to cede to categorical theories that segregate similarity and difference or to theories that rank similarity beneath difference. As with adaptation, the operations of meta-phor require both.

Metaphor may be the rhetorical figure par excellence to theorize adaptation, since it adapts internally: its vehicle adapts its tenor and vice versa. Indeed, Cathy Dent-Read and Agnes Szokolsky define metaphor as "a species of perceptually guided, *adaptive* action. . . of one kind of thing (the tenor) under the guidance of another kind of thing (the vehicle)" (1993, 227, emphasis added).

The central argument of this book, that theorization needs to adapt to and through adaptation, can be figured as a metaphorical process, in which adaptation becomes a vehicle through which theorization adapts. As a figure that maintains similarities amid differences, metaphor offers adaptation a model whereby to resist sameness with and conformity to theorization. Indeed, insisting that what it theorizes must conform to and become the *same* with itself may be humanities' theorization's greatest blind spot, as it celebrates difference and denigrates sameness everywhere else. Metaphor's insistence on a double-valanced relationship between similarity and difference not only challenges theorization's one-sided view of them but also models for theorization how to embrace differences between itself and what it theorizes.

Metaphor is not the only figure of differential similarity that can inform adaptation. Joining the central role of analogy in adaptation studies I have proposed simile as a way to reconceive, refigure, and adapt adaptation studies by defining, taxonomizing, and theorizing adaptation *as adaptation*, a self-reflexive simile that encourages the study of adaptation as itself (see Chapters 5 through 7).

Other figures further inform the processes of repetition and variation that shape relations between adaptation's other paired terms (adapted/adapting; entity/environment) and the theoretical paired terms that have sought to theorize adaptation's paired terms. The figure of antithesis ("opposed placement") not only constructs a contrast between two things but also constructs their difference from each other as an opposition. Historically, humanities theorization has tended to hierarchize oppositions; antithesis democratizes them, positioning them horizontally. My upbringing and academic training have conditioned me, when faced with an opposition, to rush in and do something to resolve it—to choose sides, to reconcile it, or to dismantle it. Antithesis maintains oppositions, holding them in tension for extended critical scrutiny. Antithesis offers an important pause to sit with opposition, contemplate it, and learn from it: a space to focus less on the two sides, or the opposition of one side to the other, and more on their mutual opposition to each other. Antithesis has enabled me to see that the opposition between adaptation and theorization has been a mutual one. Antithesis has also informed particular theoretical oppositions between theories, epistemologies, methodologies, ideologies, and cultures. For all the championing of difference as a cardinal theoretical principle *within* each theory, theoretical differences *between* theories are rarely tolerated, let alone championed. Antithesis offers a position to treat the opposition less reductively and with less hostility; it invites us to sit with unresolved oppositions, pondering them more even-handedly, at greater length, and in greater depth. In lieu of hasty dismissals, top-down hierarchies, and one-way revolutions, antithesis asks scholars to face the opposition head on and view it as a mutual opposition, rather than solely from the side that we occupy.

Although we have seen that the interpenetrations between adaptation's paired terms—adapted and adapting entities, repeating and varying in new environments—are immensely complex and resist binary opposition, antithesis can nevertheless provide a conceptual space in which to ponder the ways in which they may oppose each other, even as they also interpenetrate and cooperate. Antithesis reminds that exchanges and alliances between adaptation's paired terms do not necessarily do away with their oppositions. Staying with oppositions a bit longer, even if our goal is to resolve them, can help us to locate deeper insights into these oppositions that can help to resolve them. Antithesis also calls scholars like myself, who may be too eager to resolve conflicts, to embrace oppositions that may be necessary and productive for adaptation studies. Just as we respect cultural differences, so too antithesis can teach us to respect theoretical differences in adaptation studies.

How antithesis might be applied in studies of specific adaptations can be illustrated through the well-known case of David O. Sezlnick's film adaptation (Fleming 1939) of Margaret Mitchell's novel *Gone with the Wind* (1936). Film censorship, and the cultural and economic environments that produced it, forbade repeating some of the novel's diction—most notably, the "N-word" and Rhett Butler's expletive exit line. Selznick fought to retain both, but was forced to compromise. Clark Gable was permitted to not "give a damn" for a fine of $50,000 (the same amount that was paid to Mitchell for the film rights to use *every* word in her book), but the "N-word" was forbidden by censors (Leff and Simmons 2001, 95–108). Rather than ending such a study with Selznick's compromise, staying with the figure of antithesis raises additional questions regarding the opposition between the two kinds of profanity—one for sale, the other not purchasable at any price. This opposition can be explicated by a further antithesis through white interiority and black exteriority: Gable's line references his own mental state, while the "N-word" is conferred by others upon others based on their physical exteriority. Staying with antithesis leads to further oppositions between the censored "N-word" and other uncensored words degrading African Americans in the film, as well as to further antitheses between racist words and non-verbal racism in the music, acting, costumes, lighting, shot sizes, framing, and editing, which were not subject to censorship. Beyond the (un)censored film, antithesis opens into larger cultural oppositions between literary censorship and film censorship in the 1930s and beyond. Thus, even as antithesis presents as a simple, dyadic opposition, the figure can multiply to produce complex and nuanced studies of oppositions in adaptation.

While horizontal antithesis is more democratic than hierarchical binarism, its temporal unfolding can create a hierarchy, in which one side is presented as superior to the other through precedence or through ideological hierarchies, as in Alexander Pope's "To err is human; to forgive, divine" (Pope 1711, 30). The related figure of antimetathesis, however, ruptures antithesis down the middle, inserting meta ("change") between its parts. Meaning a change of position or sides, metathesis is a figure in its own right, describing the transposition of sounds or syllables within a word. Metathesis has been responsible for linguistic adaptation, as in the shift from the Old English *brid* to the Modern English *bird* (Campbell 2017, 39). It also describes the inversion of parts of an antithesis. While antithesis presents two sides of an opposition for simultaneous analysis, antimetathesis alternates sides, positioning the critic first on one side, then on the other. Such positioning calls critics to *occupy* the viewpoint of the other side in the same way that we occupy our own side and to see our side as the other side sees it. Like antithesis, antimetathesis has offered invaluable vantage points and methodologies for my metacritical and metatheoretical endeavors in this book, as well as prior adaptation studies, although these arguments have generally been made at the level of discourse and dialogics rather than figurative rhetoric (e.g., Bruhn 2013). Even though it has proved impossible for me to take an entirely impartial, even-handed view of opposing terms and discourses, the final draft of this book is a far cry from where it began, thanks to antimetathesis and other rhetorical figures that have offered variable points of view.

Antimetathesis has also informed this book's study of the opposition between adaptation and theorization. Their oppositions are not the same, nor have the two sides been given equal voice. Antimetathesis offers a conceptual and rhetorical framework through which to articulate and redress their opposed asymmetry. In the context of this discussion of similarity and difference, antimetathesis underscores that the ways in which difference has opposed similarity are not the same as those in which similarity has opposed difference. Antimetathesis furthermore clarifies that oppositions between adapted and adapting entities, entities and environments, and repetition and variation are rarely symmetrical in practice or theory: the opposition of what is adapted to what is adapting it is rarely identical to the opposition of what is adapting to what is adapted, nor is an entity's opposition to its environment identical to an environment's opposition to that entity, nor are the oppositions of repetition to variation the same as variation's opposition to repetition.

How these asymmetrical oppositions might be applied to a specific adaptation can be illustrated by a discussion of Patricia Rozema's film (1999) of Jane Austen's *Mansfield Park* (1814). As with opposed theoretical positions, antimetathesis asks scholars to view the opposition of the film(maker) to the novel and of the novel (reader) to the film and to set them in dialogue, while understanding that their opposition to each other is unlikely to be the same. Screenwriter and director Rozema opposed repeating the novel's characterization of its heroine in the new environment of late twentieth-century film on both formal and cultural grounds, nominating Austen's Fanny Price "insufferable" and unable to "carry" the novel into film "for 1999–2000 audiences" (Museum of the Moving Image 1999, n.p.). In the novel, Fanny gains social power through steadfast morality and adherence to submissive female gender roles, rendering her romantically attractive to several men, even though she is not particularly beautiful, intelligent, or gifted. Rozema opposed this characterization, which is equally opposed to Rozema's feminist ideology. Rozema turned to Austen's letters and juvenilia to infuse Fanny with the author's "wit and irreverence" (Museum of the Moving Image 1999, n.p.) and to carry Fanny's romantic triumphs into professional triumphs.[4]

Turning to antimetathesis again, Rozema's adaptive oppositions to the novel subsequently garnered opposition from reviewers and audiences. While Rozema insisted, "I didn't change her behavior . . . her behavior is pretty much what it is in the book" (Museum of the Moving Image 1999, n.p.), critics and audiences countered that making the mousy, unassuming Fanny "as attractive, forward, and personable as Mary Crawford" did indeed change her behavior and also changed her *relationships* with other characters.

Making Fanny attractive and personable rendered her suitors' overtures less remarkable, while obviating the importance of morality and gender conformity to Regency courtship. Making her forward, outgoing, and assertive made Fanny's oppressors seem less cruel, and her female antagonist in the novel, Mary, more sympathetic as a fellow-feminist in the film (*Jane Austen Today* 2010, n.p.). Such dynamics extend beyond mainstream feature films to the productions of Austen prosumers (consumers who make and disseminate their own adaptations), who also undertake differential oppositions to the novel and mainstream adaptations of it (Mirmohamadi 2014).

Antimetathetical studies not only spin out into larger networks of adaptation, they equally illuminate microscopic, internal oppositions between repeating and varying, adapted and adapting entities in media environments. For example, pictorial initials internally adapt graphemes and pictorial lines, often in oppositional ways (Elliott 2003a, 56–76). Here, processes of adapting and being adapted, of repetition and variation, and of entity and environment fuse, as the same line constructs both part of a grapheme and part of a picture, repeating and varying the line in the different environments of verbal and pictorial representation. Yet, even as they fuse, antimetathesis allows opposition to remain, enabling scholars to ponder it further, from both sides of the fusion in turn.

However, if we are to move beyond understanding and explicating oppositions to creating more mutual and reciprocal relationships between opposed forces such as adaptation and theorization, we also need the figure of antimetabole. A figure conjoining opposition (anti-) with inversion (metabole, turning about), it constructs this book's two parts, "Theorizing Adaptation" and "Adapting Theorization." Antimetabole creates space for both opposition *and* mutuality, obviating the hierarchies, one-way revolutions, and separate spheres commonly proposed to theorize adaptation through a process of reciprocal inversion and mutual exchange. Antimetabole does not dissolve oppositions but repeatedly inverts the two sides and, crucially, *their relation to each other*. Through a process of reciprocal inversion, antimetabole renders oppositions mutual and equal. The two halves of the antimetabole, same difference/different sameness, may not *mean* the same thing, but their rhetorical structures differ from each other *in exactly the same way*: in each phrase, an adjective precedes and modifies a noun; antimetabole inverts the terms and parts of speech. The reciprocal, inverse parts of antimetabole can reverberate endlessly, as two facing mirrors create a hall of mirrors.

Antimetabole does not eradicate opposition: rather, it makes the opposition between two things mutual and reciprocal through processes of inversion. The two continue to oppose each other, but inversion constructs that opposition *identically*: it makes them oppose each other *in exactly the same way*. Through antimetabole, "Theorizing Adaptation" and "Adapting Theorization" mirror—that is, reflect and invert—their opposition to each other. Through antimetabole, theorization and adaptation occupy the same grammatical, conceptual, and rhetorical positions in their opposition to each other.

Beyond the asymmetries of metaphor, antithesis, and antimetathesis, antimetabole calls theorization and adaptation to receive each other's opposition *as part of their identity* and to perceive their inherence in what they oppose. In the process, theorization and adaptation become more like each other—more adapted to each other, a process that also changes their relationship. Antimetabole describes not so much what we have done as what we need to do in adaptation studies to respond to "the problem of theorizing adaptation."

Refiguring Medium Specificity Theory

My history of theorizing adaptation documents the remarkable persistence of categorical medium specificity theory in adaptation studies, especially in structuralist theorization:

> Structuralism favors a way of approaching media which has its origins in Lessing's *Laokoön* (1766), even if Lessing's views have been much modified and qualified: a medium is something with its own inalienable being, its own complex structures of constitution and operation, its own codes, which individualize and separate it. (Scott 2011, 39)

One of the reasons that medium specificity has been so resistant to poststructuralist deconstruction is that Lessing's distinctions between the arts are predicated on phenomenological interactions between formal properties and the human senses. It is therefore insufficient to deconstruct oppositions between aesthetic forms; one must also deconstruct Lessing's categorical oppositions of the senses, which he separated just as categorically as he did the arts.[5]

The figure of synaesthesia does just this, challenging theories that make the senses "significantly separate and independent" (Keeley 2002, 25). Synaesthesia ("union of the senses") describes a psychological process in which the stimulation of one sense arouses the involuntary stimulation of another, as when listening to music raises goosebumps. Arguing that "we perceive the universe with the totality of our bodies, with the concerted operation of *all* our senses, not through their *separate* activities," Clive Scott has proposed a synesthetic theory of intermedial adaptation (2011, 39, emphasis in original). For Scott, adaptation

> is not primarily to be conceived of as a process of transfer of one medium to another; it is the translation of one medium *out of itself into multisensory, or cross-sensory, consciousness*; put another way, it is the translation of one medium back into whole-body experience. . . . I want to call this translation synesthetic. (39–40, emphasis added)

Synesthetic adaptation forges connections not only between the senses but also between percepts and concepts, just as figuration does:

> [It is] the aiding of one sense by another, and the aiding of percept by concept; that is, one sense functions as the prosthetic extension of another, just as concept functions as the prosthetic extension of percept. We do not just mix senses; we encourage the senses to cooperate in acts of reciprocal prosthetization. (Scott 2011, 40)

Aiding synaesthesia are figures more sensory than semantic—figures such as alliteration, assonance, consonance, and onomatopoeia, which repeat and vary sounds. These figures are not limited to verbal rhetoric but have been discussed in their musical, visual, tactile, and kinetic media manifestations.[6] Within a form such as film, multiple media forms (shot size, camera angle, camera movement, focal length, lighting, color/black and white film stock, editing, set design, acting, costume, makeup and hair, props, written and spoken words, dialogue and voiceover narration, music, sound effects, and special effects) unfold simultaneously, interacting with each other in multifarious ways. Synesthetic analysis would push formal studies of these interactions into studies of how the senses perceive them unfolding *simultaneously*.

Synaesthesia can also synthesize rhetorical figures to inform the study of adaptation. Marcus Nichols's study of how decadent literary theories and practices present new possibilities for adaptation theorization includes analysis of the synaesthetic relations produced by interart analogies, as "the analogies of art forms are mapped to the body" (2018, 195). Cristina Cacciari's metacritical study of relations forged between the figures of synaesthesia and metaphor finds that "metaphorical language is pervaded by cross-modality references" (2008, 436). While scientists theorize synaesthesia as a rare neurological condition, conventional synesthetic metaphors such as "loud colors" and "sweet music" attest to its widespread cultural presence.

For scientist-blogger "molivares," synaesthesia not only links media forms and human senses but also generates synaesthetic thinking and theorization:

Art itself, whether it is in the form of poetry, painting, sculpture, or music, is a synesthetic experience that bridges the senses and relates seemingly unrelated concepts. In its broadest definition, synaesthesia . . . can be viewed as the mind's metaphor and creative release. Thoughts, emotions, and the immaterial, somehow get transformed into the material. Poetry, paintings, and music are materialized analogies and metaphors that link together our senses and seemingly unrelated ideas. (2010, n.p.)

In a study such as mine that seeks to bridge the gaps and rifts of categorical and warring theories and the particularly troubling impasse between theorization and adaptation, synaesthesia joins other rhetorical figures to "bridge the senses" in ways that not only connect "seemingly unrelated concepts" but also transform "thoughts, emotions, and the immaterial . . . into the material." What theorization has torn asunder, let synaesthesia join together.

Figures of Contiguity

Adaptation Studies and Metonymy

Thus far, I have argued that adaptation studies suffers from humanities theorization's overemphasis on difference and denigration of similarity. Yet *within* adaptation studies, adaptation studies' historical roots in translation studies, the twentieth-century formalist turn, and the prominence of comparative value judgments continuing in cultural adaptation studies have led to an overemphasis on comparative methodologies and comparative figures at the expense of contiguous ones.

Prioritizing the comparative figure of analogy, as adaptation studies has done, has set it at odds not only with modernist theories, which privilege metaphor, but also with postmodern, poststructuralist, and new media theories, which privilege metonymy. This is one area where adaptation studies would benefit from adapting more to the theoretical mainstream. Adaptation does not live by similarity and difference alone: it also unfolds through contiguous relationships between entities and environments and between entities within environments. Comparison foregrounds adaptation's processes of change (repetition with variation); contiguity prioritizes its contextual relations (between entities and environments). Just as the first stage of theorization, definition, proceeds by both comparative and contiguous processes (a word is defined by both synonyms and its contextual usage within sentences), so too adaptation requires both comparative and contiguous analyses to understand it.

Metonymy, we have seen, has become the most prominent figure in humanities theorization in recent decades. In rhetoric, metonymy is defined as the substitution of the name of one object for another from which it is distinct, but to which it is connected by some contiguous relationship such as effect for cause, producer for product, object for agent, substance for form, or place for event. Metonymy, then, does not just describe a grammatical sequence or associative chain but also involves a degree of displacement by a near relation. Such usurpation does not take the form of radical revolution to overthrow one side of a binary with its subjected underling: its shifts are much more insidious and subtle.

Metonymy has been more implicitly than explicitly present in adaptation studies. When a scholar considers adaptations in their contexts, that is studying adaptation contiguously. Often, however, the focus of contextual adaptation studies has been on making comparative assessments of aesthetics, politics, cultures, and forms. As comparative arguments predominate over contiguous ones, metonymy becomes the subtext, the unconscious of adaptation studies. Returning to *Rethinking the Novel/Film Debate* (2003a), I see that I was discussing metonymic processes without acknowledging them as such, focused as I was on a comparative study of words and images in hybrid media and intermedial adaptation. Metonymic processes were at work in the early film adaptations of Victorian fiction I analyzed in Chapter 3. When producers placed their company names on the film set, they made metonymic substitution of film producer for film product. The anachronistic insertion of a real twentieth-century film company name into a fictional Victorian setting made further metonymic substitutions of literary with filmic ownership and effect for cause. There are metonymic displacements of object for agent in films such as *Scrooge, Or Marley's Ghost* (Booth, 1901), as the literary words that were agents generating the film adaptation are framed as objects on the film set: Tiny Tim's "GOD BLESS US EVERYONE" hangs as a huge placard in the Cratchit family parlor; Fred's "A MERRY XMAS" becomes a framed picture in his living room.

Metonymy has featured more didactically in adaptation studies' near relation, translation studies: adaptation studies can learn from this. For example, the contiguous processes of adaptation are not limited to relations between texts and contexts. For Charles Denroche, the relationship between a source and target text is rarely metaphorical: the process of translation is better described as one of metonymic near approximation and partial overlap (2015, 157).[7] For Maria Tymoczko, "A basic feature of rewritings and retellings is that they are metonymic" both textually and contextually (2016, 42). Stories rewritten and retold unfold contiguously over time and across cultures as well as texts:

> Metonymy in literary rewritings and retellings is also an important aspect in cultural continuity and change. It permits the adaptation of traditional content and form to new circumstances, allowing change while still maintaining a predominant sense of the preservation of larger elements of tradition. (Tymoczko 2016, 46)

These theories are descendants of Restoration and Augustan theories of translation and adaptation.

Metonymy also informs how recent theories have developed adaptation studies. Postmodern theories, with their emphasis on pluralism and diversity, have been contiguous, annexing ever more media forms, cultures, disciplines, and theories into their pluralist pastiches (Hutcheon 2006). Pressing adaptation studies beyond the dyads, binaries, divides, and feuds of prior theories, postmodern cultural studies has constructed adaptation studies as an ever-expanding, never-ending, metonymic, add-on field. At a microscopic level, my rhetorical experiments with hyphenated verb endings (adapt-ed-ing-ed, etc.) have forged contiguous relationships between processes of verb tenses that, in their attachment to spatial processes of adaptation's environments, construct temporo-spatial contiguities. Clearly, there is immense potential for metonymy to illuminate prior adaptation theories and to open up new methodologies and generate new arguments in adaptation studies, carrying the field beyond our predominantly comparative methodologies to engage contiguous ones. The next subsection illustrates some of this potential in a study of adaptation and synecdoche.

Adaptation, Synecdoche, and Part–Whole Relations

Synecdoche, the exchange of a part for a whole or a whole for a part, has been categorized as both near relation to and subcategory of metonymy (Nerlich 2009). Dudley Andrew has argued that "the study of adaptation is logically tantamount to the study of the cinema as a whole" (1980, 458). Even so, just as adaptation scholars have favored analogy over metaphor, so too we have favored synecdoche over metonymy, albeit more implicitly than explicitly. Even when adaptation methodologies are overtly comparative, cataloguing similarities and differences, they often take a synecdochal view, assessing what *parts* of a prior work have been adapted to the *whole* of a new work or what *parts* have been repeated and what *parts* have been varied. Reading adaptation synecdochally is so pervasive that it took me less than ten minutes to locate two essays in recent issues of *LFQ* and *Adaptation* that do just that. Melissa Elliot's essay documents "The consensus among critics and scholars . . . that major themes of the novel have been lost in the translation from page to screen" (2018, n.p.); David Evan Richard's article draws on recent phenomenological theory to argue that screen adaptations bring their less sensory sources to life as "products that appeal to the eyes, ears, skin, and viscera" (2018, 144) and that attention to embodied spectatorship "as a lived *whole*" (150) "is critical to a more *holistic* understanding of adaptation" (145, emphasis added). These and other discourses of adaptation are keenly concerned with the relation of adapted to adapting works in terms of parts and wholes, yet these scholars, and the field more generally, have not didactically theorized—or figured—them as such.

A synecdochal approach to adaptation focuses on exchanges between parts and wholes rather than on what's the same and what's different. Synecdoche therefore offers another way to conduct comparative adaptation studies— one that is less subject to the problematic binaries and hierarchies inflicted by theorization on similarity and difference. Contiguous studies of parts in relations to wholes can be partnered with comparative studies. For example, Robert Louis Stevenson's *The Strange Case of Jekyll and Hyde* ([1886] 2005) is filled with a rhetoric of binary oppositions: good/evil, higher-class/ lower-class, classical dualism, human/animal, male/female, English/ethnic other, heterosexual/homosexual, fit/degenerate, and so forth (Nollen 1994; Kane 1999, 11; 17–19). Yet the novella attests that the relationship of Jekyll to Hyde is not a binary but one of part and whole: "Although I now had two characters as well as two appearances, one was wholly evil, and the other was still the old Henry Jekyll, that incongruous compound" (Stevenson [1886] 2005, 82). I have often wondered, where does the rest of Jekyll go when Hyde takes over? This is not a question that can be answered logically or scientifically. But synecdoche answers it: the transformation from one to the other is a synecdochal process: when Jekyll transforms to Hyde, the part displaces the whole; when Hyde turns back into Jekyll, the whole displaces the part.

Synecdochal adaptation studies would go beyond substitutory exchanges of wholes and parts between adapting entities to consider exchanges between entities as parts of whole environments. At a rhetorical level, "texts" is part of the word "contexts." But texts are also environments for other texts in processes of adaptation that take parts of whole texts to create a new whole text. Just as Jekyll is not simply an individual changing within his environment with Hyde but is also an environment for Hyde, so too we have seen that the production of any adaptation is a synecdochal process in which whole texts become part of new texts and the consumption of adaptation is a synecdochal process that alternates between parts and wholes of adapting and adapted texts. Beyond individual texts, aesthetic styles constitute environments for each other: modernist authors alluding to parts of prior works within their wholes and modernist painters disassembling prior styles so that the whole remains an assemblage of disjunctive parts are adapting synecdochally. Media forms more generally adapt to each other within a shared environment, as so many scholars have argued of novels, theater, and film (Nicoll 1936; Chatman 1978; Cohen 1979). Theorizing adaptation synecdochally supports "a textual contextualism [that] would consider the textuality of contexts" and "a contextual textualism [that] would attend ... to the ways in which contexts ... inhere in texts" (Elliott 2014b, 585–86). The rhetoric here is not only one of antimetabole but also one of synecdoche. I was not thinking of synecdoche at all when I wrote this article, but it was lurking there all the same: "The task before us is ... to find ways to study adaptations *holistically* across formal-cultural and textual-contextual divides amid ideological disagreements" (584, emphasis added).

Synecdoche has not only revealed my theoretical blind spots but has also exposed my theoretical partialities. For all my personal preference for mutuality, reciprocity, and equality in the relationship between adaptation and theorization, synecdoche reminds that adaptation is not always an equitable affair: more often than not, it deals asymmetrically in parts and wholes. Far from promoting democratic relations, for Roland Barthes, "Synecdoche is totalitarian: it is an act of force. 'The whole for the part' . . . means: one part *against* another part" ([1975] 1989, 218, emphasis in original). Synecdoche articulates how theorists have subjugated whole theories on which they build as parts of their new wholes, as when postmodernism made modernism a part of its new whole. Within adaptation studies, theorists have similarly subjugated rival theories as parts of their wholes when, for example, they reduce aesthetics to operations of power and politics.

Synecdoche also describes how adaptation has been theorized partially as a part of other disciplines and subjected to their wholes (Chapter 6) and how totalizing theoretical principles have sought to subject adaptation as a part of their universal wholes (Chapter 7). Adaptation's resistance to these attempts to reduce it to being a part of other things can be conceived as refusing to concede its own status as a whole, even though it takes part in many things. It is adaptation's refusal to become part to theorization's whole that has, in part, constructed it as a rival process to theorization. Each chapter in "Retheorizing Theorization" concludes with a recommendation that scholars set adaptation and theorization in synecdochal exchanges, in which adaptation is studied as a part of other things, disciplines, and theories, alternating with studies of these as parts of adaptation's whole. Synecdoche comes ready-made as a two-way figure, denoting both the exchange of a whole for a part and the exchange of a part for a whole. The dialogue between these two purviews is a synecdochal one. However, since synecdoche does not require a reversal of parts and wholes, what I am arguing for is a hybrid figure of *antimetabolic synecdoche*, which engages in reciprocal shifts between one kind of synecdoche (part for whole) and the other (whole for part)—between the study of adaptation as part of other things and adaptation as whole, in which other things are parts. The exchanges of Jekyll and Hyde serve as cautionary tale for adaptation scholars, warning us against allowing parts of adaptation studies to subsume adaptation studies as a whole.

The synecdochal relationship between Jekyll and Hyde further informs larger theoretical debates in adaptation studies. When the part becomes the whole, it is represented as an evil, aberrant, dangerous monstrosity; when the part returns to its rightful place within the whole, order is restored. Over the course of the novella, the part, Hyde, grows more powerful than the whole, Jekyll, and threatens to take over the whole by means of a permanent synecdochal usurpation. Only Hyde's body remains at the end. Adaptation threatens the totalization of theoretical wholes by refusing to play its part within their systems; adaptation threatens their definitions, taxonomies, and principles in only partially adhering to them. Additionally, adaptation threatens the identity of whole arts as defined by medium specificity theory and the wholeness and unity of the single disciplines that study them.

Turning to the central question of this book, the hybrid figure of antimetabolic synecdoche promotes more reciprocal relations between adaptation and theorization. Viewing each as a part of the other's whole constructs a more mutual, inherent relationship between them, in which each inhabits and informs the other as part. For too long, adaptation theorization has functioned in Barthes's formulation as a totalitarian act of force, in which "the whole for the part" has meant one part against another part. As antimetabolic synecdoche renders adaptation a part of theorization's whole and theorization a part of adaptation's whole, inversely and reciprocally, it joins figures of similarity that make adaptation and theorization more like each other to create contiguous-comparative connections between adaptation and theorization that allow them to be theorized as parts of each other vying ongoingly to displace each other in endless reversals of parts and wholes.

Metalepsis, Metafigurality, and the Mysteries of Adaptation

My history and theory of theorizing adaptation in this book have been metahistorical and metatheoretical; my rhetoric of theorizing adaptation, while it has been metacritical, has not yet been metafigural. For Derrida, such discourse is impossible. Pondering "Metaphor in the Text of Philosophy," he concluded: "Concept is a metaphor . . . theory is a metaphor; and there is no meta-metaphor for them" ([1971] 1974, 23). His argument is predicated on a definition of all language as metaphorical: there is no position outside of language from which to critique language. For Madhavi Menon, there is a meta-figural figure: metalepsis is "the figure of figurality" (2004, 75); Mark Staff Brandl too has nominated it "the trope of tropes" ("Metalepsis" n.d., n.p.). For Menon, "metalepsis both denies us a face that we can recognize, and provides us with a form that continually changes shape. It is the figure of figurality and, in a sense, the essence of rhetoric" (2004, 75).

Its etymology articulates its redoubled figuration—both "meta" and "lepsis" denote substitution—so that the *Oxford English Dictionary* defines metalepsis as a "rhetorical figure consisting in the metonymical substitution of one word for another which is itself a metonym" (*OED*, 2nd rev. ed., s.v. "metalepsis," accessed April 29, 2018, https://www-oed-com/view/Entry/ 117228). Here, metalepsis is a figure that metonymizes metonymy.

Metalepsis, however, is not limited to metonymizing metonymy: the Roman rhetorician Marcus Fabius Quintilian (35–96 AD) defined metalepsis more generally as "a transition from one trope to another" ([ca. 95 AD] 1920–22, 3.37); today it encompasses any figure that "refers us to yet another figure . . . to establish its relevance" (Baldick 2008, 204). Beyond metonymy and verbal language, Brandl has identified a metalepsis comprised of simile and metaphor in painting:

> Vincent van Gogh plays a metaphor on the brushstroke of the Impressionists—their stroke was modelled after dappled sunlight. . . [and is] thus a simile. Vincent makes it into a flame-like stroke, a metaphor played on a simile[.] ("Metalepsis," n.d., n.p.)

Its redoubled figurality and extension from redoubling one figure to many figures has made metalepsis a difficult figure to define. For Quintilian, metalepsis resists definition because it has no meaning of its own: "It is the nature of metalepsis to form a kind of intermediate stop between the term transferred and the thing to which it is transferred, having no meaning in itself, but merely providing a transition" ([ca. 95] 1920, 3.37). In a study such as mine, where each figure has a definition as a figure, metalepsis can be defined as a double figurative transition. Yet in practice, specific metalepses move away from semantic definition through synonymity with other words. As the metaleptic play of a metaphor upon a simile moves further from literal meaning to a redoubled figural meaning—as the brushstroke-like-dappled-sunlight simile metamorphoses into a brushstroke-like-flame—the metalepsis represents a shift from established painting techniques to new ones. As with Restoration and Augustan theories of adaptation, metalepsis here not only references but also brings about progress in art.

While specific metalepses engaging specific figures (metaphor and simile, metonymy and metonymy, etc.) may produce readings generating meaning, scholars continue to struggle with what metalepsis *itself* means. For Douglas Robinson, it is "a confusing trope, a hard trope to define with any usefulness. . . . I am still not sure exactly what it is . . . [n]or are many other people" (1991, 181). For Terence Hawkes, "Something in the mind withers at the prospect of unfolding the mysteries of" metalepsis ([1972] 2017, 4). Even the otherwise confidently definitive *Oxford Dictionary of Literary Terms* concedes, "In rhetoric, the precise sense of metalepsis is uncertain" (Baldick 2008, 204). Although adaptation and metalepsis share a problematic relationship to definition, while adaptation's problematic definitional status has generated a host of alternate terminologies (Chapter 5), the problems of defining metalepsis have pressed it toward meaninglessness, uselessness, and mystery.

Metalepsis also occupies a liminal position in taxonomies. Like adaptation, metalepsis has been taxonomized as that which crosses taxonomical boundaries: when structuralist narratologist Gérard Genette defined metalepsis as "the passage from one narrative level to another" (1983, 243), even as he named, taxonomized, and theorized it, it crossed every border of his whole categorical system, violating it *as* system (1983, 245). Metalepsis does not exist in a categorical relationship to other categories but rather enables one categorical entity to *become* another—to pass from one category to another. Adaptation too has been defined as a passage from one category to another—from book to film, from Renaissance play to Restoration play, from good aesthetics to bad aesthetics, from bad politics to good politics, and so forth.

Genette was particularly interested in metalepsis as a transition from extradiegetic narrative to diegetic narrative, and vice versa. Postmodern theorists have built on Genette's discussion of metalepsis to argue that it collapses the boundaries between fiction and reality generally (Malina 2002). In its postmodern formulations, metalepsis does not change one thing into another but destabilizes the identity of both, and categoricity more generally. While for some theorists, metalepsis casts both fiction and reality into the single category of fiction, for others, it is the *distinction between them* that is destabilized (or "metalepsized") so that neither is either and, at the same time, both are both. A postmodern metaleptic view of a literary film adaptation would not be one in which the book becomes a film but one in which both lose their categorical identities. In a postmodern metaleptic formulation of literary film adaptation, the adaptation is neither book nor film, at the same time that it is both.

For Menon, metalepsis "has neither a clearly defined ontological status nor a sharply delineated physical form; its existence is purely relational." Because of this, "[m]etalepsis is the rhetorical term designated to bridge the gap between two worlds even as it is the trope that undermines any absolute opposition between the two" (2004, 73; 68). Figured as a bridge, metalepsis spans a gap, but even as it does, it questions the need for its bridging by revealing the "always already" affinities between what it bridges. In adaptation's closely related field of translation, Robinson has argued that metalepsis is not

> a bridge. . . . Nothing solid or sturdy. Nothing permanent. Rather, a *bridging*—or even a feeling-as-if-one-were-bridging, a feeling-about-being-caught-in-the-middle-in-terms-of-a-bridging. . . . [I]f all you have is a bridging that cannot guarantee a safe crossing, you have to learn to deal with uncertainty. (1991, 181; 184, emphasis in original)

Discourses of metaleptic processes and principles have been linked to practices of literary adaptation. For Harold Bloom, metalepsis explains how literary allusion carries canonical literature "from origins to repetition and continuity, and thence to the discontinuity that marks all revisionism" (1975, 47). For Bloom, metalepsis is a process of repetition with variation: violating temporal borders and orders, it creates a state in which "the present vanishes and the dead return, by a reversal, to be triumphed over by the living" (1975, 74). For Bloom, the past triumphs over the present when it is adapted it; conversely, for Augustan adaptation theorists, the living triumph over the dead when their adaptations of prior works surpass them. For Brandl, "This trope-of-tropes becomes the tool for an allusive yet affirmative struggle of reversals" ("Subsumption and Misprision" n.d., n.p.). In each example, metalepsis and adaptation cross categories in ways that assert one side over the other.

Like adaptation, metalepsis also asserts itself against the inaccuracies and constraints of theorization: "Want to change a constricting, seemingly somehow-incorrect conception in any field of human thought?" Brandl has asked. "Then attack it not by simple inversion, but by . . . creative, purposeful . . . misprision of the earlier metaphor" ("Subsumption and

Misprision" n.d., n.p.). Inversion, epitomized by the figure of antimetabole, proves insufficient to redress theorization's constraints upon and failures of adaptation; metalepsis, however, carries adaptation beyond the inversions of antimetabole into less formulaic, more creative refigurations of what is already figurative: "Metalepsis can be important way to rethink history, one's own history and one's work, in our continuing struggle to revitalize art" ("Subsumption and Misprision" n.d., n.p.).

In my struggle to revitalize adaptation theorization, metalepsis has brought me to understand—and accept—that adaptation passes understanding and exceeds theorization's attempts to explicate it. Metalepsis articulates the mysteries of relations between adaptation's paired terms—the adapted/adapting, repeating/varying, textual/contextual processes of adaptation. What remains most elusive is *what lies between* them—what happens there. In biology, scientists know that the base pairs of DNA are held together by hydrogen bonds. We have no such information or means of analyzing our pairs. We have only rhetoric. The redoubled figure of metalepsis is "both elusive and allusive at once" as a process in which "one or more unstated, but associated or understood figures, [are] transumed by the trope" (Hollander 1984, 115–16; 140). In classical rhetoric, transumption is a synonym for metalepsis. For John Hollander, "A transumptive style . . . involves an ellipsis, rather than a relentless pursuit, of further figuration" (140). In rhetoric, the etymology of ellipsis is omission or falling short; in writing, ellipsis is constructed by three periods (. . .) that do not conclude, as a single period does a sentence, but mark what has gone before as unfinished and inconclusive, a space where words have been cut or cannot be written. It is a mark of what is not there, cannot be known, or cannot be written. But that absence, that unknowability has been written.

While transumption and adaptation both articulate processes of change in relation to environments, transumption moves and removes, transfers something to another place, takes something for something else. In so doing, that something recedes from view and becomes inaccessible to rhetoric: "the transumed . . . is precisely that which is not mentioned . . . and yet which is refashioned" (Schirmeister 1990, 35). In the same way, the mysteries of adaptation elude and allude simultaneously: at the very moment of refashioning, they too become unmentionable. Metalepsis calls me to accept that adaptation passes understanding and that theorization, my own included, will continue to fail adaptation. Indeed, for Menon, "failure is the hallmark of metalepsis" (82).

Conclusion

When I began this study, my arguments were governed by the figure of antimetabole: it was *my* one figure to rule them all. Subsequently, other rhetorical figures offered other ways to explicate and redress impasses between adaptation and theorization. Figures such as paradox, periphrasis, parallelism, and oxymoron describe their problematic relations; comparative figures such as analogy, simile, and metaphor configure theorization and adaptation as more like each other; contiguous figures such as synecdoche and metonymy connect them temporo-spatially. Hybridized with inverting figures such as antimetabole and chiasmus, these and other figures can help us to reconfigure the relationship between adaptation and theorization. In the final analysis, however, metalepsis underscores the limitations of theorizing adaptation, pointing simultaneously to the failure of rhetoric and language to theorize adaptation and to the limitless potential of figuration to adapt theorization and adaptation studies. Figures that straddle the material and abstract, the rational and irrational, factuality and imagination offer hybrid conceptual structures in which scholars can probe hybrid theories, epistemologies, and methodologies, which have been particularly illuminating for conceptualizing the hybridities of adaptation, with potential for theorizing adaptation further across media, disciplines, nations, and epochs.

Even as adaptation remains a mystery that can never be fully understood or theorized, in their multifarious forms and their innumerable applications, figures offer diverse conceptual structures in which scholars of all theoretical persuasions can continue to explore this mystery and refigure the relationship between adaptation and theorization, as well as particular theoretical problems in adaptation studies. Experimental and creative themselves, rhetorical figures foster theoretical, conceptual, and methodological experimentation that is itself adaptive. Some figurative experiments may fail and be discarded; others may be revisited and adapted. The past limitations of theorizing adaptation lie within rhetoric itself; so too do its future possibilities.

Postscript/Coding Coda

Key questions remain: does the shift from analogical to digital media require us to rethink figuration in adaptation studies, particularly the primacy of analogy? Has the digital age rendered the figure of analogy as outdated as analogical media technologies in adaptation studies? Has the 0/1, on/off, yes/ no coding of digital media reinscribed the categoricity and binaries that both adaptation and figuration resist? Yes and no. While programmers work with bits and digits, users of digital media engage them analogically: we open file folders by double-clicking on images of them; we place documents in the folders by pointing at, clicking on, and dragging images of documents until they overlay the folder images; we then place them in those folders by lifting our finger off the keyboard mouse or touch-screen.

Annette Vee's *Coding Literacy: How Computer Programming Is Changing Writing* acknowledges the illiteracy of most digital users in computer coding and looks forward to a future in which new technologies and educational systems will improve digital literacy (2017, 23). Even so, rather than theorize the relationship between computer language and verbal language in terms of the digital and the analogical, she resorts to metaphors and analogies of literacy, reading, writing, and translation to create dialogues between academic disciplines: science and literature, mathematics and literature, and philosophical and technical disciplines. Moreover, in so doing, she too treats digital media analogically.

Carolyn Handa's *The Multimediated Rhetoric of the Internet: Digital Fusion*, which examines "the ways [figurative] rhetoric impacts various digital media" (2014, 4), also stays at the level of digital media's analogical surface representations, making no mention of the relationship between binary computer coding and figurative rhetoric. Indeed, her main argument is that figurative rhetoric functions in much the same way in digital media as it does in analogical media. Considering only the words and images of digital media, her case studies engage the same linguistic and aesthetic methodologies that scholars have used to study words and images in analogical and print media.

By contrast, David N. Rodowick's *Reading the Figural, or, Philosophy after the New Media* sees figuration in new media as rendering some traditional humanities theories obsolete: "New media [are] emerging from a new logic of sense—the figural—and [cannot] be understood within the reigning norms of a linguistic or aesthetic philosophy" (2001, x). Like Handa, Rodowick engages the figural to override binary oppositions of word and image, discussing "the concept of the figural . . . as a semiotic theory that comprehends what the image becomes when freed from the opposition of word to image" (2001, xi). Yet, in spite of his radical claims about the challenges that new media figuration's "new logic of sense" bring to older formal theories, the "new logic" does not apply to the older political and cultural theories (by Kant, Hegel, Derrida, Benjamin, Foucault, Deleuze, and Lyotard) that he champions: like Handa, he applies the figural and these theories as they have been applied to analogical media, to propose "a theory of power that unlocks the figural as a historical image or social hieroglyph wherein the spatial and temporal parameters of contemporary collective life can be read as they are reorganized by the new images and new communications technologies" (2001, xi). As with analogy, "the figural" has not refigured theorization; rather, figuration has been constrained by theorization, used here to support some theories over others.

N. Katherine Hayles has turned to psychoanalytic and post-humanist theory to conceptualize the relationship between computer coding and language: "As the unconscious is to the conscious, so computer code is to language" (2013, 39–40). This argument also uses familiar theories to explain the relationship. Yet pushing beyond classical psychoanalysis, Hayles engages posthuman theory to ponder how computer algorithms engage in *non-human* adaptation and the challenges that presents to interpretation: "In the case of evolutionary algorithms where the code is not directly written by a human but evolves through variation and selection procedures carried out by a machine, the difficulty of understanding the code is . . . notorious" (40). These "evolutionary algorithms" produce adaptations that bypass human understanding, agency, and control: in the process, they join the mysteries of metalepsis.[8]

Mike DeHaan has worked ingeniously to align biological adaptation with computer coding. Both discourses engage the literal rhetoric of linguistics, literature, and communications disciplines (transcription, translation, copying, reading, writing, expression, messenger, and information) and apply it figuratively within biology and computing disciplines. DeHaan goes further, however, to forge computational connections between DNA and computer coding, linking biological cell division and replication (2015, 1–2) to the binary arithmetic of computer coding. His computations redress concerns about the potential reassertion of binaries by the digital, since even the simplest computer command requires multiple, complex configurations of digits. In the same way, although DNA is restricted to paired chemicals, the National Human Genome Research Institute has identified three billion base pairs in human DNA, with potential to create $4^{3,000,000,000}$ possible base sequences (DeHaan 2015, n.p.). Here, biology joins metalepsis and computer codes to affirm the unknowability of adaptation through its microscopic immensities and immeasurable potential variations. And yet we continue to study it.

The future of humanities adaptations, however, will not be determined by the binary bits of classical computing: adaptations will not be stripped of their multiplicities and reduced to binaries when we dig more deeply beneath the analogical surfaces that we engage as users into the underlying processes of computer coding. The future lies in quantum computing, which works not by binary either/or bits but by qubits, which are not limited to being one of two options (0 or 1) but can be both at the same time, a process called *superposition* (Kaye, Laflamme, and Mosca 2007). Superposition allows for both/ and as well as either/or; so too, I have argued, does adaptation: a literary film adaptation is can be seen as either a revised book or a film in its own right, or as neither one, or as both.

Qubits are linked not by linear, inverting chains but by a process called entanglement, which in physics articulates a "correlation between the states of two separate quantum systems such that the behaviors of the two together is different from the juxtaposition of the behaviors of each considered alone" (*OED*, 2nd rev. ed., s.v. "entanglement" (*Physics*), accessed September 24, 2019, https://www-oed-com/view/Entry/62785). Not only does this describe the relations of adapt-ed-ing (etc.) entities and environments, it also describes the relations between adaptation and theorization in the humanities. Correlating them has revealed behaviors—processes—that differ from their processes when considered alone. Although this has long been known, understood, accepted, and pursued in practices of theorizing adaptation, what this book has sought to add to that discourse is an inverse discourse of adapting theorization, as well as to demonstrate some correlations between those two discourses.

Conclusion

Adaptation and Theorization

So what *is* the problem of theorizing adaptation? Part I's history of "Theorizing Adaptation" finds that it is a relatively recent problem: prior to the late eighteenth century, adaptation was a good theoretical object, both formally and culturally, and was considered relatively unproblematic to theorize. Even after the theoretical alliance of Romantic original creation and medium specificity theory against adaptation in the second half of the eighteenth century, adaptation continued to be valued theoretically during the nineteenth century, albeit equivocally and selectively. While bourgeois critics theorized adaptation as a regrettably downwardly mobile affair from higher to lower classes, intellects, aesthetics, ethics, prices, media, and consumers (see also Starker 1989), adaptation's proponents apotheosized adaptation as the word made flesh and, more pragmatically, theorized adaptation a means of raising the low and colonizing the world. Today, adaptation remains valued for educating children and selling media products: franchise entertainment "depends on a concept of adaptation that is almost, but not quite, what it adapts. As long as an adaptation or tie-in product is not quite what it adapts, more adaptations need to be made" (Elliott 2014a, 207).

In the early twentieth century, alliances between aesthetic originality and medium specificity were refueled by modernism's slogan, "Make it new!" The formalist turn and structuralist semiotics forged a lethal alliance against adaptation, rendering it aesthetically undesirable and logically impossible, but adaptation nevertheless survived and thrived in cultural practice and in industry and lay discourses. Even when adaptation became a thoroughly bad theoretical object in the humanities mainstream, there were always dissenting theoretical voices defending it. Following the failure of formal theories to theorize adaptation, some scholars pioneered industry, sociological, and popular cultural studies of adaptation. André Bazin, the true father of adaptation studies, went further to valorize and defend adaptation via formal theories, foreseeing radical futures in adaptation theorization that we have still not quite attained (Bazin [1948] 2000, 26). (We have until 2050!)

Theorizing Adaptation. Kamilla Elliott, Oxford University Press (2020). © Oxford University Press.
DOI: 10.1093/oso/9780197511176.001.0001

The theoretical turn in the humanities in the late twentieth century, more focused on revolutionizing theorization than on theorizing adaptation, only partially rescued adaptation from prior theoretical neglect and abuses, continuing some, exacerbating others, and introducing new forms of neglect and abuse. Radical political theories rescued adaptation from the opprobrium of high-art aestheticism and high modernism and the neglect of aesthetic formalism and structuralist semiotics, but not from dichotomous value judgments, chastising it when it supported right-wing politics and celebrating it when it supported left-wing politics. Postmodern pluralism rescued adaptation from modernist isolationism and structuralist binarisms, but overrode the processes and principles of adaptation with its own principles of pluralism, pastiche, and palimpsest. Poststructuralism worsened the fortunes of adaptation: while Brian McFarlane engaged neo-structuralist narratology to rescue adaptation from the structuralist semiotics that had rendered it a theoretical impossibility, poststructuralist semiotics atomized adaptation, displacing its processes with those of deconstruction. Adaptation helps entities to survive and thrive in new environments; although it has never ceased to thrive in culture, in twentieth-century theoretical environments it has not always thrived and survived. That said, as my history attests, adaptation studies is indubitably on the rise in the twenty-first century, engaging new theories and grappling with questions of theoretical progress versus theoretical return and theoretical pluralism versus theoretical abandonment. The problematic relationship between adaptation and theorization has survived.

Turning from metacritical history to metatheoretical theory, Part II, "Adapting Theorization," finds that the problem of theorizing adaptation is not simply that adaptation has been recently theorized as a bad theoretical object, but is also a problem that manifests even when it is theorized as a good theoretical object. It is a problem of theorization's relationship to adaptation generally—of how theorization in the humanities has been theorized in relationship to what it theorizes. That the sciences and social sciences do not consider adaptation to be a theoretical problem speaks volumes. Humanities theorization has taken a pseudo-theological stance with regard to adaptation, objecting to it via the same theories of original creation and separate species that continue to oppose biological adaptation even today. Its roots in theology have theorized humanities theorization as a top-down affair of mind over matter, as higher truth impervious to evidence of practice. Its relationship to adaptation has been a godlike one that subjects adaptation to its laws: when it conforms to them, it is rewarded; when it deviates from them, it is condemned. In practice, adaptation—like everything else that theorization theorizes—serves as an illustration to prove its principles, a cautionary tale for those who violate them, and a weapon wielded in theoretical, disciplinary, and cultural wars. Adaptation exceeds and resists its theoretical abuses and uses: it is a rival process akin to, and yet resistant to, theorization. As a process akin to theorization, adaptation engages in acts of theorization, criticism, and interpretation that are threatening to humanities scholars. Indeed, adaptation is far more likely than other subjects to provoke lay discourses that impinge on scholarly territory (McFarlane 1996, 3), a dynamic that has increased exponentially with the rise of fan-adaptation culture (Pearce and Weedon 2017).

As a process resistant to theorization, adaptation refuses to conform to theorization's definitions, taxonomies, principles, epistemologies, and methodologies. As a rival process to theorization, it is at work on everything addressed by humanities scholars, and much more: it is also at work upon theorization, adapting it. The problem of theorizing adaptation, therefore, is a relational one between rival processes. Theorizing adaptation efficaciously requires theorization to adapt to adaptation and to theorize adaptation *as adaptation* rather than as an exemplum of theoretical tenets developed to address other things in which adaptation participates, but which are not themselves "adaptation." Each chapter of "Retheorizing Theorization," therefore, concludes with a call to theorize adaptation as adaptation, recommending ways to define, taxonomize, and theorize adaptation according to its own characteristics, processes, and principles, as well as ways to adapt theorization and adaptation to each other by setting their processes in dialogue. Beyond theoretical dialogue, creative-critical adaptation practices, in which scholars produce adaptations to inform their scholarship (Scott 2011; Chapter 6), offer great promise for forging more mutual relations between adaptation and theorization.

Adaptation has long lurked as a prime underminer of humanities theorization's legacy from theology. Just as biological adaptation studies undermined theology and redefined what it means to be human in the sciences, so too humanities adaptation studies can redefine what it means to theorize in the humanities. Adaptation does not care if it is true or untrue, ethically good or bad, aesthetically pleasing or distasteful, politically correct or incorrect: it is concerned only with adapting—only with its processes of repetition and variation that adapt entities and environments to each other to foster survival.

Adaptation is the ultimate form of the uncanny—that disconcerting merger of the (un)familiar, the varied, and the repeated. Adaptation never completely lets go of the past or entirely embraces the new: it refuses to forget, even as it moves on. It never allows anything to die completely or to be completely reborn. It is always holding us back at the same time that it is always pushing us forward. It does not allow us to discard anything finally and yet never allows us to remain the same: something old always comes with something new; something borrowed is always made new. Adaptation does not allow scholars to stay with familiar theories, favored epistemologies, or accustomed methodologies. When we do, we fail to theorize adaptation because we are failing to adapt as scholars. Adaptation refuses to let us be comfortable where we are or to ever leave home once and for all. A hybrid itself, adaptation favors hybrid theorization—even (perhaps especially) logically contradictory and ideologically incongruous hybrids and theoretical hybrids that not only inhabit but also occupy the *spaces* between theories. As such, adaptation is more in line with theories of metamodernism and technologies of quantum computing (see Chapter 9) than with modernism, postmodernism, or classical computing (although my perception that it is so is almost certainly the product of my living in a metamodern, quantum age). Metamodernism arose in the 2010s in response to global crises such as climate change, financial collapse, and refugee migrancy in the wake of revolutions and wars (Vermeulen and Akker 2010). Occupying a middle ground between modernism and postmodernism that rejects their extremes, it integrates their oppositions in hybrid concepts such as "informed naivety, pragmatic idealism, [and] moderate fanaticism" and engages in quantum oscillations between "sincerity and irony, deconstruction and construction, [and] apathy and affect." Even as it rejects modernist grand theory, it refuses to collapse into postmodern skepticism and relativism. Rather, it marks "the resurgence of sincerity, hope, romanticism, [and] affect" and entertains "the potential for grand narratives and universal truths," without being certain of either (Turner 2015, n.p.).

Yet adaptation remains more mysterious than metamodern and quantum principles. Adaptation not only eludes final answers (Hutcheon 2006; Leitch 2017c), it also refuses to reveal its questions. All too often, scholars rush in with answers for adaptation given to us by theories and disciplines that we already know, theories and disciplines developed to study other things, before we have understood the questions that adaptation asks. Instead, we ask questions of adaptation that we have already asked and answered about things that are not adaptation. Those questions, those answers, rest uneasily upon adaptation. Even after writing an entire book about adaptation theorization, even after spending much of my career pondering it, I am still not sure that I have asked the right questions of adaptation.

Figurative rhetoric, however, has enabled me to ask new questions of adaptation and posit new answers to the problem of theorizing adaptation that I had not considered before, as well as ways to adapt my prior thinking. Setting figuration in dialogue with adaptation and theorization generally has helped me to reconceive their relationship, while particular rhetorical figures have explicated and redressed particular problems in theorizing adaptation better than all my theoretical wrestling along logical and empirical lines, offering new concepts and methodologies for studying adaptation. Like so many scholars before me, figurative rhetoric has given me new ways of thinking about and approaching my research questions, allowing me to break out of theoretical systems and rhetorical structures that have created trammels in my mind, where everything I theorize falls into their ruts.

Postmodern scholars have rightly drawn attention to the need for theorists to be self-reflexively aware of our cultural and ideological situatedness. Yet that situatedness is not static. In any given moment, we too are undergoing processes of adaptation: we too are adaptations. At any point, something is repeating and something is varying in our thinking, in our fields, and in our cultural contexts. Adaptation calls us beyond declarations of particular theoretical situatedness to adapt to what we theorize, to what we study ongoingly.

Writing this book has been a process of adaptation for me. More than any other book I have written, I have returned to this one to rethink, re-write, and adapt what I have thought and written before. I have tried to adapt to adaptation and to write adaptation in its own image, fully aware that I am failing, while knowing that I must continue to try. All the time I have been (re)thinking and (re)writing, I have been keenly aware that the field that I am writing about is itself changing and adapting. Between the date that this manuscript leaves my hands and the date of its publication, more changes will have taken place in the field and in my mind. My thinking will not be final with the final page of this book. I too am modeling the ways in which humanities theorization fails adaptation and adaptation fails theorization, even as I seek to redress these failures.

When speaking of this book to friends over the many years that it has taken to write, I have nominated it "the never-ending book." While that name reflects my impatience with the project and despair of ever finishing it, this conclusion does not conclude this book. It will remain the never-ending book because it is a book about adaptation, which never ends.

Notes

Introduction

1. "The humanities" has changed over time. Today, it encompasses philosophy, religion, politics, history, classical and modern languages and literatures, and a variety of audio, visual, and performing arts and media. It used to include archaeology, anthropology, philosophies of mind, and law (jurisprudence), now classified as social sciences, with psychology also studied as a science. The lines between the humanities and social sciences have thus remained unclear.
2. Search date December 23, 2019. All *MLA International Bibliography* searches in this book exclude dissertations.
3. Although the search also locates studies of linguistic adaptation (3.155 hits for "language adaptation," 347 for "phonological adaptation," and 61 for "semantic adaptation"), adaptation studies has focused primarily on the adaptation of creative and imaginative works, with an emphasis on adaptations made in the performing arts and media. A subject term search for "cultural adaptation" yielded 762 hits: most of these address media adaptation; a few are purely sociological and anthropological studies.
4. The epigraphs are selective: titles, subtitles, and chapter headings of many other publications also nominate adaptation a "problem," including Bluestone 1956; McCaffrey 1967; Murray 1973; Mitry 1971; Manvell 1979; Sobchack and Sobchack 1987; Bullen 1990; G. Jenkins 1997; McKee 1997; Kidnie 2009; Jameson 2011; Pagello 2011; Venkatesh 2012; and Friedmann 2014. Scholars writing of the "problem" of adaptation in the body of their works are legion.
5. The theoretical turn in the humanities is a turn that involved, among other things, a philosophical shift from positivism to skepticism, a political shift from high-art humanism to left-wing cultural studies, a historical shift from chronological to New Historicism and ahistorical postmodernism, and a formal shift from New Criticism and structuralism to poststructuralism. Patricia Waugh (2006) offers a rigorous, concise summary, with suggestions for further reading.

Chapter 1

1. For more detailed accounts of interchanges between history and theory in the humanities, see Von Mises 2007; Elizabeth A. Clark 2009; Banaji 2010; and L. Burke 2015.
2. Linda Hutcheon did subsequently historicize adaptation in an essay co-authored with Michael Hutcheon, nominating opera, with its four-hundred-year history, in which adaptation features as its "life-blood," the "Ur-adaptive" art (2017a, 305).

3. For example, Andrew 1984, 100; McFarlane 1996, 9, 37; Stam 2000, 54; Hutcheon 2006, 7; Leitch 2007, Chapter 6; Cartmell and Whelehan 2010, 6; Stam 2005, 15.
4. See also D. Johnson 2011, 62; Minier 2013, 42–67.
5. Leitch subsequently wrote a longer history of adaptation studies (2017b).
6. Jillian Saint Jacques's overview of adaptation theory in *Adaptation Theories* (2011a) begins in 1996 and ends in 2008, treating even this brief period sparsely.
7. Forthcoming volumes in this series include histories of German, Russian, French, and sub-Saharan African literatures on film.
8. Russell discussed older debates to contextualize contemporary ones.
9. I am aware that my limited knowledge of literature and film in these nations will have produced omissions in these tables.

Chapter 2

1. Although the catalogues I cite were published in the 1890s and 1900s, they reprint titles and wording of earlier publications.
2. Richard Hooker (1554–1600) was one of the most significant Reformation theologians of the sixteenth century.
3. Terminologies varied: for example, William Clubbe aspired to metaphrase when he positioned his *Six Satires of Horace* mid-spectrum, "in a Style between Free Imitation and Literal Version" (1795).
4. Classical literary adaptation was given greater latitude than biblical texts: paraphrase was too free for Hooker but constituted a perfect middle way for Dryden.
5. For a more detailed discussion of relations between adaptation and translation, including triadic models of adaptation, see Minier 2013.
6. Following the republication of his chapter in 1984, Andrew's taxonomy of adaptation became the most widely reprinted and cited work in the field. However, the influence of Wagner's taxonomy lingers in formalist and pedagogical scholarship.
7. After Dryden's death, Alexander Pope's *The Second Epistle of the Second Book of Horace, Imitated by Mr. Pope* (1737), which adapts Horace to contemporary issues and historical individuals in a modern style of writing, led to Pope being nominated the English Horace, widely congratulated for improving on his source.
8. In 1820, Planché adapted John Polidori's *The Vampyre* to the stage. In 1830, his insistence on using historically accurate costumes in Shakespeare's *King John* revolutionized stage practice, a practice that continued in British television and film adaptations. In the late 1820s and early 1830s, he campaigned with others successfully for dramatic copyright laws more favorable to playwrights.
9. These modes of adaptation extended to reworkings of the picaresque novel in Europe in the seventeenth and eighteenth centuries (Van Gorp 1985).
10. The first full English translation was by William Ross in 1836, but Lessing's theories of poetry and painting were discussed in English periodicals from at least the 1780s. See Lipking 1970.
11. When it came to intramedial (as opposed to intermedial) adaptation, Kames adopted the Augustan view of adapting Shakespeare (2.502).

12. Laudér's arguments were largely buried by the scandal he caused by forging documents and claiming that Milton had plagiarized Latin works.

13. These examples are illustrative: the practice was prevalent.

14. Meisel's date for this article, 1856, appears to be a typographical error.

15. Unaccountably, W. J. T. Mitchell does not discuss the nineteenth century in *Iconology: Image, Text, Ideology* (1986), leapfrogging from the eighteenth to the twentieth century, which reinscribed eighteenth-century oppositions between words and images.

16. Prior to that, copyright privileges and patents were issued by royals, popes, and aristocrats to printing collectives, such as the Stationers' Company in England.

17. The first US copyright law protected only maps, charts, and books; in 1802 prints, cuts, and engravings were added; in 1831 printed music was included, but dramatic works were not protected until 1856, and performance rights were only given legal protection in 1897.

18. In the case of *Toole v. Young* a novelist dramatized his own novel and sold its performance right to a second party. When a third party dramatized and staged the novel without purchasing the rights, the judge determined that the third party had not violated copyright because neither dramatist had printed the play.

19. For more information on Reade's copyright wars, see Lauriat 2009.

20. Other International Copyright Acts were passed in Britain in 1844, 1862, 1875, and 1886; the United States did not pass an International Copyright Act until 1891.

21. Hierarchical classifications of the arts go back at least as far as the ancient Greeks and the Zhou Dynasty of China and continue to the present day.

22. Progressivist theories of adaptation extended from literature to other art forms.

23. Britain was by no means the only nation to vaunt itself via adapting foreign works: other nations also proclaimed superiority through discourses and practices of adaptation (Del Villano 2012; Gifford 2012; Bayliss 2015).

24. Despite his Germanic name, Shoberl was an English author, journalist, editor, and translator, best known for his translation of *The Hunchback of Notre Dame*.

25. Other critics have challenged this view. Ian Donaldson has written: "Shakespeare is no longer viewed as a timeless and transhistorical genius, but as a textual phenomenon that is constantly reconstructed, constantly reinvented, constantly reinterpreted by every age according to its needs, priorities, and preconceptions" (1997, 197). Even so, Shakespeare's universality persists in academic theory and dominates pedagogical and media discourses.

26. Other national literary heroes include Homer, Sophocles, and Aeschylus in Greece; Virgil in ancient Rome; Dante in Italy; Goethe in Germany; Molière, Racine, and Rabelais in France; Cervantes and Vega in Spain; Pushkin, Dostoevsky, and Tolstoy in Russia; Ibsen in Norway; Kivi in Finland; Swift, Joyce, Shaw, Wilde, and Beckett in Ireland; Monzaemon in Japan; Xueqin in China; Assis in Brazil.

27. Wright also authored other articles about mass culture, including "On a Possible Popular Culture" (1881).

28. See also Greenwood 1869, 105.

29. Del Villano is discussing Giulio Marra.

30. I examine James Griffith's attempts to revive Augustan theories of adaptation (1997) in Chapter 3.

Chapter 3

1. The second edition of *The Cambridge Companion to Modernism* (Levenson [1999] 2011) provides an introduction to a variety of modernisms in a variety of media, and its appendix offers extensive further reading.
2. This view is so widely held that it appears in the Tate Gallery's online introduction to modernism in art (https://www.tate.org.uk/art/art-terms/m/modernism).
3. Kurt Heinzelman has shown that Pound did not publish this statement early in his career, as other scholars have claimed, but that it was first published in 1940 (2003, 131).
4. In 1914–1915, Georg Lukács would influentially recuperate the novel as art in *Theory of the Novel*.
5. See, for example, Brooks 1939; 1947.
6. Although Woolf saw potential for cinema to serve high art, she scorned both mass culture and literary film adaptation.
7. All of these scholars held degrees in English literature. Perkins began writing about film as an Oxford undergraduate and co-founded the Joint School of Film and Literature at Warwick University, where his auteurist theory of film, deemed compatible with literary theories of authorship, helped to make film an acceptable subject for academic study, although it continues to be marginalized by elite academic institutions.
8. These theories constitute the basis of adaptation pedagogy in many universities and books (e.g., Desmond and Hawkes 2006, reprinted in 2015), although the book has only been cited twice, according to Google Scholar, December 23, 2019.
9. Other books in this period also address adaptation: the last section of Morris Beja's *Film and Literature* accords one quarter of its word count to adaptation; Harrington's student reader reprints essays on adaptation by Balázs ([1952] 1970), Bazin ([1952] 1967), Eidsvik (1974), and Battestin (1967).
10. *MLA International Bibliography*, search date December 23, 2019.
11. See also Jan Baetens (2018).
12. As a subject term, "postmodernism" yields 1806 hits for the 1980s, 1418 for the 1990s, 1354 for the 2000s, and 838 for the 2010s. Search date December 23, 2019.

Chapter 4

1. Search date December 23, 2019.
2. Tables of contents and archives for the three journals are available online.
3. *Trash Culture, Adaptations,* and *Classics in Film and Fiction* are devoted entirely to adaptation; adaptations feature prominently in *Pulping Fictions, Sisterhoods,* and *Retrovisions*; however, although many of its case studies are adaptations, *Aliens* pursues a generic "representations of" methodology. Its title is therefore misleading: it does not seize the opportunity to attend to theoretical notions of literature and film as alien *to each other.*

4. The synonymity was affirmed from the other side of the theoretical divide by James M. Welsh (2003, 4).

5. Leitch's fallacies include the Romantic, aesthetic formalist, and New Critical tenets that novels are verbal and films are visual; that novels deal in concepts, while films deal in percepts; that novels create more complex characters than films; that cinema's visual specificity usurps audience imagination; that fidelity is the most appropriate criterion for analyzing adaptations; and that source texts are more original than adaptations. Medium specificity theory also features prominently in several of Leitch's fallacies.

6. Chatman's *Story and Discourse: Narrative Structure in Fiction and Film* (1978) does not address adaptation, but, as a point of comparison, had been cited 6,698 times as of January 22, 2019. That it continues to be cited (citations rose to 7,517 by December 23, 2019) indicates the ongoing presence of structuralist narratology in literature-and-film studies.

7. As of December 23, 2019, Hutcheon's second edition (2012) had a higher Amazon sales ranking than the first edition, but still ranked below Cahir's at 3,408,133.

8. Search date December 23, 2019. I am aware that Amazon sales rankings are by no means comprehensive, but presses will not release sales figures and the Nielsen Book Scan only includes print sales from shops, excluding library sales.

9. These include essay collections by Albrecht-Crane and Cutchins (2010a), Cutchins, Raw, and Welsh (2010a; 2010b), Elleström (2010), and Frus and Williams (2010). Although none undertakes the radical political critique championed by Cartmell and Whelehan, all include essays engaging newer formal theories or forging dialogues between newer and older theories.

10. Citations are from Google Scholar; sales rankings are from Amazon.co.uk.

11. Research into new media adaptation studies (Voigts 2018a; 2018b; Meikle 2019), however, democratizes scholarship through open access online resources.

12. Cartmell and Whelehan omit "Where?" from their list, intimating a rather cursory engagement with her book.

13. Search date December 23, 2019.

14. Fortier (1996) is an exception.

15. Leitch is an exception: medium specificity theory features prominently in his "Twelve Fallacies in Contemporary Adaptation Theory" (2003a).

Section I

1. Arthur Bradley, in conversation with me, October 12, 2015.

2. Citations are selective rather than exhaustive: I adapt a host of adaptation scholarship here.

Chapter 6

1. They are celebrations (curatorial, replication, heritage, pictorial realization, liberation, or literalization), adjustments (engaging in compression, expansion, correction, updating, superimposition), neoclassic imitations, revisions, colonizations,

metacommentaries or deconstructions, analogues, parodies, pastiches, allusions, and secondary, tertiary, and quaternary imitations (adaptations of adaptations).

2. See the tables in Chapter 2 and the bibliography.

3. Timothy Corrigan's literature and film reader also privileges literary over film categories in its segmentation, while expanding to consider historical and theoretical taxonomies as well (2011 edition, table of contents).

4. For example, Luhr and Lehman (1977) have critiqued adaptation for aesthetic and intellectual failure; Higson (2004) has critiqued it for its political shortcomings.

5. See also Elliott 2003a, 130–31.

6. It is notoriously difficult for panels and papers treating film adaptation to gain acceptance at SCMS conferences. The year 2010, when Dudley Andrew and Tim Corrigan agreed to be on an adaptation panel, was a notable exception.

7. Search date November 5, 2018.

8. Speranza 1979, n.p.

9. Quoted in T. White 1983, 52.

Chapter 7

1. Leitch is one of few to grapple with the "how" of adaptation in ways that ponder the principles of adaptation itself in "To Adapt or to Adapt To?" (2009), where he probes transitive versus intransitive modes of adaptation in the humanities.

2. Marcus Nichols has undertaken a brilliant study of microscopic adaptations in decadent French literature, going further to demonstrate how they mirror macroscopic adaptations (2018, 284).

3. The 2015, 2016, 2017, and 2018 issues of the English Association's publication *The Year's Work in Critical and Cultural Theory* not only include essays on familiar theoretical topics of popular culture, economics, feminisms, queer theory, black critical and cultural theory, postcolonial theory, poetics, psychoanalysis, modern European philosophy, and translation studies but also explore literature's relationship to visual culture, film, media, theater, and music, and developing theories of religion and secularism, animal studies, ecocriticism, disability studies, science and medicine, affect, and the digital humanities.

4. For a fuller summary of post-theory debates, see Vladimir Biti (2018).

Chapter 8

1. More recently, post-human scholars have pondered the limitations of rhetoric to account for non-human forms (Grusin 2015). Post-humanism, dubbed "the non-human turn" in the humanities, ponders how humanity can be transformed, transcended, or eliminated by the metaphysical, biological evolution, or technology, as post-human theories inhabit religious and spiritual studies, animal studies, ecocriticism, technological and digital studies, systems theories, and neo-formalist studies of media as objects.

2. Stam's *re-* words are rewriting, recreation, resuscitation, re-envisioning, and re-accentuation.

3. Terms engaging prefixes in Leitch's grammar of adaptation are replication, realization, revision, exposition, superimposition, metacommentary, deconstruction, and analogue.

4. In physics, reflection articulates a process whereby light, heat, sound, and other waves bounce off a surface that does not absorb it, while refraction describes a process of waves passing through a medium, so as to deflect and divert them from their previous course.

5. *Genetics for Dummies* (T. Robinson 2005).

6. "Language can be compared with a sheet of paper: thought is the front and the sound the back; one cannot cut the front without cutting the back at the same time; likewise in language, one can neither divide sound from thought nor thought from sound" (Saussure [1910] 2011, 113).

7. Elliott 2003a, 136–61.

Chapter 9

1. I am by no means the first scholar to recommend a particular rhetorical figure to resolve problems in theorizing adaptation. In 2013, Mark Rowell Wallin recommended the figure of eurhythmia to do so.

2. This discussion repeats and varies arguments made in Elliott 2012b.

3. Ever subversive, Deleuze restored metaphor to film studies ([1985] 1989, 155–56).

4. The myth that requited erotic desire is essential to literary success is prevalent in literary biopics of the period, including *Shakespeare in Love* (1998), *Becoming Jane* (2007), and *Bright Star* (2009).

5. When Zoë Shacklock defined synaesthesia as "the adaptation of one sensory mode by another" (2015, 270), she pursued the same phenomenologically based argument as Lessing: that adaptation from one medium to another requires adaptation to different senses. This is not synaesthesia: not even Lessing argued that each medium evokes only one sense.

6. See Dani Cavallaro, *Synaesthesia and the Arts* (2013).

7. For Denroche, metonymy also trumps theories of translation as equivalence, action, intercultural communication, ideological engagement, and mental processes (2015, 153).

8. Eckart Voigts (2019) has discussed humanities media adaptations (poetry, music, fiction) produced by artificial intelligence.

Bibliography

Addison, Joseph. (1711–1712) 1868. *Criticism on Milton's Paradise Lost. From "The Spectator" 31 Dec., 1711–3 May, 1712.* Edited by Edward Arber. London: Bloomsbury Press.

Addison, Joseph. 1712. "Defects." Sixth Paper on *Paradise Lost. The Spectator* 297 (Feb. 9): n.p.

Agane, Ayaan. 2015. "Conflations of 'Queerness' in Twenty-First-Century Adaptations." In *Gender and the Modern Sherlock Holmes: Essays on Film and Television Adaptations since 2009,* edited by Nadine Farghaly, 160–73. Jefferson, NC: McFarland Press.

Aikin, John. 1774. *Essays on Song-Writing: With a Collection of Such English Songs as Are Most Eminent for Poetical Merit.* 2nd ed. Warrington: William Eyres.

Albrecht-Crane, Christa, and Dennis Cutchins. 2010a. *Adaptation Studies: New Approaches.* Cranberry, NJ: Associated University Press.

Albrecht-Crane, Christa, and Dennis Cutchins. 2010b. "Introduction: New Beginnings for Adaptation Studies." In *Adaptation Studies: New Approaches,* edited by Christa Albrecht-Crane and Dennis Cutchins, 11–22. Cranberry, NJ: Associated University Press.

Albright, Daniel, ed. 2004. *Modernism and Music: An Anthology of Sources.* Chicago: University of Chicago Press.

Alcoff, Linda, and Elizabeth Potter. 1993. "Introduction: When Feminisms Intersect Epistemology." In *Feminist Epistemologies,* edited by Linda Alcoff and Elizabeth Potter, 1–14. London: Routledge.

Amala, P. Annie, P. Anupama, and D. Bhaskara Rao. 2004. *History of Education.* New Delhi: Discovery Publishing House.

Andrew, Dudley. 1980. "The Well-Worn Muse: Adaptation in Film History and Theory." In *Narrative Strategies: Original Essays in Film and Prose Fiction,* edited by Syndy M. Conger and Janice R. Welsch, 9–17. Macomb: Western Illinois University Press.

Andrew, Dudley. 1984a. *Concepts in Film Theory.* New York: Oxford University Press.

Andrew, Dudley. 1984b. "Adaptation." In *Concepts in Film Theory,* edited by Dudley Andrew, 96–106. New York: Oxford University Press.

Andrew, Dudley. 2010. *What Cinema Is! Bazin's Quest and Its Charge.* Chichester: Wiley-Blackwell Press.

Andrew, Dudley. 2011. "The Economies of Adaptation." In *True to the Spirit: Film Adaptation and the Question of Fidelity,* edited by Colin MacCabe, Kathleen Murray, and Rick Warner, 27–40. Oxford: Oxford University Press.

Anon. 1758. "Review of Richard Hurd, *A Letter to Mr. Mason: On the Marks of Imitation.*" *The Monthly Review* 18 (Jan.): 114–25.

Anon. 1761. "Review of *Giphantia.*" *The Monthly Review* 24 (Mar.): 222–26.

Anon. 1765. "Review of David Erskine Baker, *The Companion to the Play-House.*" *The Monthly Review* 32, no. 3 (Mar.): 205–16.

Anon. 1769. "The British Theatre." *The London Magazine, Or, Gentleman's Monthly Intelligencer* 38 (Aug.): 403–7.

Anon. 1769. "Review of A Four Days Tour through Part of the Land of Dumplings by Peregrine Post." *The London Magazine, Or, Gentleman's Monthly Intelligencer* 38 (Jun.): 324–25.

Anon. 1800. "Remarks on the Genius and Writings of Allan Ramsay." In *The Poems of Allan Ramsay*, 1: lix–clvii. London: T. Cadell and W. Davies.

Anon. 1826. "Reviews of New Music." *The Monthly Magazine, or British Register of Literature, Sciences, and the Belles-Lettres* 1 (Apr.): 421.

Anon. 1826. "Review of Scott's *Lives of the Novelists*." *The Quarterly Review* 34, no. 68 (Sep.): 349–78.

Anon. 1829. "Drama: Drury Lane." *London Literary Gazette* 675 (Dec. 26): 847–48.

Anon. 1831. Review of *The Keepsake*. *The Olio; or, Museum of Entertainment* 6, no. 27 (Dec. 18): 430.

Anon. 1833. "Fashion in Music." *The Lady's Book Magazine of Fashions and the Arts* 6: 269–72.

Anon. 1841. "Review of Henry Austin's Thoughts on the Abuses of the Present System of Competition in Architecture." *The Athenaeum* 729 (Oct. 16): 787–89.

Anon. 1841. "The Theatres." *The Spectator* 14, no. 665 (Mar. 27): 302.

Anon. 1844. "Mrs. Butler's Poems." *The United States Magazine and Democratic Review* 15, no. 77 (Nov.): 507–12.

Anon. 1860. "To the Reader." *The Players* 1 (Jan. 2): 2.

Anon. 1864. "Theatrical Reflections." *Punch* 47 (Nov. 5): 187.

Anon. 1866a. "The Drama." *Nature and Art* 1 (Nov. 1): 185–88. Edited by F. B. Ward. London: Day & Son.

Anon. 1866b. "The Drama and the Stage." *Nature and Art* 1 (Jun. 1): 26. Edited by F. B. Ward. London: Day & Son.

Anon. 1866c. "Theatric Art." *Nature and Art* 1 (Aug. 1): 88. Edited by F. B. Ward. London: Day & Son.

Anon. 1869. "Originality." *Every Saturday* 8 (Sep. 18): 364–65.

Anon. 1870. "Literary Intelligence." *The Publishers' Circular* 33, no. 783 (May 2): 259–64.

Anon. 1875. "Recent Legislation on the Law of Contracts Compared with the American Law." *Law Magazine and Review: A Monthly Journal of Jurisprudence and International Law, For Both Branches of the Legal Profession at Home and Abroad* 4: 427–34. London: Stevens & Hayne.

Anon. 1907. "Trade Notes." *Moving Picture World* 1, no. 41 (Dec. 14): 663–68.

Aragay, Mireia. 2005a. *Books in Motion: Adaptation, Intertextuality, Authorship*. Amsterdam: Rodopi Press.

Aragay, Mireia. 2005b. "Reflection to Refraction: Adaptation Studies Then and Now." In *Books in Motion: Adaptation, Intertextuality, Authorship*, edited by Mireia Aragay, 11–34. Amsterdam: Rodopi Press.

Aragay, Mireia, and Gemma López. 2005. "Inf(l)ecting Pride and Prejudice: Dialogism, Intertextuality, and Adaptation." In *Books in Motion: Adaptation, Intertextuality, Authorship*, edited by Mireia Aragay, 201–20. Amsterdam: Rodopi Press.

Aram, John D. 2004. "Concepts of Interdisciplinarity: Configurations of Knowledge and Action." *Human Relations* 57, no. 4: 379–412.

Archer, Neil, and Andreea Weisl-Shaw, eds. 2012. *Adaptation: Studies in French and Francophone Culture*. New York: Peter Lang.

Arnheim, Rudolph. (1932) 1971. *Film as Art*. Berkeley: University of California Press.

Arnold, Matthew. 1869. *Culture and Anarchy: An Essay in Political and Social Criticism*. London: Smith, Elder & Co.

Asheim, Lester. 1949. "From Book to Film: A Comparative Analysis of the Content of Selected Novels and the Motion Pictures Based upon Them." PhD diss., University of Chicago, Illinois.

Asheim, Lester. 1951a. "From Book to Film: Simplification." *Hollywood Quarterly* 5, no. 3 (Spring): 289–304.

Asheim, Lester. 1951b. "From Book to Film: Mass Appeals." *Hollywood Quarterly* 5, no. 4 (Summer): 334–49.

Asheim, Lester. 1951c. "From Book to Film: The Note of Affirmation." *The Quarterly of Film, Radio, and Television* 6, no. 1 (Autumn): 54–68.

Asheim, Lester. 1952. "From Book to Film: Summary." *The Quarterly of Film, Radio, and Television* 6, no. 3 (Spring): 258–73.

Attridge, Derek, and Jane Elliott. 2011. *Theory after "Theory."* London: Routledge.

Aycock, Wendell, and Michael Schoenecke, eds. 1988. *Film and Literature: A Comparative Approach to Adaptation*. Lubbock: Texas Tech University Press.

Babbitt, Irving. 1910. *The New Laokoon: An Essay on the Confusion of the Arts*. Boston: Houghton Mifflin.

Backhouse, Roger E., and Philippe Fontaine, eds. 2010. *The History of the Social Sciences since 1945*. Cambridge: Cambridge University Press.

Baetens, Jan. 2018. *Novelization: From Film to Novel*. Chicago: Ohio State University Press.

Bakhtin, Mikhail. 1981. *The Dialogic Imagination: Four Essays*. Austin: University of Texas Press.

Bal, Mieke. 2002. *Travelling Concepts in the Humanities: A Rough Guide*. Toronto: University of Toronto Press.

Bal, Mieke. 2007. "Working with Concepts." In *Conceptual Odysseys: Passages to Cultural Analysis*, edited by Griselda Pollock, 1–10. New York: Palgrave Macmillan.

Bal, Mieke. 2017a. Comment on her article "Intership." Publications/Articles/2010s. Mieke Bal website. Accessed August 31, 2017. http://www.miekebal.org/publications/articles/2010s/.

Bal, Mieke. 2017b. "Intership: Anachronism between Loyalty and the Case." In *The Oxford Handbook of Adaptation Studies*, edited by Thomas Leitch, 179–96. Oxford: Oxford University Press.

Balázs, Béla. (1924) 2010. "Visible Man, or The Culture of Film." In *Béla Balázs: Early Film Theory: Visible Man and The Spirit of Film*, edited by Erica Carter and translated by Rodney Livingstone, 1–90. Oxford: Berghahn Books.

Balázs, Béla. (1952) 1970. *Theory of the Film: Character and Growth of a New Art*. Translated by Edith Bone. New York: Dover Books.

Baldick, Chris. 2008. *The Oxford Dictionary of Literary Terms*. Oxford: Oxford University Press.

Baldwin, Edward. 1805. *Fables Ancient and Modern, Adapted for the Use of Children from Three to Eight Years of Age*. London: T. Hodgkins.

Balkin, J. M. 1987. "Deconstructive Practice and Legal Theory." *Yale Law Journal* 96, no. 4: 743–86.

Banaji, Jairus. 2010. *Theory as History: Essays on Modes of Production and Exploitation*. Leiden: Brill Press.

Barnett, Morris. 1850. "The Tempest as a Lyrical Drama." *Fraser's Magazine for Town and Country* 42 (July): 38–43.

Barthes, Roland. (1957) 1972. *Mythologies*. Translated by Annette Lavers. New York: Farrar, Straus and Giroux.

Barthes, Roland. (1967) 1977. "The Death of the Author." In *Image—Music—Text*, edited and translated by Stephen Heath, 142–48. New York: Hill & Wang.

Barthes, Roland. 1974. *S/Z: An Essay*. Translated by Richard Miller. New York: Hill & Wang.

Barthes, Roland. (1975) 1989. "Brecht and Discourse: A Contribution to the Study of Discursivity." In *The Rustle of Language*, edited and translated by Richard Howard, 212–22. Berkeley: University of California Press.

Barthes, Roland. 1977. *Image—Music—Text*, edited and translated by Stephen Heath. New York: Hill & Wang.

Bartlett, Randolph. 1917. "A Boy Named Kelly." *Photoplay* 11, no. 5 (April): 83–4; 152.

Bassnett, Susan. 2013. *Translation*. London: Routledge.

Bastin, George L. 2009. "Adaptation." In *The Routledge Encyclopedia of Translation Studies*, edited by Mona Baker and Gabriela Saldanha, 3–6. London: Routledge.

Battestin, Martin C. 1967. "Osborne's Tom Jones: Adapting a Classic." In *Man and the Movies*, edited by W. R. Robinson, 31–45. Baton Rouge: Louisiana State University Press.

Battestin, Martin C. 1998. "*Tom Jones* on the Telly: Fielding, the BBC, and the Sister Arts." *Eighteenth-Century Fiction* 10, no. 4 (July): 501–5.

Bayliss, Robert E. 2015. "Thinking Globally, Acting Locally, and Performing Nationalism: Local, National, and Global Remakes of the *Comedia*." In *Remaking the Comedia: Spanish Classical Theater in Adaptation*, edited by Harley Erdman and Susan Paun De García, 65–74. Woodbridge, Suffolk: Tamesis.

Bazin, André. (1948) 1997. "Adaptation, or the Cinema as Digest." Translated by Alain Piette. In *Bazin at Work: Major Essays and Reviews from the Forties and Fifties*, edited by Bert Cardullo, 41–52. London: Routledge.

Bazin, André. (1952) 1967. "In Defense of Mixed Cinema." In *What Is Cinema?* Translated by Hugh Gray, 1:53–75. Berkeley: University of California Press.

Beja, Morris. 1979. *Film and Literature: An Introduction*. New York: Longman.

Benjamin, Walter. (1936) 1968. "The Work of Art in the Age of Mechanical Reproduction." In *Illuminations: Essays and Reflections*, edited by Hannah Arendt, and translated by Harry Zohn, 217–52. New York: Harcourt Brace Jovanovich.

Berger, Richard. 2010. "Converting the Controversial: Regulation as 'Source Text' in Adaptation." In *Adaptation Studies: New Approaches*, edited by Christa Albrecht-Crane and Dennis Cutchins, 150–59. Madison: Fairleigh Dickinson University Press.

Bergman, Ingmar. 1966. "Each Film Is My Last." *The Tulane Drama Review* 11, no. 1 (Autumn): 94–101.

Berman, Marshall. 1988. *All That Is Solid Melts into Air*. New York: Penguin Books.

Berninger, Mark, Jochen Ecke, and Gideon Haberkorn. 2010. *Comics as a Nexus of Cultures: Essays on the Interplay of Media, Disciplines and International Perspectives*. Jefferson, NC: McFarland Press.

Bettini, Giovanni. 2017. "Where Next? Climate Change, Migration, and the (Bio)politics of Adaptation." *Global Policy* 8, supplement S1: 33–9.

Biti, Vladimir. 2018. "After Theory: Politics against the Police?" In *Policing Literary Theory*, edited by Călin-Andrei Mihăilescu and Takayuki Yokota-Murakami, 15–30. Leiden: Brill Rodopi Press.

Blackwell, Anna. 2018. "Tweeting from the Grave: Shakespeare, Adaptation, and Social Media." In *The Routledge Companion to Adaptation*, edited by Dennis Cutchins, Katja Krebs, and Eckart Voigts, 287–300. London: Routledge.

Blankier, Margot. 2014. "Adapting and Transforming *Cinderella*: Fairy-Tale Adaptations the Limits of Existing Adaptation Theory." *Interdisciplinary Humanities* 31, no. 3 (Fall): 108–23.

Bloom, Harold. 1973. *The Anxiety of Influence: A Theory of Poetry*. New York: Oxford University Press.

Bloom, Harold. 1975. *A Map of Misreading*. New York: Oxford University Press.

Bloom, Harold. 1998. *Shakespeare: The Invention of the Human*. New York: Riverhead Books.

Bluestone, George. 1956. "Word to Image: The Problem of the Filmed Novel." *The Quarterly of Film, Radio, and Television* 11, no 2: 171–80.

Bluestone, George. 1957. *Novels into Film*. Berkeley: University of California Press.

Bolter, J. David, and Richard A. Grusin. 1999. *Remediation: Understanding New Media*. Cambridge, MA: MIT Press.

Bolton, H. Philip. 1987. *Dickens Dramatized*. London: Mansell Press.

Bolton, H. Philip. 2000. *Women Writers Dramatized: A Calendar of Performances from Narrative Works Published in English to 1900*. London: Mansell Press.

Bolton, Matthew. 2017. "'Like Oil and Water': Adaptation as Textuality, Intertextuality, and Metatextuality in Lady Snowblood (Fujita, 1973)." *Studies in Twentieth and Twenty-First Century Literature* 42, no. 1 (Fall): 1–20.

Booth, Walter. R., director. 1901. *Scrooge, or Marley's Ghost*. R. W. Paul.

Boozer, Jack. 2017. "The Intratextuality of Film Adaptation: From *The Dying Animal* to *Elegy*." In *The Oxford Handbook of Adaptation Studies*, edited by Thomas Leitch, 197–213. New York: Oxford University Press.

Bordwell, David. 1985. *Narration in the Fiction Film*. Madison: University of Wisconsin Press.

Bordwell, David. 1996. "Contemporary Film Studies and the Vicissitudes of Grand Theory." In *Post-Theory: Reconstructing Film Studies*, edited by David Bordwell and Noël Carroll, 3–36. Madison: University of Wisconsin Press.

Bordwell, David, and Noël Carroll, eds. 1996. *Post-Theory: Reconstructing Film Studies*. Madison: University of Wisconsin Press.

Bortolotti, Gary R., and Linda Hutcheon. 2007. "On the Origin of Adaptations: Rethinking Fidelity Discourse and 'Success'—Biologically." *New Literary History* 38, no. 3: 443–58.

Boucicault, Dion. 1866. Testimony of Dion Boucicault to the Theatrical Licensing Review Committee, May 4, 1866. *Theatrical Licenses and Regulations. Reports from Committees*, vol. 16, 149–57. London: The House of Commons.

Bowker, Richard Rogers. 1886. *Copyright, Its Law and Literature; Being a Summary of the Principles and Law of Copyright, with Especial Reference to Books*. New York: Office of the Publishers' Weekly.

Boyd, Brian. 2009. *On the Origin of Stories: Evolution, Cognition, and Fiction*. Cambridge, MA: Belknap Press of Harvard University Press.

Boyd, Brian. 2017. "Making Adaptation Studies Adaptive." In *The Oxford Handbook of Adaptation Studies*, edited by Thomas Leitch, 587–606. New York: Oxford University Press.

Boyer, Carl B., and Uta C. Merzbach. 2011. *A History of Mathematics*. 3rd ed. New Jersey: John Wiley & Sons.

Boyum, Joy Gould. 1985. *Double Exposure: Fiction into Film*. New York: Plume Press.

Bradley, C. B. 1886. "The Classification of Rhetorical Figures." *Modern Language Notes* 1, no. 8 (Dec.): 140–42.

Brady, Ben. 1994. *Principles of Adaptation for Film and Television*. Austin: University of Texas Press.

Brandl, Mark Staff. n.d. "Metalepsis, The Trope of Tropes." *Metaphor and Art: The Linguistics and Embodiment of Metaphor and Visual Art*. Accessed August 31, 2017. http://www.metaphorandart.com/articles/metalepsis.html.

Brandl, Mark Staff. n.d. "Subsumption and Misprision: Transumption/Metalepsis as a Thought Process." *Metaphor and Art: The Linguistics and Embodiment of Metaphor and Visual Art*. Accessed August 31, 2017. http://www.metaphorandart.com/articles/sub-sumption.html.

Braudy, Leo, and Marshall Cohen. 1999. *Film Theory and Criticism: Introductory Readings*. Oxford: Oxford University Press.

Brinch, Sara. 2013. "Tracing the Originals, Pursuing the Past: *Invictus* and the 'Based-on-a-True-Story' Film as Adaptation." In *Adaptation Studies: New Challenges, New Directions*, edited by Jørgen Bruhn, Anne Gjelsvik, and Eirik Frisvold Hanssen, 223–44. London: Bloomsbury Press.

Brooks, Cleanth. 1939. *An Approach to Literature: A Collection of Prose and Verse, with Analyses and Discussions*. New York: F. S. Crofts & Co.

Brooks, Cleanth. 1947. *The Well Wrought Urn: Studies in the Structure of Poetry*. New York: Raynal and Hitchcock.

Brown, James Robert. 2008. *Philosophy of Mathematics: A Contemporary Introduction to the World of Proofs and Pictures*. 2nd ed. London: Routledge.

Brown, Kathleen L. 2009. *Teaching Literary Theory Using Film Adaptations*. Jefferson, NC: McFarland Press.

Brown, Terry. 2012. *Introduction to Genetics: A Molecular Approach*. New York: Garland Science.

Brownlee, Shannon. 2018. "Fidelity, Medium Specificity, (In)determinacy: Identities That Matter." In *The Routledge Companion to Adaptation*, edited by Dennis Cutchins, Katja Krebs, and Eckart Voigts, 157–68. London: Routledge.

Bruhn, Jørgen. 2013. "Dialogizing Adaptation Studies: From One-Way Transport to a Dialogic Two-Way Process." In *Adaptation Studies: New Challenges, New Directions*, edited by Jørgen Bruhn, Anne Gjelsvik, and Eirik Frisvold Hanssen, 69–88. London: Bloomsbury Press.

Bullen, J. B. 1990. "Is Hardy a 'Cinematic Novelist'? The Problem of Adaptation." *Yearbook of English Studies* 20: 48–59.

Bulwer-Lytton, Edward. (1863) 1864. "Certain Principles of Art in Works of Imagination." In *Caxtoniana: A Series of Essays on Life, Literature, and Manners*, 305–29. New York: Harper.

Burg, Jennifer. 2009. *The Science of Digital Media*. New York: Prentice Hall.

Burke, Edmund. (1759) 1761. *A Philosophical Enquiry into the Origin of Our Ideas of the Sublime and Beautiful*. 3rd ed. London: R. & J. Dodsley.

Burke, Liam. 2015. *The Comic Book Film Adaptation: Exploring Modern Hollywood's Leading Genre*. Jackson: University Press of Mississippi.

Burney, Charles. 1782. *A General History of Music: From the Earliest Ages to the Present Period*. 4 vols. London: J. Robson.

Buss, D. M. 1999. *Evolutionary Psychology: The New Science of the Mind*. Boston: Allyn and Bacon.

Butler, Judith. 1993. *Bodies That Matter: On the Discursive Limits of "Sex."* London: Routledge.

C., W. "Fine Arts." 1819. *The New Monthly Magazine and Universal Register* 11 (Feb.1): 50–53.

Cacciari, Cristina. 2008. "Crossing the Senses in Metaphorical Language." In *The Cambridge Handbook of Metaphor and Thought*, edited by Raymond W. Gibbs, Jr., 425–44. Cambridge: Cambridge University Press.

Cahir, Linda Costanzo. 2006. *Literature into Film: Theory and Practical Approaches*. Foreword by James M. Welsh. Jefferson, NC: McFarland Press.

Caldwell, John Thornton. 1995. *Televisuality: Style, Crisis, and Authority in American Television*. New Brunswick, NJ: Rutgers University Press.

Campbell, Laura Chuhan. 2017. *The Medieval Merlin Tradition in France and Italy: Prophecy, Paradox, and "Translatio."* Cambridge: D. S. Brewer.

Campbell, Thomas. 1851. *The Poetical Works of Thomas Campbell*. Edited by W. A. Hill. London: Edward Moxon.

Campion, Jane, director. 2009. Bright Star. Jane Campion and Caroline Hewitt, Warner Brothers.

Canterbery, E Ray. 2001. *A Brief History of Economics: Artful Approaches to the Dismal Science*. Singapore: World Scientific.

Cardullo, Bert, ed. 2011. *Stage and Screen: Adaptation Theory from 1916 to 2000*. New York: Continuum Press.

Cardwell, Sarah. 2002. *Adaptation Revisited: Television and the Classic Novel*. Manchester: Manchester University Press.

Cardwell, Sarah. 2007. "Adaptation Studies Revisited: Purposes, Perspectives, and Inspiration." In *The Literature/Film Reader: Issues of Adaptation*, edited by James M. Welsh and Peter Lev, 51–64. Lanham, MD: Scarecrow Press.

Cardwell, Sarah. 2018. "Pause, Rewind, Replay: Adaptation, Intertextuality and (Re) Defining Adaptation Studies." In *The Routledge Companion to Adaptation*, edited by Dennis Cutchins, Katja Krebs, and Eckart Voigts, 7–17. London: Routledge.

Carroll, Noël. 1996. *Theorizing the Moving Image*. Cambridge: Cambridge University Press.

Carroll, Noël, and Jinhee Choi. 2005. *Philosophy of Film and Motion Pictures: An Anthology*. Oxford: Blackwell Publishing.

Carroll, Rachel, ed. 2009. *Adaptation in Contemporary Culture: Textual Infidelities*. London: Continuum.

Carter, Ronald, and John McRae. 1997. *The Routledge History of Literature in English: Britain and Ireland*. Foreword by Malcolm Bradbury. London: Routledge.

Cartmell, Deborah, series ed. 2008–2014. *Screen Adaptations* series. London: Bloomsbury Press.

Cartmell, Deborah. 2009. "Review of Christine Geraghty, *Now a Major Motion Picture*, and Jack Boozer, ed., *Authorship in Film Adaptation*." *Screen* 50, no. 4 (Winter): 463–64.

Cartmell, Deborah, ed. 2012a. *A Companion to Literature, Film, and Adaptation*. Oxford: Wiley-Blackwell Press.

Cartmell, Deborah. 2012b. "Familiarity versus Contempt: Becoming *Jane* and the Adaptation Genre." In *Adaptation and Cultural Appropriation: Literature, Film and the Arts*, edited by Pascal Nicklas and Oliver Lindner, 26–33. Spectrum Literature 27. Berlin: Walter de Gruyter Press.

Cartmell, Deborah. 2012c. "100+ Years of Adaptations, or, Adaptation as the Art Form of Democracy." In *A Companion to Literature, Film, and Adaptation*, edited by Deborah Cartmell, 1–13. Oxford: Wiley-Blackwell Press.

Cartmell, Deborah. 2015. *Adaptations in the Sound Era, 1927–37*. Bloomsbury Adaptation Histories. London: Bloomsbury Press.

Cartmell, Deborah, series ed. From 2015. *Bloomsbury Adaptation Histories* series. London: Bloomsbury Press.

Cartmell, Deborah. 2017. "Adaptation as Exploitation." *Literature/Film Quarterly* 45, no. 2. http://www.salisbury.edu/lfq/_issues/first/adaptation_as_exploitation.html.

Cartmell, Deborah, Timothy Corrigan, and Imelda Whelehan. 2008. "Introduction to Adaptation." *Adaptation* 1, no. 1 (Mar.): 1–4.

Cartmell, Deborah, I. Q. Hunter, Heidi Kaye, and Imelda Whelehan, eds. 1996. *Pulping Fictions: Consuming Culture across the Literature/Media Divide*. London: Pluto Press.

Cartmell, Deborah, I. Q. Hunter, Heidi Kaye, and Imelda Whelehan, eds. 1997. *Trash Aesthetics: Popular Culture and Its Audience*. London: Pluto Press.

Cartmell, Deborah, I. Q. Hunter, Heidi Kaye, and Imelda Whelehan, eds. 1998. *Sisterhoods across the Literature/Media Divide*. London: Pluto Press.

Cartmell, Deborah, I. Q. Hunter, Heidi Kaye, and Imelda Whelehan, eds. 1999. *Alien Identities: Exploring Differences in Film and Fiction*. London: Pluto Press.

Cartmell, Deborah, I. Q. Hunter, Heidi Kaye, and Imelda Whelehan, eds. 2000. *Classics in Film and Fiction*. London: Pluto Press.

Cartmell, Deborah, I. Q. Hunter, and Imelda Whelehan, eds. 2001. *Retrovisions: Reinventing the Past in Film and Fiction*. London: Pluto Press.

Cartmell, Deborah, Jeremy Strong, and Imelda Whelehan. 2018. "A Brief History of the Association of Adaptation Studies." In *Where Is Adaptation? Mapping Cultures, Texts, and Contexts*, edited by Casie Hermansson and Janet Zepernick, 259–70. Amsterdam: John Benjamins.

Cartmell, Deborah, and Imelda Whelehan, eds. 1999. *Adaptations: From Text to Screen, Screen to Text*. London: Routledge.

Cartmell, Deborah, and Imelda Whelehan. 2007a. *The Cambridge Companion to Literature on Screen*. Cambridge: Cambridge University Press.

Cartmell, Deborah, and Imelda Whelehan. 2007b. "Introduction: Literature on Screen: A Synoptic View." In *The Cambridge Companion to Literature on Screen*, edited by Deborah Cartmell and Imelda Whelehan, 1–12. Cambridge: Cambridge University Press.

Cartmell, Deborah, and Imelda Whelehan. 2010. *Screen Adaptation: Impure Cinema*. New York: Palgrave Macmillan.

Cartmell, Deborah, and Imelda Whelehan, eds. 2014. *Teaching Adaptation*. New York: Palgrave Macmillan.

Cattrysse, Patrick. 1992. "Film (Adaptation) as Translation: Some Methodological Proposals." *Target: International Journal of Translation Studies* 4, no. 1: 53–70.

Cattrysse, Patrick. 2014. *Descriptive Adaptation Studies: Epistemological and Methodological Issues*. Antwerp: Garant.

Cattrysse, Patrick. 2018. "An Evolutionary View of Cultural Adaptation: Some Considerations." In *The Routledge Companion to Adaptation*, edited by Dennis Cutchins, Katja Krebs, and Eckart Voigts, 40–54. London: Routledge.

Caughie, John. 1998. "A Culture of Adaptation: Adaptation and the Past in British Film and Television." *Journal for the Study of British Cultures* 5, no. 1: 55–66.

Cavallaro, Dani. 2010. *Anime and the Art of Adaptation: Eight Famous Works from Page to Screen*. Jefferson, NC: McFarland Press.

Cavallaro, Dani. 2013. *Synesthesia and the Arts*. Jefferson, NC: McFarland Press.

Chambers, Montagu, Francis Towers Streeten, and Freeman Oliver Haynes, eds. 1863. *The Law Journal Reports for the Year 1863: Comprising Reports of Cases in the House of Lords, and in the Courts of Chancery and Appeal in Bankruptcy, Probate, Divorce and Matrimonial Causes, Admiralty, Queen's Bench and the Bail Court, Common Pleas, Exchequer, Exchequer Chamber, and Crown Cases Reserved. From Michaelmas Term 1862, to Trinity Term, 1863*. London: Edward Bret Ince.

Chan, Leo. 2012. "A Survey of the 'New' Discipline of Adaptation Studies: Between Translation and Interculturalism." *Perspectives: Studies in Translatology* 20, no. 4 (Sep.): 411–18.

Chatman, Seymour. 1978. *Story and Discourse: Narrative Structure in Fiction and Film*. Ithaca, NY: Cornell University Press.

Chatman, Seymour. 1980. "What Novels Can Do That Films Can't (and Vice Versa)." *Critical Inquiry* 7, no. 1 (Autumn): 121–40.

Chemla, Karine, ed. 2005. *History of Science, History of Text*. Netherlands: Springer.

Chettiparamb, Angelique. 2007. "Interdisciplinarity: A Literature Review." The Higher Education Academy Interdisciplinary Teaching and Learning Group, University of Southampton.

Chun, Tarryn Li-Min. 2014. "Adaptation as Hospitality: Shanghai Theatre Academy Winter Institute 2013 Performance Series." *The Drama Review* 58, no. 1 (Feb.): 108–17.

Clark, Burton. R. 1983. *The Higher Education System: Academic Organisation in Cross-National Perspective*. Berkeley: University of California Press.

Clark, Elizabeth A. 2009. *History, Theory, Text: Historians and the Linguistic Turn*. Cambridge, MA: Harvard University Press.

Clark, James G., Frank T. Coulson, and Kathryn L. McKinley, eds. 2011. *Ovid in the Middle Ages*. Cambridge: Cambridge University Press.

Clement, Jennifer. 2015. "Introduction." In "Adaptation and Early Modern Culture: Shakespeare and Beyond." Special issue, *Shakespeare* 11, no. 1 (April): 1–9.

Clubbe, William. 1795. *Six Satires of Horace, in a Style between Free Imitation and Literal Version*. London: George Jermyn.

Clüver, Claus. 2017. "Ekphrasis and Adaptation." In *The Oxford Handbook of Adaptation Studies*, edited by Thomas Leitch, 459–76. New York: Oxford University Press.

Coatman, Anna. 2018. "Dire Straights." *Sight and Sound* 28, no. 10 (Oct.): 36–38.

Cobb, Shelley. 2015. *Adaptation, Authorship, and Contemporary Women Filmmakers*. Basingstoke: Palgrave Macmillan.

Cochrane, Bernadette. 2018. "Blurring the Lines: Adaptation, Transmediality, Intermediality, and Screened Performance." In *The Routledge Companion to Adaptation*, edited by Dennis Cutchins, Katja Krebs, and Eckart Voigts, 340–48. London: Routledge.

Cohen, Keith. 1979. *Film and Fiction: The Dynamics of Exchange*. New Haven: Yale University Press.

Collard, Christophe. 2014. "Mediaturgy's Troubled Tensions with Adaptation: Convergence or Divergence?" *Adaptation* 7, no. 3 (Dec.): 265–74.

Collins, Wilkie. 1858a. "Dramatic Grub Street." *Household Words* 17, no. 415 (Mar. 6): 265–70.

Collins, Wilkie. 1858b. "The Unknown Public." *Household Words* 18, no. 439 (Aug. 21): 217–22.

Comstock, George, and Erica Scharrer. 2005. *The Psychology of Media and Politics.* Amsterdam: Elsevier Academic Press.

Conroy, Thom. 2018. "Adaptation as Salvage: Transcoding History into Fiction in *The Naturalist.*" In *Where Is Adaptation? Mapping Cultures, Texts, and Contexts,* edited by Casie Hermansson and Janet Zepernick, 15–30. Amsterdam: John Benjamins.

Constable, Catherine. 2009. *Adapting Philosophy: Jean Baudrillard and the Matrix Trilogy.* Manchester: Manchester University Press.

Constandinides, Costas. 2010. *From Film Adaptation to Post-Celluloid Adaptation: Rethinking the Transition of Popular Narratives and Characters across Old and New Media.* New York: Continuum.

Constantinescu, Cătălin. 2015. "Intermedialität and Literature: What Is Filmic Rewriting?" *Philologica Jassyensia* 11, no. 1: 165–74.

Continental Congress. (1914) 2016. "2 May 1783." *Journals of the Continental Congress, 1774–1789,* 24:326. Washington: US Government Printing Office.

Cooke, Will. 1775. *The Elements of Dramatic Criticism.* London: G. Kearsly.

Copinger, Walter Arthur. 1870. *The Law of Copyright, in Works of Literature and Art: Including That of the Drama, Music, Engraving, Sculpture, Painting, Photography and Ornamental and Useful Design, Together with International and Foreign Copyright, with the Statutes Relating Thereto, and References to the English and American Decisions.* London: Stevens & Haynes.

Corliss, Richard. 1975. *Talking Pictures: Screenwriters of Hollywood.* Hollywood: David & Charles.

Corrigan, Timothy. 1999. *Film and Literature: An Introduction and Reader.* New York: Prentice Hall. 1st ed. London: Routledge.

Corrigan, Timothy. 2007. "Literature on Screen, a History: In the Gap." In *The Cambridge Companion to Literature on Screen,* edited by Deborah Cartmell and Imelda Whelehan, 29–43. Cambridge: Cambridge University Press.

Corrigan, Timothy. 2010. "Adaptations, Refractions, and Obstructions: The Prophecies of André Bazin." Presented at the SCMS Conference, Los Angeles, March.

Corrigan, Timothy. 2011. *Film and Literature: An Introduction and Reader.* New York: Prentice Hall. 2nd ed. London: Routledge.

Corrigan, Timothy. 2017. "Defining Adaptation." In *The Oxford Handbook of Adaptation Studies,* edited by Thomas Leitch, 23–35. New York: Oxford University Press.

Crocco, Francesco. 2014. *Literature and the Growth of British Nationalism: The Influence of Romantic Poetry and Bardic Criticism.* Jefferson, NC: McFarland Press.

Crowe, Catharine. 1868. *Uncle Tom's Cabin for Children.* London: Routledge.

Culler, Jonathan. 1997. *Literary Theory: A Very Short Introduction.* Oxford: Oxford University Press.

Culler, Jonathan. 1981. *The Pursuit of Signs: Semiotics, Literature, Deconstruction.* London: Routledge.

Cunningham, Valentine. 2002. *Reading After Theory.* Oxford: Blackwell Publishing.

Curtis, Gerard. 1995. "Dickens in the Visual Market." In *Literature in the Marketplace: Nineteenth-Century British Publishing and Reading Practices,* edited by John O. Jordan and Robert L. Patten, 213–49. Cambridge: Cambridge University Press.

Cutchins, Dennis. 2017. "Bakhtin, Intertextuality, and Adaptation." In *The Oxford Handbook of Adaptation Studies*, edited by Thomas Leitch, 71–86. Oxford: Oxford University Press.

Cutchins, Dennis. 2018. "Introduction." In *The Routledge Companion to Adaptation*, edited by Dennis Cutchins, Katja Krebs, and Eckart Voigts, 1–4. London: Routledge.

Cutchins, Dennis, Katja Krebs, and Eckart Voigts, eds. 2018. *The Routledge Companion to Adaptation*. London: Routledge.

Cutchins, Dennis, Laurence Raw, and James M. Welsh, eds. 2010a. *The Pedagogy of Adaptation*. Lanham, MD: Scarecrow Press.

Cutchins, Dennis, Laurence Raw, and James M. Welsh, eds. 2010b. *Redefining Adaptation Studies*. Lanham, MD: Scarecrow Press.

Cutchins, Dennis, and Kathryn Meeks. 2018. "Adaptation, Fidelity, and Reception." In *The Routledge Companion to Adaptation*, edited by Dennis Cutchins, Katja Krebs, and Eckart Voigts, 301–10. London: Routledge.

Daly, Augustin. 1868. *Hazardous Ground: An Original Adaptation in Four Acts, from Victorien Sardou's "Nos Bons Villageois."* New York: W. C. Wemyss.

Darwin, Charles. (1859) 2009. *On the Origin of Species: by Means of Natural Selection, or, the Preservation of Favoured Races in the Struggle for Life*. London: Penguin Classics.

Darwin, Charles. (1871) 2004. *The Descent of Man, and Selection in Relation to Sex*. London: Penguin Classics.

Davidson, Phebe, ed. 1997. *Film and Literature: Points of Intersection*. Lewiston, NY: Edwin Mellen Press.

Davies, Stephen. 2003. *Themes in the Philosophy of Music*. Oxford: Oxford University Press.

Davis, Colin. 2004. *After Poststructuralism: Reading, Stories and Theory*. London: Routledge.

Davis, Tony. 2017. *Humanism*. London and New York: Routledge.

Davison, Carol Margaret, and Marie Mulvey-Roberts, eds. 2018. *Global Frankenstein*. London: Palgrave Macmillan.

Davy, Christopher. 1827. "On the Improvements of Windsor Castle. No. II." *Mechanics' Magazine, Museum, Register, Journal & Gazette* 8, no. 209 (Aug.): 146–48.

Dawkins, Richard. 2006. *The Selfish Gene*. Oxford: Oxford University Press. (Orig. pub. 1976.)

De Man, Paul. 1973. "Semiology and Rhetoric." *Diacritics* 3, no. 3 (Autumn): 27–33.

De Man, Paul. 1979. *Allegories of Reading: Figural Language in Rousseau, Nietzsche, Rilke, and Proust*. New Haven, CT: Yale University Press.

De Man, Paul. 1986. "The Resistance to Theory." In *The Resistance to Theory*, 3–20. Theory and History of Literature 33. Minneapolis: University of Minnesota Press.

Deazley, Ronan. 1833. "Dramatic Literary Property Act of 1833." Primary Sources on Copyright. AHRC. http://www.copyrighthistory.org/cam/tools/request/showRecord?-id=commentary_uk_1833#_edn3.

DeBona, Guerric. 2010. *Film Adaptation in the Hollywood Studio Era*. Urbana: University of Illinois Press.

DeHaan, Mike. 2015. "Comparing the Genetic Code of DNA to Binary Code." *Decoded={science . . . }*, Aug. 25. https://www.decodedscience.org/comparing-genetic-code-dna-binary-code/55476.

Del Villano, Bianca. 2012. "Dramatic Adaptation, Authorship, and Cultural Identity in the Eighteenth Century: The Case of Samuel Foote." *Journal of Early Modern Studies* 1, no. 1: 175–91.

Deleuze, Gilles. (1968) 1994. *Difference and Repetition*. Translated by Paul Patton. London: Continuum.

Deleuze, Gilles. (1983) 1986. *Cinema 1: The Movement-Image*. Translated by Hugh Tomlinson and Robert Galetta. New York: Continuum.

Deleuze, Gilles. (1985) 1989. *Cinema 2: The Time-Image*. Translated by Hugh Tomlinson and Robert Galetta. New York: Continuum.

Deleuze, Gilles, and Félix Guattari. (1980) 1988. *A Thousand Plateaus: Capitalism and Schizophrenia*. Translated by Brian Massumi. London: Athlone Press.

Deleuze, Gilles, and Félix Guattari. (1991 French) 1994. *What Is Philosophy?* Translated by Graham Burchell and Hugh Tomlinson. London: Verso.

Della Coletta, Cristina. 2012. *When Stories Travel: Cross-Cultural Encounters between Fiction and Film*. Baltimore: Johns Hopkins University Press.

Deltcheva, Roumiana. 1996a. "Beyond the Boundaries of the Medium." *Canadian Review of Comparative Literature* 23, no. 3 (Sep.) 639–44.

Deltcheva, Roumiana. 1996b. "Literature-Film Relations: Selected Bibliography (1985–1996)." *Canadian Review of Comparative Literature* 23, no. 3 (Sep.): 853–71. https://journals.library.ualberta.ca/crcl/index.php/crcl/article/view/3902/3154.

Deltcheva, Roumiana, Waclaw M. Osadnik, and Eduard Vlasov. 1996. "Liminaire." In "Literature and Film: Models of Adaptation." Special issue, *Canadian Review of Comparative Literature* 23, no. 3 (Sep.): 637.

Demory, Pamela. 2018. "Queer Adaptation." In *The Routledge Companion to Adaptation*, edited by Dennis Cutchins, Katja Krebs, and Eckart Voigts, 146–56. London: Routledge.

Demory, Pamela, ed. 2019. *Queer/Adaptation: A Collection of Critical Essays*. Palgrave Studies in Adaptation and Visual Culture. London: Palgrave Macmillan.

Dench, Ernest A. 1916. *Advertising by Motion Pictures*. Cincinnati: Standard Press.

Denroche, Charles. 2015. *Metonymy and Language: A New Theory of Linguistic Processing*. New York: Routledge.

Dent-Read, Cathy H., and Agnes Szokolszky. 1993. "Where Do Metaphors Come From?" *Metaphor and Symbolic Activity* 8, no. 3: 227–42.

Deppman, Hsiu-Chuang. 2010. *Adapted for the Screen: The Cultural Politics of Modern Chinese Fiction and Film*. Honolulu: University of Hawaii Press.

Derrida, Jacques. (1971) 1974. "White Mythology: Metaphor in the Text of Philosophy." Translated by F. C. T. Moore. *New Literary History* 6, no. 1 (Autumn): 5–74.

Derrida, Jacques. 1989a. *Signéponge/Signsponge*. Translated by Richard Rand. New York: Columbia University Press.

Derrida, Jacques. 1989b. "How to Avoid Speaking: Denials." Translated by Ken Frieden. In *Languages of the Unsayable: The Play of Negativity in Literature and Literary Theory*, edited by Sanford Budick and Wolfgang Iser, 3–70. New York: Columbia University Press.

Derrida, Jacques. 1991. *A Derrida Reader: Between the Blinds*. Edited by Peggy Kamuf. New York: Columbia University Press.

Derrida, Jacques. 2005. *Rogues: Two Essays on Reason*. Translated by Pascale-Anne Brault and Michael Naas. Stanford: Stanford University Press.

Desmond, John M., and Peter J. Hawkes. 2006. *Adaptation: Studying Film and Literature*. New York: McGraw-Hill. Reprinted 2015.

Deutelbaum, Marshall. 2016. "The Social Network Screenplay: Adaptation as (Re)Interpretation and (Re)Creation." *Journal of Screenwriting* 7, no. 1 (Mar.): 29–44.

Diamond, Suzanne. 2010. "'Whose Life Is It, Anyway?' Adaptation, Collective Memory, and (Auto)Biographical Processes." In *Redefining Adaptation Studies*, edited by Dennis Cutchins, Laurence Raw, and James M. Welsh, 95–110. Lanham, MD: Scarecrow Press.

Dicecco, Nico. 2011. "On Truth and Falsity in Their Intertextual Sense: Adaptation as Dissimulation." *Pivot: A Journal of Interdisciplinary Studies and Thought* 1, no. 1. http://pivot.journals.yorku.ca/index.php/pivot/article/view/32159.

Dicecco, Nico. 2015. "State of the Conversation: The Obscene Underside of Adaptation." *Adaptation* 8, no. 2 (Aug.): 161–75.

Dickens, Charles. 1839. *The Life and Adventures of Nicholas Nickleby*. 8 vols. London: Chapman & Hall.

Dickens, Charles. 1865. *Our Mutual Friend*. 2 vols. London: Chapman & Hall.

Diekmann, John. 1874. *Dryden's Virgil Compared with the Latin Original*. Rostock: Charles Bolt.

DiPaolo, Marc. 2007. *Emma Adapted: Jane Austen's Heroine from Book to Film*. New York: Peter Lang.

Dix, Hywel. 2018. "There by Not Being There: Adaptation, Intertextuality and the Multicultural Trace." In *Multicultural Narratives: Traces and Perspectives*, edited by Mustafa Kirca and Hywel Dix, 41–65. Newcastle upon Tyne: Cambridge Scholars.

Dixon, Wheeler Winston, and Gwendolyn Audrey Foster. 2008. *A Short History of Film*. New Brunswick, NJ: Rutgers University Press.

Doane, Mary Ann. 2007. "The Indexical and the Concept of Medium Specificity." *Differences: A Journal of Feminist Cultural Studies* 18, no. 1: 128–52.

Dobson, Michael. 1992. *The Making of the National Poet: Shakespeare, Adaptation, and Authorship, 1660–1769*. Oxford: Clarendon.

Docherty, Thomas. 1996. *After Theory*. Edinburgh: Edinburgh University Press.

Dogan, Mattei, and Robert Pahre. 1990. *Creative Marginality: Innovation at the Intersections of Social Sciences*. Oxford: Westview Press.

Donaldson v. Becket, London. (1774). *Primary Sources on Copyright (1450–1900)*. Edited by L. Bently and M. Kretschmer. Accessed February 3, 2017. http://www.copyrighthistory.org/record/uk_1774.

Donaldson, Ian. 1997. "'Not of an Age': Jonson, Shakespeare, and the Verdicts of Posterity." In *New Perspectives on Ben Jonson*, edited by James Hirsh, 197–214. Madison, NJ: Farleigh Dickinson University Press.

Donaldson-Evans, Mary. 2009. *Madame Bovary at the Movies: Adaptation, Ideology, Context*. Amsterdam: Rodopi Press.

Donaldson-McHugh, Shannon, and Don Moore. 2006. "Film Adaptation, Co-Authorship, and Hauntology: Gus Van Sant's *Psycho* (1998)." *Journal of Popular Culture* 39, no. 2 (April): 225–33.

Dovey, Lindiwe. 2009. *African Film and Literature: Adapting Violence to the Screen*. New York: Columbia University Press.

Dovey, Lindiwe. 2013. "Fidelity, Simultaneity and the 'Remaking' of Adaptation Studies." In *Adaptation and Cultural Appropriation: Literature, Film, and the Arts*, edited by Pascal Nicklas and Oliver Lindner, 162–85. Spectrum Literature 27. Berlin: Walter de Gruyter Press.

Dryden, John. 1709. *Preface to All for Love: Or, The World Well Lost. A Tragedy, Acted by Her Majesty's Servants. Written in Imitation of Shakespear's Stile* [sic]. London: J. Tonson.

Dryden, John. (1680) 1795. "Preface Concerning Ovid's Epistles." In *The Works of the British Poets, with Prefaces, Biographical and Critical*, edited by Robert Anderson, 6:346–50. London, John & Arthur Arch.

Duff, William. 1767. *An Essay on Original Genius and Its Various Modes of Exertion in Philosophy and the Fine Arts, Particularly in Poetry*. London: Edward and Charles Dilly.

Dworkin, Martin S. 1974. "The Writing on the Screen." In *Graham Greene: The Films of His Fiction*, edited by Gene D. Phillips, vii–xvii. New York: Teachers College Press.

Eagleton, Terry. 1996. *Literary Theory: An Introduction*. Oxford: Wiley-Blackwell Press.

Edel, Leon. 1977. "Novel and the Cinema." In *The Theory of the Novel: New Essays*, edited by John Halperin, 177–88. New York: Macmillan.

Eidsvik, Charles. 1974. "Soft Edges: The Art of Literature, the Medium of Film." *Literature/Film Quarterly* 2, no. 1 (Winter): 16–21.

Eidsvik, Charles. 1975. "Toward a 'Politique des Adaptations.'" *Literature/Film Quarterly* 3, no.3 (Summer): 255–63.

Eikhenbaum, Boris M. (1926) 1973. "Literature and Cinema." In *Russian Formalism: A Collection of Articles and Texts in Translation*, edited by Stephen Bann and John E. Bowlt, 122–27. New York: Barnes & Noble.

Eisenstein, Sergei. 1931. "The Principles of Film Form." Translated by I. M. *Close up: Cinema and Modernism* 8, no. 3 (Sep.): 167–81.

Eisenstein, Sergei. (1931 Russian; 1944 English) 1949. "Dickens, Griffith, and the Film Today." In *Film Form: Essays in Film Theory*, edited and translated by Jay Leyda, 195–255. New York: Harcourt, Brace & World.

Elbow, Peter. 1973. *Writing without Teachers*. Oxford: Oxford University Press.

Eliot, Samuel A. 1840. "Mr. Eliot's Lecture before the Musical Convention." *The Musical Magazine; or, Repository of Musical Science, Literature and Intelligence* 2, no. 48 (Oct.) 337–55.

Eliot, T. S. *The Waste Land and Other Poems*. 2010 [1922]. Toronto: Broadview Press.

Elleström, Lars, ed. 2010. *Media Borders, Multimodality and Intermediality*. London: Palgrave Macmillan.

Elleström, Lars. 2013. "Adaptations within the Field of Media Transformations." In *Adaptation Studies: New Challenges, New Directions*, edited by Jørgen Bruhn, Anne Gjelsvik, and Eirik Frisvold Hanssen, 113–32. London: Bloomsbury Press.

Elleström, Lars. 2017. "Adaptation and Intermediality." In *The Oxford Handbook of Adaptation Studies*, edited by Thomas Leitch, 509–526. Oxford: Oxford University Press.

Elliot, Melissa. 2018. No Need for Words: The Role of Music in Volker Schlöndorff's *Der Junge Töleß* (*Young Törless*). *Literature/Film Quarterly* 46, no. 4. https://lfq.salisbury.edu/_issues/46_4/no_need_for_words_the_role_of_music_in_volker.html.

Elliott, Kamilla. 2003a. *Rethinking the Novel/Film Debate*. Cambridge: Cambridge University Press.

Elliott, Kamilla. 2003b. "Cinematic Dickens and Uncinematic Words." In *Dickens on Screen*, edited by John Glavin, 113–21. Cambridge: Cambridge University Press.

Elliott, Kamilla. 2004. "Literary Film Adaptation and the Form/Content Dilemma." In *Narrative across Media: The Languages of Storytelling*, edited by Marie-Laure Ryan, 220–43. Lincoln: Nebraska University Press.

Elliott, Kamilla. 2005. "Novels, Films, and the Word/Image Wars." In *A Companion to Film and Literature*, edited by Robert Stam and Alessandra Raengo, 1–22. Oxford: Blackwell, 2005.

Elliott, Kamilla. 2006. "The Deconstruction of Fundamental Christianity." *Textual Practice* 20, no. 4: 713–38. Republished in the first virtual special issue of *Textual Practice*, May 2012.

Elliott, Kamilla. 2008. "Gothic—Film—Parody." *Adaptation* 1, no. 1 (Mar.): 24–43.

Elliott, Kamilla. 2010. "Adaptation as Compendium: Tim Burton's *Alice in Wonderland*." *Adaptation* 3, no. 2 (Sep.): 193–201.

Elliott, Kamilla. 2012a. "The Adaptation of Adaptation: A Dialogue between the Arts and Sciences." In *Adaptation and Cultural Appropriation: Literature, Film, and the Arts*, edited by Pascal Nicklas and Oliver Lindner, 145–61. Spectrum Literature 27. Berlin: Walter de Gruyter Press.

Elliott, Kamilla. 2012b. *Portraiture and British Gothic Fiction: The Rise of Picture Identification, 1764–1835*. Baltimore: Johns Hopkins University Press.

Elliott, Kamilla. 2013. "Theorizing Adaptations/Adapting Theories." In *Adaptation Studies: New Challenges, New Directions*, edited by Jørgen Bruhn, Anne Gjelsvik, and Eirik Frisvold Hanssen, 19–45. London: Bloomsbury Press.

Elliott, Kamilla. 2014a. "Tie-Intertextuality, or, Intertextuality as Incorporation in the Tie-in Merchandise to Disney's *Alice in Wonderland* (2010)." *Adaptation* 7, no. 2 (Aug.): 191–211.

Elliott, Kamilla. 2014b. "Rethinking Formal-Cultural and Textual-Contextual Divides in Adaptation Studies." *Literature/Film Quarterly* 42, no. 4 (October): 576–93.

Elliott, Kamilla. 2014c. "Doing Adaptation: The Adaptation as Critic." In *Teaching Adaptations*, edited by Deborah Cartmell and Imelda Whelehan, 71–86. London: Palgrave Macmillan.

Elliott, Kamilla. 2016. "The Illustrated Book." In *Late Victorian into Modern, 1880–1920*, edited by Laura Marcus, Michèle Mendelssohn, and Kirsten Shepherd-Barr, 539–64. Twenty-First Century Approaches to Literature, edited by Paul Strohm. Oxford: Oxford University Press.

Elliott, Kamilla. 2017. "Adaptation Theory and Adaptation Scholarship." In *The Oxford Handbook of Adaptation Studies*, edited by Thomas Leitch, 679–97. Oxford: Oxford University Press.

Elliott, Kamilla. 2018. "The Theory of Badaptation." In *The Routledge Companion to Adaptation*, edited by Dennis Cutchins, Katja Krebs, and Eckart Voigts, 18–27. London: Routledge.

Ellis, John. 1982. "The Literary Adaptation." *Screen* 23, no 1: 3–5.

Emig, Rainer. 2012. "Adaptation in Theory." In *Adaptation and Cultural Appropriation: Literature, Film, and the Arts*, edited by Pascal Nicklas and Oliver Linder, 14–24. Spectrum Literature 27. Berlin: Walter de Gruyter.

Emig, Rainer. 2015. "Fatal Analogies? Some Words of Caution on Adaptation's Expanding Remit." Paper presented at the conference on "Adaptation and Perception: Media Convergence," Johannes Gutenberg University, Mainz, Germany, December.

Emig, Rainer. 2018. "Adaptation and the Concept of the Original." In *The Routledge Companion to Adaptation*, edited by Dennis Cutchins, Katja Krebs, and Eckart Voigts, 28–39. London: Routledge.

English Association, The. 2015. *The Year's Work in Critical and Cultural Theory*. Edited by Neil Badmington and David Tucker. Oxford: Oxford Academic Press.

English Association, The. 2016. *The Year's Work in Critical and Cultural Theory*. Edited by Neil Badmington and David Tucker. Oxford: Oxford Academic Press.

English Association, The. 2017. *The Year's Work in Critical and Cultural Theory*. Edited by Neil Badmington and Emma Mason. Oxford: Oxford Academic Press.

Erdmann, Johann Eduard. (1890) 2002. *A History of Philosophy*. London: Routledge.

Esrock, Ellen J. 1994. *The Reader's Eye: Visual Imaging as Reader Response*. Baltimore: Johns Hopkins University Press.

Faulkner, Sally. 2004. *Literary Adaptations in Spanish Cinema*. London: Tamesis Press.

Fay, Brian. 1996. *Contemporary Philosophy of Social Science: A Multicultural Approach*. New York: Wiley.

Ferris, Suzanne, and Mallory Young. 2010. "'Marie Antoinette': Fashion, Third-Wave Feminism, and Chick Culture." *Literature/Film Quarterly* 38, no. 2: 98–116.

Field, Syd. "Adaptation." 2003. In *The Definitive Guide to Screenwriting*, 323–48. London: Ebury Press.

Fischer, Lucy, and Patrice Petro. 2012. *Teaching Film*. New York: MLA.

Fischer, Steven Roger. 2004. *History of Language*. London: Reaktion.

Fischlin, Daniel, and Mark Fortier, eds. 2000. *Adaptations of Shakespeare: A Critical Anthology of Plays from the Seventeenth Century to the Present*. London: Routledge.

Fitzgerald, Percy. 1891. *The History of Pickwick: An Account of its Characters, Localities, Allusions, and Illustrations*. London: Chapman & Hall.

Flanagan, Kerrie. 2010. "From Book to Big Screen: An Interview with Screenwriter Robin Swicord." *Wow* 39 (May-June). http://www.wow-womenonwriting.com/39-FE2-RobinSwicord.html.

Flanagan, Kevin. 2017. "Videogame Adaptation." In *The Oxford Handbook of Adaptation Studies*, edited by Thomas Leitch, 441–56. Oxford: Oxford University Press.

Fleming, Victor, director. 1939. *Gone with the Wind*. David O. Selznick, MGM US.

Foltz, Jonathan. 2017. *The Novel after Film: Modernism and the Decline of Autonomy*. Oxford: Oxford University Press.

Fortier, Mark. 1996. "Shakespeare as 'Minor Theater': Deleuze and Guattari and the Aims of Adaptation." *Mosaic* 29, no. 1 (Mar.): 1–18.

Fortier, Mark. 2014. "Beyond Adaptation." In *OuterSpeares: Shakespeare, Intermedia, and the Limits of Adaptation*, edited by Daniel Fischlin, 372–86. Toronto: University of Toronto Press.

Fortier, Mark. 2016. "Translation, Adaptation, 'Tradaption.'" In *The Cambridge Guide to the Worlds of Shakespeare*, edited by Bruce R. Smith and Katherine Rowe, 1046–50. Cambridge: Cambridge University Press.

Foucault, Michel. (1963) 2003. *The Birth of the Clinic: An Archaeology of Medical Perception*. Translated by A. M. Sheridan. London: Routledge.

Friedmann, Anthony. 2014. "The Problem of Adaptation." In *Writing for Visual Media*, 3rd ed., edited by Anthony Friedmann, 202–22. Oxford: Focal Press.

Frus, Phyllis, and Christy Williams, eds. 2010. *Beyond Adaptation: Essays on Radical Transformations of Original Works*. Jefferson, NC: McFarland Press.

Gambier, Yves, and Henrik Gottlieb, eds. 2001. *(Multi) Media Translation: Concepts, Practices, and Research*. Amsterdam: John Benjamins.

Garrick, David. 1750. *Romeo and Juliet. By Shakespear* [sic]. *With Alterations, and an Additional Scene: As It Is Performed at the Theatre-Royal in Drury Lane*. London: J. and R. Tonson and S. Draper.

Gaudreault, André, and Philippe Marion. 2018. "An Art of Borrowing: The Intermedial Sources of Adaptation." In *The Routledge Companion to Adaptation*, edited by Dennis Cutchins, Katja Krebs, and Eckart Voigts, 327–49. London: Routledge.

Geal, Robert. "Dialogism's Radical Texts and the Death of the Radical Vanguard Critic." 2018. In *The Routledge Companion to Adaptation*, edited by Dennis Cutchins, Katja Krebs, and Eckart Voigts, 80–86. London: Routledge.

Geal, Robert. 2019. *Anamorphic Authorship in Canonical Film Adaptation*. Palgrave Studies in Adaptation and Visual Culture. London: Palgrave Macmillan.

Geerts, Walter. 2017. "Adaptation as In-Depth Dialogue: The Cortázar-Antonioni Case Reconsidered." *Romance Studies* 35, no. 4: 260–70.

Gelder, Ken. 1999. "Jane Campion and the Limits of Literary Cinema." In *Adaptations: From Text to Screen, from Screen to Text*, edited by Deborah Cartmell and Imelda Whelehan, 157–71. London: Routledge.

Gelder, Ken, and Imelda Whelehan, eds. 2016. "Adapting Australia." Special issue, *Adaptation* 9, no. 1 (Mar.).

Genette, Gérard. (1982) 1997. *Palimpsests: Literature in the Second Degree*. Translated by Channa Newman and Claude Doubinsky. Lincoln: University of Nebraska Press.

Genette, Gérard. 1983. *Narrative Discourse: An Essay in Method*. Translated by Jane E. Lewin. Foreword by Jonathan Culler. Ithaca: Cornell University Press.

Genette, Gérard. 1992. *The Architext: An Introduction*. Translated by Jane E. Lewin. Berkeley: University of California Press.

Geraghty, Christine. 2008. *Now a Major Motion Picture: Film Adaptations of Literature and Drama*. Lanham, MD: Rowman and Littlefield.

Geraghty, Christine. 2012. *Bleak House*. BFI TV Classics. London: Bloomsbury.

Gerard, Alexander. 1774. *An Essay on Genius*. London: W. Strahan; T. Cadell.

Giannakopoulou, Vasso, and Deborah Cartmell, eds. "Intersemiotic Translation as Adaptation," special issue, *Adaptation* 12, no. 3 (Dec.).

Giannetti, Louis D. 1975. *Godard and Others: Essays on Film Form*. Madison, NJ: Fairleigh Dickinson University Press.

Gibson, Pamela Church. 2004. "Otherness, Transgression and the Postcolonial Perspective: Patricia Rozema's *Mansfield Park*." In *Janespotting and Beyond: British Heritage Retrovisions since the Mid-1990s*, edited by Eckart Voigts-Virchow, 51–63. Tübingen: Gunter Narr Verlag.

Giddings, Robert, Keith Selby, and Chris Wensley. 1990. *Screening the Novel: The Theory and Practice of Literary Dramatization*. London: Macmillan.

Giddings, Robert, and Erica Sheen, eds. 2000. *The Classic Novel: From Page to Screen*. Manchester: Manchester University Press.

Gifford, James. 2012. "Dramatic Text, Music Text: Competing Nationalist Styles in Restoration Opera." *Interdisciplinary Literary Studies* 14, no. 1: 21–37.

Godwin, William. 1824. *Fables Ancient and Modern, Adapted for the Use of Children by Edward Baldwin, Esq.* 10th ed. London: M. J. Godwin & Co.

Goodman, Nelson. 1984. *Of Mind and Other Matters*. Cambridge, MA: Harvard University Press.

Google Scholar. https://scholar.google.com.

Gordon, Richard A. 2009. *Cannibalizing the Colony: Cinematic Adaptations of Colonial Literature in Mexico and Brazil*. West Lafayette, IN: Purdue University Press.

Grafton, Anthony, Glenn W. Most, and Salvatore Settis, eds. 2010. *The Classical Tradition*. Cambridge, MA: The Belknap Press of Harvard University Press.

Graham, G. F. 1837. *First Steps to Latin Writing: A Practical Illustration and Companion to Latin Grammar, Intended for the Use of the Lower Classes and Adapted to the Youth of Both Sexes*. London: A. H. Baily & Co.

Gratch, Lyndsay Michalik. 2017. *Adaptation Online: Creating Memes, Sweding Movies, and Other Digital Performances*. New York: Lexington Books.

Greenberg, Clement. (1939) 1961. "Avant-Garde and Kitsch." In *Art and Culture: Critical Essays*, 3–21. Boston: Beacon Press.

Greene, Edward Burnaby. 1763. *The Satires of Juvenal Paraphrastically Imitated, and Adapted to the Times*. London: J. Ridley.

Greenwood, James. 1869. *The Seven Curses of London*. Boston: Fields, Osgood & Co.

Grene, Marjorie, and David Depew. 2004. *The Philosophy of Biology: An Episodic History*. Cambridge: Cambridge University Press.

Griffith, James. 1997. *Adaptations as Imitations: Films from Novels*. Newark: University of Delaware Press.

Griffiths, Devin. 2016. *The Age of Analogy: Science and Literature between the Darwins*. Baltimore: Johns Hopkins University Press.

Griggs, Yvonne. 2016. *The Bloomsbury Introduction to Adaptation Studies: Adapting the Canon in Film, TV, Novels, and Popular Culture*. London: Bloomsbury Press.

Grossi, Paolo. 2010. *A History of European Law*. Translated by Laurence Hooper. Oxford: Wiley-Blackwell.

Grossman, Julie, and R. Barton Palmer, series eds. 2015–2020. *Palgrave Studies in Adaptation and Visual Culture* series. London: Palgrave Macmillan.

Grossman, Julie, and R. Barton Palmer, eds. 2017. *Adaptation in Visual Culture: Images, Texts, and Their Multiple Worlds*. London: Palgrave.

Grube, G. M. A. 1965. *The Greek and Roman Critics*. Indianapolis: Hackett Press.

Grusin, Richard, ed. 2015. *The Nonhuman Turn*. Minneapolis: University of Minnesota Press.

Guida, Fred. 2000. *A Christmas Carol and Its Adaptations: A Critical Examination of Dickens's Story and Its Productions on Screen and Television*. Jefferson, NC: McFarland Press.

Guzzetti, Alfred. 1973. "Christian Metz and the Semiology of the Cinema." *Journal of Modern Literature* 3, no. 2: 292–308.

H. 1836. "The Drama: Historically Considered in Reference to Its Moral and Intellectual Influence on Society." *The Knickerbocker: Or, New York Monthly Magazine* 7 (Jan. 1): 7–12.

Hagberg, Garry L., and Walter Jost, eds. 2010. *A Companion to the Philosophy of Literature*. Oxford: Wiley-Blackwell.

Halliwell, Martin. 2007. "Modernism and Adaptation." In *The Cambridge Companion to Literature on Screen*, edited by Deborah Cartmell and Imelda Whelehan, 90–106. Cambridge: Cambridge University Press.

Hand, Richard. 2012. "Adaptation and Modernism." In *A Companion to Literature, Film, and Adaptation*, edited by Deborah Cartmell, 52–69. Oxford: Wiley-Blackwell Press.

Handa, Carolyn. 2014. *The Mulitmediated Rhetoric of the Internet: Digital Fusion*. Routledge Studies in Rhetoric and Communication. New York: Routledge.

Hankin, Kelly. 2009. "Adapting Lesbians: Maria Maggenti and the Practice of Lesbian Screenwriting." *Adaptation* 2, no. 2 (Sep.): 110–24.

Hansard's Parliamentary Debates: Third Series, Commencing with the Accession of William IV. 1831. Vol. 13 (May 24–July 3). London: Hansard.

Hansard's Parliamentary Debates: Third Series, Commencing with the Accession of William IV. 1866. Vol. 184 (June 8–Aug.10). London: Cornelius Buck.

Hansen, Miriam. 1991. *Babel and Babylon: Spectatorship in American Silent Film*. Cambridge, MA: Harvard University Press.

Hardy, Philip Dixon, ed. 1832. "The Age of Brass." *The Dublin Penny Journal* 1, no. 1 (June 20): 3.

Harrington, John, ed. 1977. *Film and/as Literature*. Englewood Cliffs, NJ: Prentice-Hall.

Harte, Walter. 1764. *Essays on Husbandry*. London: W. Frederick.

Hasenfratz, Bob, and Greg M. Colón Semenza, series eds. 2015–19. *The History of World Literatures on Film* series. London: Bloomsbury Press.

Hassan, Ihab Habib. 2001. "From Postmodernism to Postmodernity: The Local/Global Context." *Philosophy and Literature* 25, no. 1 (April): 1–13.

Hassler-Forrest, Dan, and Pascal Nicklas, eds. 2015. *The Politics of Adaptation: Media Convergence and Ideology*. London: Palgrave Macmillan.

Hausman, Daniel M. 2008. *The Philosophy of Economics: An Anthology*. 3rd ed. Cambridge: Cambridge University Press.

Hawkes, Terence. (1972) 2017. *Metaphor*. London: Routledge.

Hayles, N. Katherine. 2013. "Traumas of Code." In *Critical Digital Studies: A Reader*, 2nd ed., edited by Arthur Kroker and Marilouise Kroker, 39–58. Toronto: University of Toronto Press.

Hayton, Natalie. 2011. "Unconscious Adaptation: *Hard Candy* as *Little Red Riding Hood*." *Adaptation* 4, no. 1 (Mar.): 38–54.

Haywood, Ian. 2004. *The Revolution in Popular Literature: Print, Politics, and the People, 1790–1860*. Cambridge: Cambridge University Press.

Heinzelman, Kurt. 2003. "'Make It New': The Rise of an Idea." In *Make It New: The Rise of Modernism*, edited by Kurt Heinzelman, 131–34. Austin: University of Texas Press.

Heath, Stephen. 1981. *Questions of Cinema*. Bloomington: Indiana University Press.

Helman, Alicja, and Waclaw M. Osadnik. 1996. "Film and Literature: Historical Models of Film Adaptation and a Proposal for a (Poly)System Approach." *Canadian Review of Comparative Literature* 23, no. 3 (Sep.): 645–57.

Hermansson, Casie. 2015. "Flogging Fidelity: In Defense of the (Un)Dead Horse 1." *Adaptation* 8, no. 2 (Aug.): 147–60.

Hermansson, Casie, and Janet Zepernick, eds. 2018. *Where Is Adaptation? Mapping Cultures, Texts, and Contexts*. Amsterdam: John Benjamins.

Herrmann, Vanessa. 2018. "Adaptation as City Branding: The Case of Dexter and Miami." In *Where Is Adaptation? Mapping Cultures, Texts, and Contexts*, edited by Casie Hermansson and Janet Zepernick, 71–86. Amsterdam: John Benjamins.

Higson, Andrew. 2003. *English Heritage, English Cinema: Costume Drama since 1980*. Oxford: Oxford University Press.

Higson, Andrew. 2004. "English Heritage, English Literature, English Cinema: Selling Jane Austen to Movie Audiences in the 1990s." In *Janespotting and Beyond: British Heritage Retrovisions since the Mid-1990s*, edited by Eckart Voigts-Virchow, 35–50. Tübingen: Gunter Narr Verlag.

Higson, Andrew. 2006. "Fiction and the Film Industry." In *A Concise Companion to Contemporary British Fiction*, edited by James F. English, 58–82. Oxford: Blackwell Publishing.

Hodgkins, John. 2013. *The Drift: Affect, Adaptation and New Perspectives on Fidelity*. London: Bloomsbury Press.

Hollander, John. 1984. *The Figure of Echo: A Mode of Allusion in Milton and After*. Berkeley: University of California Press.

Hooker, Richard. (1636) 1821. *The Works of Mr. Richard Hooker, in Eight Books, of the Laws of Ecclesiastical Polity, with Several Other Treatises and a General Index*. 3 vols. London: W. Clarke.

Hopkins, David. 2000. "Classical Translation and Imitation." In *A Companion to Literature from Milton to Blake*, edited by David Womersley, 76–93. Oxford: Blackwell Publishing.

Hopton, Tricia, Adam Atkinson, Jane Stadler, and Peta Mitchell, eds. 2011. *Pockets of Change: Adaptations and Cultural Transitions.* Plymouth: Lexington Books.

Horton, Andrew, and Joan Magretta, eds. 1981. *Modern European Film-Makers and the Art of Adaptation.* New York: Frederick Ungar.

Horwatt, Eli. 2009. "A Taxonomy of Digital Video Remixing: Contemporary Found Footage on the Internet." In *Cultural Borrowings: Appropriation, Reworking, Transformation,* edited by Iain Robert Smith, 76–91. N.p.: Scope ebook.

Hunter, Madeline. 2018. "Bric[k]olage: Adaptation as Play in *The Lego Movie* (2014)." *Adaptation* 11, no. 3 (Dec.): 273–81.

Hurd, Richard. 1757. *A Letter to Mr. Mason; On the Marks of Imitation.* Cambridge: Thurlbourn and Woodyer.

Hurst, Rochelle. 2008. "Adaptation as an Undecidable: Fidelity and Binarity from Bluestone to Derrida." In *In/fidelity: Essays on Film Adaptation,* edited by David L. Kranz, and Nancy Mellerski, 172–96. Newcastle: Cambridge Scholars.

Hutcheon, Linda. 1985. *A Theory of Parody: The Teachings of Twentieth-Century Art Forms.* New York: Methuen.

Hutcheon, Linda. 1988. *A Poetics of Postmodernism: History, Theory, Fiction.* New York: Routledge.

Hutcheon, Linda. 2006. *A Theory of Adaptation.* 1st ed. London: Routledge.

Hutcheon, Linda. 2007. "In Defence of Literary Adaptation as Cultural Production." *Journal of Media and Culture* 10, no. 2 (May). http://journal.media-culture.org.au/0705/01-hutcheon.php.

Hutcheon, Linda. 2012. *A Theory of Adaptation.* 2nd ed. London: Routledge.

Hutcheon, Linda, and Michael Hutcheon. 2017a. "*Literature/Film Quarterly* Contribution to Roundtable Discussion." *Literature/Film Quarterly* 45, no. 2. http://www.salisbury.edu/lfq/_issues/first/lfq_contribution_to_roundtable.html.

Hutcheon, Linda, and Michael Hutcheon. 2017b. "Adaptation and Opera." In *The Oxford Handbook of Adaptation Studies,* edited by Thomas Leitch, 305–23. New York: Oxford University Press.

Inkster, Ian, ed. 2004–2012. *History of Technology.* 34 vols. London: Bloomsbury.

Ireland Commissioners of National Education. 1835. *Sacred Poetry Adapted to the Understanding of Children and Youth.* Dublin: P. D. Hardy.

J. V. P. 1860. "The Dramatic and Musical World of London." *Bailey's Magazine* 1 (Aug.): 369–76.

Jackson, S. B. 2013. "Is the Book Always Better than the Movie?" Yahoo! Books. 6 June. http://voices.yahoo.com/is-book-always-better-than-movie-12171952.html?cat=38.

Jakobson, Roman, and Morris Halle. 1956. "Two Aspects of Language and Two Types of Aphasic Disturbances." *Fundamentals of Language,* by Roman Jakobson and Morris Halle, 55–82. The Hague: Mouton.

Jakobson, Roman, and Morris Halle. 1956. "The Metaphoric and Metonymic Poles." *Fundamentals of Language,* by Roman Jakobson and Morris Halle, 90–96. The Hague: Mouton.

James, V. C. 1870. "Wood v. Chart. 27, 29 April 1870." *The Law Journal Reports* 39: 641–43.

Jameson, Fredric. 1991. *Postmodernism: or, The Cultural Logic of Late Capitalism.* Durham, NC: Duke University Press.

Jameson, Fredric. 2011. "Afterword: Adaptation as a Philosophical Problem." In *True to the Spirit: Film Adaptation and the Question of Fidelity,* edited by Colin MacCabe, Rick Warner, and Kathleen Murray, 215–33. Oxford: Oxford University Press.

Jane Austen Today. "Two Interviews with Patricia Rozema, Director of Mansfield Park." May 27, 2010. http://janitesonthejames.blogspot.com/2010/05/two-interviews-with-patricia-rozema.html.

Janson, H. W. (1981) 2001. *History of Art: The Western Tradition.* 6th ed. New York: Prentice-Hall.

Jarrold, Julian, director. 2007. Becoming Jane. Graham Broadbent, Robert Bernstein, and Douglas Rae, Miramax Films.

Jeffers, Jennifer. 2011. *Britain Colonized: Hollywood's Appropriation of British Literature.* London: Palgrave Macmillan.

Jeffrey, David L. 2017. *In the Beauty of Holiness: Art and the Bible in Western Culture.* Grand Rapids, MI: William B. Eerdmans Publishing Co.

Jellenik, Glenn. 2017a. "On the Origins of Adaptation, as Such: The Birth of a Simple Abstraction." In *The Oxford Handbook of Adaptation Studies,* edited by Thomas Leitch, 37–52. New York: Oxford University Press.

Jellenik, Glenn. 2017b. "The Task of the Adaptation Critic." In *Adaptation in Visual Culture: Images, Texts, and Their Multiple Worlds,* edited by Julie Grossman and R. Barton Palmer, 37–52. Palgrave Studies in Adaptation and Visual Culture. London: Palgrave.

Jellenik, Glenn. 2018. "Adaptation's Originality Problem: Grappling with the Thorny Questions of What Constitutes Originality." In *The Routledge Companion to Adaptation,* edited by Dennis Cutchins, Katja Krebs, and Eckart Voigts, 182–93. London: Routledge.

Jenkins, Greg. 1997. *Stanley Kubrick and the Art of Adaptation: Three Novels, Three Films.* Jefferson, NC: McFarland Press.

Jenkins, Henry. 2006. *Convergence Culture: Where Old and New Media Collide.* New York: New York University Press.

Jess-Cooke, Carolyn. 2009. *Film Sequels: Theory and Practice from Hollywood to Bollywood.* Edinburgh: Edinburgh University Press.

Jinks, William. 1971. *The Celluloid Literature: Film in the Humanities.* Beverly Hills: Glencoe Press.

Johnson, Barbara. 1984. "Metaphor, Metonymy and Voice in Zora Neale Hurston's *Their Eyes Were Watching God.*" In *Black Literature and Literary Theory,* edited by Henry Louis Gates, Jr., 205–19. New York: Methuen.

Johnson, David T. 2011. "Windows onto Disciplines." Review of *True to the Spirit: Film Adaptation and the Question of Fidelity. Literature/Film Quarterly* 39, no. 3: 162–64.

Johnson, David T. 2017. "Adaptation and Fidelity." In *The Oxford Handbook of Adaptation Studies,* edited by Thomas Leitch, 87–100. New York: Oxford University Press.

Johnson, Mark. 2008. "Philosophy's Debt to Metaphor." In *The Cambridge Handbook of Metaphor and Thought,* edited by Raymond W. Gibbs, Jr., 39–52. Cambridge: Cambridge University Press.

Johnson, Samuel. (1755) 1812. *A Dictionary of the English Language.* London: A. Wilson.

Johnson, Samuel. (1781) 1830. "Life of Alexander Pope, Esq." In *The Poetical Works of Alexander Pope.* Philadelphia: J. J. Woodward. iii–xlii.

Jones, Doris Arthur. 1930. *Taking the Curtain Call: The Life and Letters of Henry Arthur Jones.* New York: Macmillan.

Jonze, Spike, director. 2002. Adaptation. Jonathan Demme, Vincent Landay, Edward Saxon. Sony Pictures.

Jonson, Ben. 1623. "To the Memory of My Beloved, the Author, Mr. William Shakespeare." In *Mr. William Shakepeares* [sic] *Comedies, Histories, & Tragedies*, edited by John Heminge and Henry Condell. London: Isaac Jaggard and Ed Blount.

Kames, Henry Home, Lord. (1762) 1785. *Elements of Criticism*. 6th ed. 3 vols. Edinburgh: John Bell and William Creech.

Kane, Michael. 1999. *Modern Men: Mapping Masculinity in English and German Literature, 1880–1930*. London: Bloomsbury.

Kant, Immanuel. (1790) 2000. *Critique of the Power of Judgment*. Translated by Eric Matthews, edited and translated by Paul Guyer. Cambridge: Cambridge University Press.

Kaplan, David M. 2009. *Readings in the Philosophy of Technology*. 2nd ed. New York: Rowman & Littlefield.

Kauffman, Stuart. 1993. *The Origins of Order: Self Organization and Selection in Evolution*. New York: Oxford University Press.

Kaye, Heidi. 1996. "Feminist Sympathies vs. Masculine Backlash: Kenneth Branagh's Mary Shelley's Frankenstein." In *Pulping Fictions: Consuming Culture across the Literature/Media Divide*, edited by Deborah Cartmell, I. Q. Hunter, Heidi Kaye, and Imelda Whelehan, 57–72. London: Pluto Press.

Kaye, Phillip, Raymond Laflamme, and Michele Mosca. 2007. *An Introduction to Quantum Computing*. Oxford: Oxford University Press.

Keeley, Brian L. 2002. "Making Sense of the Senses: Individuating Modalities in Humans and Other Animals." *The Journal of Philosophy* 99, no. 1: 5–28.

Kelly, Douglas. 1978. *Medieval Imagination: Rhetoric and the Poetry of Courtly Love*. Madison: University of Wisconsin Press.

Kennedy, George A. 1994. *A New History of Classical Rhetoric*. Princeton: Princeton University Press.

Kennedy-Karpat, Colleen, and Eric Sandberg, eds. 2017. *Adaptation, Awards Culture, and the Value of Prestige*. Palgrave Studies in Adaptation and Visual Culture. London: Palgrave Macmillan.

Kenner, Hugh. 1972. *The Pound Era*. Los Angeles: UCLA Press.

Kidnie, Margaret Jane. 2009. *Shakespeare and the Problem of Adaptation: Forms of Possibility*. London: Routledge.

Kilbourne, Frederick Wilkinson. 1906. *Alterations and Adaptations of Shakespeare*. Boston: Poet Lore.

Klein, Michael, and Gillian Parker. 1981. "Introduction." In *The English Novel and the Movies*, edited by Michael Klein and Gillian Parker, 1–13. New York: Frederick Ungar.

Kline, Karen E. 1996. "*The Accidental Tourist* on Page and on Screen: Interrogating Normative Theories about Film Adaptation." *Literature/Film Quarterly* 24, no. 1: 70–83.

Koff, Leonard Michael. 2018. "Adaptation as Translation: A Fifteenth-Century Chaucerian Case." *The Medieval Translator* 14: 395–409.

Kousser, Rachel. 2015. "Adapting Greek Art." In *A Companion to Roman Art*, edited by Barbara E. Borg, 114–29. Hoboken, NJ: Wiley-Blackwell.

Kracauer, Siegfried. 1960. "Interlude: Film and Novel." In *Theory of Film: The Redemption of Physical Reality*, 232–44. Oxford: Oxford University Press.

Krämer, Lucia. 2017. "Adaptation in Bollywood." In *The Oxford Handbook of Adaptation Studies*, edited by Thomas Leitch, 251–67. Oxford: Oxford University Press.

Krämer, Peter. 2015. "Adaptation as Exploration: Stanley Kubrick, Literature, and *A. I. Artificial Intelligence*." *Adaptation* 8, no. 3 (Dec.): 372–82.

Kranz, David L., and Nancy Mellerski, eds. 2008. *In/fidelity: Essays on Film Adaptation*. Newcastle: Cambridge Scholars.

Krasilovsky, Alexis. 2018. *Great Adaptations: Screenwriting and Global Storytelling*. New York: Routledge.

Krebs, Katja. 2012. "Translation and Adaptation: Two Sides of an Ideological Coin?" In *Translation, Adaptation, and Transformation*, edited by Laurence Raw, 42–53. New York: Continuum.

Krebs, Katja. 2013. "Introduction: Collisions, Diversions, and Meeting Points." In *Translation and Adaptation in Theatre and Film*, edited by Katja Krebs, 1–10. London: Routledge.

Krebs, Katja. 2018. "Adapting Identities: Performing the Self." In *The Routledge Companion to Adaptation*, edited by Dennis Cutchins, Katja Krebs, and Eckart Voigts, 207–17. London: Routledge.

Krings, Matthias. 2015. *African Appropriations: Cultural Difference, Mimesis, and Media*. Bloomington: Indiana University Press.

Kuhn, Thomas S. 1962. *The Structure of Scientific Revolutions*. Chicago: University of Chicago Press.

Lacan, Jacques. 1992. *The Ethics of Psychoanalysis 1959-1960: The Seminar of Jacques Lacan*. Edited by Jacques-Alain Miller. Translated by Dennis Potter. Book VII. London: Routledge.

Laera, Margherita, ed. 2014. *Theatre and Adaptation: Return, Rewrite, Repeat*. London: Bloomsbury Press.

Lakoff, George, and Mark Johnson. 1980. *Metaphors We Live By*. Chicago: University of Chicago Press.

Lakoff, George, and Mark Johnson. 1999. *Philosophy in the Flesh: The Embodied Mind and Its Challenge to Western Thought*. New York: Basic Books.

Lamb, Charles, and Mary Lamb. 1807. *Tales from Shakespeare. Designed for the Use of Young Persons*. 2 vols. London: Thomas Hodgkins.

Lanzi, Luigi Antonio. 1831. *History of Painting in Upper and Lower Italy*. Translated by G. W. D. Evans. 2 vols. London: J. Hatchard & Son.

Lardner, Dionysius. 1838. *The Cabinet Cyclopaedia*. London: Longman.

Larson, Randall D. 1995. *Films into Books: An Analytical Bibliography of Film Novelizations, Movies, and TV Tie-Ins*. Metuchen, NJ: Scarecrow Press.

Larsson, Donald F. 1982. "Novel into Film: Some Preliminary Reconsiderations." In *Transformations in Literature and Film: Selected Papers from the Sixth Annual Florida State University Conference on Literature and Film*, edited by Leon Golden, 69–83. Tallahassee: University Press of Florida.

Latour, Bruno. 1988. *The Pasteurization of France*. Translated by Alan Sheridan and John Law. Cambridge, MA: Harvard University Press.

Laudér, William. 1750. *An Essay on Milton's Use and Imitation of the Moderns in his Paradise Lost*. London: J. Payne and J. Bouquet.

Lauriat, Barbara. 2009. "Charles Reade's Roles in the Drama of Victorian Dramatic Copyright." *Columbia Journal of Law and the Arts* 33, no. 1: 1–35.

Le Page, Michael. 2008. "Evolution Myths: Everything Is an Adaptation." *New Scientist* April 16. https://www.newscientist.com/article/dn13615-evolution-myths-everything-is-an-adaptation/.

Lee, Klaudia. 2016. "Audience Response and from Film Adaptation to Reading Literature." *Comparative Literature and Culture* 18, no. 2 (June): 1–6.

Lee, Sung-Ae, Fengxia Tan, and John Stephens. 2017. "Film Adaptation, Global Film Techniques, and Cross-Cultural Viewing." *International Research in Children's Literature* 10, no. 1 (July): 1–19.

Leff, Leonard J., and Jerold L. Simmons. 2001. *The Dame in the Kimono: Hollywood, Censorship, and the Production Code.* 2nd ed. Lexington: University Press of Kentucky.

Leitch, Thomas. 2003a. "Twelve Fallacies in Contemporary Adaptation Theory." *Criticism* 45, no. 2 (Spring): 149–71.

Leitch, Thomas. 2003b. "Where Are We Going, Where Have We Been?" *LFA News* 1, no. 1 (Sep.): 2, 6, 8.

Leitch, Thomas. 2005. "Everything You Always Wanted to Know about Adaptation Especially If You're Looking Forwards Rather than Back." *Literature/Film Quarterly* 33, no. 3: 233–45.

Leitch, Thomas. 2007. *Film Adaptation and Its Discontents: From* Gone with the Wind *to* The Passion of the Christ. Baltimore: Johns Hopkins University Press.

Leitch, Thomas. 2008a. "Adaptation, the Genre." *Adaptation* 1, no. 2: 106–20.

Leitch, Thomas. 2008b. "Adaptation Studies at a Crossroads." *Adaptation* 1, no. 1: 63–77.

Leitch, Thomas. 2009. "To Adapt or to Adapt to? Consequences of Approaching Film Adaptation Intransitively." *Studia Filmoznawcze* 30: 91–103.

Leitch, Thomas. 2010. "Adaptation and/as/or Postmodernism." *Literature/Film Quarterly* 28, no. 3: 244–46.

Leitch, Thomas. 2011. "Vampire Adaptation." *Journal of Adaptation in Film & Performance* 4, no. 1: 5–16.

Leitch, Thomas. 2012a. "Adaptation and Intertextuality, or, What Isn't an Adaptation, and Does It Matter?" In *A Companion to Literature, Film, and Adaptation*, edited by Deborah Cartmell, 85–104. Oxford: Wiley-Blackwell Press.

Leitch, Thomas. 2012b. "Is Adaptation Studies a Discipline?" *Germanistik in Ireland* 7: 13–26.

Leitch, Thomas. 2013a. "'New! Expanded! Unimproved!' Review of *A Theory of Adaptation*, by Linda Hutcheon, 2nd ed." *Literature/Film Quarterly* 41, no. 2: 157–60.

Leitch, Thomas. 2013b. "What Movies Want." In *Adaptation Studies: New Challenges, New Directions*, edited by Jørgen Bruhn, Anne Gjelsvik, and Eirik Frisvold Hanssen, 155–76. London: Bloomsbury Press.

Leitch, Thomas. 2015. "History as Adaptation." In *The Politics of Adaptation: New Media Convergence and Ideology*, edited by Dan Hassler-Forest and Pascal Nicklas, 7–20. London: Palgrave Macmillan.

Leitch, Thomas, ed. 2017a. *The Oxford Handbook of Adaptation Studies.* New York: Oxford University Press.

Leitch, Thomas. 2017b. "Introduction." In *The Oxford Handbook of Adaptation Studies*, edited by Thomas Leitch, 1–20. New York: Oxford University Press.

Leitch, Thomas. 2017c. "Against Conclusions: Petit Theories and Adaptation Studies." In *The Oxford Handbook of Adaptation Studies*, edited by Thomas Leitch, 698–709. New York: Oxford University Press.

Leitch, Thomas. 2018. "Not Just the Facts: Adaptation, Illustration, and History." In *The Routledge Companion to Adaptation*, edited by Dennis Cutchins, Katja Krebs, and Eckart Voigts, 67–79. London: Routledge.

Leitch, Thomas. 2019. *The History of American Literature on Film.* London: Bloomsbury Press.

Leitch, Thomas, and Patrick Cattrysse. 2018. "A Dialogue on Adaptation." *Literature/Film Quarterly* 46, no. 3. http://www.salisbury.edu/lfq/_issues/46_3/a_dialogue_on_adaptation.html.

Leitch, Vincent B. 2014. *Literary Criticism in the 21st Century: Theory Renaissance.* London: Bloomsbury Press.

Leitch, Vincent B., and Nicholas Ruiz III. 2005. "Theory, Interdisciplinarity, and the Humanities Today. An Interview with Vincent B. Leitch." InterCulture 2 (May). http://www.fsu.edu/_proghum/interculture/homepage20Interview.htm.

Lellis, George, and H. Philip Bolton. 1981. "Pride but No Prejudice." In *The English Novel and the Movies*, edited by Michael Klein and Gillian Parker, 44–51. New York: Ungar.

Lentz, Rex A. 2002. *An Abridged History of World Religions.* New York: Writer's Showcase.

Lessing, Gotthold Ephraim. (1766) 1962. *Laocoön: An Essay upon the Limits of Painting and Poetry.* Translated by Edward Allen McCormick. Indianapolis: Bobbs-Merrill.

Lev, Peter. 2003. "The Future of Adaptation Studies." *LFA News* 1, no. 1 (Sep.): 7.

Lev, Peter. 2017. "How to Write Adaptation History." In *The Oxford Handbook of Adaptation Studies*, edited by Thomas Leitch, 661–78. Oxford: Oxford University Press.

Levenson, Michael. (1999) 2011. "Introduction." In *The Cambridge Companion to Modernism*, 2nd ed., edited by Michael Levenson, 1–8. Cambridge: Cambridge University Press.

Lewis, Pericles. (2007) 2011. "Modernism and Religion." In *The Cambridge Introduction to Modernism*, 2nd ed., edited by Michael Levenson, 178–96. Cambridge: Cambridge University Press.

Lewis, Wyndham, ed. 1914. "Long Live the Vortex!" *Blast* 1 (June 20): 7. London: John Lane.

Ley, Graham. 2009. "'Discursive Embodiment': The Theatre as Adaptation." *Journal of Adaptation in Film & Performance* 2, no. 3: 201–9.

Lhermitte, Corinne. 2004. "Adaptation as Rewriting: Evolution of a Concept." *Revue LISA e-journal* 2, no. 5: 26–44. https://journals.openedition.org/lisa/2897.

Lindsay, Vachel. (1915) 1922. *The Art of the Moving Picture.* rev. ed. New York: Macmillan.

Lipking, Lawrence I. 1970. *Ordering of the Arts in Eighteenth-Century England.* Princeton: Princeton University Press.

(Litchfield, John?). 1796. *Remarks on Mr. Colman's Preface; also a Summary Comparison of the Play of The Iron Chest with the Novel of Caleb Williams.* London: Miller.

Little, Daniel. 2010. *New Contributions to the Philosophy of History.* New York: Springer.

Lofgren, Erik R. 2016. "Adapting Female Agency: Rape in *The Outrage* and *Rashōmon.*" *Adaptation* 9, no. 3 (Dec.): 284–306.

Loock, Kathleen, and Constantine Verevis, eds. 2012. *Film Remakes, Adaptations and Fan Productions: Remake/Remodel.* London: Palgrave Macmillan.

Low, Linda. 2000. *Economics of Information Technology and the Media.* Singapore: Singapore University Press.

Luhr, William, and Peter Lehman. 1977. *Authorship and Narrative in the Cinema: Issues in Contemporary Aesthetics and Criticism.* New York: Putnam.

Lukács, Georg. (1914–1915) 1971. *The Theory of the Novel: A Historico-Philosophical Essay on the Forms of Great Epic Literature.* Translated by Anna Bostock. Cambridge, MA: MIT Press.

Lyotard, Jean-François. 1979. *The Postmodern Condition: A Report on Knowledge.* Minneapolis: University of Minnesota Press.

MacCabe, Colin. 2011. "Introduction. Bazinian Adaptation: *The Butcher Boy* as Example." In *True to the Spirit: Film Adaptation and the Question of Fidelity*, edited by Colin MacCabe, Rick Warner, and Kathleen Murray, 3–25. Oxford: Oxford University Press.

MacCabe, Colin, Rick Warner, and Kathleen Murray, eds. 2011. *True to the Spirit: Film Adaptation and the Question of Fidelity*. Oxford: Oxford University Press.

Macdonald, Robert. 1835. *French Cookery, Adapted to English Tastes and English Pockets*. London: Gadsden & Percival.

MacFarlane, Robert. 2007. *Original Copy: Plagiarism and Originality in Nineteenth-Century Literature*. Oxford: Oxford University Press.

Mackenzie, Robert Shelton. 1870. *Life of Charles Dickens*. Philadelphia: T. B. Peterson & Bros.

Madden, John, director. 1998. Shakespeare in Love. Harvey Weinstein and Marc Norman, Miramax Films.

Magny, Claude-Edmonde. 1948. *L'Age Du Roman American*. Paris: Editions du Seuil. Translated by Eleanor Hochman in *The Age of the American Novel: The Film Aesthetic of Fiction between the Two Wars* (New York: Frederick Ungar, 1972).

Malina, Debra. 2002. *Breaking the Frame: Metalepsis and the Construction of the Subject*. Columbus, OH: Ohio State University Press.

Manovich, Lev. 2001. *The Language of New Media*. Cambridge, MA: MIT Press.

Manvell, Roger. 1979. *Theatre and Film: A Comparative Study of the Two Forms of Dramatic Art, and of the Problems of Adaptation of Stage Plays into Films*. Rutherford, NJ: Fairleigh Dickinson.

Marcsek-Fuchs, Maria. 2015. *Dance and British Literature: An Intermedial Encounter*. Leiden: Brill Rodopi Press.

Marcus, F. H. 1971. *Film and Literature: Contrasts in Media*. Scranton, PA: Chandler Publishing.

Margulis, Lynn, and Dorion Sagan. 2002. *Acquiring Genomes: A Theory of the Origins of Species*. New York: Basic Books.

Marlow, Christopher. 2009. "The Folding Text: Doctor Who, Adaptation and Fan Fiction." In *Adaptation in Contemporary Culture: Textual Infidelities*, edited by Rachel Carroll. London: Continuum. 46–60.

Marsden, Jean. 1995. *The Re-Imagined Text: Shakespeare, Adaptation, and Eighteenth-Century Literary Theory*. Lexington: University of Kentucky Press.

Marsh, Huw. 2011. "Adaptation of a Murder/Murder as Adaptation: The Parker-Hulme Case in Angela Carter's 'The Christchurch Murder' and Peter Jackson's 'Heavenly Creatures'." *Adaptation* 4, no. 2: 167–79.

Marsh, Joss, and Kamilla Elliott. 2005. "The Victorian Novel in Film and on Television." In *The Blackwell Companion to the Victorian Novel*, edited by Patrick Brantlinger and William B. Thesing, 458–77. Oxford: Blackwell Publishing.

Martin, Cathlena. 2009. "Charlotte's Website: Media Transformation and the Intertextual Web of Children's Culture." In *Adaptation in Contemporary Culture: Textual Infidelities*, edited by Rachel Carroll, 85–95. London: Continuum.

Maskelyne, Edmund Story. 1868. "Wood v. Boosey and Another." 3–4 Feb. *The Law Journal Reports for the Year 1868: Cases Argued and Determined in the Court of Queen's Bench and in the Exchequer Chamber on Error and on Appeal from the Queen's Bench*. Vol. 37, edited by Mongtagu [sic] Chambers, 84–88. London: Edward Bret Ince.

Masson, David, ed. 1874. *The Poetical Works of John Milton*. Vol. 3. London: Macmillan.

Mathews, Charles James. 1852. *Letter from Mr. Charles Mathews to the Dramatic Authors of France*. Translated by Charles James Mathews. London: J. Mitchell.

Matthews, James Brander. 1894. *Studies of the Stage*. New York: Harper & Bros.

Mayer, S. R. T. 1866. Letter to the editors. 17 Dec. 1866. *Athenaeum* 2, no. 2043 (22 Dec.): 841.

McCaffrey, Donald W. 1967. "Adaptation Problems in Two Unique Media: The Novel and the Film." *The Dickinson Review* 1: 11–17.

McDougal, Stuart Y. 1985. *Made into Movies: From Literature to Film*. New York: Rinehart & Winston.

McFarlane, Brian. 1996. *Novel to Film: An Introduction to the Theory of Adaptation*. Oxford: Clarendon Press.

McFarlane, Brian. 2007. "Reading Film and Literature." In *The Cambridge Companion to Literature on Screen*, edited by Deborah Cartmell and Imelda Whelehan, 15–28. Cambridge: Cambridge University Press.

McGann, Jerome. 1983. *The Romantic Ideology: A Critical Investigation*. Chicago: University of Chicago Press.

McKechnie, Kara. 2009. "*Gloriana*—The Queen's Two Selves: Agency, Context, and Adaptation Studies." In *Adaptations: Performing across Media and Genres*, edited by Monika Pietrzak-Franger and Eckart Voigts-Virchow, 193–209. Contemporary Drama in English 16. Trier: Wissenschlaftlicher Verlag Trier.

McKee, Robert. 1997. "The Problem of Adaptation." In *Story: Style, Structure, Substance, and the Principles of Screenwriting*, 364–70. New York: HarperCollins.

McLuhan, Marshall. 1970. "Education in the Electronic Age." *Interchange* 1, no. 4: 1–12.

Meikle, Kyle. 2013. "Rematerializing Adaptation Theory." *Literature/Film Quarterly* 41, no. 3: 174–83.

Meikle, Kyle. 2017. "A Theory of Adaptation Audiences." *Literature/Film Quarterly* 45, no. 4. http://www.salisbury.edu/lfq/_issues/45_4/a_theory_of_adaptation_audiences.html.

Meikle, Kyle. 2019a. *Adaptations in the Franchise Era: 2001–16*. London: Bloomsbury Press.

Meikle, Kyle. 2019b. "Is Adaptation Sustainable?" Presented at the 13th Annual Association of Adaptation Studies Conference, "Adaptation and Modernisms: Establishing and Dismantling Borders in Adaptation Practice and Theory," University of Masaryk, September 19.

Meisel, Martin. 1983. *Realizations: Narrative, Pictorial, and Theatrical Arts in Nineteenth-Century England*. Princeton: Princeton University Press.

Mellet, Laurent. 2011. "From Defining to Categorising: A History of Film Adaptation Theory." *Interfaces: Image—Texte—Language* 32: 99–110.

Mendel, Johann Gregor. 1865 [1866]. "Versuche über Pflanzen-Hybriden" [Experiments Concerning Plant Hybrids]. In *Verhandlungen des naturforschenden Vereines in Brünn* [Proceedings of the Natural History Society of Brünn] IV (1865): 3–47.

Menon, Madhavi. 2004. *Wanton Words: Rhetoric and Sexuality in English Renaissance Drama*. Toronto: University of Toronto Press.

Messier, Vartan. 2014. "Desire and the 'Deconstructionist': Adaptation as Writerly Praxis." *Journal of Adaptation in Film & Performance* 7, no. 1: 65–82.

Metz, Christian. (1974) 1991. *Film Language: A Semiotics of the Cinema*. Translated by Michael Taylor. New York: Oxford University Press.

Metz, Christian. (1975) 1977. *The Imaginary Signifier: Psychoanalysis and the Cinema*. Translated by Celia Britton, Annwyl Williams, Ben Brewster, and Alfred Guzzetti. Bloomington: Indiana University Press.

Michaels, Lloyd. 1998. Review of James Griffith, Adaptations as Imitations: Films from Novels and Brian McFarlane, Novel to Film: An Introduction to the Theory of Adaptation. Screen 39, no. 4 (Winter): 425–32.

Mill, John Stuart. 1846. "Resemblance." In A System of Logic, Ratiocinative and Inductive; Being a Connected View of the Principles of Evidence and the Methods of Scientific Investigation, 46–47. New York: Harper & Brothers.

Millar v. Tayler, London. (1769) 4 Burr. 2303, 98 ER 201. Accessed February 3, 2017. http://www.commonlii.org/uk/cases/EngR/1769/44.pdf.

Miller, Jonathan. 1986. Subsequent Performances. London: Faber.

Milton, John. 2009. "Between the Cat and the Devil: Adaptation Studies and Translation Studies." Journal of Adaptation in Film & Performance 2, no. 1 (May): 47–64.

Minier, Márta. 2013. "Definitions, Dyads, Triads and Other Points of Connection in Translation and Adaptation Discourse." In Translation and Adaptation in Theatre and Film, edited by Katja Krebs, 34–78. London: Routledge.

Mirmohamadi, Kylie. 2014. The Digital Afterlives of Jane Austen: Janeites at the Keyboard. New York: Palgrave Macmillan.

Mitchell, W. J. T. 1986. Iconology: Image, Text, Ideology. Chicago: University of Chicago Press.

Mitry, Jean. 1971. "Remarks on the Problem of Cinematic Adaptation." Midwest Modern Language Association Bulletin 4, no. 1: 1–9.

Mittell, Jason, and Todd McGowan. 2017. Narrative Theory and Adaptation. London: Bloomsbury Press.

Modern Language Association International Bibliography. n.d. EBSCO. https://www.ebsco.com/products/research-databases/mla-international-bibliography-full-text.

Modern Language Association, n.d. "Frequently Asked Questions." Accessed December 11, 2018. https://www.mla.org/Publications/MLA-International-Bibliography/Frequently-Asked-Questions.

Moeller, Hans-Bernhard, and George Lellis. 2002. Volker Schlöndorff's Cinema: Adaptation, Politics, and the "Movie-Appropriate." Carbondale: Southern Illinois University Press.

molivares. 2010. "The Key to Artistic Creativity: Synesthesia, the Mind's Metaphor." Serendip Studio. June 5. https://serendipstudio.org/exchange/molivares/key-artistic-creativity-synesthesia-mind's-metaphor.

Moore, Michael Ryan. 2010. "Adaptation and New Media." Adaptation 3, no. 2: 179–92.

Morris, Michael. 2006. An Introduction to the Philosophy of Language. Cambridge: Cambridge University Press.

Morrissette, Bruce. 1985. Novel and Film: Essays in Two Genres. Chicago: University of Chicago Press.

Morse, Ruth. 1991. Truth and Convention in the Middle Ages: Rhetoric, Representation, and Reality. Cambridge: Cambridge University Press.

Munslow, Alun. 2012. A History of History. London: Routledge.

Münsterberg, Hugo. (1916) 2002. The Photoplay: A Psychological Study and Other Writings, edited by Allan Langdale. London: Routledge.

Murray, Edward. 1973. "In Cold Blood: The Filmic Novel and the Problem of Adaptation." Literature/Film Quarterly 1, no. 2 (Spring): 132–37.

Murray, Michael J., and Michael C. Rea. 2008. An Introduction to the Philosophy of Religion. Cambridge: Cambridge University Press.

Murray, Simone. 2008. "Materializing Adaptation Theory: The Adaptation Industry." *Literature/Film Quarterly* 36, no. 1: 4–20.

Murray, Simone. 2012a. *The Adaptation Industry: The Cultural Economy of Contemporary Literary Adaptation.* London: Routledge.

Murray, Simone. 2012b. "The Business of Adaptation: Reading the Market." In *A Companion to Literature, Film, and Adaptation,* edited by Deborah Cartmell, 122–39. Oxford: Wiley-Blackwell Press.

Museum of the Moving Image. "A Pinewood Dialogue with Patricia Rozema." Moderated by David Schwartz. Nov. 9, 1999. http://www.movingimagesource.us/files/dialogues/2/96168_programs_transcript_html_217.htm.

Naremore, James. 1999. "Film and the Reign of Adaptation." September 24. Distinguished Lecturer Series 10. Lecture of the Indiana University Institute for Advanced Study.

Naremore, James, ed. 2000a. *Film Adaptation.* New Brunswick, NJ: Rutgers University Press.

Naremore, James. 2000b. "Introduction." In *Film Adaptation,* edited by James Naremore, 1–16. New Brunswick, NJ: Rutgers University Press.

Nealon, Jeffrey T. 2012. *Post-Postmodernism: Or, The Cultural Logic of Just-in-Time Capitalism.* Stanford: Stanford University Press.

Neblett, Robert L., ed. 2014. "Re-Imagining, Re-Remembering and Cultural Recycling: Adaptation across the Humanities." Special issue, *Interdisciplinary Humanities* 31, no. 3 (Fall).

Nerlich, B. 2009. "Metonymy." In *Concise Encyclopedia of Pragmatics,* 2nd ed., edited by Jacob L. Mey, 631–34. Amsterdam: Elsevier Press.

Newell, Kate. 2010. "'We're off to See the Wizard' (Again): Oz Adaptations and the Matter of Fidelity." In *Adaptation Studies: New Approaches,* edited by Christa Albrecht-Crane and Dennis Cutchins, 78–96. Cranberry, NJ: Associated University Presses.

Newell, Kate. 2017. *Expanding Adaptation Networks: From Illustration to Novelization.* Palgrave Studies in Adaptation and Visual Culture. London: Palgrave Macmillan.

Newstok, Scott L., and Ayanna Thompson, eds. 2010. *Weyward Macbeth: Intersections of Race and Performance.* New York: Palgrave Macmillan.

Nichols, Marcus. 2018. "Examining Adaptation Studies in and through the Decadent Aesthetics of J. K. Huysmans's *À Rebours.*" PhD diss., University of West London.

Nicklas, Pascal. 2015. "Biopolitics of Adaptation." In *The Politics of Adaptation: New Media Convergence and Ideology,* edited by Dan Hassler-Forrest and Pascal Nicklas, 229–42. London: Palgrave Macmillan.

Nicklas, Pascal, and Sibylle Baumbach. 2018. "Adaptation and Perception." *Adaptation* 11, no. 2 (Aug.): 103–110.

Nicklas, Pascal, and Arthur M. Jacobs. 2017. "Rhetoric, Neurocognitive Poetics, and the Aesthetics of Adaptation." *Poetics Today* 38, no. 2 (June) 393–412.

Nicoll, Allardyce. 1936. *Film and Theatre.* New York: Thomas Y. Crowell.

Niemeyer, Paul J. 2003. *Seeing Hardy: Film and Television Adaptations of the Fiction of Thomas Hardy.* Jefferson, NC: McFarland Press.

Nietzsche, Friedrich. (1873) 1997. "On Truth and Falsity in Their Extramoral Sense." Translated by Maximilian A. Mügge. In *Philosophical Writings: Friedrich Nietzsche,* edited by Reinhold Grimm and Caroline Molina y Vedia, 87–102. New York: Continuum.

Nissen, Annie. 2018. "To Adapt or Not to Adapt? Writers and Writing across Prose Fiction, Theatre, and Film, 1823–1938." PhD diss., Lancaster University.

Nollen, Scott Allen. 1994. *Robert Louis Stevenson: Life, Literature, and the Silver Screen.* Jefferson, NC: McFarland Press.

North, Julian. 1999. "Conservative Austen, Racial Austen: *Sense and Sensibility* from Text to Screen." In *Adaptations: From Text to Screen, from Screen to Text*, edited by Deborah Cartmell and Imelda Whelehan, 38–50. London: Routledge.

Nünning, Ansgar. 2003. "Narratology or Narratologies? Taking Stock of Recent Developments, Critique and Modest Proposals for Future Usages of the Term." In *What Is Narratology: Questions and Answers Regarding the Status of a Theory*, edited by T. Kindt and H.-H. Müller. Berlin: De Gruyter. 239–75.

O'Connor, Ralph. 2014. "Irish Narrative Literature and the Classical Tradition, 900–1300." In *Classical Literature and Learning in Medieval Irish Narrative*, edited by Ralph O'Connor, 1–24. Cambridge: D. S. Brewer.

O'Flynn, Siobhan. 2012. "Epilogue." In *A Theory of Adaptation*, 2nd ed., by Linda Hutcheon, 179–206. London: Routledge.

Orr, Christopher. 1984. "The Discourse on Adaptation." *Wide Angle* 6, no. 2: 72–76.

Orr, John, and Colin Nicholson, eds. 1992. *Cinema and Fiction: New Modes of Adapting 1950–1990.* Edinburgh: Edinburgh University Press.

Orzack, Steven Hecht, and Patrick Forder. 2010. "Adaptationism." In *The Stanford Encyclopedia of Philosophy*. Spring 2017 ed., edited by Edward N. Zalta. https://plato.stanford.edu/archives/spr2017/entries/adaptationism/.

Osteen, Mark, ed. 2014. *Hitchcock and Adaptation: On the Page and on the Screen.* Lanham, MD: Rowman & Littlefield.

O'Thomas, Mark. 2010. "Turning Japanese: Translation, Adaptation, and the Ethics of Trans-National Exchange." In *Adaptation Studies: New Approaches*, edited by Christa Albrecht-Crane and Dennis R. Cutchins, 46–60. Cranberry, NJ: Associated University Press.

Pagello, Federic. 2011. "True to *The Spirit*? Film, Comics, and the Problem of Adaptation." *OI3Media* 4, no. 10 (June). http://host.uniroma3.it/riviste/Ol3Media/Pagello.html.

Paine, Thomas. (1791–1792) 1999. *Rights of Man: Being an Answer to Mr. Burke's Attack on the French Revolution.* Mineola, New York: Dover.

Papazian, Gretchen, and Joseph Michael Sommers, eds. 2013. *Game On, Hollywood! Essays on the Intersection of Video Games and Cinema.* Jefferson, NC: McFarland.

Park, Julie. 2010. *The Self and It: Novel Objects and Mimetic Objects in Eighteenth-Century England.* Stanford: Stanford University Press.

Parker, J. 2002. "A New Disciplinarity: Communities of Knowledge, Learning and Practice." *Teaching in Higher Education* 7, no. 4: 373–86.

Parody, Clare. 2011. "Franchising Adaptation." *Adaptation* 4, no. 2: 210–18.

Park-Finch, Heebon. 2012. "Hypertextual Adaptation: Humanistic Enquiry through Transfocalization in Stoppard's Rosencrantz and Guildenstern Are Dead." *Journal of Adaptation in Film & Performance* 5, no. 2: 183–96.

Parrill, Sue. 2002. *Jane Austen on Film and Television: A Critical Study of the Adaptations.* Jefferson, NC: McFarland Press.

Partridge, Samuel. 1805. *Sermons, Altered and Adapted to an English Pulpit from French Writers.* 2nd ed. London: F. C. & J. Rivington.

Pasanek, Brad. 2015. *Metaphors of Mind: An Eighteenth-Century Dictionary.* Baltimore: Johns Hopkins University Press.

Payne, Michael, and John Schad, eds. 2003. *Life. After. Theory: Jacques Derrida, Frank Kermode, Toril Moi, and Christopher Norris.* London: Bloomsbury.

Pearce, Samantha, and Alexis Weedon. 2017. "Film Adaptation for Knowing Audiences: Analysing Fan On-line Responses to the end of Breaking Dawn—Part 2 (2012)." *Participations: Journal of Audience & Reception Studies* 14, no. 2 (Nov.): 175–98.

Peeters, Heidi. 2007. Review of Linda Hutcheon's *A Theory of Adaptation*. Image and Narrative: Online Magazine of the Visual Narrative 16 (Feb.) http://www.imageandnarrative.be/inarchive/house_text_museum/peeters.htm.

Pelling, Mark. 2011. *Adaptation to Climate Change: From Resilience to Transformation*. London: Routledge.

Percy, Thomas. 1765. *Reliques of Ancient English Poetry: Consisting of Old Heroic Ballads, Songs, and Other Pieces of Our Earlier Poets*. 3 vols. London: J. Dodsley.

Perkins, V. F. 1972. *Film as Film: Understanding and Judging Movies*. London: Penguin Mass Market.

Phillips, Gene D., ed. 1974. *Graham Greene: The Films of His Fiction*. New York: Teachers College Press.

Phillips, Gene D. 1980. *Hemingway and Film*. New York: Frederick Ungar.

Phillips, Gene D. 1986. *Fiction, Film, and F. Scott Fitzgerald*. Chicago: Loyola University Press.

Phillips, Gene D. 1988. *Fiction, Film, and Faulkner: The Art of Adaptation*. Knoxville: University of Tennessee Press.

Pickering & Chatto. (1789) 1896. *A Catalogue of Old and Rare Books, Being a Portion of the Stock of and Offered for Sale by Pickering and Chatto*. London: Pickering & Chatto.

Pickering & Chatto. (1800?). *Catalogue*. London: Pickering & Chatto. Google Books. Accessed December 8, 2018. https://books.google.co.uk/books?id=5yBXAAAAIAAJ&source=gbs_navlinks_s.

Pickering & Chatto. (1825) 1903. *English literature, Noted Bibliographically and Biographically. A Catalogue with Prices Affixed, of a Very Extensive Collection of the First and Early Editions of Ancient and Modern English Literature*. London: Pickering & Chatto.

Pittman, L. Monique. 2011. *Authorizing Shakespeare on Film and Television: Gender, Class, and Ethnicity in Adaptation*. Studies in Shakespeare 19. Berne, Switzerland: Peter Lang.

Planché, J. R. 1872. *The Recollections and Reflections of J. R. Planché: A Professional Autobiography*. London: Tinsley Bros.

Plowman, Richard. 1824. *An Essay on the Illustration of Books*. London: J. Plummer.

Poague, Leland A. 1976. "Literature vs. Cinema: The Politics of Aesthetic Definition." Journal of Aesthetic Education 10, no. 1: 75–91.

Pollock, Griselda, ed. *Conceptual Odysseys: Passages to Cultural Analysis*. New York: Palgrave Macmillan.

Ponzanesi, Sandra. 2014. "The Adaptation Industry: The Cultural Economy of Postcolonial Film Adaptations." In *The Postcolonial Cultural Industry: Icons, Markets, Mythologies*. 109–55. London: Palgrave Macmillan.

Poole, Adrian. 2004. *Shakespeare and the Victorians*. London: Arden Shakespeare.

Pope, Alexander. 1711. *An Essay on Criticism*. London: W. Lewis.

Pope, Alexander. 1737. *The Second Epistle of the Second Book of Horace, Imitated by Mr. Pope*. London: R. Dodsley.

Pope, Johnathan. 2020. *Shakespeare's Fans: Adapting the Bard in the Age of Media Fandom*. Palgrave Studies in Adaptation and Visual Culture. London: Palgrave Macmillan.

Poplawski, Paul. 2003. *Encyclopedia of Literary Modernism*. London: Greenwood Press.

Pound, Roscoe. 1954. *An Introduction to the Philosophy of Law*. New Haven: Yale University Press.

Prasad, Pushkala. (2005) 2015. *Crafting Qualitative Research: Working in the Postpositivist Traditions*. London: Routledge.

Price, Stephen. 2010. *The Screenplay: Authorship, Theory, and Criticism*. London: Palgrave Macmillan.

Primorac, Antonija. 2012. "Corsets, Cages, and Embowered Women in Contemporary Victoriana on Film." *Film, Fashion & Consumption* 1, no. 1: 39–53.

Punzi, Maddalena Pennacchia. 2007. "Literary Intermediality: An Introduction." In *Literary Intermediality: The Transit of Literature through the Media Circuit*, edited by Maddalena Pennacchia Punzi, 9–26. Bern, Switzerland: Peter Lang.

Quintilian, Marcus Fabius. (ca. 95 AD) 1920–1922. *Institutio Oratoria*. 4 vols. Translated by Harold Edgeworth Butler. Loeb Classical Library. Cambridge, MA: Harvard University Press.

Rabaté, Jean-Michel. 2014. *Crimes of the Future: Theory and Its Global Reproduction*. London: Bloomsbury Press.

Raines, Melissa. 2018. "Uncanny Adaptations: Revisionary Narratives in Bryan Fuller's *Hannibal*." *Adaptation* 11, no. 3 (Dec.): 252–72.

Rajewsky, Irina O. 2002. *Intermedialität*. Tübingen: Francke.

Rajewsky, Irina O. 2005. "Intermediality, Intertextuality, and Remediation: A Literary Perspective on Intermediality." *Intermédialités* 6 (Autumn): 43–64.

Raw, Laurence, ed. 2012. *Translation, Adaptation and Transformation*. New York: Continuum.

Raw, Laurence, ed. 2013. *The Silk Road of Adaptation: Transformations across Disciplines and Cultures*. Newcastle: Cambridge Scholars.

Raw, Laurence. 2014. "Psychology and Adaptation: The Work of Jerome Bruner." *Linguaculture* 1 (Feb.): 89–101.

Raw, Laurence. 2017. "Aligning Adaptation Studies with Translation Studies." In *The Oxford Handbook of Adaptation Studies*, edited by Thomas Leitch, 494–508. Oxford: Oxford University Press.

Raw, Laurence, and Defne Ersin Tutan, eds. 2012. *The Adaptation of History: Essays on Ways of Telling the Past*. Jefferson, NC: McFarland.

Raw, Laurence, and Tony Gurr. 2013. *Adaptation Studies and Learning: New Frontiers*. New York: Rowman & Littlefield.

Ray, Robert B. 2000. "The Field of 'Literature and Film.'" In *Film Adaptation*, edited by James Naremore, 38–53. New Brunswick, NJ: Rutgers University Press.

Ray, Robert B. 2001. *How a Film Theory Got Lost and Other Mysteries in Cultural Studies*. Bloomington: University of Indiana Press.

Reade, Charles. 1860. *The Eighth Commandment*. London: Trübner & Co.

Reilly, Kara. 2017. "Preface." In *Contemporary Approaches to Adaptation in Theatre*, edited by Kara Reilly, xxi–xxix. London: Palgrave Macmillan.

Reisz, Karel. 1952. "Shadow into Substance." In *The Cinema 1950*, edited by Roger Manvel, 188–205. New York: Pelican Books.

Rentschler, Eric. (1986) 2015. "Introduction: Theoretical and Historical Considerations." In *German Film and Literature: Adaptations and Transformations*, edited by Eric Rentschler, 1–8. London: Routledge.

Rescher, Nicholas. 2006. *Studies in the Philosophy of Science: A Counterfactual Perspective on Quantum Entanglement*. Berlin: Walter de Gruyter.

Rhodes, Neil. 2013. *English Renaissance Translation Theory*. London: MHRA.

Rice, Jenny, and Carol Saunders. 1996. "Consuming *Middlemarch*: The Construction and Consumption of Nostalgia in Stamford." In *Pulping Fictions: Consuming Culture across the Literature/Media Divide*, edited by Deborah Cartmell, I. Q. Hunter, Heidi Kaye, and Imelda Whelehan, 85–98. London: Pluto Press.

Richard, David Evan. 2018. "Film Phenomenology and Adaptation: The "Fleshly Dialogue" of Jane Campion's *In the Cut*." *Adaptation* 11, no. 2 (Aug.): 144–58.

Richards, I. A. (1936) 2001. *The Philosophy of Rhetoric. I. A. Richards's Selected Works, 1919–1938*, edited by John Constable. Vol. 7. London: Routledge.

Richardson, Robert D. 1969. *Literature and Film*. Bloomington: Indiana University Press.

Ricoeur, Paul. 1990. *Time and Narrative*. Translated by Kathleen Blamey and David Pellauer. 3 vols. Chicago: University of Chicago Press.

Ricoeur, Paul. 2003. *The Rule of Metaphor: The Creation of Meaning in Language*. Translated by Robert Czerny, Kathleen McLaughlin, and John Costello. London: Routledge. Originally published as La Métapore Vive (Paris: Éditions du Seuil, 1975).

Rimmon-Kenan, Shlomith. 2002. *Narrative Fiction: Contemporary Poetics*. 2nd ed. London: Routledge.

Ritchie, Leigh. 1856. "The Perambulatory Movement." *Chambers Journal of Popular Literature, Science, and Arts* 5 (Jan.-June): 116–18.

Rizk, Laila. 2015. "Adaptation as Critique: Gender and Politics in the Plays of Effat Yehia and Amel Fadgy, Caridad Svich and Christine Evans." *Journal of Adaptation in Film & Performance* 8, no. 3: 213–32.

Robinson, Douglas. 1991. *The Translator's Turn*. Baltimore: Johns Hopkins University Press.

Robinson, Tara Rodden. 2005. *Genetics for Dummies*. Indianapolis, IN: Wiley Publishing.

Rodowick, David N. 2001. *Reading the Figural, or, Philosophy after the New Media*. Durham, NC: Duke University Press.

Rodowick, David N. 2007. *The Virtual Life of Film*. Cambridge, MA: Harvard University Press.

Rodowick, David N. 2014. *Elegy for Theory*. Cambridge: Harvard University Press.

Roglieri, Maria Ann. 2001. *Dante and Music: Musical Adaptations of the* Commedia *from the Sixteenth Century to the Present*. Aldershot: Ashgate Press.

Ropars-Wuilleumier, Marie-Claire. 1970. *De la littérature au cinéma: Genèse d'une écriture*. Paris: A. Cohn.

Rosch, Eleanor. 1978. "Principles of Categorization." In *Cognition and Categorization*, edited by Eleanor Rosch and Barbara B. Lloyd, 27–48. Hillsdale, NJ: Lawrence Erlbaum.

Ross, Harris. 1987. *Film as Literature, Literature as Film: An Introduction to and Bibliography of Film's Relationship to Literature*. New York: Greenwood Press.

Rothwell, Kenneth S. 2004. *A History of Shakespeare on Screen: A Century of Film and Television*. 2nd ed. Oxford: Blackwell Publishing.

Routledge Encyclopedia of Translation Studies. 1998 (2nd ed.). Edited by Mona Baker and Gabriela Saldanha. London: Routledge.

Rowe, Rebecca. 2018. "'The More Accuracy the Better'? Analysing Adaptation Reception in Reaction Videos." *Adaptation* 11, no. 3 (Dec.): 193–208.

Royle, Nicholas. 1999. "Déjà vu." In *Post-Theory: New Directions in Criticism*, edited by Martin McQuillan, Graeme MacDonald, Robin Purves, and Stephen Thomson, 3–20. Edinburgh: Edinburgh University Press.

Rozema, Patricia, director. 1999. Mansfield Park. Sarah Curtis, Miramax HAL Films.

Ruhe, Edward. 1973. "Film: The 'Literary' Approach." *Literature/Film Quarterly* 1, no. 1 (Winter): 76–83.

Russell, Edward R. 1869. "'Thorough' in Criticism." *Belgravia, A London Magazine.* Conducted by M. E. Braddon. 7: 39–48.

Ruud, Amanda. 2018. "Embodying Change: Adaptation, the Senses, and Media Revolution." In *The Routledge Companion to Adaptation*, edited by Dennis Cutchins, Katja Krebs, and Eckart Voigts, 245–55. London: Routledge.

Ryan, Frank. 2002. *Darwin's Blind Spot: Evolution beyond Natural Selection.* New York: Houghton Mifflin.

Ryan, Marie-Laure. 2017. "Transmedia Storytelling as Narrative Practice." In *The Oxford Handbook of Adaptation Studies*, edited by Thomas Leitch, 527–41. Oxford: Oxford University Press.

Sabey, Josh, and Keith Lawrence. 2018. "The Critic-as-Adapter." In *The Routledge Companion to Adaptation*, edited by Dennis Cutchins, Katja Krebs, and Eckart Voigts, 169–81. London: Routledge.

Saint Jacques, Jillian, ed. 2011a. *Adaptation Theories.* Maastricht: Jan Van Eyck Academie.

Saint Jacques, Jillian. 2011b. "Preface: Four Fundamental Concepts in Adaptation Studies." In *Adaptation Theories*, edited by Jillian Saint Jacques, 9–45. Maastricht: Jan Van Eyck Academie.

Saint Jacques, Jillian. 2011c. "Route Awakening." In *Adaptation Theories*, edited by Jillian Saint Jacques, 317–65. Maastricht: Jan Van Eyck Academie.

Sanders, Julie. (2006) 2017. *Adaptation and Appropriation.* 2nd ed. London: Routledge.

Sanders, Julie. 2007. *Shakespeare and Music: Afterlives and Borrowings.* Cambridge: Polity.

Sartre, Jean Paul. 1963. *The Problem of Method.* London: Methuen.

Saussure, Ferdinand de. (Lecture date 1910; 1959) 2011. "Linguistic Value." In *Course in General Linguistics*, edited by Perry Meisel and Haun Saussy, translated by Wade Baskin, 111–22. New York: Columbia University Press.

Schäfke, Werner, and Johannes Fehle, eds. 2019. *Adaptation in the Age of Media Convergence.* Amsterdam: University of Amsterdam Press.

Schirmeister, Pamela. 1990. *The Consolations of Space: The Place of Romance in Hawthorne, Melville, and James.* Stanford: Stanford University Press.

Schmidt, Siegfried J. 1980. "Fictionality in Literary and Non-Literary discourse." *Poetics* 9, no. 5–6 (Dec.): 525–46.

Schober, Regina. 2013. "Adaptation as Connection: Transmediality Reconsidered." In *Adaptation Studies: New Challenges, New Directions*, edited by Jørgen Bruhn, Anne Gjelsvik, and Eirik Frisvold Hanssen, 89–112. London: Bloomsbury Press.

Scholz, Anne-Marie. 2009. "Adaptation as Reception: How a Transnational Analysis of Hollywood Films Can Renew the Literature-to-Film Debates." *American Studies* 54, no. 4 (Jan.): 657–82.

Scholz, Anne-Marie. 2013. *From Fidelity to History: Film Adaptations as Cultural Events in the Twentieth Century.* Transatlantic Perspective Series. New York: Berghahn Books.

Scott, Clive. 2011. "From the Intermedial to the Synaesthetic: Literary Translation as Centrifugal Practice." *Comparative Critical Studies* 8, no. 1: 39–59.

Scott, Walter. (1825) 1852. "Biography of Henry Fielding." In *The Miscellaneous Prose Works*, 1:253–61. Edinburgh: Robert Cadell.

Scrutton, Thomas Edward. 1896. *The Law of Copyright.* 3rd ed. London: William Clowes & Sons.

Seager, Nicholas. 2018. "Pouring Out of One Vessel into Another: Originality and Imitation in Two Modern Adaptations of *Tristram Shandy*." *Adaptation* 11, no. 3 (Dec.): 228–51.

Seger, Linda. 1992. *The Art of Adaptation: Turning Fact and Fiction into Film*. New York: Henry Holt.

Seldes, Gilbert. 1924. *The Seven Lively Arts*. New York: Harper & Bros.

Seldes, Gilbert. (1937) 1978. *The Movies Come from America*. New York: Arno Press Reprint.

Semenza, Greg M. Colón, and Bob Hasenfratz. 2015. *The History of British Literature on Film, 1895–2015*. The History of World Literatures on Film. London: Bloomsbury Press.

Semenza, Gregory. 2018. "Towards a Historical Turn? Adaptation Studies and the Challenges of History." In *The Routledge Companion to Adaptation*, edited by Dennis Cutchins, Katja Krebs, and Eckart Voigts, 58–66. London: Routledge.

Setiawan, Dwi. 2017. "Post-Colonialism From Within: Repoliticisation and Depoliticisation in Ifa Isfansyah's Adaptation of Ahmad Tohari's *The Dancer*." *Adaptation* 10, no. 1 (Mar.): 18–33.

Shacklock, Zoë. 2015. "'A Reader Lives a Thousand Lives before He Dies': Transmedia Textuality and the Flows of Adaptation." In *Mastering the Game of Thrones: Essays on George R. R. Martin's A Song of Ice and Fire*, edited by Jes Battis and Susan Johnston, 262–80. Jefferson, NC: McFarland Press.

Shanahan, Timothy. 2004. *The Evolution of Darwinism: Selection, Adaptation, and Progress in Evolutionary Biology*. Cambridge: Cambridge University Press.

Shaughnessy, Nicola. 1996. "Is S/He or Isn't S/He? Screening *Orlando*." In *Pulping Fictions: Consuming Culture across the Literature/Media Divide*, edited by Deborah Cartmell, I. Q. Hunter, Heidi Kaye, and Imelda Whelehan, 43–55. London: Pluto Press.

Shelley, Percy Bysshe. (1821) 1840. "A Defence [*sic*] of Poetry." In *Essays, Letters from Abroad: Translations and Fragments*, edited by Mary Shelley, 1–57. London: Edward Moxon.

Shoberl, Frederic. 1819. *The Patriot Father, A Play in Five Acts; Freely Translated from the German of Augustus von Kotzebue*. Truro: F. Shoberl.

Simonova, Natasha. 2015. *Early Modern Authorship and Prose Continuations: Adaptation and Ownership*. Early Modern Literature in History, edited by Cedric C. Brown and Andrew Hadfield. London: Palgrave.

Sims, Robin. 2016. "Theory on Theory." *The Year's Work in Critical and Cultural Theory* 24, no. 1: 246–68.

Sinyard, Neil. 1986. *Filming Literature: The Art of Screen Adaptation*. New York: St. Martin's Press.

Sisley, Joy. 2007. "Writing, the Body, and Cinema: Peter Greenaway's *The Pillow Book*." In *Literary Intermediality: The Transit of Literature through the Media Circuit*, edited by Maddalena Pennacchia Punzi, 27–42. Bern, Switzerland: Peter Lang.

Slethaug, Gordon E. 2014. *Adaptation Theory and Criticism: Postmodern Literature and Cinema in the USA*. New York: Bloomsbury.

Smith, Iain Robert. 2016. *The Hollywood Meme: Transnational Adaptations in World Cinema*. Edinburgh: Edinburgh University Press.

Smol, Anna. 2018. "Adaptation as Analysis: Creative Work in an English Classroom." In *Fandom as Classroom Practice: A Teaching Guide*, edited by Katherine Anderson Howell, 17–31. Iowa City: University of Iowa Press.

Snyder, Mary H. 2011. *Analyzing Literature-to-Film Adaptations: A Novelist's Exploration and Guide*. London: Continuum.

Snyder, Mary H. 2017. "Adaptation in Theory and Practice: Mending the Imaginary Fence." In *The Oxford Handbook of Adaptation Studies*, edited by Thomas Leitch, 101–15. Oxford: Oxford University Press.

Sobchack, Thomas, and Vivian Carol Sobchack. 1987. "Film and Literature: The Problem of Adaptation." In *An Introduction to Film*, 312–24. Boston: Little, Brown.

Sommer, Robin Langley, and David Rago. 1995. *The Arts and Crafts Movement*. New York: Chartwell Books.

Speranza, Gary. 1979. Review of *Sam & Dave*. *Time Barrier Express* (Sep.-Oct.): n.p.

Spivak, Gayatri. 1985. "Can the Subaltern Speak? Speculations on Widow-Sacrifice." *Wedge*, nos. 7–8: 120–30.

Stam, Robert. (1985) 1992. *Reflexivity in Film and Literature: From* Don Quixote *to Jean-Luc Godard*. 2nd ed. New York: Columbia University Press.

Stam, Robert. 2000. "Beyond Fidelity: The Dialogics of Adaptation." In *Film Adaptation*, edited by James Naremore, 54–76. New Brunswick, NJ: Rutgers University Press.

Stam, Robert. 2004. *Literature through Film: Realism, Magic, and the Art of Adaptation*. London: John Wiley & Sons.

Stam, Robert. 2005. "Introduction: The Theory and Practice of Adaptation." In *Literature and Film: A Guide to the Theory and Practice of Film Adaptation*, edited by Robert Stam and Alessandra Raengo, 1–52. Oxford: Blackwell Publishing.

Stam, Robert. 2017. "Revisionist Adaptation: Transtextuality, Cross-Cultural Dialogism, and Performative Infidelities." In *The Oxford Handbook of Adaptation Studies*, edited by Thomas Leitch, 239–50. Oxford: Oxford University Press.

Stam, Robert, and Alessandra Raengo, eds. 2005a. *Literature and Film: A Guide to the Theory and Practice of Film Adaptation*. Oxford: Blackwell Publishing.

Stam, Robert, and Alessandra Raengo, eds. 2005b. *A Companion to Literature and Film*. Oxford: Blackwell Publishing.

Starker, Steven. 1989. *Evil Influences: Crusades against the Mass Media*. New Brunswick, NJ: Transaction Publishers.

Stecker, Robert. 2005. *Aesthetics and the Philosophy of Art: An Introduction*. New York: Rowman & Littlefield.

Steiner, T. R. 1975. *English Translation Theory, 1650–1800*. Leiden: Brill.

Stevenson, Randall. 2016. "Broken Mirrors: The First World War and Modernist Literature." The British Library. May 25, 2016. https://www.bl.uk/20th-century-literature/articles/broken-mirrors-the-first-world-war-and-modernist-literature.

Stevenson, Robert Louis. (1886) 2005. *The Strange Case of Dr. Jekyll and Mr. Hyde*, 2nd ed. Edited by Martin A. Danahay. New York: Broadview Press.

Stewart, Garrett. 2012. "Literature and Film—Not Literature on Film." In *Teaching Film*, edited by Lucy Fischer and Patrice Petro, 164–76. New York: MLA.

Stobbart, Dawn. 2018. "Adaptation and New Media: Establishing the Video Game as an Adaptive Medium." In *The Routledge Companion to Adaptation*, edited by Dennis Cutchins, Katja Krebs, and Eckart Voigts, 382–29. London: Routledge.

Strang, David, and John W. Mayer. 1993. "Institutional Conditions for Diffusion." *Theory and Society* 22, no. 4: 487–511.

Straumann, Barbara. 2015. "Adaptation—Remediation—Transmediality." In *Handbook of Intermediality: Literature-Image-Sound-Music*, edited by Gabriele Rippl, 249–67. Berlin: De Gruyter.

Strong, Jeremy, ed. 2019. "Adaptation and History," special issue, *Adaptation* 12, no. 2 (Aug.).

Szwydky, Lissette Lopez. 2018. "Adaptations, Culture-Texts, and the Literary Canon on the Making of Nineteenth-Century 'Classics.'" In *The Routledge Companion to Adaptation*, edited by Dennis Cutchins, Katja Krebs, and Eckart Voigts, 128–42. London: Routledge.

Tate, Nahum. (1681) 1761. *The History of King Lear, Revived with Alterations.* London: Eugene Swiney.

Telesforo de Truera y Cosío. 1831. "The Musical Drama." Letter to *The Tatler* 3, no. 405, (Dec.): 607.

Thagard, Paul, ed. 2007. *Philosophy of Psychology and Cognitive Science.* Amsterdam: Elsevier.

Thalberg, Sigismund. 1852. "Pianofortes." In Exhibition of the Works of Industry of All Nations, 1851. Reports by the Juries on the Subjects in the Thirty Classes into Which the Exhibition Was Divided, 326–30. London: William Clowes & Sons.

Thompson, John O. 1996. "'Vanishing' Worlds: Film Adaptation and the Mystery of the Original." In *Pulping Fictions: Consuming Culture across the Literature/Media Divide*, edited by Deborah Cartmell, I. Q. Hunter, Heidi Kaye, and Imelda Whelehan, 11–28. London: Pluto Press.

Tinsley v. Lacy. (1863) 1 Hem. & M. 747.

Tomlins, Frederick G. 1840. *A Brief View of the English Drama: From the Earliest Period to the Present Time, with Suggestions for Elevating the Present Condition of the Art, and of Its Professors.* London: C. Mitchell.

Trapp, Joseph. 1742. *Lectures on Poetry Read in the Schools of Natural Philosophy at Oxford.* London: C. Hitch and C. Davis.

Truffaut, François. (1954) 1976. "A Certain Tendency of the French Cinema." In *Movies and Methods: An Anthology*, edited by Bill Nichols, 1:224–35. Berkeley: University of California Press.

Turner, Luke. 2015. "Metamodernism: A Brief Introduction." January 12. http://www.metamodernism.com/2015/01/12/metamodernism-a-brief-introduction/.

Tutan, Defne Ersin. 2017. "Adaptation and History." In *The Oxford Handbook of Adaptation Studies*, edited by Thomas Leitch, 576–86. Oxford: Oxford University Press.

Tymoczko, Maria. 2016. *Translation in a Postcolonial Context: Early Irish Literature in Translation.* London: Routledge.

Umrani, Safdar Imam. 2012. *Literature and Film Adaptation: Hindi Cinema: A Case Study.* N.p.: Lambert Academic Publishing.

Underhill, James. 2011. *Creating Worldviews: Metaphor, Ideology, and Language.* Edinburgh: Edinburgh University Press.

Universal Film Manufacturing Company. 1916. Advertisement for *Two Mothers. Moving Picture World* 28, no. 3 (May 20): 1260.

Uricchio, William, and Roberta E. Pearson. 1993. *Reframing Culture: The Case of the Vitagraph Quality Films.* Princeton: Princeton University Press.

Urrows, David Francis, ed. 2008. *Essays on Word/Music Adaptation and on Surveying the Field.* Amsterdam: Rodopi Press.

Van Gorp, Hendrick. 1985. "Translation and Literary Genre: The European Picaresque Novel in the 17th and 18th Centuries." In *The Manipulation of Literature: Studies in Literary Translation*, edited by Theo Hermans, 136–48. New York: St Martin.

Van Parys, Thomas. 2007. Review of Thomas Leitch, *Film Adaptation and Its Discontents: From Gone with the Wind to The Passion of the Christ. Image & Narrative: Online Magazine of the Visual Narrative.* 20 (Dec.). http://www.imageandnarrative.be/inarchive/affiche_findesiecle/vanparys.htm.

Van Parys, Thomas. 2011. "Against Fidelity: Contemporary Adaptation Studies and the Example of Novelization." In *Adaptation Theories*, edited by Jillian St. Jacques, 407–43. Maastricht: Jan Van Eyck Academie.

Vattimo, Gianni. 1988. *The End of Modernity: Nihilism and Hermeneutics in Postmodern Culture.* Translated by J. R. Snyder. Baltimore: Johns Hopkins University Press.

Vee, Annette. 2017. *Coding Literacy: How Computer Programming Is Changing Writing.* Cambridge, MA: MIT Press.

Venkatesh, Vinodh. 2012. "Perspectives, Problems, and Processes in Contemporary Spanish Adaptations." *Hipertexto* 16 (Summer): 41–53.

Venuti, Lawrence. 2007. "Adaptation, Translation, Critique." *Journal of Visual Culture* 6, no. 1: 25–43.

Verevis, Constantine. 2006. *Film Remakes.* Edinburgh: Edinburgh University Press.

Vermeulen, Timotheus, and Robin van den Akker. 2010. "Notes on Metamodernism." *Journal of Aesthetics & Culture* 2, no. 1: 1–13.

Verrone, William. 2011. *Adaptation and the Avant-Garde: Alternative Perspectives on Adaptation Theory and Practice.* New York: Continuum.

Voigts, Eckart. 2018a. "Memes, GIFs, and Remix Culture: Compact Appropriation in Everyday Digital Life." In *The Routledge Companion to Adaptation*, edited by Dennis Cutchins, Katja Krebs, and Eckart Voigts, 390–402. London: Routledge.

Voigts, Eckart. 2018b. "Why Will You Think That I am Wrong about Adaptation?" Presented at the 12th Annual Association of Adaptation Studies Conference, "Facts: True, Alternative, Evolving," University of Amsterdam, September 28.

Voigts, Eckart. 2019. "Digimodernism? Auto-Modernity? Posthuman Adaptation and the Case of *Sunspring*." Presented at the 13th Annual Association of Adaptation Studies Conference, "Adaptation and Modernisms: Establishing and Dismantling Borders in Adaptation Practice and Theory," University of Masaryk, September 19.

Voigts-Virchow, Eckart, ed. 2004. *Janespotting and Beyond: British Heritage Retrovisions since the Mid-1990s.* Tübingen: Gunter Narr Verlag.

Voigts-Virchow, Eckart. 2006. "Adaptation, Adaptation and Drosophilology, or Hollywood, Bio-Poetics and Literary Darwinism." In *Proceedings Anglistentag 2005*, edited by Christoph Houswitschka, Gabriele Knappe, and Anja Müller, 247–63. Trier: Wissenschaftlicher Verlag Trier.

Voigts-Virchow, Eckart. 2009. "Metadaptation: Adaptation and Intermediality—Cock and Bull." *Journal of Adaptation in Film & Performance* 2, no. 2 (Sep.): 137–52.

Voigts-Virchow, Eckart. 2013. "Anti-Essentialist Versions of Aggregate Alice: A Grin without a Cat." In *Translation and Adaptation in Theatre and Film*, edited by Katja Krebs, 63–82. Routledge Advances in Theatre and Performance Studies. London: Routledge.

Von Mises, Ludwig. 2007. *Theory and History: An Interpretation of Social and Economic Evolution.* 2nd ed. Auburn, AL: Ludwig Von Mises Institute. (Orig. pub. 1957.)

W. C. "Fine Arts." 1819. *The New Monthly Magazine and Universal Register* 11 (Feb.1): 50–53.

Wagner, Geoffrey. 1975. "Three Modes of Adaptation." In *The Novel and the Cinema* 219–31. Rutherford, NJ: Farleigh Dickinson University Press.

Wallin, Mark R. 2013. "Eurhythmatic Analysis: A Rhetoric of Adaptation." *Journal of Adaptation in Film & Performance* 6, no. 1 (Sep.): 125–39.

Warton, Joseph. (1782) 2004. "An Essay on the Genius and Writings of Pope." 4th ed. In *Alexander Pope and His Critics*, edited by Adam Rounce. Vol. 1. London: Routledge.

Watson, J. D., and F. H. C. Crick. 1953. "Genetical Implications of the Structure of Deoxyribonucleic Acid." *Nature* 171, no. 4361: 964.

Waugh, Patricia, ed. 2006. "Introduction: Criticism, Theory, and Anti-Theory." In *Literary Theory and Criticism: An Oxford Guide*, edited by Patricia Waugh, 1–34. Oxford: Oxford University Press.

Wavresky, François, and Seok-Won Lee. 2016. "A Methodology towards the Adaptization of Legacy Systems Using Agent-Oriented Software Engineering." In *Proceedings of the 31st Annual ACM Symposium on Applied Computing.* April 4–8: 1407–14. https://dl.acm.org/citation.cfm?id=2851776.

Welch, Jeffrey Egan. 1981. *Literature and Film: An Annotated Bibliography, 1909–1977.* New York: Garland.

Welch, Jeffrey Egan. 1993. *Literature and Film: An Annotated Bibliography, 1978–1988.* New York: Garland.

Wells, Karen. 2009. "Embodying Englishness: Representations of Whiteness, Class and Empire in *The Secret Garden.*" In *Adaptation in Contemporary Culture: Textual Infidelities*, edited by Rachel Carroll, 123–33. London: Continuum.

Wells-Lassagne, Shannon, and Ariane Hudelet, eds. 2013. *Screening Text: Critical Perspectives on Film Adaptation.* Jefferson, NC: McFarland Press.

Welsh, James M. 2003. "Journal of a Journal: *Literature/Film Quarterly* and the Little College on the Shore." *LFA News* 1, no. 1 (Sep.): 1, 4, 5.

Welsh, James M. 2006. Foreword. In *Literature into Film: Theory and Practical Approaches*, by Linda Costanzo Cahir, 1–5. Jefferson, NC: McFarland Press.

Welsh, James M. 2007. "Introduction: Issues of Screen Adaptation: What Is Truth?" In *The Literature/Film Reader*, edited by James M. Welsh and Peter Lev, xiii–xxviii. Lanham, MD: Scarecrow Press.

Welsh, James M., and Peter Lev, eds. 2007. *The Literature/Film Reader: Issues of Adaptation.* Lanham, MD: Scarecrow Press.

Wertheimer, Michael. 2012. *A Brief History of Psychology.* 5th ed. New York: Psychology Press, Taylor & Francis Group.

Westbrook, Brett. 2010. "Being Adaptation: The Resistance to Theory." In *Adaptation Studies: New Approaches*, edited by Christa Albrecht-Crane and Dennis R. Cutchins, 25–45. Cranberry, NJ: Associated University Presses.

Whale, John. 1977. *The Politics of the Media.* Manchester: Manchester University Press.

Whelehan, Imelda. 1999. "Adaptations: The Contemporary Dilemmas." In *Adaptations: From Text to Screen, Screen to Text*, edited by Deborah Cartmell and Imelda Whelehan, 3–19. London: Routledge.

Whelehan, Imelda. 2000. *Overloaded: Popular Culture and the Future of Feminism.* London: The Women's Press.

White, Hadyn. 1973. *Metahistory: The Historical Imagination in Nineteenth-Century Europe.* Baltimore: Johns Hopkins University Press.

White, Richard Grant. 1857. "Introduction to The Merchant of Venice." In The Works of William Shakespeare: The Plays Edited from the Folio of MDCXXIII, with Various Readings from All the Editions and All the Commentators, Notes, Introductory

Remarks, a Historical Sketch of the Text, an Account of the Rise and Progress of the English drama, a memoir of the Poet, and an Essay upon his Genius 4:131–45. Boston, Little Brown & Co.

White, Richard Grant. 1865. *Memoirs of the Life of William Shakespeare, with an Essay toward the Expression of His Genius, and an Account of the Rise and Progress of the English Drama*. Boston: Little Brown & Co.

White, Timothy. 1983. "A Man out of Time Beats the Clock." *Musician*, no. 60: 52.

Whittington, William. 2008. "Review of Linda Hutcheon, *A Theory of Adaptation*." *Comparative Literature Studies* 45, no. 3: 404–6.

Williamson, Timothy. 2007. *The Philosophy of Philosophy*. Oxford: Blackwell Publishing.

Winch, Christopher, and John Gingell. 1999. *Key Concepts in the Philosophy of Education*. Key Concepts Series. London: Routledge.

Wollen, Peter. 1972. *Signs and Meaning in the Cinema*. Bloomington: Indiana University Press.

Woodmansee, Martha. 1984. "The Genius and the Copyright: Economic and Legal Conditions of the Emergence of the 'Author.'" In "The Printed Word in the Eighteenth Century." Special issue, *Eighteenth-Century Studies* 17: 425–48.

Woolf, Virginia. (1926) 1966. "The Cinema." In *Collected Essays*, 2:268–72. London: Hogarth Press.

Worthen, W. B. 2014. *Shakespeare Performance Studies*. Cambridge: Cambridge University Press.

Wright, Thomas. 1881. "On a Possible Popular Culture." *Contemporary Review* 40: 25–44.

Wright, Thomas. 1883. "Concerning the Unknown Public." *Nineteenth Century* 13, no. 72 (Feb.): 279–96.

Yang, Jing, and Xiaotian Jin. "Imagining Globalization in a Chinese Chick Flick." *Literature/Film Quarterly* 47, no. 1. https://lfq.salisbury.edu/_issues/47_1/imagining_globalization_in_a_chinese_chick_flick.html.

Young, Edward. 1759 [1918]. *Edward Young's Conjectures on Original Composition*. Manchester: Manchester University Press.

Younge, Edward, and John Collyer. 1836. "D'Almaine v. Boosey." Mar. 3, 1835. *Reports of Cases Argued and Determined in The Court of Exchequer in Equity*, 1:288–303. London: S. Sweet.

Zaiontz, Keren. 2009. "The Art of Repeating Stories: An Interview with Linda Hutcheon." In *Performing Adaptations: Essays and Conversations on the Theory and Practice of Adaptation*, edited by Michelle MacArthur, Lydia Wilkinson, and Keren Zaiontz, 1–9. Newcastle upon Tyne: Cambridge Scholars.

Zatlin, Phyllis. 2005. *Theatrical Translation and Film Adaptation: A Practitioner's View*. Topics in Translation 29. Clevedon, UK: Multilingual Matters.

Zhen, Zhang. 2005. "Cosmopolitan Projections: World Literature on Chinese Screens." In *A Companion to Literature and Film*, edited by Robert Stam and Alessandra Raengo, 144–46.

Index

Tables are indicated by *t* following the page number.

For the benefit of digital users, indexed terms that span two pages (e.g., 52–53) may, on occasion, appear on only one of those pages.